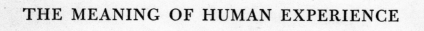

THE MEANING OF HUMAN EXPERIENCE

LYNN HAROLD HOUGH

THE MEANING

of

HUMAN EXPERIENCE

THE THIRD ANNUAL
SOUTHWESTERN UNIVERSITY LECTURES
GEORGETOWN, TEXAS, 1945

ABINGDON-COKESBURY PRESS
NEW YORK · NASHVILLE

THE MEANING OF HUMAN EXPERIENCE

Scriptural quotations are from the American Standard Version of the Revised Bible, copyright renewal, 1929, by the International Council of Religious Education.

K

PRINTED IN THE UNITED STATES OF AMERICA

CONTENTS

Part One

⇶ BASIC CONSIDERATIONS ⇷

Part Two

>>>THE HEBREW-CHRISTIAN WITNESS<<<

Part Three

⇒⇒ THE HUMANISTIC TRADITION ⇐⇐

in the Enlightenment. 8. The Debacle of the French Revolution. 9. The Debacle in the Society of Science. 10. The Debacle of the Society of Social Blueprints. 11. The Debacle in the Society of the Machine Age. 12. The Debacle of the Great Reversion. 13. Democracy Faces Fate. 14. The Judgment of the Christian Sanctions.

Part Four

>>> THE EVANGELICAL SYNTHESIS <<<

CONTENTS

CHAPTER I

Confronting the Human

THE introductory verses of *The Panchatantra* declare:

> One Vishnusharman, shrewdly gleaning
> All worldly wisdom's inner meaning,
> In these five books the charm compresses
> Of all such books the world possesses.[1]

Arthur W. Ryder, its translator from the Sanskrit into English, claims that *The Panchatantra* contains the most widely known stories in the world. And he inclines to the opinion that they are also the best. Here we have a textbook of the wise conduct of life. Curiously enough, most of the characters are animals. It is, of course, a fascinating as well as an ancient device. And the important thing to remember is that these stories of the lions, the bull, the two jackals, the mouse, the turtle, and the deer are interesting just because these animals behave like human beings. It is not as beasts that they are intriguing. It is as beasts who by some strange magic exercise human qualities. It is the human which is the significant.

The same thing is true of Dean Swift's brilliant satire. He thought he was exercising the most mordant irony when he suggested that horses might be wiser than men. But the horses are arresting just because they reveal essentially human qualities at a high level of excellence. So what was supposed to be a deadly attack upon humanity becomes a tribute to the definitively human qualities. The tale of the talking beasts, whether in *The Panchatantra* or in Aesop's *Fables,* is always unconsciously an expression of man's interest in man. Even the beast is made a man beast in order to capture human attention. Men's experiences in the world are of exhaustless fascination and, as it turns out, of endless importance. Men's ways with nature, men's ways with other men, men's ways with their own minds, and men's ways with the great world of the unseen make up the very warp and woof of that experience which we would confront and seek to understand.

1. The Men We Can Scarcely See

Our far-off cousins, the prehistoric men and women and little children, are scarcely visible in their distant habitations. They left no

[1] Tr. A. W. Ryder (Chicago: University of Chicago Press, 1925), p. 3.

11

written record. But they left a few tools, a few works of their hands, and strange glimpses of their art. The cave at Altamira in northern Spain, which in 1879 revealed its secret of animals painted in bright colors many centuries ago, brought a bit of the experience of ancient man to men of the late nineteenth century. And the tools once held in ancient hands have stirred the imagination of anthropologists without number. The men we meet in this odd fashion were already beginning to turn the world of natural objects to their own purposes. And they were beginning to have a sense of harmony and beauty. We cannot see the light which flashed in their ancient eyes. We cannot hear the sounds of their far-off speech. But we know enough to recognize them as our kin. They observed. They thought. They turned things to their own uses. They were haunted by dreadful fears. But they mastered the fears and the things of which they were afraid. And they had begun to dream bright dreams.

2. The Men of the River Valleys

We begin to have a clearer sense of the life of men five thousand years ago. We see them thronging the river valleys. There are the men of the Tigris and Euphrates valleys. There are the men of the valley of the Nile. James Henry Breasted used to walk about Chicago with the busy life of ancient Egypt filling his mind. There was, no doubt, a fertile imagination at work. But there was also the man who had seen and touched and handled the remains of an ancient life. And the brightness of its color, the quality of its achievements, and some sense of its lovelier and more subtle thoughts pursued him to the end of his days.

Always there was the sense of power. Always there grew a deeper and deeper appreciation of man mastering nature for his own purposes. The building of the pyramids is a fascinating mystery just because it is a story of man solving difficult problems in controlling his world. He is becoming a mathematician. He is becoming an engineer. He is learning to master other men and to use them for his own purposes. He is a hunter. He is a builder. He is a farmer. He is a maker of beautiful places bright with colors which satisfy his eye. He lifts eyes toward the mystery beyond this world. He sees powers like his own, only greater. He sees deathless people, wielding divine energies, the masters and judges of the world and of men. By the time of Ikhnaton he becomes a spiritual idealist. The dreamers of lofty dreams confront the skillful manipulator of men and events. Great thoughts battle with little shrewdnesses. There is a sense of mystery and a sense of hope. The Nile Valley is splendid and haunting, noble and ignoble, good and evil.

The Tigris and Euphrates valleys have their own pageant of brave and cruel men, of masters and lawgivers, of men like Hammurabi, who can turn experience into a code. They fight for a place in the world.

They march through blood to power. They inscribe words as did the men of the Nile Valley. They have mastered time as they make it tell its tale in recorded language. The great river valleys become the homes of libraries. Man learns to remember as he has never remembered before. Each land gets into art in its own fashion. Fresh insight fights with hardening convention. Most men live poor lives. But they form human pyramids at the apex of which a few powerful people stand. The strange secret by which the few control the many has been learned already and learned too well.

3. The Men of Masterful Mind

Hills continue to be hills. Trees continue to be trees. Rivers still flow to the sea. But man changes. And always he secures a firmer control over nature and a surer use of his own intelligence. He has discovered that he can observe and think and decide and remember. This invisible mind of his is the man. Not his weight. Not the play of his muscles. Not the energy of his physical vitality. But his power to know and to think and to decide makes him a man. The man who knows the most and thinks the most quickly and acts with the swiftest understanding is the master. You see his fierce, clear eyes in Egypt. You see his strong, suddenly moving hand in Babylonia and Assyria. And back of all you see is the mind. It is not matter thinking. It is thought dominating matter. Or better, it is a thinker mastering things.

The anthropologists dig and dig and dig. And the things they find quicken into interest at one bright point of revelation. They show the working of ancient minds. They reveal the handicraft of ancient hands. They are always saying: "Men walked this way. These men had mental powers like yours. They were full of the yeast of a great unrest of the brain. Always they asked questions. Always they found answers. Always they revealed the strange powers of creatures who were kings because they could think."

4. The Man Who Controls Other Men

Man mastered his world by slow and memorable stages. He invented the sharp instrument for cutting. He built boats and manufactured oars. He lifted sails and caught the unsuspecting wind. He began to tame the creatures among which he lived. Dogs, oxen, horses, camels, felt the power of his eye, the strength of his hand, and most of all the power of the mind and the will behind the eye.

Then this strange creature became a tamer of other men. Men were taught to serve other men. They were enslaved by other men. The masters made a mythology to uphold their claims to authority. They tasted the subtle intoxication of bending other men to do their will. The ruler might be wise and gracious. He might bring good to the men he ruled. The ruler might be cruel and arrogant and full of the hard, selfish lust of power. The face of the mighty patrician began to appear in the valley of the Nile and the valleys of the Tigris and the Euphrates. The rulers taught other men to honor them. At their best they taught men to trust them. At their all too often worst they taught men to cower and to tremble before them. They made men the servants of their pleasure, of their lust, and of their power. They taught men the ugly acts of servility and flattery. The cult of the supermen began to be a power in the world.

5. The Everlasting Barbarian

The men who fell behind in the race were the men who fed and fought for and supported the victors. They could not think so quickly. They could not act so effectively. They had no quicksilver qualities of sparkling and energetic mind. They seemed at times to look backward and downward toward the beast rather than onward toward the heights of achievement which lay before man's conquering mind. They were creatures of habit rather than creatures of insight. They felt the biological urges more insistently than the stirrings of questioning and adventurous intelligence. They gathered a slow and curious wisdom of their own. They had folklore and custom and their new, slowly ripening tales of gods and men. Some sullen sense of inadequacy poured a kind of slow poison through their blood. Or they sank into sluggish, dull content with the fate of human beasts of burden. They hewed the wood. And they drew the water. But you never could be sure when the light of wild and demanding intelligence would shine in the eyes of a slave. Once and again from the slave race came the master man. Often he fought cruelly for his own place and held it as cruelly when it was won. But in odd and curious ways the sense of comradeship grew. There was the comradeship of the lords. There was the comradeship of the slaves. Each group came to have passwords which the members of the group shared and used with a kind of satisfied understanding.

The common stuff of the life of the lowly came to represent a human soil of greater richness than anyone really understood.

But if there was a ripening of wisdom, there was a maturing of ugliness and sloth and beastliness, too. In every land there was an ignoble tradition of all that was unlovely and of bad report. Cumulative evil had its own sordid tales to tell. And in the most bewildering fashion the evil twined about the good and crept into the pattern of the noble. In high places and in low the dark light of lawlessness was all too often seen on sea and land.

6. The Men of Slippery Mind

Partly because the men who had no physical force or driving power could often accomplish their desires by shrewdness, the men of slippery mind appeared. They were adroit and plausible people, skillful in flattery, knowing every secret of appeal to the complacency, the self-love, and the passions of the men whose ways they wanted to guide for their own purposes. They never asked what was true but always what would serve the exigencies of their own desires. When they were weak they learned how to master the strong by the subtlety of their persuasion. When they were in a hopeless minority, they knew how to confuse the majority by the crosslight of their unexpected arguments and because they knew just what they wanted, to drive a dull majority by their own quick wit. Sometimes they were inverted idealists, members of the tribe of Machiavelli before Machiavelli was born, telling lies to others and sometimes telling lies to themselves to further what they believed to be noble ends. They liked to believe that they practiced peripheral vices in the name of central virtues. So they corrupted their own natures and the natures of others for the sake of an idealism discredited by their own falseness. Often they were bad and ruthless men of utter selfishness bending every argument to their own evil ends and cynically using even goodness to do the bidding of evil. The men of the slippery mind belong to a powerful choir invisible whose music is the moral madness and badness of the world.

7. The Men Who Made Words Slaves

From the time when sounds became freighted with ever sharper and more incisive meaning, men have been fascinated by words. In the days of magic and of magical religions there was a sense that mysterious power inhered in the words themselves. So in many a religion whose main quality belonged to a level below the intelligence, magical formulas had their astonishing place. They could curse and they could bless. They could kill and they could heal. There were collections of them. There were volumes of them. There were libraries of them. They constitute perhaps the greatest mass of literary rubbish past centuries have left behind.

But very early the sense of the wonder of words associated itself with the relation between meaning and expression, and so words were taught to cut like swords, to bloom like flowers, to sing lovely songs, and to run all the complicated register of the music of human experience. The savage was full of a sense of the fresh new wonder of words. The civilized man was full of a sense of the sophisticated and disciplined speech which caught an echo of every evasive experience and brought to clear and sharp focus every thought.

So words became the instruments of good and the instruments of evil, the servants of truth and the servants of falsehood. They could be used for every sort of purpose. The men who made words slaves were of every variety of character, and they lived on every level of intelligence.

The ignoble and deceptive use of words led to a psychopathic dislike of powerful and effective speech, as if it were necessarily ignoble. Ages which misused the arts of expression first disliked and then despised them. But this was only a reflection of their own moral quality. When great men believed great things and expressed them in great ways, the orator was a royal person. Demosthenes made speech kingly. Cicero made the cause of the civilized man and the speech replete with civilized insights one and the same thing. Quintilian distilled the experience and judgment of men to whom rhetoric was the noblest of arts because it found for all meanings an adequate expression. When ethical religion came upon great days, as in the Israel of the eighth century B.C., the orator became the prophet, his words burning with a sense of their power to set forth the will and purposes of the God of moral character. Whenever men have come upon days of crisis and living insights have cried for masterful speech, the men who make words their slaves have appeared. Winston Churchill became more than a prime minister, more than a political leader. In the days of his nation's most critical experiences he found words which were mightier than armies with banners.

8. The Men Who Enshrined Memories

Increasingly men used the materials of the past to build the houses of the present. The uncivilized man was one who lived as if he had no ancestors. He thought as if reasoning had begun with his arrival. He had the crass assurance of the incompetent. He was full of the unblushing confidence of the ignorant. But the fraternity of the wise came to be a real power in every land. The wise were those who remembered. They enshrined the memory of the best. They endeavored to become masters of the noblest that had been thought and done in the world. They had the freedom of the libraries because they brought understanding to the past. They did not remember uncritically. They did not look back without intelligence. They did not appropriate without judgment. Their sharpest weapons were for those who would resuscitate ancient evils. Their greatest foes were the scholars who would not let old follies and old confusions rest in their ancient graves but brought them forth for the deception of living men. They knew the power of discrimination as well as the power of memory.

They gave themselves to the great endeavor to keep alive that which ought not to die, to remember that which ought not to be forgotten, always to see the age in the light of the ages. They learned that if we are to understand investigating intelligence and subtly integrated harmony we must all be Greeks, that if we are to understand how custom ripens into law we must all become Romans, that if we are to understand ethical religion, we must all be men of Israel. They came to know that if we would understand and use the forces of nature we must become men of mathematics, that if we would understand and guide human life we must become men who ask what other men have done with their freedom. We must understand the ancient paths if we are to build the great new roads. The best of the past deserves to be immortal. It knocks at the door of every age asking that it may be allowed to live again. The men who belong to the fraternity of wisdom hear the knocking and open the door. Homer made a Bible for the Greeks because he put their greatest memories into noble speech. Vergil did the same thing for the Romans because in *The Aeneid* tradition became the glorious interpretation of a nation's sense of its own genius. Dante turned memory into moral and spiritual judgment.

9. The Men Who Captured Dreams

Man remembers. He also hopes. And when hope finds words which move like wings and lift men's dreams to lofty heights, we behold another aspect of this many-sided human drama. To see the meaning of what is a part of immediate experience is the constant work of man's mind. To re-create the past and fathom its significance is the perpetual work of historical investigation and the historical imagination. To picture what might be is the far-flung achievement of the adventurous mind. The land of heart's desire began to call men early. The land of mind's desire seemed to summon from afar. So the fraternity of those who captured dreams increased all about the world. The cult of poetry began to be a part of the life of man. And it became clear that there was something infinite in man's desires. His feet were always marching to new lands. He was always sensing things as a part of a dream of perfection. And so ideas became ideals and thoughts became radiant dreams. There was often bitter disappointment and disillusionment when the men who captured dreams came back to the world of actuality. So satire arose. For the masters of irony were always finding this mordant way to measure the world of daily experience by the world of ideal truth and beauty. In some strange fashion your Lucian is always a disillusioned poet. Your Juvenal can only be indignant because of the high standards of the country of his mind. Ben Jonson's brilliant hatred of evil is a love of good set in reverse.

But there comes the time when the dreamers—at least some of them —see their dreams come true in the sky and by faith find in eternity what has not become real in time. Plato, when he fails as a political prime minister, flings his unrealized ideals into the world of eternal truth and goodness and beauty—or rather, looking into the region of ultimate being, finds there in perfection all that which at its best this world only suggests. So he becomes the philosopher poet of the eternal ideas. And so philosophy itself becomes a religious faith.

10. The Men Who Were Disturbed by the Moral Voice

Very early men came to have not only a sense of what had been, what was, and what might come to exist, but also a compelling and masterful sense of what had a right to be. It might express itself at first in lowly and strange taboos. It might become entangled in intellectual confusion and moral obfuscation. But the thing itself would not die. This sense of what had a right to be was deep, and it became imperial. It became the moral voice. It was the genius of the conscience of humanity.

To Sophocles it was a law eternal in the heavens. To the Roman Stoic it involved a life according to principles written deep in nature itself. To the Hebrew prophet it was the moral character of God made vocal in its demand for moral character in men. But whatever form it took, it was a sense of that which had a right to be. It was a voice saturated with moral demand.

And just as the dreamers looked into eternity to find what was lacking in time, so the men who were disturbed and driven and mastered by the moral voice saw religion itself become ethical. Zoroaster saw the universe as a stage for the battle between good and evil. The Hebrew prophet Amos looked up and beheld God as the One who was righteousness alive.

So in every way man was pursued by a kind of theology implicit in his own life. He was made for truth. He was made for goodness. He was made for beauty. He was haunted by imperishable splendors never more inevitable than when they seemed out of his reach.

11. The Men Who Made Nations

Families, clans, tribes, nations—so the human story goes. And the nation builders are particularly impressive examples of the power of man. Men began to stand together to resist something. They knew that they must be stronger than their fears. And despite the strange and shaking fears of the black mystery which surrounded them, their practical fears were fears of other men. Looking at it all in the largest perspective, we may say that they fought other men for food, they fought other men for land, they fought other men for security, and they fought other men for power. And they made their victories secure by building states and nations and empires. The minds of men moved in ever larger areas of thought and action in their practical affairs. They became students of human relations. They became students of customs which make nations strong. They became students of military art. They became organizers for peace and organizers for war. The sheer brain power demanded in the men controlling a vast empire almost staggers thought. There was ruthlessness, and there was exploitation. But there was also a growing practical idealism. The Pax Romana was a noble thing, and Roman rule developed a sense of human qualities and human rights transcending geographical and racial boundaries. The gains of civilization were preserved in powerful states. And the quiet maintained in powerful civilized states, even when that quiet was intermittent—and most of all when it was prolonged—gave all the arts and what we may now call the humanities a new chance at life. The politician became a statesman. And Rome itself came upon its Augustan age.

There was the story of disintegration and decadence, too. Gibbon found the inevitable words in his title *The Decline and Fall.* ... What men built, men could destroy. And when the building was so great as to be magnificent, the fall came with a tragedy like the impact of colliding planets destroying each other by the very velocity of their movement.

12. The Men Who Made Republics

The idea that every man is an important man was inevitable, but it came to its own slowly and fitfully. Ezekiel's revelation that the individual soul is of value to God—"all souls are mine"—was startling in its possibilities. Protagoras' individual man as the "measure of all things" opened doors upon great vistas. The Athenian democracy saw men who were political equals working together even if their edifice of democracy rested on slavery. The Renaissance came like a breath of spring with its confidence in man. And the Reformation, with every man his own priest having direct access to God, caused rusty doors to move on ancient hinges. England kept moving in its own sure but illogical fashion from the time of the Great Charter. Human rights became sacred in the thought of men. Two revolutions in the seventeenth century worked with a kind of finality with respect to despotism in England. On the Continent even absolute monarchs like Frederick the Great became benevolent servants of the state in the eighteenth century. England broadened its sense of individual rights. The little states in America made themselves into a federal republic based on democratic sanctions. The French Revolution burned many things to ashes. The nineteenth century saw successive reform bills in England with ever-increasing rights belonging to larger and larger numbers of individual men. The twentieth century saw political democracy expanding into industrial democracy. And so the makers of republics reaped mighty returns from their sowing.

To be sure, there was resurgent absolutism. The totalitarian state began to lift its banners, its exponents sneering at the inefficiency of democracies. All the old urges of blood and lust for power moved forth upon the world—ancient evils with new names. But the tigers from ancient jungles found a humanity not taught in vain by the makers of the republics. The beasts may be unleashed, but the little creature with moral conviction and intelligent eyes reveals unexpected power. Everyman is proving stronger than the superman.

13. The Men Who Made Machines

You can put your finger into the human past and find the promise of science in many places. Athens accomplished more in this direction than most people know. Aristotle had the very spirit and method of the observing and classifying of facts which belong to the scientist. As centuries went by, acute observation was oddly mixed with magic. The Arabs were sometimes both mathematicians and magicians. Roger Bacon in the thirteenth century saw very clearly the possibilities of moving from individual facts to general principles. The seventeenth century revealed developments in mathematics which had profound significance for science. But the great Scientific Revolution came in the nineteenth century. A kind of scientific world view where everything from the smallest atom to the largest star belonged to one great system was the gradual achievement of multitudes of men busy with experiment and classification. We are not at the moment principally concerned with the fact that these brilliant results came from preoccupation with one territory, the territory of the measurable. We only pause to call attention to the fact that every achievement of science was and is the result of the action of the free intelligence of man. We are, however, just now very much concerned with the practical control man attained by means of his scientific achievements. Inventions multiplied in the most bewildering fashion. The age of steam transportation came. Electricity was harnessed. The telegraph operator was found in every village. The telephone became ubiquitous. The study of combustion and the invention of new techniques made possible astounding advances in manufacturing. The automobile began to appear on all roads. Radio activity was studied. Broadcasting developed. The airplane appeared in the sky. Air fleets for commerce and air fleets for war became possible and actual. New inventions and new analyses of the soil produced a new agriculture. The Machine Age had indeed arrived. The men who made and used the machines were the masters of a new empire.

All this reveals human power in striking fashion. Many of the results were good. Many were evil. The slums about the factories, the gangsters with automatics and swiftly moving cars, were in their own way the product of the Machine Age. Problems of distribution became acute. Overproduction in one part of the world and starvation in another made part of the anomaly of modern life.

14. The Men Who Became Machines

Of course, you can never really drive out the human. But the Machine Age did tend to produce men whose preoccupation with the mechanical affected their own quality. The automatic worker became more and more automatic. The typist grew like the typewriter. The world became obsessed by the mechanized aspects of life. The qualities which enabled men to invent and use machines fell into the background of their thought. Sociology often became a study of impersonal laws applied to human relationships. Dialectical materialism became an increasingly powerful political philosophy. War seemed to become a battle of machines. Peace seemed likely to become the harmonious adjustment of mechanical activities. The cinema produced thrills with mathematical precision. One industrial leader was said to have played with the idea of producing a novel by classified piecework such as that which obtained in his factory. For some men religion degenerated into a series of altruistic blueprints for a new social order. The human machines were to be made comfortable by formula. It was evident that the battle of man for his manhood had reached a new crisis.

15. The Interpreters of the Battle of Impulses and Ideas

In this new world biology came to its own. To countless men the biological impulse became more important than the moral insight coming from clear understanding. The novel, the drama, and the poem became the vehicles of biological urges. In all this resurgence of conscious animality Oscar Cargill has been inclined—in spite of some hesitation —to see a notable renaissance which he has described in *Intellectual America*. The discussion reads more like a case book of abnormal psychology. The decadent, the primitive, the Freudian elements in our literature are traced with masterful erudition to their European sources. The result is a series of adventures in slime, the slime glowing at times with the malignant vitality of the swamps.

Centuries ago Cicero had seen appetite and reason in conflict. And he had seen and said with all clarity and vigor that reason must conquer. The contemporary victories of impulse over intelligence are a part of the inverted saga of man's march back toward the jungle.

However, the prophets of unmastered appetites and subconscious urges have not had the field all to themselves. The prophets of Baal have been vociferous and energetic, but there have been Elijahs to recall men to a nobler loyalty. The Socratic tradition has never been without witnesses. The examined life has had its wise interpreters. The criticism which has been like a voice of gentle stillness after the wild tempest of unleashed passion has been heard. And by many truly thoughtful men it has been heeded.

16. The Alluring and Betraying Utopias

If one asks what religion has been doing in the midst of this contemporary debacle, the reply is curious and not a little startling. The cult of the body is surely the foe of ethical religion. And one might suppose that the voice of religion would be clear and unhesitating. But as a matter of fact the dream of giving a spiritual basis to the Marxist dialectic has obsessed the minds of many of the bright young leaders in the religious field. It has all been very noble in a way. Indignation against social wrong, a chivalrous devotion to the rights of the down-trodden, a dream of a better distribution of the things which make the physical basis of the good life, have filled the minds of eager idealists, and so busy have they been with the new society that many of them have forgotten the decaying individual. In some cases religious ideal-ism has sought for a world of comfortable bodies rather than a world of free minds where the freedom is nobly used. Eager idealism un-mastered by disciplined and critical intelligence has sought to create the utopian state without facing the problem of the very unutopian men who are the material for the new order—or, for that matter, of any order. So the alluring utopias have hovered before the imagination and all too often have betrayed the conscience. Something with genuine qualities of good has filled men's thoughts until often they have ignored the more fundamental good upon which all social good must rest.

17. The Men Who Have Seen Individuals Sharply

The spectacle of humanity is not the sight of an abstraction—if such a thing were possible. It is the view of a great number of concrete in-dividuals. Everything which is said is said by individuals. Everything which is thought is thought by individuals. Everything which is done is done by individuals. Even what is called social action is always action by individuals for the good of society. So the men who have seen the individuals sharply have been the clear and dependable thinkers. They have been saved from that fallacy of the abstract which has confused and betrayed so many.

All the things we have considered in this introductory survey have been characteristic not of some curiously integrated man of abstraction but of concrete human beings. Individuals have lived in this world. They have observed and classified and mastered and used what they have found. They have been individual centers of that masterful intelli-gence which is the significant matter in respect of the life on this planet. Sometimes they have used their full intelligence wisely. Sometimes they have used it unwisely. They have voted for the good. They have voted for the evil. They have been their own friends. They have been their own foes. They have been other men's friends. They have been other men's foes. They have quickened their intelligence. They have dulled their intelligence. They have made the most of their freedom. They have sunk back into a state where freedom was first betrayed and then lost. So noble, so ignoble, so great and so tragic is man.

18. *The Man Everyman Sees*

Man is actual. He is what he is at every stage. Man is potential. He is what he may become. He is the possible knocking at the door of life. This pull of the possible is his most distinctive experience. It creates his intellectual restlessness. It accounts for his moral ambition. It is the secret of his spiritual aspiration. It is the basis of his endless curiosity. It has seeds of splendor in it. It contains seeds of tragedy. And whenever you meet man—rich or poor, wise or foolish, good or evil—he is this strange creature of measureless possibilities. His eye shines suddenly, and you know that there has come to his imagination the light of some far-off port. He never fully understands himself. But he feels an instinctive anger when his tale is told in such a way that the strange power of his mind to see, to think, to choose, to decide is forgotten. This creature meant for mastery is the man every man sees who truly sees his fellow. And he is able to see this capacity for mastery in other men because he finds it at the center of his own life.

CHAPTER II

Knowing and Thinking

IN a striking sentence in *The Testament of Beauty*, Robert Bridges spoke of what would happen to

> . . . a wolf that all his life
> had hunted after nightfall neath the starlit skies
> should he suddenly attain the first inklings of thought.[1]

This sense of a new awareness and a new capacity has never, so far as we know, come to a wolf. But it is actually the defining matter regarding man. Here we are not dealing with matters of fancy or imagination. We are dealing with what has actually happened. And so we do not need to fear the test suggested by Aristotle in the *Nicomachean Ethics* when he says, "The test of truth in matters of practice is to be found in the facts of life; for it is in them that the supreme authority resides." [2] Man becomes aware of himself as a creature knowing and thinking. He has always become aware of himself as a creature knowing and thinking. Man the knower and man the thinker belong to the realm of fact and not to the realm of speculation. And here we find not only something which meets the test of the factual; we meet the defining fact. The beginning of all human discussion is man the knower. The essential matter in all discussion is that man is a thinker as well as a knower. It is here that our discussion of the meaning of human experience must really begin. If man were not a knower, there would be no human experience to discuss. If man were not a thinker, there would be no human story to tell.

Thus it becomes clear that we must always have a theory of knowledge before we have a theory of reality. We must always have an epistemology before we have a metaphysic. We must see what is involved in the fact that man is a knower and a thinker before we raise the far-reaching questions which have to do with that which he knows and that of which he thinks.

When man becomes aware of himself, he always finds that he is knowing and thinking. He does not argue about it. He does not create a process of dialectic by means of which he reaches and then exercises these powers. He finds that they are given to him. They are his own.

[1] New York: Oxford University Press, 1930, ll. 319-21.
[2] 1179*a* 17-20.

24

They are a part of himself. He accepts them. He uses them. And by accepting and using them he carries on the whole great human adventure in the world.

At first he accepts them quite naïvely. He uses his powers of awareness without analyzing them. He uses his powers of thought without subjecting them to critical scrutiny. Indeed, he may go on being quite naïve as to the nature of his powers after he has learned to use them most brilliantly. There are men in many fields of intellectual achievement who have won high place in using their mental powers without ever inspecting critically the nature of those powers. And some of the oddest confusions of thought century after century have been the product of the minds of men who have had a theory of reality but have never faced the problems of knowledge which lie back of all consideration of the nature of that which we know.

If we are to do anything with this power to be aware, we must accept it as a major premise never to be denied. If we are to do anything with the power of thought, we must see it as a fundamental assumption never to be questioned. It is not our task to prove that men can know. For unless we assume that they can know there is such a blackout that there is nothing left to discuss. It is not our task to prove that men can think. For unless they can think there are no instruments by which one can prove anything at all. Man has to be able to know before he can set about dealing with knowledge. He has to be able to think before he can set about dealing with thought.

1. The Necessary Assumptions

When we come to anything like critical self-consciousness, we find that intelligence is already controlling the materials of experience. Man does not invent his mind. He wakes from the darkness of the unconscious—to put it so—already possessing and using his mind. Of course, in the nature of things this must be so. For if he constructed his mind by a brilliant process of creative activity he would have to have another mind to use for the purposes of the creative process. And this other mind would be his real mind. He can discipline his mind. He can develop its powers. He can misuse it. He can use it effectively and wisely. But he begins to think, aware of its presence, and he assumes its powers as naturally as an infant assumes the dependable strength of its mother's arms. It is an organ of awareness. And it is an organ of consideration. By it he preceives and through it he weighs and estimates the meaning of that of which he is aware. But we have used an unnecessarily cumbersome form of words when we have said that the mind is an organ by means of which man is aware and by means of which he considers. Actually he is not aware first of himself, then of an organ of awareness, and then of things of which he is aware. He is just aware of himself perceiving and of himself considering. He uses—when at last he does come to use—the word "mind" to describe himself knowing and himself thinking. And after our most sophisticated flights of thought and our filling of abstract words with the greatest variety of meaning, we must always come back to this *self* which becomes aware that it knows and thinks and that in some real way the materials of experience are subject to it. Much of our difficulty about thought comes from the fact that, in order to express a certain meaning, we sharpen a word which may have had a rather checkered experience. Then we argue about its previous history or its possible connotations and create such a general confusion that we think we have discredited the idea we were using the word to express. So a good deal of philosophy comes to be a battle in the dark about irrelevant etymologies. The critical thinker must continually ask just what particular freight a word is meant to carry. Most discussions would be in infinitely simpler if the disputants would just make sure before the argument becomes too heated that they are actually talking about the same thing.

Man begins, then, with his experience of himself as a controlling intelligence. This experience enlarges until it becomes one of the great and necessary assumptions he must make about himself and his world. He can know. He can consider. And in no end of ways he can use much of what he knows and much of what he considers. This he can never deny without inner and outer stultification. For only by being aware can he conduct a process discrediting awareness. And only by considering can he create a skepticism which discredits his powers of consideration. Only by the use of intelligence can he create an argument to cast doubt upon intelligence. It is always characteristic of writers like that most brilliant and wholly fascinating and often disconcertingly powerful thinker Reinhold Niebuhr that when they speak slightingly of the capacity of the human mind, their skepticism never causes them to hesitate in writing their books to assume that their own minds possess the very dependability which they are inclined to deny to the mind of humanity. You cannot construct an argument without assuming the essential validity of the knowing process. Karl Barth and all the psychopathic theologians flounder on this rock. For the purposes of a very noble sense of man's dependence on God, they discredit the very power without which all argument—and especially their own—is made invalid. The major premise of all thought is the essential validity of the knowing process.

You may invert this insight with some mental gain and with no intellectual loss by saying that a necessary assumption of all thought and action is just the apprehension that experience is by its very nature subject to the uses of critical intelligence. Here you go beyond the thinker and begin to have an objective reference. Man comes to consciousness in a world over which he has some sort of control. In some way it was made for him. And he was made for it. At once he knows that he has keys which will unlock some of its doors—if we may use words borrowed from his later experience—and as time goes on he discovers that he is all the while able to make keys which fit more locks. Man is a controller. Man lives in a world where he can exercise control. These things he assumes implicitly before he begins to analyze their meaning. These things he can never deny without self-stultification. You can call them truths made sure by experience if you like that form of words. Or you can more critically call them necessary assumptions, that is, assumptions involved in the validity of the knowing and thinking process. We have, then, as man becomes aware of himself entangled in the actualities of experience, a thinker, thoughts, and things about which to think. All these words express actualities whose qualities must be subjected to the closest critical scrutiny. But at least they mean a self capable of awareness, thoughts by which that awareness is made articulate to the self, and some sort of experience of that which is other than the self, which is the reflection of a world beyond the self and in a real way subject to its control.

2. The Possibility of Universal Skepticism

Gamaliel Bradford once wrote a little poem which runs thus:

> If you removed my thyroid gland,
> I should become an ox,
> Without the power to command
> A single paradox.

> The interest I feel in God
> Is all my thyroid gland.
> My quick inventions quaint and odd,
> The glorious works I planned,

> The splendid sweep my fancy takes
> Wide over sea and land,
> Also my various mistakes,
> Are all my thyroid gland.

Here in a few bright lines you have thought reduced to stuff, and the thinker reduced to things. It is an old game. Many people have played it in ages past. And many people will play it in ages to come. It represents the apotheosis of matter. It celebrates the dethronement of mind.

But such skepticism, clever and paradoxical though it is, turns out to be rather vain and incomplete. Real skepticism must be more thorough-going. It is the universal skeptic who goes the whole length of the skeptical mood. We do not say the whole length of the argument. For of course the universal skeptic has no materials for argument left. He has only a mood. And that mood dissolves while he inspects it.

Universal skepticism is always possible. And to universal skepticism there is no answer. The whole scheme of questioning and answering falls into the abyss when you become a universal skeptic. You cannot be driven to it by a process of reasoning, for it abolishes reasoning. You cannot be forced to it by logic, for it denies all logic. It is the everlasting substitute of a period for the sentence. It leaves no language. It leaves no alphabet. It leaves no subject or predicate or object. It is as evasive as the smile of the Cheshire cat after the cat has gone.

The insight that skepticism carried to its final conclusion inevitably becomes suicidal is one of the three or four insights which lie at the basis of all truly critical thought. For once this is seen it becomes clear that *faith* is the basis of all significant experience. The man of religion may tell us that the just shall live by faith. The philosopher has attained mature wisdom only when he has realized that the rational must also live by faith. It is because of the faith inherent in the understanding of the ultimate meaning of skepticism that the critical inspection of the universal skeptic is so important.

In a certain institution for the mentally unsound, I once saw a man standing quite nude with his back toward the entrance of the cell where he was detained and his face to the wall. He was a symbol of many things, most of all of the universal skeptic, who also stands quite nude with his back toward the world of living experience and his face turned finally and conclusively toward the wall.

We cannot accept his fate. So we must refuse to follow the destructive processes of his thought. We must have faith in life if we are to live at all. We must have faith in meaning if we are to find significances in experience. We must walk in the way of the great assertions which come to us as a part of the mind's invincible surmise. And just because we see the meaning of the great denials, we must deny their validity.

3. The Mistakes of the Thinkers

Yet we cannot deny man's capacity to misuse his power to think. We cannot deny his power to misinterpret his experience. The possibility of error is itself a matter of the utmost significance. Professor Borden P. Bowne, that subtle and corrosive thinker, was convinced that this fact of error is a rock upon which all impersonal philosophies break and fall apart. An impersonal process cannot make mistakes. Forces cannot make mistakes. They are what they are. And that is what you can say of them. To find an agent capable of making mistakes you must transcend the world of things and the world of forces and enter the world of conscious selves.

We cannot, however, avoid the problem of a world where the knowing process is made for truth and yet may fall into error. There seems, at least at first, to be something paradoxical in a mind made to be an organ of truth and yet becoming an organ of error. It is, however, a paradox and not a contradiction. And even the paradox becomes less disconcerting as you examine the experience of the knowing person. The real trouble is that some thinkers insist on thinking of persons as things, and because they know that things and forces are free from the problems of intelligence they are inclined to deny the existence of intelligence.

The most immediate way to deal with this problem is to make an appeal directly to experience. If man did not possess the power of finding truth, all the achievements of even a material experience would be impossible. If there were not obstacles in the way of using that power, all the long tale of progress by trial and error in the physical and the biological sciences would never have been told. If there is a direct insight into the nature of all reality, this does not belong to man. He is a self in the midst of an adventure of knowing. He loses his way and he finds it again. But—speaking for a moment of man as synonymous with mankind—he never loses it completely. One of the oddest things about man is his tendency to regard his capacity to go wrong in the use of his mind as if there were something fatal about it. In the *Spoon River Anthology,* Edgar Lee Masters put into the voice of Calvin Campbell speaking from the tomb the words:

> You may blame Spoon River for what it is,
> But whom do you blame for the will in you
> That feeds itself and makes you dock-weed,
> Jimpson, dandelion or mullen
> And which can never use any soil or air
> So as to make you jessamine or wistaria? [3]

These words subtly persuasive with a kind of deadly appeal are actually a contradiction of the facts of life. The most constant fact of experience lies just in man's power to turn from errors and so to find truth, to turn from one thing and to become another. Speaking in terms of the figure of speech in Edgar Lee Masters' little poem, we may say that probably Calvin Campbell had never heard of Luther Burbank.

4. Freedom

This leads us at once to the heart of the whole matter. Man is a creature who in some sense is a master of "either-or." He can go one way; he can go another. He is not only a self; he is a free self.

There is a vast literature based on the belief that man is the victim

[3] New York: The Macmillan Co., 1916, p. 179.

and not the master of the events of his life. Sometimes the thought runs like a subtle poison of suggestion through writing of rare beauty and power. John Masefield's *The Daffodil Fields* is a story of two men and a woman. It is told with sensitive sympathy, and their dilemma becomes a haunting tragedy. But, for all the loveliness of the poem, it represents the abdication of personality and not the assertion of true personal qualities. You feel all the while that these people are driven by an invisible force which they cannot resist. But the very glory of human life lies actually in man's capacity to master himself and to master his world. And when men surrender their freedom, that surrender itself is an act of freedom.

Free men who have some knowledge which they are all the while increasing, and not full knowledge with no possibility of adding more to what they know, will inevitably proceed by a trial-and-error method. Intellectual mistakes are a natural part of the experience of a sound, free mind dealing with a body of experience it has not yet fully mastered.

Freedom is often discounted for the sake of making men more comfortable by disclaiming responsibility for evil acts. Indeed, an enormous part of the literary attack on freedom can be charged to the account of this motive. Many novels and plays say little else than this: "True, these persons did these things, but they were not responsible." And they are read and imbibed by many people who avidly accept the false gospel of irresponsibility because they have done many things of which they must be ashamed unless they can settle quietly into the conviction that they have been the victims of fate. The argument is really psychological and not logical.

Freedom is also discounted by those who somehow feel that they pay tribute to the glory of God by denying the freedom of man. The consideration of the Deity belongs to a later stage of our discussion. But surely if God made the world and man, if they continue to exist only because He supports them at every instant, if His own character provides the goals for their conduct and His own reign of righteous love determines their destiny, His sovereignty is not less glorious because He gives men power to choose freely to do His will. Actually, He gives men freedom in order that they may choose to be sons and not slaves.

There are limitations pertaining to the freedom of a finite person in this vast universe. There are limitations of a moral character which will come in for later discussion. Just now we are claiming that some actual and indubitable freedom must belong to the self if all experience is not to dissolve into a mist. A man has to be free even to conduct an argument against freedom.

5. The Great Correlation: Thinker, Thought, Thing

The stream-of-consciousness literature which has made such a curious and indeed fantastic place for itself in the contemporary world is busy with the uncontrolled contents of consciousness and quite ignores the self who is conscious and the strategy of the controlling position of the self in all its experiences. That the stream-of-consciousness literature has revealed to us many obscure, not to say muddy, aspects of human experiences, no one would deny. But it misses the essential matters. It is like an account of the forest and the wild beasts which ignores the hunter and his gun. There are plenty of facts. But there is a curious disinclination to speak of the fact that matters. Without attempting a thorough discussion of that stream of consciousness which flows along uncontrolled, we can see that we need not be too much impressed by it when we remember that the stream of consciousness can be studied only by a controlled consciousness. It becomes an object of scientific knowledge only when it is subjected to the investigation of a disciplined intelligence. The passive contemplation of a stream of consciousness would never build a house or a boat. It would never produce a civilization. The thinker is not, when he is a true thinker, merely the witness of his thoughts. He is the controller of his thoughts. Out of the control of thought comes civilization. But out of the control of thought comes also the winning of life on the part of primitive people from what is often a hostile nature.

The thinker must never be confused with the instrument of his thought. You say just nothing when you call him a thinking reed. The reed contributes nothing to the thinking or the thinker. There is a difference in quality here. The thinker uses the reed, but he is not the reed.

So the study of the functioning of the brain is never a study of any significant matter at the center of the process of thought. If you move from the thinker outward, you can say many significant things about the brain. When you try to move from the brain inward, you end in a state of complete intellectual chaos. And you only escape from this chaos by going back to the insight that the thinker is something different from the brain which he uses. Physiological psychology begins by standing the whole process of experience on its head. And it succeeds in maintaining this insane equilibrium only by using aspects of experience which come, not from the body, but from the thinker who uses the body.

As we shall see, the thinker comes to consciousness in a material world. But he is aware of himself as in some sense its master, in some sense different from it, and in some sense above it. To lose the thinker in the thing is, in the long run, to make sense neither of the thinker nor of the thing. The very fashion in which, historically, men have moved from experience with things to the thought of ideas is one of the most definite of the proofs that the thinker transcends the things with which he has to do. Indeed, his immediate world is a world of thought even when things form in some way the stuff by means of which he makes images of his thoughts. It is by means of thought that he uses things. It is by means of thought that he controls things.

While the things seem immediate, the thought is always implicit in the experience of the things. The thinker has his own intimate and characteristic world, where thought is monarch. It is because of this primacy of thought that he is impatient and restless in the presence of things until he subjects them to his knowledge and to his control. He is always saying to himself: "I touch this, but I am other than this. I feel this, but I am other than this." And even his sense of his own body at its clearest is always a sense of something which he inhabits and not of something which he is. In the invisible corridors of his thought something happens which is more subtle and important than the movement of the blood and the beating of the heart and the ticking of the brain. The true significance of the word "organic" is found in the complete possession of something by something else. The organ belongs to the mind. The mind does not belong to the organ. The interrelations of thinker and thought and thing are so intricate that it is easy to lose oneself in the attempt to unravel their relationships. But one always moves toward darkness when one tries to explain thoughts by things. And when one moves through things and thoughts to a controlling self busy with the activities of thinking, one always enters a world of light.

The whole method by which the thinker gets words to express this intricate process is a tribute to that invisible realm of the self which can have commerce with a world of color and light and sound and hard material and yet be something other even in the act of controlling. Indeed, the self would at once cease to be the controller were it not something different from that which it controls. A man is only putting together words without meaning when he cries mystically, "I am both the thinker and the thing of which I think." You can put words together in that way, but you simply cannot unite meanings in that fashion. Pantheism is always a form of words. It is never a collection of meanings.

The analysis of awareness is, of course, a subtle enough process. But it is man's most critical business. If he goes wrong here, he will go wrong everywhere. If he goes right here, there is at least the hope that he will go right everywhere.

6. What the Mind Brings to Experience

Ever since the time of Immanuel Kant—to go back no farther—it has been clear that the human thinker is so constituted that experience must come to him in a certain fashion. Indeed, when we have analyzed the contribution of the mind to experience, it is clear that this contribution is definite and far-reaching. The "thing in itself" becomes the thing as the mind is constituted to receive it. All human experience is mental experience. The mind imposes its own powers upon the whole cluster of sensations. The objective reference is always a matter of faith. It turns out to be a matter of well-buttressed and justified faith.

Of course, it is conceivable that human minds might be of such a nature as constantly to falsify experience. But in that case there would be an inevitable breakdown between the mind and the world other than itself, and ultimately there would be a breakdown between the mind and other minds. The fact that the process goes on successfully century after century is proof of its essential validity. The thinker, the thought process, and the thing belong to a universe capable of genuine correlation. Here the great word is "coherence." It is not "unity." The word "unity" is what Theodore Roosevelt used to call a weasel word. In philosophy it is likely to be used to represent a number of different meanings. Some of them are quite harmless and even helpful. But it has a way of coming to mean "identity." And then the results are bad indeed. The panpsychist is likely in his vain way to think that if he has said that a man is identical with that objective world which he has experienced, he has explained the man's understanding and use of his world. But, of course, precisely the opposite is true. If man were identical with the world he experiences, he could have no relations with it. He must be separate from it and yet capable of relations with it. And the relation between a man and his world is best expressed by the word "coherence" just because it is not a slippery word, going from one meaning to another while you are not watching.

The fact that the mind imposes its own laws upon the objective world as a condition of that world's becoming a part of human experience is the fundamental fact in epistemology. This involves far-reaching problems, the most important of which we shall consider later. Just now it is the fact itself which is important. These laws which the mind imposes upon things in order to make them the subject of experience can never be contradicted in interpreting experience, for without these laws the experience itself would fall apart and cease to be. It is because of this fact that the word "categories" has been used to express the necessities the mind imposes upon its world. Lack of clarity at this point has confused no end of clever thinkers. There is nothing more important than to know what it is you cannot deny without the stultification of the whole process of living experience. The moment it is seen that experience is always mental and always conforms to the implicit laws of the mind, the fog begins to lift and the sun to shine. The investigation of this process is the task of the whole discipline we call epistemology.

It is important to observe that men often use the word "epistemology" to denote a study of the physiological accompaniments of experience rather than a study of the implicit laws of the knowing mind. In this way all the real problems are ignored, and a number of interesting matters irrelevant to the main matter are introduced. To confuse a man with physiology when he is supposed to be studying psychology is a characteristic indoor sport of men who are trying to reduce the world of thought to the world of things.

The mental forms include experiences in relations of succession and in relations of extension. Whatever these things are in themselves, they are a necessary part of experience. They belong to the format of the mind. Identity and difference, change and causality are a part of the pattern the mind impresses upon experience. And the successful ongoing of experience proves that they have some sort of dependable objective reference. The important matter now, however, is not the detailed consideration of these numerous categorical imperatives but the fact that they are implicit in experience itself. They may require critical inspection. But they cannot be denied without the breakdown of all experience.

It becomes increasingly clear that the path of progress in thought lies in the closer and closer inspection of experience as a living fact and not in the attempt to secrete consciousness and thought from the material aspects of experience which actually become real in experience only as they become mental facts.

Though all these insights are involved in the very ongoing of experience, it is only in a highly civilized mind that their significance becomes clear. And many extremely clever people never discover them at all. It is easier to keep the world as it appears to the senses in motion and to call the result thought than really to think. The Greeks began with things and mounted to thought and mind. This was the real Pilgrim's Progress of the intelligence. By a tragic sort of Pilgrim's Regress the modern world has tended to begin with a depreciation of intelligence and then to try to find the meaning of experience in things and forces. The kingly man is dead. Long live the electron!

But the fallacy is clear when once one begins to use one's intelligence. For only minds discover electrons. Electrons never discover minds. Only intelligence discovers forces. Forces never discover intelligence. Only men control the world with conscious purpose. The hills do not plan to lift men to their own height. The valleys do not plan to bring men down to their own level. It is only human beings who in the Rockies say, "We must have men to match the mountains."

The tendency of the human mind to use what it is willing to admit to be the most sophisticated intelligence to depreciate its own powers is one of the extraordinary phenomena of history. Man alone uses his brain to foul his own nest. But even this perverse use of his intelligence is the inverted proof of the possession of that free mind which can go so desperately wrong as well as so nobly right. Bertrand Russell, denying the free intelligence which made him a stupendous mathematician in order that he may be brave in a sense only possible to free men and master a despair only possible to kingly intelligence, is the final and splendid proof of the actual validity of all that which he so vehemently denies.

When one follows Oscar Cargill's brilliantly documented analysis of modern authors' adventures in the underworlds of experience in what with unconscious irony he calls *Intellectual America,* one becomes conscious that the very decadence sweeping on toward the death of the sense of genuine moral value is only possible to those who have used the intelligence of men to dramatize the experiences of beasts. These lurid studies in the moral confusion produced by men who have used their minds to betray their bodies give their own strange testimony to the dignity of the powers of awareness, of knowing and thinking, which have been so tragically misused. Man can misuse in just these dark and devastating fashions his free intelligence. But as a conflagration lights up the very destruction which it is achieving, so, when man sets fire to his own manhood, in that lurid light he stands amazingly and doubly regal even in the hour when he reveals that his own choices have made him a man only fit to be a king in hell.

Sometimes it appears that that fierce English dramatist Ben Jonson revealed the honor in which he held humanity more by his excoriations of man's misuse of his powers than in his delight in man's good use of his noble capacities. How the play *Sejanus* burns with hatred of treachery and lustful falseness. And how the comedies like *Volpone* and *Bartholomew Fair* echo with scornful laughter in the description of human duplicity. But as you read, as last you begin to understand why Ben Jonson is so angry and why he is so scornful. In strange negative fashion he is painting a picture of the men who are the opposite of the scoundrels he so mercilessly uncovers. There is no softness about his love of goodness. And there is a great hardness about his hatred of the rotting evils which man hugs to his bosom. These men are not caught in the clutches of circumstances over which they have no control. If a house of fate falls upon them, they themselves have built that house of fate. The days which produced the Invincible Armada were days when men believed deeply in man's awful power. And the scorn of Ben

Jonson is the scorn of a man who is a great believer in the powers which so often men accept only to drag them in the dust. Only men of great faith can be men of great indignation.

However you come upon it, the virile and vital and dependable sense of man always treats him as the master of great powers. He may be worthy of them. He may be unworthy of them. But there he stands knowing and thinking and controlling, the master of fate even when he brings ruin upon himself.

CHAPTER III

The Nature of the Real

IN the year 1915 Vachel Lindsay received the Levinson Prize signalizing the judgment that his poem "The Chinese Nightingale" was the best contribution for that year, to *Poetry, A Magazine of Verse*. It tells the tale of a night in a Chinese laundry. Chang, the laundryman, goes on with his work of ironing all through the night.

> "While the monster shadows glower and creep,
>   What can be better for man than sleep?"

> "I will tell you a secret," Chang replied;
> "My breast with vision is satisfied,
> And I see green trees and fluttering wings,
> And my deathless bird from Shanghai sings." [1]

Then comes the wonder and glamour of the strange night, with the nightingale singing, the Chinese lady of high degree and her songs of love fulfilled long ago, and the joss in the corner singing impolitely as though to himself. Old days, old ways, old beauty, and old struggles come into the room where Chang irons hour after hour, with impassive face.

> "Years on years I but half-remember . . .
>   Man is a torch, then ashes soon,
>   May and June, then dead December,
>   Dead December, then again June.
>   Who shall end my dream's confusion?
> Life is a loom, weaving illusion . . ." [2]

The whole subtle and beautiful poem, with its Chinese laundryman and his impassive face and all the exotic world of his imagination and his mind, in curious fashion brings to the reader the sense of the secrets hidden beneath the commonplace surface of things. And back of all the contrast, the old questions emerge: What is real? What is illusion? What is the nature of that which actually exists?

These are questions of which men inevitably think in their deeper moods. They are questions of which poets dream. And they point the direction of those speculations and processes of thought by means of

[1] From *The Chinese Nightingale, and Other Poems*, 1917, p. 3. Used by permission of The Macmillan Co., publishers.
[2] *Ibid.*, p. 12.

which philosophers try to answer the deepest questions regarding existence.

There is stuff; there is thought. There is the material; there is the
mental. And so we begin quickly to get at positions inevitably taken by
men who try to answer the question, What is the nature of the real?

1. Materialism

The materialist says, "The real is matter." And he gets his name from
his answer. Stuff seems so inevitably and indubitably present that this
answer may be said to be the first possible answer of the thoughtless.
You use material legs to transport a material body over the material
earth. You use material arms to lift material objects or to put them
down or to throw them from you. You use material eyes to look upon a
material landscape. You have a body, and you never meet other people
without meeting bodies like your own. It is matter, matter everywhere.
So it may seem inevitable that the materialist shall have the first day in
court. "The material," he asserts, "is the real." And he reverses the
statement with a good deal of gusto, "The real is always material."

If the materialist is reminded that you cannot get very far in the way
of explanation by means of static matter, he conveniently remembers
that his most ordinary experience is that of objects in motion. "Give me
matter and motion," he cries, "and I can explain everything." So, although he may require some centuries for the process, he constructs a
conception beginning with a nebular hypothesis and ending in the
subtler motions which he ascribes to the brain of man, this brain which
in his idea "secretes thought as the liver secretes bile." All this becomes
a vast picture covering all space and all time. The great god matter and
the great god motion are truly married, and from the union comes an
explanation of everything in the world.

It is all very bright, and it may seem very satisfying if you do not think
too critically or ask questions which are too difficult.

The idea, however, is sure to come to someone that there is a
difference between quantity and quality, that there is a difference between the existence of things and the consciousness of their existence,
that all the while the materialist is using powers which do not belong
to the world of matter and making distinctions which are not accounted
for by the world of motion.

The one fact about which a man is sure is his awareness. And he
moves from that to considering the experiences which this awareness
brings to him. Stuff is not delivered ready-made to his consciousness.
It must somehow become a mental fact before it has any reality for him.
To ignore the mental quality of awareness and to begin with things is
not only to put the cart before the horse, but it is fairly sure to mean the
denial of the existence of the horse. The answers to the questions, What

is real? and What is the nature of this reality?—if these answers are to
be critical—must always be based upon a prior investigation of how
things become real to us, such as we indicated in the last chapter.
Things only become things to us through thought. Thought is only real
to us as the action of the mind. All facts have to become mental facts before they are a part of human experience. So the materialist is not
merely standing on one leg. He is mistaking the nature of the leg on
which he stands. To be significant for thought, it must become a mental leg.

Of course, by means of agile figures of speech you can talk about
matter as if it were capable of all sorts of mental capers. You can even
talk about matter as if it were capable of all the work of the mind.
There are evidences of mind everywhere. But matter is the only reality.
Therefore, matter thinks. It is an easy and specious syllogism. And it is
just as false as it is easy. It begs the question in its minor premise that
matter is the only reality, and it goes on begging the question through
a vast and vagrant career.

This is just about what materialism amounts to. You seem so immediately sure of the world of stuff that you say, "This at any rate is
certain." It requires mental effort involving sweat and tears to analyze
the knowing process. So you blithely assert that thought is a function
of things. But if you put only things into the mill of your thought, only
things will come out. And so by a sure revenge the matter which is the
only reality becomes a monster devouring everything else. You have
really denied mind by making its powers a function of matter. And
you must live with your denial. To be a mountain simply is not the
same thing as being aware of the existence of a mountain. To stand
like Mont Blanc magnificently against the sky is one thing. To think
inspired thoughts about Mont Blanc as its summit of snow is glorious
in the sunset is quite another. Thought and thing are two different
orders, and, however they get related, they can never be regarded as the
same without the complete breakdown of the critical intelligence. And
since the world of things can only exist in experience by means of a
mental process, true explanation must always begin with mind. It can
never begin with matter. The materialist has already transcended his
materials the moment he has become aware of their existence. And no
theories of motion will help at this point. For motion, by definition, is
always a change of place. And a change of place is by its very nature
something very different from a consciousness of change.

2. Realism

It is possible, of course, to admit all this and yet to insist on the
reality of the material. It must assume mental form to be actual in
experience, we may say, but the actually existent material entity is the

occasion of the mental experience. This position holds the name "realism" in modern thought. It is, of course, quite different from the realism of the Middle Ages, which was concerned with the reality of ideas rather than with the reality of things.

Realism in the modern sense pays tribute to a certain sharp sense of actuality which characterizes all sensations. They may be mental experiences. But surely they refer to that which is beyond the mind. Healthy common sense, especially when it is not very reflective, always leans toward realism. It has a feeling that its world would somehow vanish if it were not a world with what the philosophers would call ontological reality. Hills and houses are not phantasmagoria. This is clear enough when you are paying for the building of a house or paying the price for all the land which is the surface of a hill so that this hill will become a part of your new farm. Eating, in some way, has to do with actual food. Drinking, in some way, has to do with actual liquid. Say what you will about consciousness, there must be an external world of which you are conscious. You are not buying so many yards of thought when you purchase cloth. You are not crossing the ocean in an idea when you embark in an Atlantic liner. You are not flying over the sea in a thought when you cross to Europe by air. On what Professor Borden P. Bowne used to call the sense plane, all this is very convincing. Usually it does not occur to the man who says these things that perhaps the truth which they contain may be expressed in quite a different philosophy.

For we must not attempt to deny that the realist is talking about things which by means of either his frame of thought or some other must be held clear as a part of our assured knowledge. There must be an objective reference in mental experience. And this objective reference cannot be a will-o'-the-wisp. It cannot be a make-believe. When I go to Switzerland, I must be sure of finding the same old mountains even if I am not sure of finding the same old buildings. Even after the blitz, I must find the Thames when I go to London, though sad havoc has been played with many familiar streets. When I meet an old friend, I must not find someone else looking out of his eyes. When I read an old book, I must not find the ancient sentences gone and new forms of words in their place. Without a certain dependability in experience as it moves out beyond the self, there would be no real experience at all. The realist is quite right in declaring for the dependability of our experience of things. He may not turn out to be so completely right about the source of that dependability.

3. Idealism

When Ralph Waldo Emerson wrote, "I become a transparent eyeball," he was expressing something—or trying to express something—

which many men have felt. You seem to see the hard and heavy aspects
of life fall away and there remains only a clarity so perfect that it is
almost disembodied. It is a flash—a mood—if you like. But perhaps it
expresses more of the genius of Emerson's never clearly thought out and
never masterfully articulated idealism than many of his more pontifical
utterances. To be sure, to Emerson idealism soon became a kind of pantheism where important distinctions had a way of becoming confused
and of getting lost. He was never a coherent thinker. And he had a way
of believing that when he contradicted himself he was simply expressing another side of the truth. But from the time when the influence of
Plato became powerful in his thought, Emerson belonged to those who
see things from the side of the idea rather than from the side of the
thing.

If we have been right in saying that things must become thoughts in
order to enter into actual experience, then it is surely from the side of
the mind that we must move in trying to understand things and not
from the side of things that we must move in trying to understand the
mind.

It is true again in experience that the great Irish Bishop was right
when he declared that to be is to be perceived. Perception is a mental
act. And all the stuff in the world must become a series of mental facts
before the material is real in experience. We can move along uncritically and call our mental experience of things an actual contact with
their physical essence. But we can say this only when we call a morato-
rium on thought. A fist can never get into the brain in order to become
a material experience of a fist. A child can never wedge its way into the
cerebrum or cerebellum in order to become the experience of a child.
The country through which you ride on a train or over which you fly in
the air does not enter your head by some open door. Your experience of
nature and of people is always a mental experience. It belongs to the
mystery of the capacity of the self to be aware. And whenever you reduce this world of mental experience to a world of things, you emasculate it, and take away from it every living quality.

It is possible to try to solve the problem by putting words together
and by supposing that you have put together that for which the words
stand. You may call the universe a thought-thing world. And after you
have said this you may feel very wise. Actually you have made no contribution to critical understanding. You have put down the word
thought and you have put next to it the word thing. But nothing has
happened in the realm of intellectual apprehension. It still remains true
that things must become thoughts before they can become real in consciousness. All facts of experience are mental facts. And however big the
problem, we must begin with the mental awareness and try to find out

how it can have an objective reference, and especially how it can be the common experience of many separate minds.

In the meantime, it is important to see that by this clear assertion of the essentially mental quality of experience we have escaped many pitfalls. Once and for all we are delivered from the confusion of those who think that the existence of size is the same thing as the experience of size, that the existence of length is the same thing as the experience of length, that the existence of thickness is the same thing as the experience of thickness.

We are insisting on this because the failure to be clear here is the source of no end of philosophical fallacies. You have told something about a book when you have completely described the way in which a fountain pen writes the letters, the words, the sentences, the paragraphs, and the chapters. But you have left out everything really important. It is not merely that you must get to the fingers which hold the fountain pen and the hand which contains the fingers and the arm which reaches its consummation in the hand and the body of which the arm is a part and the brain which is the telephone center from which a message is sent out to the fingers—you can do all this and yet miss the secret. The invisible and regal mind which commands all this responsive mechanism is the important matter. The self which is aware and which moves among possibilities and decides and executes decisions is the important matter. And all the other elements are part of real experience only as they become mental facts. The world of the idea is the real world.

To say all this is to be sure to say something which leaves a perfect mass of problems unsolved. But to say it is to say the one thing which gives a promise of the solution of the problems and without which none of the problems could be solved at all.

At first it seems to the unwary that we are destroying the very world of form and color and movement which is so central in experience itself. But the unwary must be asked to be patient. We are not in any way trying to change experience. We are simply trying to change the explanation of experience. All this Berkeley saw long ago and said with a certain finality. But any time anyone fails to see this it is necessary to say it again. To say that in order to become real in experience a thing must become a thought is not to change experience one iota. It is only taking a step in understanding experience.

4. Impersonal Realism

The realists, however, insist on being heard. And there is no better way of clarifying our thought than by inspecting some of the claims which the realists make. There is impersonal realism, and with this we are immediately concerned. There is also personal realism, and of that we shall be speaking in a later section.

The impersonal realist is busy with what he sees and hears and touches. Like Dr. Johnson—who was not, however, an impersonal realist—he kicks stones and puts an end to all argument. The stones are *there*. The subtle process by which the stones on the ground become stones on the ground of the mind he never considers. But it is of another aspect of his argument that we wish now to think. He becomes so busy with what he finds the mind perceiving that he quite forgets the mind which does the perceiving. He not only ignores all the problems connected with physical objects becoming mental experience, but he completely forgets the mind which becomes aware of the objective world. So he limits his thought to this objective world. He finds there masses and masses of stuff. He finds endless change of position. And because he forgets that this world of stuff and change has no possible significance until it becomes real for a knowing mind, he reaches the conclusion that he lives in a universe where stuff and change are the only realities. The self which he ignores is, of course, the one fundamental fact in the whole situation. He leaves his stuff and change without real definition and without real meaning. When a philosophy ignores the knowing self, we call it impersonal. And so we may call this thinker who forgets his own mind in his preoccupation with things and their movements an impersonal realist.

Since the world in which he believes becomes actual only in experiences in a world whose existence he denies, it is clear that he is caught in a very confusing dilemma. As long as he keeps his mind and uses it, of course his denial of the existence of the mind upon which he depends in making the denial is not very important to any critical thinker. Unfortunately, there are a good many uncritical thinkers in the world.

But once we see the building of the uncritical realist falling to pieces before our eyes, we begin to make genuine headway. If there is a world of stuff and change in which there is no other reality, it can never be an object of thought, it can never be the basis of experience, and it can never be known to exist, since knowledge belongs to a world which transcends stuff and material change.

Volumes of discerning and acute reasoning could scarcely make the matter clearer than it becomes if we have this central insight. Stuff and change, if they exist in a universe which contains nothing else, belong forever to a blind, black world without meaning and incapable of having any relation to experience. The stuff which is conscious is more than stuff. The change which is conscious is more than change.

The impersonal realist is a master at trick card playing. When you are not watching, he always slips in the card he is going to produce later. And he does wonderful work with this card which has no right to be where he has put it—which, indeed, according to his theory of the game, has no existence at all. The process is not merely magic. It is black magic.

The impersonal realist is, of course, a materialist. And all that we have already said in criticism of the position of the materialist applies to him. He claims a title to property because he believes in the existence of the property. But he quite forgets the fact that if you have denied the existence of owners, you have no right to ask for a warranty deed from a particular owner.

He says in effect, "I do not exist, but I assert my right to believe in a universe whose defining qualities make my own existence impossible." Really he cannot have it both ways. A realist who denies the existence of a knowing self has come to a position of complete and hopeless self-contradiction. If realism is to survive, it must be in different terms than those of the impersonal thinker. For the impersonal thinker always insists on making another speech after he has been condemned to death and executed. Such a lively corpse really ceases to be a corpse.

5. Impersonal Idealism

This problem of the impersonal might seem remote enough from the the interpretation of life which bears the name idealism. But as a matter of fact there is idealism and idealism. There is a type of idealism—and one form of Hegelianism is profoundly associated with it—which bases its interpretation on the logical structure of the mind rather than on the living mind in action. This produces that very odd result, an impersonal idealism.

It is clear when you analyze the elements of logic—and it has been clear ever since the time of Aristotle—that there is a formal structure of mental relationships which we can analyze and set forth with the utmost clarity. By a process of abstraction and a development of bright figures of speech, we may speak of this logical analysis as if it were the cause of that whose character it expresses. Of course, there is nothing causal about it. The pattern of formal logic is one thing. The causal aspect of reality is another. But if you keep juggling your abstractions, you can make a tremendous impression of intellectual depth and of profound understanding. You seem to get rid of all the hard stuffiness of materialism and to inhabit a world of clear mental quality. You get away from all living quality and make your bed in a place of abstract relationships.

In the long run, it all becomes as cold and hard and rigid as materialism itself. Logic describing the dialectic of conscious intelligence is one thing. Logic as the abstract substitute for living intelligence is quite another.

One is fairly baffled by the many-sided history of the vast adventures of these abstractions which are really no more than the ghosts of thought. We shall see later that they enter theology with the most astonishing effect. The pseudo sciences thrive on them. Here we are at the root of all this confusion. The moment you substitute an abstract formula for the living action of a conscious self, you fall into a very deep pit. And you can never get out of this pit by the aid of an impersonal logical formula. Only a conscious self using the dialectic of intelligence as a living being can get out of the pit.

In a way, the whole problem emerged in the thinking of Plato. His world of ideas can easily be construed as an impersonal world. There is good evidence that by the time he wrote the *Laws* he saw that these ideas must be a part of the experience of an Ultimate Person. This aspect of the whole problem will confront us later.

The question is likely to be asked: Why all the concern which has emerged again and again as to logical forms? The answer is not simple. But we can say at once that logical forms are of the utmost importance for classifications, though they are never adequate for causal explanation. So logical forms represent a sort of double-entry bookkeeping of the mind by which no end of things get put in their proper places. It all has the greatest practical value as long as there is a bookkeeper about to make the entries. But when you try to think of the logical forms as having a certain vitality so that they record themselves, as if the figures a bookkeeper manipulates were fighting to get themselves put in proper places on the page, you are in a world of fairyland and not in a world of rational intelligence.

It is further true that the logical forms are valuable because by their means a thinker discards the adventitious and gets down to the matters of central significance. But here, too, the thinkers have to make the choices. In a way, there is a double process. In dealing with justice, for instance, the thinker abstracts the general logical quality from particular cases and does fine execution on a basis of happy subjectivity. Then, when he wants to make the principle effective in some concrete situation, he moves back from the general to the particular with a good deal of mental enrichment coming from his processes of abstract thought. But the abstract principle of justice never creates just people. It never seizes unjust people and lifts them by their hair. It is an instrument of conscious intelligence. It is helpless—indeed, it is nonexistent—apart from a consciously intelligent self.

In the same way the liberty for which men die is logically abstracted from the deeds of countless brave men. But at every crisis it has to get back into concreteness again. Our powers of abstraction are endless. And when we personify our abstractions, as we do incessantly, we feel that we have advanced our understanding. It is fascinating and precarious business. For we always have to come back from abstractions and figures of speech when we are dealing at first hand with reality. Impersonal idealism thrives on a diet of abstractions. It becomes corpulent on a diet of personifications.

6. Personal Realism

Realism itself, however, may repudiate its materialistic relations. The realist may be a thinker who sees that without a self all experience disintegrates. And he may think about the conscious agent of experience in such a fashion as to achieve a true conception of personality. He may avoid the pitfalls of materialism and the similar pitfalls of impersonal realism. He may become a personal realist.

At once we must admit that the personal realist is a very engaging thinker. He gives one a sense of having his feet on the ground. But he stands erect, and he has a sense of high places and high meanings. He seems to himself, and often he seems to others, to have all the advantages of the idealist with his emphasis on the thinker and the thought process and of the realist with his sense of actual material aspects of existence.

In any future we can foresee there will be thinkers who set the highest value on the conscious, intelligent self and yet believe that the world of things is real in its own right. And the personal realist may well turn out to be on the side of the angels as well as on the side of the atoms. We must always be prepared to treat him with respect, and he will probably be a comrade-in-arms in most of the good battles we have to fight. In a way, he seems to make the best of both worlds. He knows the importance of thoughts and ideas. He knows the tremendous value of persons. And he sets this world of people and thoughts and decisions in a material frame in which, so he is persuaded, it loses no jot or tittle of its significance. He lives in a world of seeds and a world of bullets. But he also lives in a world of ideas and ideals which give these seeds and bullets their significance. He is persuaded that if you give up the material world you live in a universe of ghosts. He is persuaded that if you give up spiritual personality you have no significant world in which to live. So he keeps a firm hand upon both.

It is not hard to meet the personal realist at a peace congress of philosophies. He seems to be eclectic in the best sense. If his thinking has dualistic aspects, the dualism is, so he tell us, a reflection of experience. He only keeps in his interpretation of experience what he finds in experience itself. He refuses to emasculate experience in the name of a false unity. He believes in persons. He believes in things. He believes that it is the function of persons to rule over things. What could be more satisfactory?

And we must be willing cheerfully to admit him to the fellowship of the thinkers who would do justice to the world of facts as well as to the world of values. Any quarrel we have with him is a family quarrel.

For a quarrel there is. At least, there are questions which we must ask. And we do not think he will find it easy to answer the questions.

First, what does he do with the fact that all experience is on the thought side and not on the side of things? The existence of the material, as he has seen, would not mean the experience of the material. And however actual they are, things must become part of the fabric of a mind, which can make them a part of experience only as they accept its laws and themselves become mental facts. For here is the crux of the whole matter. A material fact must become a mental fact before it can become a fact of experience. The order of experiences is a mental order. It is an experience which has a material reference, but the experience itself is not material. And if all this is true, does not the hard material world quite fade out as a fact apart from experience which is by its very nature always a matter of the reality of the mind? How does the world of stuff become real in experience? By the very definition of experience, the world of stuff and the world of consciousness are two different worlds. How do things get into thought? How do things become thoughts?

If the suggestion of Leibnitz as to preëstablished harmony be made, at first it seems very attractive. But pressing questions force themselves upon us. If the world of things is given connection with the world of thought only by a nexus which expresses merely a parallel and not a genuine relationship, what is it really worth? Do we really need the world of things? The question may seem shocking enough at first, but it simply will get asked.

7. Personal Idealism

So at long last we come to that personal idealism which makes such regal claims in the world of thought. And at the outset we must be clear as to just what its claims are. It not only does not deny, it asserts, the actuality of the material *as experience*. But it denies that an experience of the material is itself material. It believes in a firmly coherent order of experience with a material reference. But it believes that this experience is a *mental fact* or, if you will, a series of mental facts. And it declares that if all the minds were to be destroyed there would be nothing left. It does not believe that a world of hard stuff is necessary as a basis for experiences with an objective reference. It does not believe that stuff could ever get to minds or that minds could get to stuff. It believes in the actuality of the material as experience. But it does not believe in its ontological reality. It does not believe that it has any existence apart from minds.

Even the personal realists must have been somewhat embarrassed by the way in which physics plays with their ideas of what is real. Sir

James Jeans has half critically and half naïvely confessed that the physicist, by paths all his own, is coming to conceptions of reality not so different from those of Berkeley. The analysis of things can never proceed very far even in physics without finding that the hard qualities begin to change and the first thing you know you are living in a world consisting of something not unlike mathematical points.

But not to press this matter for the moment, the personal idealist insists on asking why, if the mind can furnish a complete pattern of experience with an objective reference—and as a matter of fact all experience does belong to just such a pattern—why you should seek a reality beyond the mind and what you should do with it if you found it?

The personal idealist, like the personal realist, begins with the conscious self. All experience is experience of a conscious self. And all experience becomes experience only by being a part of the conscious awareness which is a spiritual and not a material fact. The person—the conscious self—is real. Only the conscious self is real.

Now the hosts of critics rush in. This is all very well, they shout, if there is only one conscious self and if he creates his world in the constant process of experiencing it. But there are millions and millions of conscious selves. And they live in the same world. How do you account for this community in experience? How do you account for this common pattern of facts? A billion selves each creating his own mental environment would produce chaos worse confounded. What is the source of this community? What makes it secure? What makes it dependable? Must we not go back to the material universe after all?

The personal idealists are by no means disconcerted in the presence of this onslaught of questions. It is at least clear, they reply, that the solution must be in the realm of mind and not in the realm of matter. If the experience of the material is a mental experience for one person, it is not less a mental experience for a billion persons. You cannot go to things to piece out the limitations of intelligence. You will have to find more intelligence. The experience of every conscious self belongs to the realm of the unpicturable reality of spiritual awareness. And in this world the solution of its problems must be found. The world of minds must be held together by a Supreme Mind. It cannot be held together by inanimate matter.

The truth is that, much as we respect the personal realist, we are driven to suspect that to maintain his own position he will have to make more of personality and less of the hard world of matter. Until he does this we gladly give him the right hand of fellowship just because he has traveled so far in the great journey of metaphysics. But his journey's end is, we must assert, only a halfway house. We must go on, and we look a little anxiously at our friend the personal realist, fearing that he may be tempted to go backward. In any event there is light on the mountaintop. And toward that light we proceed to climb.

But we remind ourselves, as we go on in the clear, pure air of the heights, that no true idealist, least of all a personal idealist, denies the actuality of experience with a material reference. To all idealists daylight and dark, spring and summer and autumn and winter, food and drink, health and sickness, birth and death, are just as actual, just as much a dependable part of experience, as to the most convinced realist. The one finds the basis of all this in a world of matter. The other finds it in a world of mind. And the personal idealist authenticates his position by a series of tremendous assertions, not about a human person, but about an Ultimate Person—the source, the upholder, and the basis of all experience.

CHAPTER IV

The Ultimate Person

THE seventeenth-century poet Henry Vaughan wrote the lovely lines:

> My soul, there is a country
>   Far beyond the stars,
> Where stands a wingèd sentry
>   All skilful in the wars:
> There, above noise and danger,
>   Sweet Peace sits crown'd with smiles,
> And One born in a manger
>   Commands the beauteous files.
> He is thy gracious Friend,
>   And—O my soul, awake!—
> Did in pure love descend
>   To die here for thy sake.
> If thou çanst get but thither,
>   There grows the flower of Peace,
> The Rose that cannot wither,
>   Thy fortress, and thy ease.
> Leave then thy foolish ranges;
>   For none can thee secure
> But One who never changes—
>   Thy God, thy life, thy cure.

The last lines breathe that sense of God as the basis of life, the deep security, the great healer, which is so essentially the genius of religion. We are now to make the claim that this is truly authentic just because God is as necessary to the world of reality and to thought about it as he is to the realm of religion. Without God all experience would fall apart.

At the close of the last chapter we had come face to face with the problem of securing a community of experience in a world of separate persons. We had already seen that a hard material world is of no help here. The fact that materials exist simultaneously does not mean that they are conscious of existing simultaneously. The fact that material objects touch each other does not mean that they are conscious of touching each other. Assertions about existence never solve problems of consciousness. All material facts, as we have seen, must be transmuted into mental facts before they exist for consciousness. But if the world

of experience is a mental world, what need is there of a physical coun-
terpart? If experience with an objective reference is a secure experience
of all minds, what is added by assuming and asserting a world of stuff
apart from the mind? Here we met one great problem. How can you
have a world of common experience held secure from individual eccen-
tricity when you have such multitudes of minds? Clearly this world of
experience, however mental it may be, is not the creation of the individual human mind. He finds it when he becomes conscious. He leaves
it secure for other minds when he passes from the activities of this life.
At this point we move toward the thought of that Great Person, that
Supreme Mind, who is the source and the sustainer of all experience.

1. The Ground of a Community of Personal Experience

The only way to account for that community of personal experience
which is the first and most significant part of human life is by finding
its source in an ultimate Mind, who determines and maintains the
whole fabric of experience of all the other minds which exist. It does not
begin with any specific human individual, because its source is in God.
It does not pass with the going of any human individual from the activities of this world, because it is maintained by God. Man is a finite agent
of conscious experience and decision. God is that complete personal intelligence which is free from all the limitations of the finite. Man is a
finite mind. God is the ultimate conscious mind with an amplitude of
knowledge and power of every sort. Man is the relative mind. God is
the perfect mind. And God provides that stable structure of mental
experience with an objective reference which becomes the human experience of a material world. The experience is mental, but it has an
objective reference as secure and as dependable as the character of God.
The experience of a world of things depends not on changing and passing human individuals. It depends on the complete and perfect and all-
powerful intelligence of God, who maintains this mental experience of
a physical world and gives it security and dependability. The experience is mental, but it is an experience of a material world, though it is
not material experience. Indeed, there is no such thing as material
experience.

Now the moment one sees that this mental experience with a material
reference is just as secure as the power and the character of God, he
sees that there is no need of a world of stuff outside the mind of man
and of God and of whatever other rational beings there are in the universe. Such a world of stuff would add nothing to the definiteness and
adequacy and security of the objective experience we have already. And
it would be a rather embarassing problem, since such a material world
would have to be transmuted into mental form before it could become
real in experience. So the specter of materialism disappears even as a

specter. God, the Perfect and Controlling Mind, provides the ground for a mental experience of material things and relationships and holds that pattern of experience steady and secure.

2. *The Ground of the Existence of Persons*

If we grant the truth of what has been said, we have given some account of the experience of human persons and of its basis and security in God, who is the Ultimate Person. But if in this fashion we have given account of the experience of persons, we have said nothing at all about that other problem which arises when we consider the *existence* of persons. We have come to think of God as the author and the maintainer of the pattern of the experience of persons. The next step in our dialectic is that we can do this just because He is the creator of those persons and has immediate contact with the very texture of their minds. He is the creator and the sustainer of the life of all persons. He is the ground of their existence. All the relative persons exist because of the act of the creative will of the perfect person. He gives them *being*—to be sure, dependent upon him—but real in the most fundamental ontological sense.

Here we come upon an important distinction. God creates persons. He maintains in and through their own mental life a pattern of experience with a physical reference. The material aspects of life are real in experience. They have no ontological reality outside experience. If the Great Person, who establishes the pattern and all the conscious beings who share it as experience, ceased to be, there would be nothing left. The material exists only in and for conscious beings. Apart from them it is nonexistent.

The persons, however, have ontological reality. The power of God creates and keeps them alive, but they are real in a sense in which hills and mountains are not real. God *makes* persons; He *posits* the experience of a material world for the conscious beings whom He makes.

We begin to see, then, the whole philosophical point of view. All reality belongs to the mind. There is the eternal and perfect reality which is found in the life of God, the Eternal and Self-Existent Mind. God creates creatures who have the same qualities of awareness and knowledge and decision which characterize His own life. He possesses these things perfectly; they possess them relatively. God and all persons are ontologically real. But the relative persons come from God and depend on Him for the sustaining of their existence.

God posits for the conscious creatures He has made an objective, material world. It is as clear as the thoughts of His mind and as dependable as His purpose. It is real in the experience of conscious minds. But it is not ontologically real. That is, it has no reality apart from mental experience. God supports it as an experience for the persons He has made. But to say that it has a reality apart from experience would be to use a form of words without meaning. It would have less meaning, if such a thing were possible, than a sound no one has ever heard, a sight no one has ever seen, or an object no one has ever touched.

But within experience the material world is as real as any objects of experience could be. Day and night, summer and winter, the laws of physics and chemistry, are as secure as the character of God. He did not posit this order of experience to deceive men, but to give them an actual and a dependable experience.

Here, then, you have a rich and complete world of experience, with God over and under and moving through it all. Only through His fiat does it exist. Only through His will does it continue. But it is as actual in experience as we feel it to be when we witness the shining of the sun, the falling of the rain, or when we inhale the fragrance of spring flowers.

All this is the result of the divine thought, the divine purpose, and the divine will. It does not represent the pantheistic abyss, where everything is divine in a sense that leaves nothing with any actual significance. The world which depends on the conscious purpose of the God of good will is something very different from a hypothetical world somehow an aspect of the nature of God. In a sound philosophy the Divine Self in its perfect awareness and purpose and the human self with its relative awareness and purpose are kept in emphasis all the time.

3. Explaining the Personal by Means of the Impersonal

We are now at a point in our discussion where it ought to be possible to see very clearly that there is no more characteristic fallacy than that involved in the attempt to explain the personal by means of the impersonal. It may seem odd that anyone should even attempt to explain the conscious by means of the unconscious. But it happens often enough. It is as if some queer thinker arrived at the conviction that if you kept an unconscious object long enough, at last it would become conscious. It is as if we were to suppose that if you exercised a long enough period of patient thinking in dealing with things, at last they would become thoughts. So men have been tempted to look at brain cells and so to try to discuss ideas. They have been tempted to study glands for the purpose of finding purposes. Sometimes the fallacy takes the form of assuming that if one thing succeeds another, the first of the series has caused the form which comes later. It seems to require some intelligence to perceive that succession does not involve causality. When there is some uniformity in the succession, the case becomes more complicated, but still the cause is outside the series. Anyone playing from a music sheet a composition of Mozart would follow the same order in the production of sound. But the cause would have to be sought first in Mozart as he created the composition, and later in the musician who reproduced what Mozart had indicated. In no case would one note be the cause of the next.

Sometimes it is an impersonal abstraction which is discussed as if it were a genuine cause. There is a principle which unfolds in the processes of existence, we are told, and in this principle is the cause of what happens. If we mean by principle a clearly held purpose in the mind of a person divine or human, a purpose which dominates action, then what we say has meaning. But if we mean some unconscious entity which somehow does the work of conscious intelligence, we are talking nonsense.

This is all the more true when it is turned into a large scheme of an intelligent "unconscious." In a number of ways this sort of thinking has been carried on. We have, for instance, the very purposeful way in which a universe quite without awareness does the most intelligent things, and only becomes conscious of how intelligent it is when man appears. One is tempted to feel that a universe which does so well without consciously trying is a trick universe playing fast and loose with an intelligence which it really possesses. Again there is the furtive idea that if the universe is without intelligence a long enough time, this mental vacuum will do the work of a mind. The truth is, of course, that from the impersonal only the impersonal can come—if, indeed, there is any coming at all. A process which moves from the unconscious to the conscious is not evolution. It is magic.

4. Explaining the Impersonal by Means of the Personal

It is the most natural thing in the world, however, to explain the impersonal by means of the personal. Every time a boy makes a whistle by means of a small branch and a bit of bark, we have the personal turning the impersonal to its own ends.

In his *Technics and Civilization* Lewis Mumford has a good deal to say of mining and its processes. And much of what he has to say is not very pleasant. It is necessary to keep in mind in all such discussions that the whole story is a tale of persons getting things out of the bowels of the earth. We can never explain a mining process by means of the ore which the mine contains. We can only explain a mining process by means of the persons who see the possibilities of the mine and plan it and those who carry on its activities. A laboratory has no significance apart from the personality of the scientific investigators who use its facilities.[1] Whenever anything which has meaning happens, we have to search for the person who is responsible for the meaning. History is a tale of the adventures of persons. They have used the impersonal more

[1] See my *Personality and Science* (New York: Harper & Bros., 1930).

and more. Mechanized warfare is one of the most typical examples of man bending the impersonal to his own purposes. The person is the point of pivotal importance always.

We have been saying in this chapter that what is so obviously true in our planting and sowing, in our building and manufacturing, in our writing of books and in our impassioned speech, is most of all true of the whole order of significance. We explain the things that happen to the impersonal in the whole universe by that Great Person, Almighty God. The causal activity we know most immediately is that of a man with a purpose. The only intelligible way of explaining the universe is to take this man as a clue and to move on to a God with a purpose.

The scientists who have been moving in recent years from attempted explanations in terms of impersonal formulas to the recognition of a conscious, free master of impersonal relationships have been characterized by increasing critical insight. A formula is always abstracted from a concrete situation which gains its significance from the intention of a person. The orderly ways of the Great Master of the universe are discovered by man. Then by a process of abstraction they are discussed as if they had a life and independence of their own. But what we call the laws of nature are only what someone has wisely denominated the habits of God.

No catalogues of impersonal formulas amount to an explanation. You have got to get back to an intelligent purpose if you want to carry on a process of explanation. The impersonal formula is always the discovery of a conscious person. The law of gravitation never discovers Newton. It is Newton who discovers the law of gravitation.

In the days when materialistic scientists made a vast machine of the universe, even this cold and mechanical product was the result of their own mental activity. They made a closed system of the uniform and mathematically impersonal activities they discovered and equated this vast machine with the whole of reality. But they never could get themselves into the machine. In other words, men have never been able to construct even an incomplete or a false explanation of the universe without using their free personal consciousness. You have to be a person in order to deny personality.

All true explanation, then, comes at last to be personal explanation. Everything that really happens goes back to personal intention somewhere.

5. Human Personality

My copy of the first volume of Lord Macaulay's *Critical and Historical Essays* contains at the end the note: "Finished August 20, 1942, 2:45 A.M. London." Those days and nights in the English metropolis in 1942 with their quality of subconscious tension were given a certain color by the reading of these essays, engaged so much with powerful and brilliant and dramatic people. It was good to read of the mighty figures of other days in hours one snatched from demanding responsibilities while England was fighting for its life. Burleigh, John Hampden, William Pitt, Lord Clive, Warren Hastings, and the rest brought back a spacious life full of glory and of tragedy, of great honor and of moral vicissitudes. It gave one a sense of an imperishable splendor not untouched by the pattern of human weakness and failure. But it gave one a deep impression that it is good to be a man.

We are making this study from the standpoint of an inspection of human experience. Already we have seen what tremendous positions are implicit in that experience and must be assumed to be true if that experience is valid. We have seen that, though this experience has to do with things, it is essentially mental in its own quality. And we are beginning to see what it means to say that it is begun, continued, and ended in God.

At this point of our discussion we want to see that experience as a part of this large pattern of thought. Here stands man with an objective reference to his experience. This puts him above a world of things, which comes to him as a mental experience but which functions as a world below him which he must master, discipline, and use. Man is always tempted to make a practical abdication of his manhood like the intellectual abdication which he makes when he becomes a materialist. He is tempted to let this physical reference of his experience master and dominate all his thought and action. His physical experience may be likened to a throne. He himself may be likened to the king. The oddest thing about man is that he is constantly tempted to forget his kingliness and to worship the throne upon which he sits. But he was meant for lordship. This physical reference of experience is fascinating, useful, and at times wholly delightful. But it is always to be mastered by something higher than itself, something more real than itself, something, indeed, without which it could not become a part of experience at all.

Just because the physical aspects of man's experience may be given a place which does not belong to them, it is sometimes conceived that what is called the life of the body is really the great foe of the life of the mind. Actually this is not so. The body has its own rights as a part of experience. It has its own place in experience. It has its own wholly dignified and important and, indeed, beautiful place in human experience. And when it seems to take the bit in its teeth and go galloping down the road, it is really a victim rather than a rebel. For just as all experience of the physical is mental, so we must go on and say that only through the permission and decision of the mind can the body go wrong. It is the mind which falsely used can give to physical experience a place which never belonged to it. For it is the mind which goes wrong in mental experience just as it is the mind which goes wrong in physical experience. Indeed, it is only the mind which goes either right or wrong. The physical world provides the chessmen. The mind provides the player who decides what moves the wooden puppets on the chess-board are to make.

But the human mind itself has a place just as does the human body. For the mind of man exists only through the creative and sustaining action of that great ultimate intelligence which is the mind of God. And just as the physical aspects of man's experience must be mastered and guided and disciplined by the mind of man, so men's minds are under a great overlordship, the overlordship of the Creator and Ruler of all minds. Of this we shall have much to say in later chapters. Now we look straight at the fact that man's experience has a physical refer-ence though he is not material. And it has a divine reference though he is man and not God.

This man has relations with a world below him without becoming one with it and with a world above him while remaining a creature owing his creation and his continuing existence to God.

The uncritical thinkers are perpetually trying, as they look at the physical side of experience, to make man one with the world below him. Or when they look at his possible fellowship with God, they try to make him one with the God who made him. So man under their encourage-ment sinks into the world of beasts or tries to be a god. And disaster comes either way. The word "unity" is the most misused word in the language. Carried to its ultimate conclusion, as we shall see later, it blocks out all distinctions. Men may mean something true when they talk of man's moral unity with God, but the phrase is so open to mis-construction that it is better always to speak of moral likeness to God.

Man is over a world of experience which is below him and under a world of experience which is above him. He is to live in the light of these tremendous relationships. Forever he is able to look down with-out going down, and to look up without the strange arrogance of sup-posing that he is God and that he has made himself.

6. Divine Personality

Some years ago Dr. William Barry published a remarkable book en-titled *The Triumph of Life*. Its pages literally glow with bright flashes of penetrating thought. Sometimes insight and something not unlike perfect poetry happily combine. Toward the end of the volume the reader comes upon these phrases: "A crumpled rose-leaf, a gleam in the water lit up by sunset, a child's happy smile, waken in me the convic-tion that, as I am looking out upon Nature, so there is Another gazing on me." [2] The Great Other Person is the goal of one's thought. He is

[2] New York: Longmans, Green & Co., 1928, p. 244.

also implicit as a conviction ready to emerge whenever we understand the actual quality of the human mind. We are not trying in the ordinary sense to prove the existence of God. We are only saying that when man contemplates his own experience with anything like critical acumen he enters upon processes of thought which fall apart completely unless they are held together by the living God, Creator and Sustainer of all life. This much has surely appeared in a good many different fashions in the process of the dialectic of human experience which we have been conducting. Doubtless God is infinitely more than we perceive as a result of such an enterprise in thinking. But so much He must be. And He can never be anything which contradicts the fundamental insights which we reach when we contemplate what is involved in the very nature of human experience. However little we apprehend it in the naïve stages of our thinking, human experience is actually an adventure in partnership with God. He may be hidden from our dull eyes, but all the while He is supporting us and with a sort of divine, kindly irony supporting the very dullness which blinds our eyes and of which we are so inordinately proud.

Suddenly, then, we begin to see that, while in one way God is the great mystery, in another He is the One whom we can understand. Things, in a sense, are always alien to our deepest selves, however much commerce we have with them. But God is like us because He has made us like Himself. We are aware. God is aware. We have a sense of truth. God is truth infinitely alive. We use our wills and behold results. God's infinite will is the ultimate potency of the universe. We choose between alternatives. God's beatific life is a perpetual and perfect choice. We reach out for fellowship with other beings who are aware, who think, who decide. And God, who alone is such a being in ultimate completeness, is the final goal of our desire for fellowship.

Much light is thrown upon rather dark matters when once we realize that when we try to have fellowship with nature, we always make some aspect of nature human in order to believe in this fellowship. The nature poets of the mystical sort are constantly remaking nature, putting personal qualities into it in order to have that deep and brooding fellowship by means of which they hope to satisfy the intuitions of religion. They make an idol of nature in order that they may turn the idol into a person breathing what they like to feel is the very breath of the universe. But nature is the creation of God, not the God of creation, and any attempt to rest in nature's fellowship is little more than tossing one's loneliness into an evening cloud and so trying to see the reflection of a human face.

Not so with God. He offers more than we are yet able to desire of perfect fellowship, because all that we are in the small beginnings of personality, He is in amplitude and in final fulfillment. What we are and what God is somehow fit together. What God would have us be is written in a nature which is made like His own so that it can hear His cry across the wastes of the universe.

The Perfect Person alone can give us rest of mind and rest of spirit. Only He, more like ourselves than we have ever been able to be, can satisfy us. All this is involved in being made in the image of God.

But the sense of likeness must deepen as we realize that God, the Perfect Person, made us, the finite persons. There is nothing quite so satisfying as following the river of our life back to its source. And when we find that source in the creative act of the Perfect Person, all life begins to be suffused with light. At last we begin to see that we cannot define anything or any person except in relation to the Mighty Master of the creative act.

The Great Person is the Sustainer as well as the Creator. He is the One always and immediately present. Without that present Omnipotent Person, experience would be less than the disappearing shadow of a dream. It is only because He is sure of us that we live at all. And therefore as our awareness deepens it is the most normal thing in the world to be sure of Him. Our relation to God is immediate. Our relation to all other persons and things is secondary. Therefore faith in God always comes to the confused as a recovery and never as a discovery. The bundle of our life is perpetually involved in relationships only understood in the light of the perpetual presence of the living God.

So we have seen the Divine Person in connection with His involvement in our own experience. Doubtless there is much more to see and much more to know. But at least we are in a position of good certainty as far as we have gone.

7. *The Security of Experience in the Ultimate Person*

Now we may venture a brief summary: All experience is mental. God is Himself the Perfect Mind and the Creator and Sustainer of all other minds. God makes secure in experience that objective frame of reference which has to do with the material world. He maintains its orderliness and definitiveness and coherence. It has no existence apart from the Divine Mind and the other minds in which He makes this experience constant and secure. But it is as secure as the character of God. He does not play tricks with the minds which He has made. He maintains the whole infinitely complex fabric of the physical order of experience so that it reflects the dependableness and the orderliness and the coherence of His own mind. The actuality of the physical side of experience is maintained by that omnipotent God who has immediate access to every mind He has made and gives to these minds a great order of experience *which they share.* This gift of a "common for all" to men is one of the greatest of God's gifts. We would be strangers indeed in a strange universe if He gave to each of us a different world. But that is just what He does not do. From electrons to stars He gives us the same world of experience. And just because He is not an eternal jester but is the God of infinite good will, we can move together through this world of experience, never looking at each other with alien eyes because the mind of one has been made responsive to one mental pattern of the physical world which has been given to him, and the mind of another has been made responsive to another pattern of the physical world which has been given to him. All men find the Southern Cross in the sky when they sail the South Pacific.

One begins to see, then, how tremendously religious life is, whether or not one understands it to be so. A man may try to let God alone. A man may try to let the thought of God alone. But God never lets the man alone. One second without God and the whole fabric of experience would fall apart. All our experience is in God. None of it is apart from God.

What we call the vast, interlacing system of natural law is only a name for the uniformity in experience which is maintained by the immediate presence of the living God. It is the expression of His purpose. It is the product of His will. It is dependable because He is dependable. It is secure because of His perfection as the very essence of eternal good will.

A laboratory, then, always contains an altar, though the scientist may not see the altar. The scientist may be so busy studying the uniformities which appear in experiences that he never looks up to see the Creator and Master of Uniformity who presides over all the world of relationships, which he studies. Of course, a study of the uniformities themselves never reveals the nature of that creative act which makes them real in human experience any more than a study of a mouth organ by itself would reveal the mouth of the player of the organ. You can so hide yourself in an aspect of experience that you quite miss the other aspects of experience which give it any permanent meaning.

But all the while the really important questions have to do with the source of that uniform experience of the material world so familiar to us all. And the important answers all have to do with the Great Person who posits the frame which enables the minds of men to have experience with a constant and dependable material reference. It is in this sense that all questions are theological questions at last, and that science is a perpetual adventure in exploring the thoughts of God as they have become objective in man's experience.

8. Moving Back to the Major Premise from the World of Experience

So we have been constructing a sort of inverted series of syllogisms. We have moved from things back to the mental form they must take in order to have significance for experience. We have moved from the human mind of the individual on to the cluster of human minds. We have moved from the cluster of human minds to the Great Ultimate Mind which has made and sustains them all and which gives them a frame of experience with a dependable objective reference. It all hangs together and gives us in outline a complete and orderly account of the process of thought and its relation to the actuality of being.

It needs to be said with much firmness that we must continually be seeking not merely thoughts but a coherent corpus of thought. It is one of the curious characteristics of our bright and superficial age that men play with particular thoughts as they might play with a handful of jewels. There is much bright shining, and there is much glitter. But there is almost no sense of relationship. So we contradict ourselves with cheerful composure and with complete fatuousness without any sense that we have betrayed our minds by this playing fast and loose with the things which we conceive to be true.

Even a bad pattern of thought is better than no pattern at all. This is because you can point out the flaws in a bad pattern and move on toward the constructing of a true pattern. But the man who has no pattern at all is in such a state of intellectual chaos that the very fluidity of his thought processes in a way protects him from attack. When you point a weapon at his ideas it is like shooting into a moving stream. The drops of water at which the gun pointed have gone before the bullet arrives. And there is not in any event much point in shooting at a passing stream.

It ought to be said, however, that the man who is proud of the fact that his intellectual incoherence saves him from attack has a curious source of pride. It is a little as if a man who had never learned to use the alphabet were to be proud of the fact that he could not be caught misspelling words.

It is, as a matter of fact, the very nature of the mind when it is truly at work to unite its thoughts into a coherent system. And when we find that we can move from the experience of things to a person, to the race of persons, and on to the great Ultimate Person with all the doors opening widely as we come to them we have a certain cause for intellectual satisfaction.

9. Moving from the Ultimate Person Back to History

After moving from conclusions back through inverted syllogisms to the great Major Premise of everything else, we can reverse the process and, beginning with the Ultimate Person, we can move back to history.

The book of Genesis strikes a note of finality in its first sentence. It begins with a phrase which is a kind of literary alpha and by implication an omega too: "In the beginning God."

It is the only right beginning. For now everything else falls into proper place. The Great Person whose self-existence in perfect knowledge and power is the ultimate fact of the universe is indeed the beginning of all reality and so must be the beginning of all thought. As we have seen, He is implicit in the very process of knowing even when we fail to be aware of this tremendous freight of ultimate truth which thought carries.

The Ultimate Person, this Original and Perfect Mind, creates other minds. He gives them an entity dependent, it is true, always upon Himself, but actual with a reality of being. He creates a world of minds.

And for these minds he provides an environment. This experience comes to every one of these living minds as a mental experience. But it comes as actual and dependable experience. It has all the stoutness of objective actuality. It is objectively real without being ontologically real. That is, it is real as experience. But it has no reality apart from experience. It is vast and intricate and infinitely rich and fascinating. It has all the magnificence of the versatility of the mind of God. And it is not a phantasmagoria. It is held in constantly dependable relations to all those human minds for whom God provides it as an environment. So man made by God and sustained by God lives in a world God makes actual in and for his experience. And in this world God makes possible a fellowship of persons, as well as an experience of things.

Again and again man is tempted to think of this world of objective reference as if it somehow got into being without God. And again and again with the curious human tendency to want hard stuff, he is tempted to think that God has made a world of heavy material which would continue to exist if there were no minds divine or human to experience it. The truth is that God does not need a world of hard stuff to rearrange, calling the result creation, and God does not need to make a world of hard stuff upon which man may stand. The Great Mind can give the minds He has made a dependable mental experience of a physical world whose only reality is precisely in the dependable order of experience which God posits and maintains for men. So we begin with the Ultimate Person and move on to the created persons and then to the world of experience God makes real for all the human spirits he has made. We have, then, God, man, and the experience of things and persons. With this in mind we can paraphrase the words of John Keats and say, This is all man knows or needs to know. With these facts kept secure, we can go on in good faith and in good hope.

CHAPTER V

The Speech of the Great Person

MAN'S adventure with the Diety is a curious and checkered and amazing tale. Sometimes it is more of a tale of the limitations of man than an unfolding of the glory of God. Once in a little poem called "Natural Theology" Rudyard Kipling wrote:

> Money spent on an Army or Fleet
> Is homicidal lunacy.
>
> . . . .
>
> My son has been killed in the Mons retreat.
> Why has the Lord afflicted me?
> Why are murder, pillage and arson
> And rape allowed by the Deity?
> I will write to the *Times,* deriding our parson,
> Because my God has afflicted me.[1]

The oddities of man's thoughts about God and God's ways with men are endless. But he must keep thinking. He cannot let God alone. And he has a suspicion that God never lets him alone.

When we approach the thought of the significance of human experience in the fashion which has characterized our dialectic thus far, we find that we are indeed living in a world of conscious persons. Everything begins and continues and concludes in conscious personality. Men are relative persons. God is the Perfect Person. They have their life in Him. Without Him they would never have begun to live. Without Him they would not continue to live. Without Him life would have no meaning and no goal. They have limited minds. He is the Perfect Mind. They have limited thoughts. His thought is complete and all embracing.

Inevitably we must confront a great and penetrating question. Can such a God dealing with such men be silent? Since He has made men with minds capable in some sense of thinking His thoughts after Him, must He not speak to them? Must not the Perfect Mind share His thoughts with the imperfect minds which He has made? Must not the Perfect Person communicate with the relative persons? Must not the God who has made men's minds in some however distant sense like His own share His thoughts with them? The human and the divine are correlated in quality of being. Must they not be correlated in living experience?

[1] From *The Years Between,* copyright 1914, 1919, by Rudyard Kipling, reprinted by permission of Mrs. Bambridge and Doubleday, Doran & Co., Inc.

The very asking of these questions makes certain matters abundantly clear. Communication is involved in the genius of the relationships characteristic of a world of persons. So the idea of the speech of God to men is not some strange and difficult and barely conceivable thing. It grows in the most definite way out of the relationship as we have already seen it. The Creator and Sustainer of a company of persons who is Himself the Ultimate Person can hardly be conceived in the terms of an eternal silence without doing violence to what must be the very quality of His own life.

1. The Speech of the Creator

In that distinguished anthology *The Spirit of Man* Robert Bridges quoted from an unpublished poem of Gerard Hopkins the lines:

> God mastering me;
> Giver of breath and bread;
> World's strand, sway of the sea;
> Lord of living and dead;
> Thou has bound bones and veins in me, fasten'd me flesh,
> And after at times almost unmade me with dread,
> Thy doing; and dost Thou touch me afresh?
> Over again I feel thy finger and find Thee.[2]

In these dim and cloudy words richly interwoven you have the expression of a truth of which we must keep firm hold. As soon as God creates, He has begun to reveal Himself. As soon as He creates, in a sense He begins to speak. For creation is self-expression on the very highest level. When God creates, He does not express something which He is not but something which He is. Every contact with experience is a contact with that which owes its being to God. Human experience is His tremendous achievement. His own thought, His own character, indeed, have been put into the experience. In experience we meet that which has come from God. As we shall see later, man can so use that capacity for experience which God has given him as to discolor and distort the experience. But even then, in an inverted way, the experience bears witness to the Great Creator. Even when we are running away from God, we are running with feet which He has given us and which were meant to bring us into His presence.

There is a certain strange and beautiful feeling of being at home in the universe the moment we begin to understand that the created, in the very nature of the case, must be whispering perpetually some of the secrets of the Creator. If it cannot be said that we are meeting God directly in that which He has created, it can at least be said that we are reading a letter which He has written. Every man at least goes so far as to become familiar with the handwriting of God. Of course, we may

[2] By permission of Oxford University Press, publishers of Gerard Hopkins, *Poems*.

refuse to read the letter. We may refuse to learn the alphabet which would enable us to decipher its words. We may refuse to fit the words together into coherent meaning. We may move about in the great library of God without reading any of the books. In one way man is showing a power which is like God when he refuses to have anything to do with God. He is showing his kinship at the very moment when he is disowning that kinship. At all events the Creator cannot avoid beginning to be a revealer the very moment He begins to create.

2. God's Speech in Man

Our first and most immediate knowledge of this speech of God in creation has to do naturally enough with man. Man's awareness of himself in the process of conscious experience and decision is his most direct and immediate form of knowledge. This provides the major premise for all his thought and action. And in this most immediate experience it is that man comes to have his deepest sense of reality. To be real is to be a knowing and deciding self. In creating man an agent of knowledge and decision, God was already speaking to man about the nature of reality. As man inspects himself, he does not merely say with Descartes, "I think; therefore, I am." Rather, in a more direct fashion, he says, "I, the thinking self, am," or, "I, thinking, am."

This idea of a self who is aware is one of those seminal ideas which keep turning up everywhere. Man finds himself in a world of other selves who are aware, and he has constant relations with them. This experience goes backward as memory and then as history. It goes forward as expectation. The deepest meaning of life lies in the adventure of the self with other selves. And this experience of being a part of a world of knowing and deciding selves is all the while telling a man things God meant him to know. God is speaking not only in a man's experience with himself but in his experience with others. And all this inevitably moves backward to the Greatest Self of all. In making man a human self God is preparing him to think of the Divine Self. And all the subtle adumbrations of the experience of selfhood in their own way repesent God's speech in man.

There is a curious and almost tragic aspect to all this. It is very easy for a man to become so familiar with the self and its adventures that he takes them for granted. Having taken them for granted, he passes lightly over their significance. Having treated them casually, he forgets them. And later he denies them.

For such a man the inception and the development of the critical use of the intelligence lie largely in a recovery of a sharp sense of the self and its adventures. Man is a palimpsest, and he must erase much writing which tells of casual and uncritical experiences to get back to that first writing which sets forth the plain and simple annals of the self.

Often the later writing reflects a communal life which has ceased to ask great questions and to find great answers. There is an insistent masterfulness about this later writing. It does not want to be erased. This accounts for the fashion in which men of every period resent more than they resent almost anything else a genuine examination of the part of their own thinking which has not been subjected to criticism. The most ordinary fallacy of the human mind is the belief that because an idea is familiar, it follows that it is true. The critical thinker always has his hardest battles with the sophisticated thinkers of his period rather than with the dullards. For it is a characteristic attitude of the sophisticated to object strenuously to any intellectual analysis of the mental grounds for the positions held by those who possess sophistication rather than understanding. So it is always necessary to appeal from a man's duller second thoughts back to the freshness and powers of his primary experiences. It is in these primary experiences that God continues to speak to him.

This recall to the direct gaze at experience will have profound relations to matters of which we shall speak later. Just now we content ourselves by remarking that one of the most important things about a man is just his capacity to look at the self in action and to see it for what it is. So looking, he finds that he is becoming aware of matters which have to do with the most far-reaching relationships. He is not only seeing; he is hearing. He is hearing a voice which is talking to him about the nature of reality. He is hearing a voice which is saying, "The real is the personal." And this voice is the voice of God.

3. God's Speech in Nature

Rupert Brooke, in "The Song of the Pilgrims," wrote:

> O Thou,
> God of all long desirous roaming,
> Our hearts are sick of fruitless homing,
> And crying after lost desire.
> Hearten us onward! as with fire
> Consuming dreams of other bliss.
> The best Thou givest, giving this
> Sufficient thing—to travel still
> Over the plain, beyond the hill,
> Unhesitating through the shade,
> Amid the silence unafraid,
> Till, at some sudden turn, one sees
> Against the black and muttering trees
> Thine altar, wonderfully white,
> Among the Forests of the Night.[3]

[3] From *The Collected Poems of Rupert Brooke.* Copyright, 1915, by Dodd, Mead & Co., Inc.

The sense of finding God in nature is a very old experience. It accounts for some of the loveliest poems of the world. It accounts for experiences alluring, fascinating, and sometimes profound. It is not without its elements of treachery and betrayal. Indeed, it must be watched constantly. The first notes of the great god Pan are always tender and sweet and delightful. But Pan knows his own terrible secrets of cruelty for all that. God does speak in nature. But we can fancy we hear nature saying a great many things which in no sense come from God.

There is, for instance, a great difference between saying that God speaks in nature and saying that nature is God speaking. On one side of our nature we all have a desire to escape from God. He is too mighty, too tremendous, too glorious, too lofty. And the easiest way to escape from Him is to create another god. Nature at once offers an escape. It seems such an easy step to begin by saying, "The world which God has made tells us something of God," and to go on to say, "This world is actually the God whom we must worship." As a matter of fact, at the best, if God says no more than He says in nature, He does not say enough. And if nature is God, He cannot say more.

It was a tremendously sound insight which led St. Augustine to write in the *Confessions*: "I asked the heavens, sun, moon, stars, 'Nor (say they) are we the God whom thou seekest.' And I replied unto all the things which encompass the door of my flesh; 'Ye have told me of my God, that ye are not He; tell me something of Him.' And they cried out with a loud voice, 'He made us.' "[4]

It is one thing to recognize that God is responsible for all that we experience in respect of nature. It is quite another to say that nature is God. The worship of nature always turns out at last to be the worship of that which is not only not divine but is actually below the human. It easily becomes a worship of the biological urges with an incredible overemphasis on sex, or a worship of an impersonal order from which all sense of personal meaning has been taken away.

Our whole discussion thus far has led us to see man's experience of the physical world as a mental experience posited by the Great Mind as a common experience for all men. This means that the Great Mind makes this material reference of experience constant and dependable but that apart from His volition and His power it would have no place in experience at all. Nature would not even be a shadow apart from the volition of God.

But the very God who establishes this frame of reference to a material order does in this fashion reveal certain important things about Himself. The dependable order which, considered by itself, looks like a vast, impersonal piece of mathematics is really the making objective in experience of the orderly quality of God's own mind. What we call

4 X. vi. 9.

the laws of nature are the volitions of God. He could easily change them. But because He is a God who likes order, He maintains them. Because we have a God with a character, we have an experience of the material order which reflects that character. The uniformity of nature in its own way reflects the dependable nature of God.

The vast and manifold aspects of biological experiences, if thought of as if they are self-created and self-sustaining, easily lend themselves to an interpetation where the physical aspects of the biological experience seem pivotal in their importance. Sex is suddenly spelled with a capital and with italics. And you begin to have a biological religion.

On the other hand, when it is seen that even the vital and masterful aspects of biological experience come to be a part of experience through being made stuff of the mind, at once one begins to think of sex as a part of something larger than itself. The whole rich meaning of life becomes included in a larger mental and spiritual biology, if one may put it so. Thus all the physical vitalities become in their own way a part of the vast speech of God in nature. But this means not the apotheosis of sex, but the seeing of all these things as a legitimate and friendly aspect of something larger than themselves. God made all this a part of the life of man. And this rich vitality is to be the servant of something larger and loftier than itself. The very thought of the biological as something established and maintained by the Eternal Mind begins to clear the air. God is the author of all the vitalities. He leads men to a life which transcends them even as it welcomes and appropriates and disciplines them.

4. "Natural Theology"

Here we come to the entirely fascinating subject of "natural theology." And here it becomes most important that we shall define our terms. By "nature" we may mean everything below man. This was the meaning Matthew Arnold clearly had in mind when he wrote, "Man must begin, know this, where nature ends." This is a sound and permanent distinction. And we shall forget it, even for a moment, at our peril. The difference, clearly perceived, between the free and knowing mind of man and that phenomenal order with which he has so much to do becomes basal for all critical thinking. And it will have just that relation to all the discussion in this book.

The matter is complicated, however, by an ecclesiastical usage which has had a long history and which we cannot ignore. This usage defines natural theology as the theology of human nature apart from divine revelation. The truths man can reach by the use of his own reason constitute natural theology. The truths he reaches only through revelation constitute the unique corpus of Christian thought. Here the word "nature" is expanded to include, and specifically to refer to, human nature.

We must see at once that such a usage in no way contradicts what we have been saying about man and that which is below him. For now that is left aside, and we are considering man and that which is above him. It does involve two uses of the word "nature": one referring to that which is below man, the other referring to human nature. There is, of course, no battle between the ecclesiastical theologians who want to keep clear the distinction between man using his own powers and man receiving the divine revelation and those other thinkers who want to keep clear the distinction between man as free intelligence and the world of the thing and the world of the beast below him. The ecclesiastical theologians who make this distinction are all humanists, in the classical sense, in the value they see in the human reason—in man as an intelligent agent of thought and decision.

Much that we have already said in conducting this dialectic in respect of the meaning of human experience fits happily into the general ecclesiastical position in respect of natural theology. Without attempting to carry out a comparison, it is clear that the general frame of thought which sees God as the Creator of all persons and the One who establishes the whole coherent pattern of that experience which has a material reference, has a profound kinship with the forms of thought which a churchly theologian would use as he considers that natural theology which man may reach by means of his own reason. To be sure, the churchly theologian might—perhaps would be—a theistic realist. But his conviction that any coherent corpus of thought interpreting existence would require belief in a personal, conscious God would at that point agree with the positions we are advocating in these studies.

The discussion of what is involved in a rational interpretation of existence may be carried farther than some thinkers have realized. In a good many ways this dialectic of critical human intelligence will move in and out of our whole discussion. We are not interested in trying to make a microscopic distinction between what man can do with the faculties God has given him and his use of these faculties to recognize what we can more specifically call revelation. Like the difference between the animal and the vegetable kingdoms, it is sharp enough when you are dealing with extremes. But as the two approach each other there are many matters in which a certain insight looked at in one way may seem to be man's discovery and in another to be God's special revelation of Himself.

Just now, however, we are most concerned with the fact that when man inspects that rational life God has made possible for him and uses its powers to move Godward, in a sense, this very use of God-given powers is a part of the speech of God to men. When God makes man's intellect in such fashion that its critical activity moves Godward, that very movement is in one way God making clear to men His thought and His power.

5. Has God Spoken in the Ethnic Religions?

Professor George Foot Moore, whose vast erudition was a marvel to all who knew him, had clear convictions about the commanding position of religions in the human story:

To avoid controversy about definitions we may content ourselves here with saying that no people or tribe has been discovered which has not something that answers for it the purposes of religion, whether we think it it respectable enough to be dignified by that name or not. . . . From Greek historians and geographers we have accounts not only of the religions of the civilized peoples of their times, but of many barbarous tribes in all parts of their world. They nowhere discovered irreligious men. . . . The universality of religion within the range of our knowledge warrants the inference that it has its origin in a common motive.[5]

The moment we begin to be interested in the religious life of mankind, religions begin to confront us. And as we go on with our investigations, the tale of the ethnic religions becomes more and more engrossing. The question as to whether God Himself speaks through any or all of the ethnic religions becomes more and more insistent. Is this vast human adventure of man with an unseen world and unseen powers simply the tale of an illusion until we come to the classical stream of ethical religion? Is it simply a tale of man's seeking and never of his finding? Is it never in any sense a tale of God's seeking and of God's finding men whom He would help?

The very study of the processes by which the mind of man moves from human reason to a Divine Reason predisposes us to the view that man's adventures with religion have not been merely a tale of confusion and lost motion. On the other hand, the inspection we have already made of man's freedom prepares us for a use of man's mind which does involve profound and even tragic and betraying illusion.

If a man who has been reading in the field of the ethnic religions were to speak, he would find little difficulty in making two rather far-reaching assertions. First: There is no religion in the world which is false in the sense that in no way at all does it bear any witness to the truth. Second: There is no religion in the world which is true in the sense that some of its votaries have not set forth that which is false in its name. There is no escape from the demand for discrimination when we begin to study the ethnic religions.

The more we study the threads of gold in the vast tapestries, the less

[5] *The Birth and Growth of Religion* (New York: Charles Scribner's Sons, 1923), pp. 2, 3.

THE SPEECH OF THE GREAT PERSON 71

do we find it difficult to relate their presence to that Great Master Mind
which makes all human experience possible. All truth belongs to God,
and we never discredit God by seeing what is true in its inevitable
rootage in the mind which is Eternal Truth omnipotently alive. This
universal interrelatedness on the part of human pilgrims through the
world is a matter of the deepest significance. Every man everywhere who
has found contact with any truth is our benefactor and our friend. And
every man who is caught in the clutches of falsehood is a victim to be
delivered, or, if he has deliberately made falsehood his truth and evil
his good, is a foe to be met with unhesitating hostility. When in one
part of his thought a man is our guide to truth and in another would
betray us into the acceptance of error, the situation is complicated
enough.

But at the moment it is not the complications which are important.
It is the presence of good. And it is the source of that good in God.
From this standpoint we must claim an intimate relation between the
ethnic religions and God. Speaking in pardonably figurative language,
we may say that the ethnic religions are the children of God. When we
have faced all the facts, we shall have to add that sometimes they are
wayward children, sometimes they are children who have forgotten
their descent, and sometimes they are children who have disowned their
parentage. But related to God they are, even when that relation is one
of negation. And at their best they shine with the glory of that light
which lighteth every man coming into the world.

6. Classification of Religions

Christopher Dawson's *The Age of the Gods* is a remarkable summary
of anthropological material gathered from many sources and always
considered by a very discriminating mind. In the chapter on "The City
State and the Development of the Sumerian Culture" he makes this
observation: "Thus the god was the real ruler of the city, and the
Sumerian territories are often described not as the land of such-and-
such a city, but the land of such-and-such a god." [6]

This sentence strikes the note of the penetrating and far-reaching influence of religion. If it is religion at all, its aim is to rule. Of course,
politically minded men may use religion for their own private purposes. But their power to do this depends upon the belief of the people
in respect of certain rights and powers inherent in the religious forces
or persons they claim to represent. The god always claims the right to
be the real ruler of the city.

The religions of magic, with their appeal to formulas of incantation,
represent a low level of religious experience. Just because they do not
appeal to or submit themselves to the judgment of ideas or ideals, they

[6] Boston: Houghton Mifflin Co., 1928, p. 123.

have no power to express men's aspirations, to lift them to a higher level, or to become the vehicle of any sort of moral or spiritual advance. The literature of incantation—if literature it may be called—has an astonishing place in the history of religion. And it is not unusual for a religion which advances to a higher level to trail clouds of incantation with it for a long time and perhaps at last to leave them behind.

The religions which represent the apotheosis of the biological processes have been referred to in passing already. Here a wise remark of Professor George Foot Moore needs to be kept in mind: " 'Primitive' man is near enough a healthy animal not to be a victim of the obsession of sex, which is in fact a degenerative phenomenon of decadent civilization." [7] It remains to be said, however, that whenever biological processes have been emphasized apart from the rest of life and of a life in which the biological is the servant of the intellectual and the moral and the spiritual, religion itself has become decadent. On the other hand, a certain fear of that which belongs to a full and healthy human life has represented, when it has appeared in ethical religion, a decadence of another sort. But when religion becomes absorbed and obsessed by the world of sensation, it becomes a foe of the best life for man. In this fashion various forms of religion have put a blight upon the life of their devotees.

On the whole, religion moves at least in the direction of becoming ethical as it becomes more personal. The religion where every kind of life has its patron deity is at least an advance upon the worship of mysterious impersonal forces. The place gods, the functional gods, and all the varied deities who represent man worshiping his own interests and enthusiasms as they sharpen in personal quality suggest and at times embody a growing ethical and intellectual life on the part of the worshipers. As one watches these processes at work over the vast reaches of the varied religions, it is difficult to avoid the sense of an intelligent will at work. It is not entirely a matter of faith to say that here God Himself is speaking.

In the great pantheons of Greece and Rome you witness an amazing process. Some deities advance, if one likes to put it so, with the advancing life of their people. Zeus becomes a person of large and beneficent dignity. Athena becomes the actuality of a spirit of high and gracious intelligence. As the progress goes on, men become ashamed of some of the practices of their gods. This appears clearly enough in the writings of Euripides. And allegory offers us a convenient method by transforming bad acts into noble symbols. In a highly gifted people like the Greeks sometimes the most serious thought about subjects which really belong to religion is carried on by philosophers. Plato more than any priest represents the religious genius of the Greek people.

[7] *Op. cit.,* p. 61.

THE SPEECH OF THE GREAT PERSON

On the other hand, religion may be so busy with ethics that it almost ceases to be religion. The many human relations come in for patient and discriminating treatment in the teachings of Confucius. There almost seems to be a fear of the deeper devotions of religions with alluring deities in the shrewd and urbane practicalities of Confucianism. In the moral clarity of many an insight, in the clear, penetrating quality of many a statement of the ethical code of Confucius, one feels again that quality of moral conclusiveness which suggests roots the man of ethical religion may well inspect. If whatever is truly said in some sense represents the voice of God, here too God may be said to speak.

The attempt to make religion as vast and inclusive as all the manifold types of human experience comes to flower in Hinduism. The cosmopolitan quality of this appeal masters many minds. We shall have more to say of it in a later chapter. Here we only pause to say that if you try to say everything sympathetically you can never say anything decisively. The great gregariousness is seen to become the great relativity. And the great relativity becomes the great illusion. Even the dream becomes at last the make-believe of a dream. And so even the mysterious is pseudo-mysterious.

Over against the vast gregariousness which ultimately dissolves all values there are the religions of the masterful will. Here, of course, Mohammedanism has a place all its own. The deification of the will has a sure appeal to men of action. But in the end the only will is the will of Allah. Only God has any rights, and the submission which gives the very name to the religion becomes a submission which easily destroys the very integrity of human personality. Of course, as long as a man can think of the divine will as one with his own, or his own as bent on the execution of the divine purposes, he can run his course and be glorified.

If in a sense Mohammedanism is a glorification of the active, Buddhism is the glorification of the passive. If the Mohammedan fiercely exercises his will, the Buddhist fears the active will almost more than he fears anything else. All the hot impetuosity, whether of flesh or spirit, belongs to a world of illusion. The self is always a bad self. Complete deliverance from desire for any sort of self-assertion—indeed, from desire of every kind—comes with true enlightenment.

But inevitably the sense of life as a battle between opposing forces must have its day in religion. Zoroastrianism—still alive in the world—has always been the religion of the great conflict between good and evil, light and darkness. Something about the summons to this fight must speak deeply to the spirit of every man. The call to arms in the moral struggle will never fall upon completely dull ears.

But the warrior's code itself may become a religion. Here Shinto speaks, and we listen to the summons of the Bushido teachings as to a warrior's behavior. The crude primitivism is somehow transfigured in the cult of the military hero.

Of course, all of these religious forms are infinitely rich and manifold. In all you will find things good enough to come from God. In all you will find some things of a questionable nature, some full of danger, and, as the religion becomes a cult, some which are positively evil. If you are ready to believe that God has been sowing wheat to grow up in the ethnic religions, there is clearly the presence of growths which suggest many tares. You have to confront these ethnic religions with the hand of a friend and the weapons of a foe.

7. The Ethnic Religions and "Natural Theology"

That distinguished and vital scholar Professor Gilbert Murray, in his little book *Five Stages of Greek Religion,* takes up an astonishing preliminary position:

I shall not start with any definition of religion. Religion, like poetry and most other living things, cannot be defined. But one may perhaps give some description of it, or at least some characteristic marks. In the first place, religion essentially deals with the uncharted region of human experience. A large part of human life has been thoroughly surveyed and explored; we understand the causes at work; and we are not bewildered by the problems. That is the domain of positive knowledge. But all round us on every side there is an uncharted region, just fragments of the fringe of it explored, and those imperfectly; it is with this that religion deals.[8]

This would, of course, be to give away the whole cause of religion. Whenever material is subject to the analysis of intelligence, it ceases to be religious. As long as it belongs to regions as yet uncharted by the mind, it is religious. If this were true, the next step would be to say that as the realm under mental control is constantly increasing and the regions beyond the mastery of the intelligence are constantly decreasing, the area of religion becomes smaller and smaller all the while. And the final step would be to declare that when everything has been reduced to intelligible forms there will remain no place for religion.

As a matter of fact, precisely the opposite is true. The more materials take their place in patterns provided by critical intelligence, the more they are seen to belong to a world dominated by the perfect intelligence of God. That which has never been subjected to intelligent analysis belongs to a world of vague mystery which may be called religion. But the region has in it realms of pseudo religion. Here all magic and superstition thrive.

So that, following again the distinction of the ecclesiastical theologians between the theology reached by man's use of his reason and

[8] New York: Columbia University Press, 1925, p. 5. Reprinted by permission.

that reached by man as he accepts the divine revelation, we may say that as ethnic religions advance they more perfectly express and respond to the demands of man's intelligence. And as this happens religion is on a higher and not on a lower level. On the other hand, to just the degree that a religion ignores, forgets, or contradicts the demands of reason, it becomes more a matter of lawless emotion and of sheer magic. The ethnic religions at their best contain elements which deeply relate themselves to man as an intelligent creature. In a sense they represent a march from the subrational to the rational. They reflect the pilgrimage of minds increasingly feeling the compulsions of critical intelligence. In fact, the battle between those primitive elements unwilling to subject themselves to the disciplines of the intelligence, and those elements reflecting intelligence worshiping, is going on all the while.

8. The Ethnic Religions and Revelation.

That the processes of thought and ritual and experience are complicated and full of inner contradiction is clear enough. That at their best they have to do with that which is true and of permanent significance ought to be equally clear.

And on these higher levels we may see the building of roads leading to a great highway with which they will one day converge. This sense that the ethnic religions represent men and women who are on a journey is very important. As a matter of fact, some men living under the sanctions of the ethnic religions are taking a journey in one direction while others are taking a journey in the opposite direction. A man can use any one of the ethnic religions in such a way as to betray at last his noblest insights and his true understanding. But he may discriminate. He may accept and use those elements which point to a fulfillment beyond the religion itself. These elements in such use may surely be said to be a part of a divine plan. And in speaking of them in this process we may surely use modestly the word "revelation."

9. Is There a Higher Revelation?

In many fashions, then, we may say that the Great Person has spoken. But a searching and imperative question remains. All of this is good. But it is good enough? Must not the Great Person speak to the persons He has made and whose life He sustains in a more direct fashion? Must it not be possible to use the word "revelation" in a more complete and adequate and final fashion than we have yet found to be possible?

It is clear at once that we are here in a region of much difficulty and danger. There is nothing which gives a group of men such power as the claim that they are speaking a word to men which God Himself has given to them. When this claim is accepted and when men obey the word of those who speak, the men who speak for God become quite literally the rulers of men. That such a claim may be false and unworthy is very clear. That it has been false and unworthy is the testimony found on some of the darkest pages of the history of religion. Even ethical religion has had its charlatans, and the situation has been perhaps most tragic when by a strange inner confusion the man who claimed to speak for God, the man who claimed that his speech was God's speech, was part charlatan and part saint.

But the dangers and the difficulties and the tragedies connected with an unjustified claim to speak for God cannot remove the urgency of one main question: Has God the Person directly and definitely revealed Himself to men? Has He spoken to men in such a fashion that they in turn have had a right to speak for God? Have men had a right to use the great words, "Thus saith the Lord"?

Happily there is a test which can be applied successfully. Does that which is set forth as a divine message have a divine quality? Of the prophet, as of every other man, the principle holds true: "By their fruits ye shall know them."

And over long periods, as we see the influence of what claims to be a divine message upon men and nations, the test becomes particularly effective and the results really secure. That which is plausible yet evil does produce evil results at last. That which is tentative and not permanent does reveal its relative quality as the years go on. If what comes with the claim that it is the speech of God gets to work in the world, its quality becomes evident. If it meets the test, we can see that it is worthy of the God whose speech it claims to be. The question, then, takes on another form. Can we find a "revelation" which corresponds to the highest possible conception of God and which so vindicates its claim? There is only one stream of religion which can possibly meet the test, and to that we now turn.

CHAPTER VI

The Religious Experience of Israel

OVER a thousand years after the coming of the Christian Era, Judah Ha-Levi wrote words of proud and wistful memory and longing which have been translated by Maurice Samuel:

> Art thou not hungry for thy children, Zion,—
> Thy sons far-scattered through an alien world?
>
> . . . .
>
> We will remember till the end of time
> The cradle of our childhood, from a thousand seas
> Turn back and seek again thy hills and vales.
> Glory of Pathros, glory of Shinar,
> Compared to the light and truth that streamed from thee
> Are dust and vanity: and in all the world
> Whom shall I find to liken to thy seers,
> Thy princes, thy elect, thy anointed ones?
> The kingdoms of the heathen pass like shadows,
> Thy glory and thy name endure for ever.
> God made His home in thee.[1]

So the unique land with the unique people and the unique word has captured the imagination of its sons century after century. And all the civilized world has felt the compulsion of that which has gone out from Israel. The larger the perspective in which we see this story, the more noble and notable it is seen to be.

1. The Adventure of Man with Nature

We have already seen how vast and varied man's experiences have been. Now we remind ourselves of that series of adventures which have interlaced and intertwined to form the fabric of his life in the world. His battle with nature fairly staggered him and seemed likely to exhaust his resources. For the forces of nature, like the rough schoolboys of pioneer days, must feel the cut of the master's whip before they become friendly. Man had to use all the alertness of his eye, all the quickness of his ear, all the fleetness of his foot, all the strength of his hand, and all the keenness of his mind to turn the world from a hostile foe to a friendly servant. The people of Israel knew all about this, and some

[1] From *The Jewish Anthology* (New York: Harcourt, Brace & Co., 1925).

of their subtlest temptations had to do with those hot and unethical religions of nature whose very cults promised the productiveness of the soil and the fertility of the flocks. Sometimes—always actually—man mastered nature by the strength of his arm and the flare of his intelligence. But he was tempted to try to master it by incantations. There was a subtle illusion of power in the quotation of a magical formula when you confronted nature in one of its darker moods when it seemed not only irresponsive but angrily hostile. The struggle went on and the cultivators of the soil and the builders of houses and the builders of ships and the makers of tools did their work. The struggle still goes on, and the victories become more stupendous. Forces of which the ancient world was ignorant have become slaves of man's conquering mind and his imperial will. At whatever state you examine this struggle, you find man restless and full of unappeased desire in the midst of his victories.

2. The Adventure of Man with Men

Man has always had not only a world to conquer but other men with whom to live. And the other men can be foes as well as friends. They can hate as well as love. In fact, the impersonal hostilities of nature seem almost friendly if you have seen the bitter and unappeasable anger which can shine in a human eye. If man's life with nature has been one long struggle, it is also true that from one standpoint human relations represent century after century of strife. But there are vast areas of difference. Man can love as well as hate. Nature neither loves nor hates. You can appeal to the reason of man. You can only use the uniformities of nature so that they serve you. You can use all your force to improve human relations. On the other hand, a storm always remains a storm and a volcano remains a volcano and an earthquake remains an earthquake. Nobody has ever thought of organizing societies against earthquakes or volcanoes. The human adventure has often involved a battle for power. It has also often involved the building of a community of good will. These things, too, were happening in Israel. Its hills and its valleys were drenched with blood. Its life was bent to purposes of that civilized organization which moves from slaughter to a certain amount of federated good will. The human problem tore at men's minds and hearts in ancient Israel as it tears at men's minds and hearts today. Man's inhumanity to man was all the while confronting man's humanity to man in that far-off Palestine long ago. Both in respect of the adventures of man with nature and the adventures of man with his fellow men, the broad human background in this land was like that in all lands. And it set the stage for those great and magnificent things of which we shall speak later in this chapter.

3. The Adventure of Man with God

The third characteristic aspect of the human adventure, as we have already seen, has to do with man's adventure with God. The Unseen Companion has haunted the thought of men in every time and in every place. And so it was in ancient Israel. Just as its life was planted and grew in typical human soil in respect of man's experiences with nature and with his fellow men, so it grew in typical human soil in respect of the life of religion. A Mighty Shadow fell across the landscape. And that shadow was ascribed to a figure which was divine. But, as we shall see more fully later, the men of Israel did not come to their experience of religion empty-minded or empty-hearted. They came out of the same soil as did other peoples of their racial group. Old memories filled their minds and suffused their hearts. Nature cults had their own place in the life out of which they came. Differences, in the beginning, may well have seemed to be very small indeed. It is always important to remember this. The backsliding to which they were tempted for centuries was always literally sliding back. Their world was in one respect characterized by a sharp contrast to our own. Everybody then was religious. There were people with a bad religion. There were people with a religion which was a mixture of good and evil. And a really good religion was in process of making itself felt. But there were no secular people. There were no people who, having lost all sense of actuality in respect of religious experience, had come to live in a genuinely secular world. There were no people who had a religious vocabulary but no actual religion. And there were no people who disliked all religious vocabularies because that for which the vocabularies stood had ceased to have any meaning for them. The godless, we may say, were nonexistent. In the terms of a later type of analysis, we may say that many people were tempted to find God or gods in the subhuman. But they were sure of a realm of mighty powers with whom they had to deal. And commerce with these powers was the most important matter in their lives.

4. The Unique Adventure in Palestine

The Old Testament Scriptures tell the story of the unique thing which happened in Israel. We become sharply aware of religion as something more than man's quest for God. It is God's quest for men. Here at last we come upon the religion of the Divine Initiative. God is revealing Himself to men. He is speaking to them. He is guiding them. He is leading them. And He is doing all this in the very terms of their own experience. He does not in some strange fashion come to them from outside their experience. But *He* comes. There is a magnificent authenticity in the sense of God speaking and God acting which suffuses the Old Testament writings. Men are being led from somewhere to somewhere else. There is a genuine movement in the thought of the people. There is dramatic advance. There is always the paradox that what on the human side may look like discovery, on the divine side is revelation. And it is the divine side which is emphasized. There is no self-consciousness among the men of Isreal as to what they think about God. There is tremendous anxiety as to what God thinks about them and as to what God says to them. There is the most overwhelming conviction that they have become aware of the purpose of God, that this purpose has to do with them, and that they are to co-operate with this purpose.

The literary period in the life of Israel represents a high stage in moral and spiritual understanding. And there is no doubt a tendency to read back into earlier periods the apprehension of truths which were then implicit rather than explicit. The actual history is complex and difficult to follow. The whole tale of the unraveling of the documents J. E, D, and P is an illustration of all this. In these matters the work of Old Testament scholars has been of very great significance. They have given us a new sense of the actualities of a historical process, and they have brought to life very much which would not be a part of our memory of living experience but for their achievements. But scholars are not omnipotent, and the history of scholarship in these matters has itself been a checkered thing. The good Hebrew scholar obsessed by an idea whose shadow he sees everywhere has been a curious phenomenon; his theories have sometimes been built upon very fragile foundations. The matters of date and authorship and stages of religious apprehension are important, but the central assertions which make up the body of the message to be found in the Old Testament have a timeless quality quite apart from these questions. The scholar himself, to do his best work, must be suffused with a consciousness of the meaning of this revelation. He must feel deeply the sense of God at work. Excellent books on the Old Testament have been written whose authors have been so fully occupied with the idea of the evolution of man in religious matters that they have forgotten the dominant part of God in the whole process. It is possible to complete the study of some very learned discussions of parts or of all of the Old Testament documents feeling that man has done very well in discovering how he ought to think about God and with no overwhelming sense of the glorious action of God in revealing Himself to men. Even in Old Testament criticism one can have the play of *Hamlet* with Hamlet left out.

This is in no sense an attack upon the exercise of the true functions of historical and literary criticism. Often we must accept results which are radical enough. But if we are truly radical, we get to the root. And in this case the root is that personal conscious being whom we call God.

There is such a thing as treating YHVH in such a way that one leaves out not only the vowels but the consonants.

5. *The God with a Character*

Religion among the people of Israel is first of all a personal adventure. It has to do with man's relation with a conscious being who thinks and feels and wills. It has to do with the living God. This matter is of fundamental importance. The tendency of some able contemporary religious thinkers to use the word God as a covering term for a cluster of abstract principles is quite absent from the Old Testament. God is not the sum of good ideas held together by a name. He is not the sum of gracious ideals cemented by a few letters of the alphabet and so made into a word. He is a living, conscious, acting being. And the authenticity of the Old Testament revelation owes much to this dominate feature. The God you meet in the Old Testament is not a creation of the mind of man. He is man's Creator speaking to him in a completely commanding voice.

And He is One God. The tendency to have a deity for every thought and feeling and emotion and fact and function meets its opposite in Israel. The civil war of the gods is replaced by the vast serenity of the rule of the Most High. A world of gods of contradictory character forever fighting, forever meeting in mutual antagonism, is sure to be responsible for human anarchy. When men cast the contradictions of human character upon the heights of Olympus and then fall down to worship them, they are actually worshiping the very tensions which are tearing their inner lives apart. The One Eternal Person who makes and rules the world is seen with increasing clearness as the religious experience of Israel develops until at last His full magnificence bursts upon the astonished vision of men.

But very especially this One God is a God with a character. Jehovah is not every sort of person. He is one sort of person. All moral excellence is alive in Him. The virtues are harmonized in complete and triumphant security in His life. He is righteousness alive. He is good will alive. He is the living actuality of everything that is good.

The worship of gods who are only beings of power without the possession of noble character is one of the most devastating aspects of human experience. If conscienceless power is on the throne of the universe, it is very sure that conscienceless power will be on the human thrones. The worship of a God who is the Eternal Reality of perfect moral understanding and moral goodness makes all the difference. It is not at all disconcerting to believe that the Ten Commandments had a history which is reflected in certain documents of the Old Testament. It is of the utmost importance to see that the full representation saw a completely good God commanding goodness of His children. It is, indeed, precisely at this point that the uniqueness of the Old Testament appears. There had been fragmentary flashes of this truth here and there in many an ethnic faith. But the full light which shines on the face of the God in whom all moral excellence lives eternally is first seen shining in Israel.

Of course, in a sense all this makes life much more difficult. It is disconcerting enough to have your best self lifted to undreamed-of qualities of moral perfection gazing at you as a face in the sky. It is exasperating enough to come to know that all that you are not but ought to be is alive forever in the very life of God. Yet it is infinitely satisfying, too. If the worst could get on the throne of the universe, the most evil man in the world would not welcome the result. Something in our deepest selves desires and welcomes the rebuke of perfection. And just this a religion which is a true revelation of a God with a character inevitably brings to us.

But it also brings reassurance, and hope, and at last glorious belief. If the thought so good that we have hardly dared to think it lives securely in the mind of God, how great a thing that is. If the hope so splendid that it seemed we must discard it with bitter tears represents something forever real in God's life, how that changes the world of our own expectation. All that God is in character we may become. And the God who is infinite perfection holds out before us vistas which dazzle our imagination at the very moment when they confirm our faith.

This thing happened in Israel. This very God in whom all goodness lives entered into the mind, dominated the conscience, swept through the imagination of men in Israel, until they felt that they were really thinking His thoughts after Him, and making His purposes their very own. That such a God exists is a matter of supreme significance. That men who walk this earth have become aware of Him, have heard His voice and have accepted His commands, represents a series of facts which have transformed the very meaning of life and have transfigured history.

6. Borrowing and Transforming

That fascinating and brilliant scholar Robert William Rogers, in a volume entitled *The Religion of Babylonia and Assyria,* said with a certain finality some things regarding Israel's borrowings and its transformation of what it borrowed in the realm of religion. There is, for instance, the name "Jahweh" which cannot be regarded as a peculiar possession of the Hebrews:

It covers a large extent of territory both geographically and ethnologically, and the rapid accumulation of cases in which it appears during so few years makes reasonably probable a still wider use of the name than has yet been actually proved. . . . At first sight this may seem like a startling robbery of Israel, this taking away from her the divine name Jahweh as an exclusive possession. But it is not so. Jahweh himself is not taken away. It is only the *name* that is shown to be widespread. And the *name* matters little. The great question is, what does this name convey?—what is its theological content? The *name* came to Israel from the outside. But into that vessel a long line of prophets, from Moses onward, poured such a flood of attributes as never a priest in all Western Asia, from Babylonia to the Sea, ever dreamed of in his highest moments of spiritual insight. In this name, and through Israel's history, God chose to reveal Himself to Israel, and by Israel to the world. Therein lies the supreme and lonesome superiority of Israel over Babylonia.[2]

After a long and thoroughly documented discussion of the cosmologies and their relation to the narratives found in Genesis, Professor Rogers summed up his conclusions in these words:

But great as are the resemblances which bind these two narratives together, the differences are far greater and more important. The soberness, the dignity, the simplicity of the Hebrew account lift it far above its ancient exemplar. From it the crude nature myths have all been stripped away; no drunken gods hold revels in its solemn lines. But above even this stands monotheism. Alone and lonesome is this God whom the Hebrews knew. Hard and long was the struggle into this great faith. From the days of Moses to the days of Jeremiah the charm of polytheism held many a goodly spirit in Israel, but the great truth was latent, fighting its way to a supremacy which should here in Genesis find positive acknowledgment. To that lofty faith the Babylonians never came. This great glory belongs to Israel. Beyond the limits of her realm no other folk had attained this lofty preëminence. No other people brought forth prophets to preach, or priests to teach, this truth. Whence came this superiority? I can find no origin for it but in a personal revelation of God in human history. It was He who made Himself known to the Hebrew people through their prophets, and through their living experience of Him in their history. He had indeed not left Himself without a witness in Babylonia, but the revelation to Israel lifted her thinking to heights unknown before.[3]

All this can stand for many matters and many relationships. When the people of Israel heard their religious leaders speak, the language came with old and intimate familiarity. It came out of the stuff of their own people and of surrounding peoples. Only with such familiar quality could it have gained immediate and natural contact with their minds. There was borrowing enough. But what was borrowed was transformed. It was shot through with new and splendid meaning. Old words became the vehicle of new ideas. Old ideas shot out unexpected

[2] New York: The Methodist Book Concern, 1908.
[3] *Ibid.*, pp. 140-41.

tentacles and fastened themselves to new thoughts. And so that great religion of moral love came to be. It deeply belonged to the men who experienced it. But it had power to live because most of all it belonged to the great God who had made and was sustaining human life and was speaking through their own experience to men whom He had made.

7. Things Left Behind

Our Lord made a perennially important distinction when he declared: "It was said by them of old time, . . . but I say unto you." Indeed, long before the time of Jesus the religion of Israel was a religion of things left behind for the sake of that advance which was to capture the citadel of spiritual truth. The Old Testament documents contain many evidences of crude features of natural religion once accepted without critical thought, then appraised with discrimination and cast aside. There are certain scholars who seem to have a gleeful satisfaction in unearthing these ancient customs and practices as if they are a part of Old Testament religion. They only represent that from which Israel emerged, that which Israel left behind. The obsession of interest in the ugly insects which once crawled under the stones of ancient temples is actually not very creditable. The facts are to be looked straight in the eye, catalogued for just what they are; then we too are to pass on, leaving them behind.

But there is a sense of the tremendous vitality, of the great moral and spiritual power of true religion, which comes to the scholar as he inspects the regions from which even the noblest ethical forms of worship were digged. And there is a correspondence between this ethnic experience of a great people casting off the unworthy as it entered into the meaning of the worthy and the experience of many an individual in the modern world. In this respect, as in many others, the individual in a new land and a new day may recapitulate an ancient ethnic story.

It is difficult to say how much this adds to the conviction of the sturdy authenticity of religion. It is not the ethereal pattern of a world of lovely spiritual dreams. It has arisen in the world of men dull, hard-pressed, often beastly. It has held before them a light whose allurement they could not fail to feel. It has called them to a great experience of mountain climbing.

It has not been content to say:

> There are lives like golden clouds
> Flying above high mountains at evening time,
> Bright with the glory of a sun you cannot see.
> You're of the valley and its damp chill hands
> Are pressing on your heart,
> But as you journey toward the night
> You have a sense of sunlight from those far pure heights.

No, it is just the people of the valley who are summoned to journey toward the heights. It is just the people who feel its damp, chill hand who are to cast off that ugly grasp and journey from the night toward the morning light. In this negative sense the recurrent references which give the scholar sudden vistas of ancient depths from which Israel journeyed are in a way a part of the revelation of the glory of the heights.

8. Truths Apart from Experience

It is possible to abstract truth and to think of it apart from experience. The science of mathematics is a perfect example of abstraction reduced to a science of interlaced and perfectly analyzed relationships. The one thing which is clear is that the mind of Israel did not tend to this sort of dialectic. Its argument was never the argument of abstract thought. It was the argument of life itself.

It is fortunate, for two reasons, that it has been so. First, the dialectic of abstraction, by the very nature of the case, belongs to a world below that of freedom and of personal choice. The truth which has become abstract has already ceased to be human. And it cannot take account of the personal. There is nothing like an abstract formula for the making of a machine. For the making of a free person, there is nothing less serviceable than an abstract formula. Certain social thinkers who have failed to learn from the shrewd vitality of Israel the menace of the fallacy of the abstract are all the while constructing the formulas for a society which, if it could be brought into being, might be well fed and well clothed but which would be completely inhuman. Certain brilliant thinkers who have failed to understand the abyss into which the dialectic of abstraction leads are continually attempting to construct a theology which would be the account of the ghostly adventures of a series of noble figures of speech rather than an account of the adventures of living men with the living God.

That there are aspects of experience which relate to regions of impersonal mathematical coherence is true enough. But they do not represent the living force of either morals or religion. When you are building a bridge, you do not have to take account of the free intelligence of the bridge. When you are training a child, you do have to remember first and last and all the time the processes of a growing mind in whose free intelligence is its central and defining meaning. When God was dealing with a child nation growing into lusty youth and then into manhood, He did not lead it into a realm of abstraction. He met it in the world of living experience.

It is, of course, true that living experiences, when properly understood, can be expressed in harmonious and coherent forms so that you have what can be likened to an organism of truth. But such a philosophy or such a theology is as different from the dialectic of impersonal abstraction as an eagle on lofty flight is from a crystal imbedded in the earth.

9. Truth in Experience

When the curtain rises in the book of Genesis, you have a Great Person in the Act of Creation. This prelude in the experience of the Divine Person sets the stage for the experience of human persons. You become aware of God creating man. You become aware of man in the intimate relations of the family. You become aware of man confronting the necessity of choice. You become aware of man confronting moral obligation. You become aware of man's misuse of freedom. You see sin entering the world as the gratification of appetite takes the place of loyalty to the Great Person. It is all incredibly simple and straightforward, coming right out of living experience. And by the same token it is all utterly profound. The personal relations to which you are introduced at the beginning of the book of Genesis are never transcended. They are as significant today as when men centuries ago told these stories of their beginnings as they wistfully peered into their own souls. Murder is seen emerging at the point of tension between two persons, one of whom has no true sense of the value of human life. You have a sudden sense that man's freedom and power of control—which are his because he is made in the image of God—can lead to a vast jealousy of God. Men are so like God that they want to be gods. So the tale of Babel dramatizes that ancient form of the Faustian sin which refuses to accept the limitations of the human. Men, it is obvious, are brooding over human experience. And God is brooding over human experience. God does not forsake the man and woman who misuse their freedom. He does not forsake the race which misuses its freedom. So the long and amazing tale of redemption begins. Whenever you think anything, you are having an adventure with God whether you know it or not. Whenever you do anything, you are having an adventure with God whether you know it or not. And when you become aware of God, it is always at some point of your own experience of thinking or deciding.

10. The Striking Individuals

Dr. George Matheson was in his day one of the greatest preachers in Scotland. And in his own way he was a great thinker, too. Sometimes one is tempted to say that God made him blind in order that he might be relieved from the sight of the external and with the eyes of the spirit see the inner meaning of life. When he wrote his famous books *The Representative Men of the Bible,* with what amounted to a flash of genius he considered the portraits in the Old Testament as pictures painted by a great artist. He liked to feel that he was not trying to tell the history of the pigments—as interesting and as fascinating as that task would have been. He was setting forth the significance of the pictures. And he took the pictures as he found them.

In this way he found—and we may find—what these portraits meant as an interpretation of human experience. Was a certain portrait the slow crystallization of the experience of a tribe into the sharp figure of a person? Was it the tale of an individual told through the processes of a racial memory which dropped the incidental and retained the essential? In either case you have the portrait. And it comes as a deep and revealing representation of the meaning of personal experience in respect of the great matters which have to do with men and God. So viewed, he saw Abraham as the citizen of a cosmopolitan city who went out to take something priceless to less cultivated lands.

The dream which there burst upon the soul of Abraham was the hope of being a secular missionary, a colonist of waste places. He looked out from a scene of culture upon a scene of surrounding barbarism, or, at least, of surrounding primitiveness. There came to him the thought that his culture was a gift from God—a gift not to retain, but to bestow. Was it not the part of a benefited nation to bless those lands which had not been benefited! [4]

Perhaps more than George Matheson saw, the experience of Abraham led him to insights it was difficult to express in a decadent civilization and he went out to found a society where they could be made secure. So he lived by a great spiritual faith. After the choice of Lot, he had to build his spiritual society in a land which forced a man to conquer a difficult environment rather than to accept an environment which made life easy. And his experience with Sodom led him to know that the hot vices of a primitive town can in their own way be as terrible as the vices of a decadent culture. It was a long battle with a sense of a Divine Companion who showed the way and set the pace. A great spiritual tradition was in process of being born.

In Jacob the fight becomes terribly acute. What he inherits is good. Yet he is a person full of shrewd double-mindedness and of such treachery that he has to desert his home and flee for his life. But alone in the wilderness all that he is not summons him in the piercing power of a revealing dream. The Freudians have taught us to believe that the evils in which our hearts delight but which our wills repudiate come back to us from the realm of the subconscious in masterful dreams. The story of Jacob gives us a bit of Freudian psychology turned upside down. It is the good which he has resisted which comes back to him in dreams. The subconscious, then, may be a dwelling place of angels as well as a

4 *The Representative Men of the Bible, Adam to Job* (New York: Geo. H. Doran Co.), pp. 114-15.

den of coiling serpents. This hard and selfish young man dreams of a ladder propped against the sky with God at the top of it claiming the shrewd, double-minded man who had cared so little for things beyond himself. There is a commerce between the spiritual heights and the heart of Jacob. It is a tremendous tale. There is, then, no such thing as a secular man. If Jacob could become a man of the divine fellowship, any man who will do it may have the same experience. The tale of Israel is telling us always that the hunger for moral and spiritual heights gnaws at the heart of every worldling.

The story of Joseph tells of a vain and gifted youth chastened by adversity and finding God when men forsake him. What happens to Joseph in Egypt is dramatic. What happens in the soul of Joseph is profoundly significant. That he became a ruler in Egypt completes a tapestry of the brightness of Oriental color and magnificence. That he become a ruler of his own heart through finding his true environment in God even when he was in a prison is the defining matter.

Always there is the invisible splendor. Moses moves like a prince among great events. But he finds something in his heart and in the memories of his people which sets a standard and makes it possible for him to reject the visible gold of an external magnificence for the invisible splendor of a moral and spiritual life. This invisible thing which alone is permanent and which finally masters the visible by its tremendous power masters his imagination and dominates his will. The bush which is burning and not consumed is not merely something which he sees. It is something which becomes a deathless burning in his own life. And that fire which blazes but does not destroy is the very presence of the living God.

So in a hundred ways these ancient stories tell of men's adventures with the moral God. They are intense men with magnificent virtues. They fight terrible vices. And in them God conquers. Typical of all of them is David, so tender that he will not drink water brought to him by men who have secured it at the risk of their lives, so loyal that his friendship with Jonathan has become a perpetual lyric, so hot with passionate energy that he can turn utterly cruel at the command of lust, so honest with himself that his repentance is more terrible than the defeat of an army with banners. And in all his fierce, tempestuous, and powerful life he has one great and masterful companion, the Lordly Person whose character is his perpetual rebuke and yet, because he loves fully that which he only partly becomes, his perpetual glory.

11. The Dedicated People

The Old Testament has to do with an astonishing number of persons. And they come to life in the most vivid and individual way. But the Old Testament has to do in a very special way with a people, a people belonging to God, a people chosen by God, a people dedicated to God. From the stories of Abraham, Isaac, and Jacob on down the centuries, one has this apprehension of the making first of a family, then of a cluster of families, and then of a great people, with the sense of a unique vocation, with the sense of belonging to God.

There are long periods of training. The years under Moses in the wilderness are typical. The people are wayward. Sometimes they are positively evil. Sometimes they are darkly and deeply evil. But they never really get away from the sense of being a dedicated people. You cannot be an apostate unless you have something great and high which has a right to your loyalty and to which you turn traitor. Even when the men of Israel were most evil, they were false sons. They were not aliens. And great meanings did become bone of their bone and flesh of their flesh. Great lessons were learned. They did at last become a people of God. They did put away idolatry. They did become loyal to Jehovah. They did come to understand what it meant, in the midst of peoples who worshiped every natural impulse, to serve a God of moral love, the very genius of whose reign was found in a firm discipline which saved them from becoming beasts and made them men.

They became stiff and hard in the process. They became isolated and full of a proud sense of their difference from other men. They were required to say "No" to so much to which the peoples around them said "Yes." Their moral code was so tremendously demanding. As they walked their lonely way, they did become separate. They did become a royal race of priests. But sometimes it seemed that they might be destined to lose as much as they had gained. This proud, self-conscious cult of spiritual isolation had in it elements of the greatest danger. Sometimes—to speak for a moment in the vernacular of a later day— it seemed that they had set out to be saints and only succeeded in becoming Pharisees. Indeed, when Jesus came with the vast universality of his message, this proud and bigoted self-consciousness was one of his greatest foes. It was against it that He spoke when He told of the lost coin, and the lost sheep, and the lost son.

But even in the Old Testament period the danger and the menace were realized, and it is in protest and condemnation and hope that the greatest of the Old Testament parables was spoken, a parable spoken by one whose voice calls across the centuries to the One who so eagerly spoke of joy when the lost were found.

This Old Testament parable tells of a prophet named Jonah. Now Jonah means *dove,* and one begins to get the sad irony at once, for in the Semitic world a name was supposed to reflect the character of the one who bore it. Jonah was most undovelike. When Jehovah commissioned him to go to the great and wicked city of Nineveh and cry out against it, he was angry and sullen, and set out to go to the opposite part of the world. He did this for a very strange reason. He wanted the city to be destroyed. And he was afraid that, if his voice was heard in condemnation in its streets, it would repent. He did not have a very pleasant time running away from God—this bigoted and selfish prophet. There was a storm in which, so gentle and friendly is the author of the tale, we are told that the pagan sailors threw Jonah overboard only as a last resort. Then there is a submarine part of the tale which has been rather overemphasized in the telling of it. Some very literal readers have been so full of thoughts of the great fish that they have forgotten the point of the story.

At all events, once safe on the land, when Jonah heard the voice of Jehovah requiring him to speak words which would ring like bells of doom in the city of Nineveh, he was ready to obey. Indeed, a rather ugly thought, yet one very pleasing to the selfish prophet, had occurred to Jonah. Perhaps after all Nineveh would not repent. Then he could go outside the city at a safe distance and see it destroyed.

Soon the streets of the mighty town were ringing with the words, "Yet forty days, and Nineveh shall be overthrown." But Jonah's unpleasant, selfish fears and not his bigoted hopes were justified. The whole city repented. They "put on sackcloth, from the greatest of them even to the least of them." Even the great king sat in sackcloth and ashes and repentance.

And now Jonah was very angry. He hated above everything being the servant of a forgiving God. He was ready to declare that he hated life under such terms and that he wished he could die. He went out and sat within a booth he made under the shade of a tiny friendly vine which grew up with miraculous quickness. He rather enjoyed the experience. It was better to have the vine which he did not need to share with anyone than to have a God he had to share with Nineveh. He would not love God. He would love the sheltering vine he could have all to himself.

Then the vine died and the burning sun beat on Jonah's head, and once again the sulking, selfish child prophet declared that he wanted to die. Then Jehovah spoke to him: "Dove," he said, addressing this undovelike man, "do you do well to be angry?"

"Yes," replied Jonah, "I do well to be angry and I want to die."

Then came from Jehovah the tenderest and most wonderful words in the Old Testament: "You love a vine, which comes and goes so quickly. Should I not regard that hiving town of Nineveh with all its confused and bewildered people? Do you not know that there are one hundred twenty thousand children in the city so small that they cannot tell their right hand from their left? Ought I not to love them? And think also of the cattle!"

So the heart of God speaks at full last in the Old Testament and rebukes the bigotry of His selfish, self-conscious people.

The great truth is put in another charming story. There was a man of Bethlehem, where Jesus later was to be born, who because of a famine in Israel went to the foreign land of Moab and dwelt among its alien people. Here he died, leaving his widow, Naomi, and his two sons. The two sons married young women of the land. And then the sons died also, leaving their mother and the two alien daughters-in-law. Naomi longed for her own land and decided to return. She blessed her daughters-in-law and set out for the land of her own people. One of the daughters-in-law wept and remained. The other, Ruth, refused to leave this older woman going away in lonely sorrow and insisted on returning with her. "Thy people shall be my people, and thy God my God." George Matheson— to refer to him again—has said that the Old Testament writers are always original. So when one of them sets out to tell a love story, it is the tale of the love of a woman for her mother-in-law! It is all of that. But it is more. And we find the point farther on. Ruth behaved with such noble modesty and goodness that in the land of Naomi she became the wife of Boaz. And thus a very wonderful thing happened. For Ruth became the great-grandmother of David, the messianic King. The author of the tale is saying that so rich, so capable of good, is foreign stock that when God was preparing the messianic line, He put into it the alien Ruth so that noble foreign blood mixed with the best blood of Israel.

And thus the people who had become a separate people for the sake of God and goodness heard voices telling them that they were so chosen and so dedicated, not to condemn the world, but to save the world. The dedicated people were to carry a message for all mankind.

We have only hinted at the richness and the manifoldness of the religious experience of Israel. So these ancient men met God. So they learned to speak in the accents He taught them. And so in the very terms of their own life He revealed some of the deepest secrets of His character to them and, as we shall more fully see, through them to the world.

CHAPTER VII

The Hebrew Prophets

In Lord Dunsany's *The Book of Wonder* there is a charming bit of phantasy called "The Wonderful Window." It tells the tale of a London clerk who paid all that he possessed at the moment for a window which he bought from an old man in an Oriental-looking robe, who put the window in the shabby room he rented in a certain London house. He

rubbed his eyes, then rubbed the window, and still he saw a sky of blazing blue, and far, far down beneath him, so that no sound came up from it or smoke of chimneys, a mediaeval city set with towers; brown roofs and cobbled streets, and then white walls and buttresses, and beyond them bright green fields and tiny streams. . . . The banners floating from every tower over the idle archers had little golden dragons all over a pure white field. . . . Each day as soon as he woke he went first to the wonderful window, and there was the city, diminutive in the distance, all shining in the morning, and the golden dragons dancing in the sun. . . . And when he saw them flaunting themselves on white folds from every tower against the marvelous deep blue of the sky he dressed contentedly, and, taking one last look, went off to his work with a glory in his mind.[1]

There could hardly be a more perfect illustration of that which makes magical phantasy different from prophecy. The London clerk looked through a magical window which had no relation to his past, or to his inner life of thought or struggle, and saw in this quite external fashion wonderful things. The Hebrew prophet at the very deepest place of his own thought and struggle, of his own personal experience, found that "the thought of God took hold on him." And so profound was his awareness, so sure was his sense of the Divine Companion, so authentic was the voice which spoke to him, that he had to say, "Thus saith the Lord."

1. Elijah and Elisha

Let us look at some of these prophets whose contribution to man's sense of God is as classic as that of the Greek tragedians is to man's sense of the tragic splendor of human life. There is the man of thunder and lightning who speaks in the ninth century B.C. and bears the name Elijah. He comes flashing out of the silence with an awful voice. The battle of a growing ethical religion with a hot and cruel nature worship is on, and the tale of his struggle with the prophets of Baal has all the tense pas-

[1] Boston: John W. Luce & Co., 1915, pp. 77, 78, 79.

sion of a final and tragic spiritual conflict. They are of the earth earthy.
He is the voice of the fire from heaven. But for all his robust desert
strength he is very human; and, when after his victory the brilliant and
powerful queen, Jezebel, vows that she will accomplish his death, he flees
the length of his own land, then all across Judah, and never stops until he
is far in the wilderness hills. There, exhausted, he waits. There is a singular tenderness in the tale of how God feeds him and sends him to sleep
before He speaks to him. There in the mountains come the tempest, the
lightning, and the earthquake. But, though they are God's, God is not in
them. And at last there comes the voice of gentle stillness which is indeed
the voice of God. So there comes to Elijah an inner serenity untouched
by outer vicissitude. But there is more than the triumphant theology in
action of an ethical God. There is the sharpest sense of the moral demands of human relationships. When the king, inspired by his conscienceless wife, goes to take possession of the patrimony of the man
whom she has caused to be slain, Elijah, stern with the wrath of God,
meets him, and the startled king cries out: "Hast thou found me, O mine
enemy?"

If Elijah represents the fierce and austere aspects of ethical religion, in
Elisha we see the prophet in an intimate human aspect. He is the companion of men in their everyday experiences, in their daily work with its
problems, in their sickness and health, and in the petty forays of border
warfare. These folk stories give a happy sense of God's nearness through
His prophet to the daily life of men. When there is danger the prophet
can make his servant aware of heavenly resources making insignificant
the menace of men. The chariots and horsemen in the sky may be invisible to most men, but they are the symbols of divine help not far away
if men truly reach for it. The stories represent the curious march of men
forward, with less noble thoughts mingling with flashes of profound understanding. The tale of the bears destroying the lads who had called the
prophet "baldhead" scarcely belongs to the nobler aspects of prophecy.
But something far deeper and nobler is at work. When Elisha refuses
gifts from Naaman, whose leprosy has been healed, we see the sharp
sense of the prophet with a high conception of the nobility of his mission.
He will not be a medicine man shrewdly using his powers for personal
gain. Men are becoming more aware of God high above them as they
hear Elijah, and of God very near to them as Elisha lives among them.

2. Amos

In a sense the eighth century, with Amos and Hosea and Isaiah and
Micah, is a golden age, the classic period of Hebrew prophecy. Two centuries later Confucius is to live in China, and Gautama in India. Three
centuries later the proud age of man is to come in Athens. Here in the
hills and valleys of Israel something is happening more significant for the

good life for men and, above all, for men's knowledge of God than anything which ever happened in Greece.

Amos, keeping his stunted sheep in the wilderness of Tekoa and tend-
ing the bitter figs not too bad for the taste if they are pierced by a sharp
instrument at the right time, looks out on the caravans and gazes toward
the heights of Jerusalem. He learns with the wonderful clairvoyance of
the desert, sees everything, hears everything, is familiar with lions and
serpents in caves, meditates, opens his mind and heart, and at last cries
with a voice to be heard age after age: "The lion hath roared; who will
not fear? The Lord Jehovah hath spoken; who can but prophesy?"

He goes to the sanctuary at Bethel—a royal shrine—where vice and
worship flourish together. With the magnificent art of the Oriental orator he condemns the evils which corrode the life of surrounding nations.
For cumulative transgressions which Jehovah has beheld, He will not
turn *it* (terrible pronoun of doom) back. He condemns the sister nations'
vices. Then looking into the eyes of the men who have had a hot appetite for the promise of doom to brothers and neighbors, he analyzes their
dark deeds. And again there comes the awful reiteration: "He will not
turn *it* back." The things he condemns as he speaks against Damascus
and Gaza and Tyre and Edom and Ammon and Moab and Judah and
Israel are sins against humanity, cruel and lustful deeds which shame the
name of man. Not for a cult, but for a moral code growing out of the
character of God, does he speak.

Amaziah, the royal priest, silences him, crushing him with insulting
speech. And Amos, whose words might perhaps have gone with the wind,
writes them out, and so they are winged age by age to all lands and to all
peoples. "Seek good, and not evil, that ye may live," he declares; "and
so Jehovah, the God of hosts, will be with you, as you say. Hate the evil,
and love the good, and establish justice in the gate. . . . Let justice roll
down as waters, and righteousness as a mighty stream." Do they depend
upon the fact that God has chosen them to be His people? There is a
quick reply to that: "You only have I known of all the families of the
earth: therefore I will visit upon you all your iniquities. . . . Prepare
to meet thy God, O Israel." Do they think they can combine wickedness
and worship? "I hate, I despise your feasts, and I will take no delight in
your solemn assemblies." There is the sudden flash of tenderness, the
desire that Israel may repent and be saved. "O Lord Jehovah, forgive, I
beseech thee: how shall Jacob stand? for he is small."

There is the mighty sweep of a wider vision: "Are ye not as the children of the Ethiopians unto me, O children of Israel? . . . Have not I
brought up Israel out of the land of Egypt, and the Philistines from
Caphtor, and the Syrians from Kir?" All movements and all nations belong to God.

So the full, mighty note of prophecy sounds. The word God is so pronounced that it is synonymous with righteousness. A light from the very face of the Moral God shines upon men.

3. Hosea

The chapter on "The Sin Against Love" in the first volume of Principal Sir George Adam Smith's *The Book of the Twelve Prophets* is one of the most remarkable pieces of penetrating exposition in the English language. He is bringing together deep insights which have come from his study of the prophet Hosea:

Believe then in hell, because you believe in the Love of God—not in a hell to which God condemns men of His will and pleasure, but a hell into which men cast themselves from the very face of His love in Jesus Christ. The place has been painted as a place of fires. But when we contemplate that men come to it with the holiest flames in their nature quenched, we shall justly feel that it is rather a dreary waste of ash and cinder, strewn with snow—some ribbed and frosted Arctic zone, silent in death, for there is no life there, and there is no life there because there is no Love, and no Love because men in rejecting or abusing her have slain their own power ever again to feel her presence.[2]

What sort of person was the man whose words led Sir George Adam Smith to write his profound and searching analysis of the relation between the rejection of love and moral death?

Hosea was a sensitive and vital young man in Israel who loved and married a young woman of his people whose goodness seemed as radiant as her charm. But as time went on he began strangely to feel that, while he was giving the full devotion of a deep and abiding love, he was not receiving in return an equal eager loyalty. As he moved along the street his friends would suddenly stop talking, and he had a feeling that they were talking of him. He became aware that his wife was unfaithful. And at last she left his home for a wild and lawless life and sank lower and lower until she became a slave. But the love of Hosea for this faithless woman did not die. He could not put her out of his heart. She had thrown his love back in his face, but he loved her still. He bought her back from slavery and brought her to the old home. With infinite patience and tenderness he tried to rekindle a devotion whose fires had died. He bent before the hearthfire of his cold and cheerless home sadly yet eagerly trying to blow into flame an ancient burning. With a love that out-Arthured Arthur—who expected to be reconciled to Guinevere only after the cleansing fires of death—he himself became the instrument of moral reconciliation. Once more he would see the light of love in those vagrant and wandering eyes.

Through all this personal heartbreak and agony and despairing hope Hosea came to an overwhelming realization that what he had experi-

2 New York: Doubleday, Doran & Co., I, 354.

enced in respect of Gomer, God had experienced in respect of Israel. "When Israel was a child, then I loved him, and called my son out of Egypt." And Israel had cast Jehovah's love back in His face in falseness and treachery. But love would not die in the heart of God. "How shall I give thee up, Ephraim? . . . I will not execute the fierceness of mine anger, . . . for I am God, and not man; the Holy One in the midst of thee; and I will not come in wrath." Yet with all the heartbroken tenderness of the divine love, there is an utterly complete facing of facts: "Ephraim compasseth me about with falsehood. . . . He continually multiplieth lies and desolation." "It is thy destruction, O Israel, that thou art against me." But again there is the strange, loving call: "O Israel, return unto Jehovah thy God; for thou hast fallen by thine iniquity."

So right out of the depth of his own experience Hosea learned the meaning of suffering love, the suffering love of man and the suffering love of God. If Amos is the prophet of the God who is righteousness alive, Hosea is the prophet of a God who is love alive. But the two prophets are speaking not of two Gods but of one God. For Jehovah is the God of moral love.

4. Isaiah

Isaiah has been pictured as a member of the royal circle, as a man with the blood of kings in his veins. At all events, he was a patrician in easiest contact with the leaders of his people. And he lived at the time when, according to tradition, in far-off Italy, Rome was beginning its life. As a young man Isaiah was a member of a circle of admiring youths who were about the brilliant King Uzziah. They were joyously proud of their monarch—ruler, military leader, every inch a king.

Then a strange and tragic thing happened. The fascinating, majestic king was seized by leprosy. He went into retirement, and erelong he died. It was a staggering blow to the young men about the throne.

Isaiah felt as if life had ceased to have any meaning. He had lost his human hero. But, significantly enough, he tells us that in the year that the King Uzziah died he had a tremendous experience in the temple. He saw Jehovah. The end of the temple faded away, and all the eternal glory mastered the eye in one dazzling vista. There on a throne was Jehovah, high and lifted up, and his train filled the temple. In the year that Isaiah lost his human hero, he found his divine hero. If it was a glorious experience, it was a terrible and searching experience, too.

Facing that transcendent perfection, Isaiah felt all the pangs of repentance. And he repented not of what was evil in him but of the best thing about him, his gift of golden speech. The best of Isaiah was not good enough for God. We do not know what battles this Oriental youth in an Oriental court may have had with many sorts of evil desire. What is clear is that, when he saw the glory of the divine perfection, that of which he had been proud became that of which he was ashamed. "I am a man of unclean lips, and I dwell in the midst of a people of unclean lips." Then came the burning miracle of the transformed lips and the transformed life, and Isaiah was God's man ready to speak God's word for more than a generation.

He knew how to speak lovely and ringing words of summons to repentance: "Cease to do evil; learn to do well." "Though your sins be as scarlet, they shall be as white as snow." He knew how to speak with desperate and caustic condemnation: "Woe unto them that call evil good, and good evil; that put darkness for light, and light for darkness; that put bitter for sweet, and sweet for bitter!" He longs to see Jerusalem called "the city of righteousness, a faithful town." He knows the necessity of sharp separation from evil: "A highway shall be there, and a way, and it shall be called The way of holiness; the unclean shall not pass over it." He is full of the wonder of the divine invitation: "Therefore with joy shall ye draw water out of the wells of salvation." His sense of kingliness never leaves him. Happily he pictures the ideal king: "Behold, a king shall reign in righteousness, and princes shall rule in justice. And a man shall be as a hiding-place from the wind, and a covert from the tempest, as streams of water in a dry place, as the shade of a great rock in a weary land." His vision sweeps over the nations in appraisal and judgment. He is an international prophet, and in glorious vision he sees the day of reconciliation between the nations. He who had spoken of the highway of exclusiveness speaks of the highway of friendliness:

In that day shall there be a highway out of Egypt to Assyria, and the Assyrian shall come into Egypt, and the Egyptian into Assyria; and the Egyptians shall worship with the Assyrians. In that day shall Israel be the third with Egypt and with Assyria, a blessing in the midst of the earth; for that Jehovah of hosts hath blessed them, saying, Blessed be Egypt my people, and Assyria the work of my hands, and Israel mine inheritance.

Alas that the nations never rose to a moral height which could meet the conditions for the fulfillment of this most generous and gracious word in the Old Testament!

Ancient enemies, glorious friends! What a splendid hope it is! But people of all lands must have their hearts touched with the burning and transforming fire of God to make it come true. And that fire never touches unwilling hearts.

5. Micah

Micah is a small-town man. His village is right in the path of invading hostile armies. And you feel the terror of his time running through all his words. He sees moral meaning in it all. His people have done evil, and they are to suffer the consequences which must come in a world governed by a moral God. "Woe to them that devise iniquity and work evil upon their beds! when the morning is light, they practise it, because it is in the power of their hand." He is especially the voice of the common man oppressed by those in power. "And they covet fields, and seize them; and houses, and take them away: and they oppress a man and his house, even a man and his heritage." But Jehovah sees all this. "Therefore thus saith Jehovah: Behold, against this family do I devise an evil, from which ye shall not remove your necks." It is the leaders of the people whom he condemns: "Hear, I pray you, ye heads of . . . Israel: is it not for you to know justice? ye who hate the good, and love the evil; who pluck off their skin from off them, and their flesh from off their bones." "The godly man is perished out of the earth, and . . . they all lie in wait for blood; they hunt every man his brother with a net." False prophets inspired by wine would be the fitting prophets for this people. "But as for me," declares Micah, "I am full of power by the Spirit of Jehovah, and of judgment, and of might, to declare unto Jacob his transgression, and to Israel his sin."

Those without a voice are suddenly articulate in this great prophet. He hurls their wrongs upon the consciences of men. Those without weapons see the unsheathing of a great divine sword.

There are insights of amazing depth and moral reach and spiritual power. In a world where human sacrifice was still practiced Micah dramatically asks if he too is to offer the fruit of his body for the sin of his soul. There in a blaze of light come the words: "He hath showed thee, O man, what is good; and what doth Jehovah require of thee, but to do justly, and to love kindness, and to walk humbly with thy God?"

There is hope beyond the doom if men will walk in ways of repentance. "Who is a God like unto thee, that pardoneth iniquity, and passeth over the transgression of the remnant of his heritage? he retaineth not his anger for ever, because he delighteth in lovingkindness."

So condemnation and invitation, judgment and mercy, continue in the words of the mighty villager who speaks for God. You see the flash in his eye. You feel the tenseness of his voice. You sense the quiver of his flesh. And you are more than ready to believe that his words are words of God.

6. Jeremiah

Years ago in a lecture in New York City I remember hearing Sir George Adam Smith say that Jeremiah reminds you of one of those shells whose shriek is heard above the noise of battle and whose very mission is performed in its explosion. The eighth century with its mighty voices has passed. The seventh century has its last days, and the sixth comes on apace. Jeremiah speaks the words God gives him as his recalcitrant nation in utter rebellion repudiates Jehovah and staggers on toward its doom. It is a mission he would escape if he could: "Ah, Lord Jehovah! behold, I know not how to speak; for I am a child." Tender and sensitive, a man who would have fitted into the gentle ways of a quiet day, Jeremiah is bound to the wheel of destiny as it spins toward terrible doom. And the voice of God comes to him in his commission: "Say not, I am a child; for to whomsoever I shall send thee thou shalt go, and whatsoever I shall command thee thou shalt speak."

"Then Jehovah put forth his hand, and touched my mouth; and Jehovah said unto me, Behold, I have put my words in thy mouth: see, I have this day set thee over the nations and over the kingdoms, to pluck up and to break down and to destroy and to overthrow, to build and to plant."

All the long years of his tragic ministry he is listening to God and speaking to men. He is amazed at his people. "They are wise to do evil, but to do good they have no knowledge." When false prophets speak to them, they, God's people, "love to have it so." "How long," the prophet asks, "shall thine evil thoughts lodge within thee?" The years pass toward a climax of doom. If they really understood, they would be saying: "The harvest is past, the summer is ended, and we are not saved."

Over against this weakness and evil of men is the greatness and glory and goodness of God. "There is none like unto thee, O Jehovah; thou art great, and thy name is great in might. . . . Jehovah is the true God; he is the living God, and an everlasting King." There is only one center of security. "Blessed is the man that trusteth in Jehovah, and whose trust Jehovah is." But men have forsaken Jehovah "the fountain of living waters." It is a bitter and terrible thing to have to speak words of doom. The prophet wishes he could find a lodge in some vast wilderness and escape this hard responsibility. "Cursed be the day wherein I was born," he cries in one of his darker moods. But he goes on to tell the bitter truth: "Moreover I will take from them the voice of mirth and the voice of gladness, the voice of the bridegroom and the voice of the bride, the sound of the millstones, and the light of the lamp." But even in this approaching darkness Jeremiah can declare for God, "I know the thoughts that I think toward you, . . . thoughts of peace, and not of evil, to give you hope in your latter end. . . . Ye shall seek me, and find me, when ye shall search for me with all your heart." "It may be that the house of Judah will hear all the evil which I purpose to do unto them; that they may return every man from his evil way; that I may forgive their iniquity and their sin." Yet as the people harden in evil, he cries: "Thy hurt is incurable." "Behold, I will set my face against you for evil, even to cut off all Judah." The very fires of the ancient conflagration burn before us as we listen to Jeremiah.

Dark tragedy comes. And a bitter sense of social solidarity takes possession of the people. They are in a state of heavy, black despair. "The fathers have eaten sour grapes," they cry, "and the children's teeth are set on edge." The prophet retorts with words of hot rebuttal: "Every one shall die for *his own iniquity*: every man that eateth the sour grapes, his teeth shall be set on edge."

All the while Jeremiah's own thought is deepening and broadening. And it comes to a splendid power in the word he speaks for God about the new covenant:

This is the covenant that I will make with the house of Israel after those days, saith Jehovah: I will put my law in their inward parts, and in their heart will I write it; and I will be their God, and they shall be my people. And they shall teach no more every man his neighbor, and every man his brother, saying, Know Jehovah; for they shall all know me, from the least of them unto the greatest of them, saith Jehovah: for I will forgive their iniquity, and their sin will I remember no more.

Once and again Jeremiah comes upon bitter personal experience. He is scoffed at. He is scorned. He is hated. He is treated with ignominy. And at last we have reason to believe he met a violent death in Egypt. There remain his glorious insights, his awful condemnations, his splendid hopes. And there linger in one's ear his words: "Israel is not forsaken."

7. *Nahum*

The little book of Nahum is the taunt song of a hundred little lands, sung when the great loot city Nineveh fell with a crash which was heard all over that ancient world. Assyria had been a brilliant, brutal world power. Its career of conquest had been an achievement of sheer, unethical force. The treasures of cities and villages belonging to many lands had been poured into its waiting and capacious lap. It had been a city of cruelty in an empire of brutality. And when it fell a wild cry was lifted from the small lost peoples it had betrayed:

Woe to the bloody city! it is all full of lies and rapine; the prey departeth not. The noise of the whip, and the noise of the rattling of wheels, and prancing horses, and bounding chariots, the horseman mounting, and the flashing sword, and the glittering spear, and a multitude of slain, and a great heap of corpses, and there is no end of the bodies; they stumble upon their bodies. . . . Thy princes are as the locusts, and thy marshals as the swarms of grasshoppers, which encamp in the hedges in the cold day, but when the sun ariseth they flee away, and their place is not known where they are. Thy shepherds slumber, O king of Assyria; thy nobles are at rest; thy people are scattered upon the mountains, and there is none to gather them. There is no assuaging of thy hurt; thy wound is grievous: all that hear the report of thee clap their hands over thee; for upon whom hath not thy wickedness passed continually?

The little book might be called The City That Was Against Goodness, or The City That Was Against the Moral God. It burns with the power of an ancient passion. It sees the destruction of that which is against goodness and against God with a joy which there is no attempt to hide.

There may be sentimental people who find Nahum a difficult book. It ought to be said clearly that in the full New Testament light we are commanded to forgive evil people when they repent. We are not commanded to forgive evil people in the full and unhesitating practice of evil. And as a matter of fact, the whole subject of forgiveness needs some moral clarification. We sometimes say we hate the sin and love the sinner. That is all very well if we are speaking of the part of the sinner which hates the sin and is ashamed of it and is restless and wistful with desire to escape from it. But when a man makes evil his good and likes it and comes to love it and chooses it for his very own, you can make no distinction between the sin and the sinner.

That is, of course, a doctrine which works both ways. It would be a brave man who would state it without something of a chill moving down his own spine. For who of us can completely escape its condemnation? For all that, the book of Nahum, with its fierce wrath against a city which had become an incarnation of evil, is a part of the moral virility of ethical religion. We rejoice in its downright strength of moral energy, even though, while we rejoice, we may also tremble.

8. The Isaiah of the Exile

Charles Dickens—as Gilbert Chesterton has pointed out, and as we ought to have seen without the aid of Chesterton—so painted the life of the very poor as to fill it with a certain golden fascination. He so portrayed tragedy that somehow it ceased to be sordid tragedy and became magnificent tragedy. He always found laughter, and he often found song, where dull observers have found only meaningless boredom at best and insufferable brutality at the worst. There is quite likely to be an outburst of music just when you would expect a dirge. The Isaiah of the Exile has none of Charles Dickens' rollicking delight in life. But he does have Dickens' sense of a song in the midst of tragedy. And he does shout with triumph at the most surprising times.

The Exile was supposed to be the death of a nation. Elegy and obituary seemed the only appropriate utterances. Then suddenly the great unknown prophet of the Exile began to shout:

Speak ye comfortably to Jerusalem; and cry unto her, that her warfare is accomplished, that her iniquity is pardoned, that she hath received of

Jehovah's hand double for all her sins. . . . O thou that tellest good tidings to Zion, get thee up on a high mountain; O thou that tellest good tidings to Jerusalem, lift up thy voice with strength; lift it up, be not afraid; say unto the cities of Judah, Behold, your God!

At first it seems that we are painfully listening to a wedding march in the house of death. Then all at once we know that there has been a resurrection: a resurrection of expectation, a resurrection of hope, a resurrection of the sheer joy of living.

Right in the midst of a foreign land, with its foreign religion and its tyrannical political power, there is a sense of God so ample and so magnificent that all human oppressions become small and irrelevant in its presence:

Hast thou not known? hast thou not heard? The everlasting God, Jehovah, the Creator of the ends of the earth, fainteth not, neither is weary; there is no searching of his understanding.

Thus saith Jehovah, the King of Israel, and his Redeemer, Jehovah of hosts: I am the first, and I am the last; and besides me there is no God.

Arise, shine; for thy light is come, and the glory of Jehovah is risen upon thee.

And from this greatness of God the prophet thus passes to the glory which is to come to His disciplined and chastened children. The word which at its beginning was: "Prepare ye the way of the Lord," toward the end becomes: "Prepare ye the way of the people." And the two belong together. "Awake, awake, put on thy strength, O Zion; put on thy beautiful garments, O Jerusalem, the holy city." "Ho, every one that thirsteth, come ye to the waters, and he that hath no money; come ye, buy, and eat; yea, come, buy wine and milk without money and without price." He has not forgotten the moral problem: "Seek ye Jehovah while he may be found; call ye upon him while he is near: let the wicked forsake his way, and the unrighteous man his thoughts; and let him return unto Jehovah, and he will have mercy upon him; and to our God, for he will abundantly pardon."

The great prophet of the Exile has not forgotten the tragedy. He has transcended it by piercing its very secret. For here in the sublimest words in the Old Testament we hear of the suffering servant of God. "He was despised, and rejected of men; a man of sorrows, and acquainted with grief. . . . Surely he hath borne our griefs, and carried our sorrows. . . . He was wounded for our transgressions, he was bruised for our iniquities; . . . with his stripes we are healed."

What profound and passionate and tragic experience is sure to lie back of heavenly music! The writer of the greatest of the servant passages had probed the very depths of personality, had learned how the good can take upon himself the burden of the evil, how the just can make his own the hard pain of the unjust, and how this gift of suffering love has in it a redemptive power beyond the thought or the imagination of man.

Professor Franz Delitzsch used to say years ago that when you read these words you feel on the very edge of Calvary. The door is truly opening, and you are just about to discover the meaning of the great insight as to the suffering love of God. It is not an accident that the prophet who has the very loftiest doctrine of the divine power sees in the Servant who most perfectly represents God a great sufferer.

The prophet of the Exile has journeyed beyond tragedy to the eternal fulfillment, beyond darkness to the eternal light, beyond cynicism to the truth which makes all cynicism shabby. His song is cleansed from all sentimentality by the blood of cruel tragedy; his hope is saved from all superficiality by its utter moral realism. As you listen to his heavenly music, you feel that you have come upon something ultimate and final.

Here, as always, there is the deep note of experience. Thousands of suffering hearts have been pressed to make this wine of anticipation. Thousands of terror-stricken and broken lives have united their experience to find this resurrection of hope. The great prophet has become a tremendous seismograph to record the throbbings of an earth of woe. And then he becomes capable of recording the glory of a heaven of hope. From the tomb of the nation he comes forth with shining eyes. The Exile is not the last word. Beyond it lie the mountain peaks beautiful with the light of the new day which is to be.

Less and less is it difficult, as we go on with these gigantic men of prophecy, to accept their own claim that when they speak for God, God is speaking through them. And the most wonderful thing about it is that every word they say comes leaping from living experience. So they have known God. So has God become real to them. And so they have found the very fashion in which they must speak.

It is beyond all words vital. There is no artificial congruity. There is disagreement enough on the surface. But the deeper you go, the more you find a great correlation, the more you find indubitable harmony. Dead things must have mechanical agreement or fall apart. Living men can catch their fragments of truth and speak them out for God at last to discover that all unwittingly each has become an instrument in a great orchestra making divine music in the world. And the seeming discords but add to the harmony in this living music.

9. Ezekiel

All sorts of things meet in the amazing young man who was carried off with the exiles and became their comforter in bitter days. He had his gracious gift of speech and, much to his own distress, his fellow exiles who came to hear him were lured by the lovely music of his words rather than by their deeper meaning.

And they come unto thee as the people cometh, and they sit before thee as my people, and they hear thy words, but do them not; for with their mouth they show much love, but their heart goeth after their gain. And, lo, thou art unto them as a very lovely song of one that hath a pleasant voice, and can play well on an instrument; for they hear thy words, but they do them not.

Ezekiel tells of his visions in a complicated fashion of rich symbolism. But it is usually easy to see some central meaning lying at the heart of the symbol. The living creature dominating the wheels has naturally enough been full of suggestion for ages of machinery such as Ezekiel never knew. But when in the presence of the divine glory Ezekiel falls flat upon his face, we who have so often been afraid of a brightness too great for us well understand what it means. And when the voice of God comes with the great words, "Son of man, stand upon thy feet, and I will speak with thee," this call to meet God standing erect thrills us through and through. This sense of the value of man *standing* is very characteristic of the Old Testament revelation. There is a glorious humanism moving through all its awed sense of the glory of the divine. Ezekiel deals with ugly vices and uglier habits of mind. He understands the badness of heart which evil brings, and he promises something better. "I will give them one heart, and I will put a new spirit within you; and I will take the stony heart out of their flesh, and will give them a heart of flesh; that they may walk in my statutes, and keep mine ordinances, and do them: and they shall be my people, and I will be their God." Then come unhesitating words of repudiation of the bad-hearted. There is always a sense of the great alternatives in prophecy. The same sense of corporate life and individual responsibility with which Jeremiah had dealt comes to Ezekiel. And even more directly he deals with the proverb of the sour grapes the fathers have eaten and the teeth on edge of the children: "As I live, saith the Lord Jehovah, ye shall not have occasion any more to use this proverb in Israel. Behold, all souls are mine; as the soul of the father, so also the soul of the son is mine: the soul that sinneth, *it* shall die." Both positively and negatively Ezekiel develops the principle at some length. One great thing is to come to men of good will out of bitter experience. And this the prophet reiterates, "Ye shall know that I am Jehovah." There are no moral hesitations. If a thing is evil and a people do it: "Thus saith Jehovah: Behold, I am against thee." There is a clear sense of the meaning of disappointment with human stuff. "I sought for a man among them, that should build up the wall, and stand in the gap before me for the land, that I should not destroy it; but I found none." But there is the perpetual summons: "Say unto them, As I live, saith the Lord Jehovah, I have no pleasure in the death of the wicked; . . . turn ye from your evil ways; for why will ye die, O house of Israel?"

The prophet turns to the great hope and works out the details of his vision with infinite care. For the broken city, a new city; for the destroyed temple, a new temple. And then there comes the immortal vision of the waters which issued out from under the threshold of the temple. "Behold, there ran out waters on the right side." The stream increased as it ran—to the depth of a man's ankles—to the depth of a man's knees—to a man's loins—then a river in which one had to swim. Glorious trees grew by this river flowing from the temple. At last it rushed into the Dead Sea, healing its waters and making them sweet so that a multitude of fish lived in the Sea, so long incapable of supporting life. Now there were nets where no nets had been seen before. But— what a practical vision!—some marshes were left given up to salt that this necessity should be provided. And on this side and on that perennial trees bore new fruit every month. The place of worship was indeed the source of life.

10. God Meets Men at the Central Place of Their Own Experience

A great Old Testament scholar who was a profound student of the Hebrew prophets liked to say that prophecy was "psychologically mediated." God always met men right in some living experience. He met them where they were living. But He did not leave them there. Prophecy, indeed, was first of all an adventure of living with God. Then it was a great adventure of speaking for God.

We have listened to some of the voices. We have inspected some of the experiences which lay back of the speech. We have looked upon the faces of some of the men—sharp, clear faces, shaggy, weary faces, but always eyes clear with the light of God. And all we have seen and heard corresponds to precisely that sense of the meaning of the personal which is central in these studies. Everything we have said about God, the Creator and Preserver—God, the Great Person, and the human persons He has made—comes to more perfect focus as we confront these Hebrew prophets. We are not for a moment claiming that they were conscious of the philosophical relationships which we have described. But everything they said and did fits into those relationships, confirming our sense of their authenticity and of their meaning for the interpretation of life. And it is still true that on the mountain tops of the world we meet the Hebrew prophets.

CHAPTER VIII

"The Reign of Law"

A GOOD many years ago James Lane Allen wrote a novel entitled *The Reign of Law*. It was the story of a Kentucky boy who was a student of theology. The crisis of the book lies in the fact that when he is confronted by the uniformities of nature he finds it difficult to believe in the being of God. The dilemma seemed real enough at the time the book was written, though even then there were those who saw that there was something the matter with a process by which one used the free intelligence of man to collect data which would prove that there is no free intelligence in the universe. Men were to rise one day to the conception of laws of nature as habits of God and not as impersonal, unconscious deities controlling the world.

When we talk about law, then, we may mean the uniformities of nature. So science will teach us to regard law. We may mean the principles which lie at the basis of all sound reasoning. So logic will teach us to regard law. We may mean a code of behavior by which men succeed in living together in some sort of harmony. This is the political conception of law. We may mean the divine sanctions by means of which God would have us guide our lives. This is the religious conception of law.

As a matter of fact, all these types of law meet and intermingle so that the whole matter is not at all so simple as the above analysis might lead us to expect. The Code of Hammurabi, for instance, which comes from a time roughly two thousand years before the Christian era, is obviously the product of much practical activity in ruling men and is also the summation of long experience. But the king is seen receiving the laws from the sun-god in a relief at the top of the shaft of stone containing the laws.

1. Old Testament Laws

The Hebrew laws come through a long process of human experience. They also come with a profound sense of the divine sanction. The earlier forms have a certain crudity, even as the latest forms have perhaps a certain rigidity. It is in the period when the full tide of the consciousness of the moral character of God is at its height that the laws reflect this living experience with a certain moral magnificence.

We need not enter upon a detailed study of early commands, of the law of the Covenant, of the Deuteronomic Code, or of the later Levitical legislation. It is important to see, however, that the more we know of what may seem to be the checkered history of all this mass of legislation, the more we see God Himself moving through the vicissitudes of human thought and experience which at last are crystallized into legal form. The high, clear note of justice rings out magnificently:

Thou shalt not oppress thy neighbor, nor rob him: the wages of a hired servant shall not abide with thee all night until the morning. Thou shalt not curse the deaf, nor put a stumblingblock before the blind. . . . Thou shalt not go up and down as a talebearer among thy people. . . . Thou shalt not hate thy brother in thy heart. . . . Thou shalt love thy neighbor as thyself. . . . And if a stranger sojourn with thee in your land, ye shall not do him wrong.

Ye shall have one manner of law, as well for the sojourner, as for the home-born.

There is a glorious sense of the meaning and strategy of choice. And this comes out with especial vividness in the Deuteronomic Code. "Behold, I set before you this day a blessing and a curse." "I have set before thee life and death, . . . therefore choose life." The moral tragedy of evil is set forth in graphic form in a series of vigorous curses. And a whole moral code lies embedded in these curses.

Modern scholarship has made it possible for us to pursue the developing experience in and through which God spoke to Israel in a way which was not possible before. And all of this only makes it more clear that God was speaking through His people's history and not apart from it.

The law has its powerful human center, and this, of course, is Moses. When once one has understood that all experience is essentially personal, he is less allured by the tendency of some scholars to get away from persons to abstract principles doing battle in a fog. A law is only a law to a conscious person who thinks in terms of its sanctions and decides to obey them or to refuse to be guided by them. Naturally enough there were many lawgivers, and we are not at all surprised to find one greatest lawgiver of all. Around his name traditions would gather. Like a ship sailing a sea, he might even gather barnacles. But all this simply proves how great and overpowering a person he was.

It is all a living tradition, and just because it is a living tradition there is a certain fluidity. But through all this one sees clearly that which is not subject to the defeat of hoary time.

We will not try to rob Moses of his place in history. Through a physical wilderness and, we may be sure, through a moral and spiritual wilderness, he led his people. The Exodus stands always as a great symbol of the discipline of a nation of persons. There is no promised land without a promised mind, a promised heart, and a promised will.

Quite properly, the Ten Commandments typify law as a revelation of moral and spiritual meanings. Whatever the problem of tracing their history, there is no problem about testing them practically. The man of the Ten Commandments is a good and dependable man. The nation of the Ten Commandments would be a good and dependable nation. The world of the Ten Commandments would be a good and dependable world. These commands claimed a divine sanction. And history, both individual history and the history of nations and of races, has vindicated the claim.

The genius of the Ten Commandments is seen in the upward look, the outward look, and the inward look. The upward look sees the one true God above to be worshiped. It asserts a spirituality which must never be forgotten. And it condemns a finding of God where God is not. There is a sacredness of the words which enshrine divine meaning and a sacredness of days where every day has more meaning because of one most sacred day.

There is the outward look to social relations, the family at the heart of all this with an honor for the home life out of which new life comes. There is a sense of the sacredness of human life, and of the sacredness of marriage, and of the sacredness of truth among men in all their relations. And under God all these insights are bound together in mighty commands.

There is the inward look. For in the last commandment of the ten, attention is turned from the act to the motive, from what men do to what they want. So all the vast realm of the life within is opened up with a tremendous demand for its integrity.

2. Law as Convention

It is said that when Montesquieu had completed his famous work *L'Esprit des Lois,* he called together a group of his famous friends to hear what he had written and to give their opinion of it. Unanimously they advised against its publication. As the century scarcely produced a more significant book in France and as it must be placed among the foremost books produced in Europe during the century, the advice is a classic example of the futility of the judgment of men who would confess that their opinions should have great weight. The attempt to see the laws in relation to national governments, the manners of people, their climate, their religion, their commerce and other aspects of their life was ambitious enough. The thing ought to be done at least once in a century with the new perspective of added knowledge and the fresh angles of approach made inevitable by different philosophical presuppositions. Any discussion, however modest, of law in its relation to human experience must consider some aspects of the growth of legal sanctions and their relations to the men who accept them.

Inevitably no end of rules—and by the same token no end of laws—express conventions. They might easily have been otherwise. Their importance lies in the fact that life can move along with smooth efficiency only if large numbers of men do certain of the same things in the same way. Railroads cannot frequently change from one gauge to another without immense loss of time and unnecessary complexity in respect of equipment. Games are based upon rules which quite easily might be different, but if the game is to be played the players must accept a common convention, and if it is to be a national game there must be universal acceptance of convention in the nation. If it is to be a world-wide game, there must be acceptance of the convention everywhere in the world. The game of life has the same characteristics. There are regulations where the *sameness* is more important than the original nature of the regulation itself. You cannot have a town set forth in ten different timetables with ten different names without confusion. It does not really matter very much what the name is. But there must be one name, and it must be a name in common use. When we enter the realm of men's life together in an organized society, there are many matters which come to be of the utmost practical importance which belong to this field of necessary conventions. The recording of deeds is a necessary convention in respect of property in an organized society which recognizes individual ownership. Regulations regarding traffic lights doubtless save many lives, but they belong to the field of necessary conventions. So one might go on and on.

There is a tendency in certain quarters to depreciate all the laws which grow out of convention. This tendency itself shows a lack of discrimination. The truth is there are conventions and conventions. There are conventions which are worked out to meet genuine problems. And there are conventions which, if one may put it so, are created to solve problems which do not exist. The conventions in respect of manner of dress belong to the second class. Yet in certain societies at certain periods they have had all the force of the laws of the Medes and the Persians. There is a healthy spirit of rebellion against laws of behavior which have no secure basis in problems which arise when men try to live together in comfort and good will.

Through their relationship to deeper matters the conventions which inevitably arise in civilized life come to have an importance even beyond their practical utility. The Ishmaels of the world have a dislike of restrictions which inevitably arise in communal life. And often this dislike grows out of an inner attitude toward other people which is itself reprehensible.

The various stages of Old Testament life reflect this conventional side of law as well as the deeper aspects. Wandering tribes represent one situation, and agricultural theocracy represents another, and monarchy represents a third. The important thing to observe is that the conventions growing out of these different types of communal life do have a constant reference to human values and human needs which gives one a sense of a purpose beyond the immediate practical problem. The way in which the Eternal masters and makes use of the relative is itself an important part of revelation. And here again we see the actual human situations becoming central in all the decisions. In other words, in a noble society convention is always more than convention. And laws growing out of convention have a surprising way of expressing a deeper meaning.

3. Law as Ritual

The uniform aspects of all cults tend to crystallize and to become the laws of the cult. With the passage of time they command an intense, sometimes even a fanatical, loyalty. If the moral life of the people is advancing and deepening, the leaders with a keen sense of moral and spiritual values are likely to become the critics of the uniformities of the cult. They call attention to the habit of all too many men of substituting loyalty to the ceremonial for faithfulness to moral obligation. On the other hand, there are those who see in the cult a symbol of deep moral and spiritual values and resent any attempt to discriminate between the two. To them the ritual is the garment of religion, and the garment has some of the sacredness of religion itself. There are, of course, always those who would like to exploit the cult for their own ends. And sometimes they succeed in doing this.

Broadly speaking, the people of Israel were not inclined to make a distinction between the ceremonial law and the moral law. Law was law and came from Jehovah. The whole sacrificial system was a part of the will of God for His people, and just as much a part of it as the Ten Commandments. The priests administered the cult. The prophet administered the word of God. A man might be both a priest and a prophet, as was Ezekiel. But the two tended to drift apart. The prophet was likely to suspect and even to condemn the cult. "I hate, I despise your feasts" strikes a not uncharacteristic prophetic note. And in a sense the distinction between the ceremonial and the moral law is implicit in the tensions between priests and prophets.

The cult tended to attempt to maintain older and cruder forms of worship and more or less the thoughts which had accompanied them. To be sure, there was also a tendency to refine and to change all this. But, in a sense, a man often felt a little nearer to what he had been in dealing with a priest and a little nearer to what he ought to be in dealing with a prophet.

The sacrificial system sometimes represented a feast shared with God and sometimes a sacrifice offered to God. The sense of a constant relation to the Great Person back of the world was a profoundly important matter in the whole system. And when, as was often true, that consciousness was suffused with an apprehension of moral values, it became a very splendid and noble thing. A man with deep and sensitive ethical experience could find meanings which responded to his deepest sense of tension and struggle and forgiveness. The shedding of blood, the offering upon the altar to God, spoke very deeply to something in a man which felt that his own moral tragedy and the moral tragedy of his people must be met by something equally tragic which he confronted at the heart of his worship. The Passover had a place all its own in the religion observance of Israel; it turned men's eyes back to an ancient deliverance, but it also tended to turn them inward upon a tragic need.

If a man lived his own life upon more superficial levels, he could interpret the cult in such a way as to correspond to his own rather casual relation to the deeper struggles belonging to life and religion.

There is here also a good deal that is fluid. As is perpetually true in a religion always grasping for the deepest moral meanings and sometimes contented with something less, it was possible to give first-class loyalties to secondary distinctions and second-class loyalties to first-class distinctions. It was possible to use the cult as a method to escape confronting the character of the Moral God. It was also possible to find the Moral God in the cult.

There was a sense in which the cult could be so interpreted as to move away from those personal relations between men and God which lie at the heart of true religion. The cult could gradually become impersonal. It could even be so interpreted that it became little more than magic. And the constant slaying and burning of beasts could easily become a rather heavy vehicle of a materialism less and less conscious of spiritual values.

For all these reasons one can understand how one day, if only in the terms of the Christian religion which fulfilled and transcended the Old Testament religion, the distinction between the ceremonial and the moral law was sure to emerge. And the cult was bound to pass. But there would be no complete end of ritual. The symbol must not become the substitute for that which it symbolizes. But the symbol has a place, if only a subordinate one, for all that. And our symbols do get profoundly related with that which they symbolize. This is true of political as well as spiritual symbols. A man who throws a flag upon the ground and tramples it underfoot does something more than step upon a fabric woven by the hand of man. He insults a fabric woven by the heart of man.

The religious ritual deals with the tangible and the visible. It represents the invisible and the eternal. So at its best the law of the ritual does have its share in revealing the nature of God.

4. Natural Law

The Stoics put an emphasis on living according to nature which finally bloomed out into the whole conception of natural law. They saw in the world a co-ordinated and harmonious and orderly, indeed a determined, system of things. This was nature. The good life consisted in living according to nature. And when Stoicism entered into Roman law it carried with it the conception of law as that which expresses the orderliness of nature. This easily grew into a sense of those common features of human nature which could be united in such a fashion that from them came a sense of orderly human life. The Roman liked to believe that his law corresponded to the law of nature. There are incoherent elements in these interlacing ideas. Above all, the willing acceptance of necessity, which appears again and again in Stoic thought, when critically inspected, is seen to be self-stultifying. But the whole emphasis on an order revealed in nature and an order revealed in human nature and a human order wrought out to conform to these is of the most far-reaching significance.

When in ecclesiastical thought it is related to the conception of revelation, you will have the natural law and the revealed law. Natural law will deal with those sanctions you can reach without the special intervention of the Divine Grace. Revealed law will express that divine will which becomes articulate to us as a result of a special action of God. Ecclesiastical administration with all this at the root of it will have to do with statutes formally set forth by the church and will become canon law.

The conception of something God has written in man's experience of nature and in man's own nature which expresses a sense of order to be understood and made articulate in authentic human laws is one which possesses both dignity and truth. Speaking from the positions set forth in this book, we can see how the uniformities of nature are not impersonal realities but are the result of the volition of God and an expression of the character of God. And as man attempts to secure the same orderliness and dependability for human life by the adopting of sanctions which will promote this order, he is both imitating nature and constructing a natural law and imitating God and constructing a law whose ultimate source is in God.

The same things may be said of human nature on a higher level. When God created free persons to live together in mutual good will, He put in the very structure in their lives the requirement of truth and loyalty and honor and integrity. The free choice of goodness is man's exercise of his most distinctive power as a human being in relation to the highest of which he can think. The Stoics missed the pivotal significance of freedom in all this. They quite too casually moved from the natural order on the subhuman level, which is mechanical, to the order on the level of human nature, which expresses the loyalty of free persons. We can correct their mistake and come to have a conception of law based on human nature which is essentially sound and is the very outgrowth of the nature of personality in man, and so in a relative human way a reflection of something which is eternal in the personality of God. So human law is a summons to free men to choose to obey the behests of that good order whose quality is written in the very structure of their own nature.

It must be confessed that the Old Testament writers thought very little, if at all, of all this. But what they did think fits in with all that we have been saying about natural law. And in their moment of shrewd sagacity reflected in weary sentences in the books of Proverbs and Ecclesiastes, we have ideas which fit neatly enough into this pattern of thought. The Old Testament writers were too busy thinking of the will of God to analyze the philosophical basis of the human will or to think objectively of the order of nature. And as we can see now, they were on solid ground when they thought of God as the Author of the book of life. A personal philosophy only gives a formal pattern to their essential insights. Nevertheless the conception of natural law, if we do not forget the roots of all nature in the will of God—if we may put it so—has values all its own.

5. Law as the Correlation of Human Sanctions

The laws by which human societies are governed are of two classes. There is that large body of legal experience and practice never made secure by parliamentary enactment which is called the common law. There is that body of statutes coming directly from the enactment of a parliamentary body of some sort which, of course, bears the name statutory law. Some years ago Dean Pound of Harvard wrote a book entitled *The Spirit of the Common Law*. Agreeing with many other interpreters, Dean Pound felt and argued that the common law, which is the crystallization of actual human experience, is much nearer to the needs of the people and responds much more quickly to the elements of living situations than does the statutory law.

Revolutionary thinkers—especially those on the extreme left socially—have made much of the tendency of legislators to make statutory law an implement by which the strong maintain their hold on the weak. In other words, they have found it an instrument of exploitation. The tendency to think of property rights as more fundamental and more binding than human rights would be relevant here. Soapbox orators of a certain type have been able to wax very eloquent as they have contemplated the tragic situation when law itself becomes an implement of injustice. That this has happened historically it would be a brave man who would deny. That such tendencies are to be watched in autocracies and oligarchies is also true. But in a democracy where the people themselves make the laws it is clear that any weakness in the laws is first of all a weakness in the people themselves. That Demos can become either a beast or a tyrant or both is true enough. But it is also true that in a democracy when the people go wrong they have the cure in their own hands. They are themselves the source of power. They are themselves the source of law. Any betrayal is self-betrayal.

Dean Pound's contention as to the vitality and sound responsiveness of the common law is not, however, to be taken lightly. But here there are important explanations, if not qualifications, to be made. Experience itself may be a mere will-o'-the-wisp changing and fluctuating in the most irresponsible way. A collection of customs turned into legal sanctions which reflected merely men's successive and changing moods would not be very valuable. It might be not only ineffective but dangerous. Yet human experience may represent a commerce with sound and stable principles which express themselves in as many forms as there are people but which are themselves timeless. They are written deep in the structure of human life. And as we have said before, they are so written by God. This contact through experience with the manifold expressions as unchangeable as the essential structure of human nature represents the common law at its best. When men think of this body of principles emerging at the point of men's contact with the source of their own deepest life in the very structure of their nature and contrast it with the changeable and undependable rule of tyrants, they are likely to say that society should be ruled by laws and not by men. They do not mean by this that unconscious abstractions are more dependable than living persons. The real contrast is between the fluctuating behavior of persons without sound character, and the stable behavior of persons whose conduct is the reflection of qualities of character which have been set forth in good laws and not in passing moods which possess only the autocracy of the irresponsible.

That much human experience is reflected in the legal literature of the Old Testament no one would deny. And as we have already seen, no one who believes that God works through human experience and not apart from it will be disconcerted by that fact. But the Old Testament emphasis is clearly on what God is doing in the process and not on the process apart from the activity of God.

The study of sanctions related to that law which is deeply grounded in the nature of human beings leads on naturally to a consideration of a law applicable to all human beings, in other words, to international law. Hugo Grotius is usually considered the founder of international law, and his famous work *De jure belli ac pacis* its first classic. Significantly enough, he finds at the basis of everything else a law based on the essential qualities of man as a rational and social being. This law has a right to be applied universally. And in experience we approach it through the actual practice of the nations.

All this represents a good beginning. But it would by no means be a good conclusion. The existing practice of nations is often the existing anarchy of nations in their international relationships. There are sanctions based on man's own nature which have the right to be universally applied. But how can they be enforced? How can the recalcitrant nations which misled by the lust of selfish interest, refuse to be guided by sanctions be brought to heel? Clearly if international law is to get beyond the stage of an international debating society, there must be methods of enforcing the true international sanctions. And if experience teaches anything, it is that the nations of good will must be stronger at the point of military force than the nations of bad will if there is to be any peace founded on justice and not merely a temporary cessation of hostilities while conscienceless nations gather their resources to enslave those whose only strength is their good will. When goodness is combined with weakness, you have futility. When strength is combined with unscrupulous selfishness, you have tyranny. When good will is combined with military strength, you have a good life for the nations. And when the cluster of nations of good will is adequately strong, you have the situation necessary for the establishment of international law.

This strength in the world of fact as well as goodness in the world of conception rests on the good will of living persons, and is an attempt in some manner to realize in time what God is in eternity, namely, power and good will in equal fruition. God has written something of His own nature in the nature of man. And studying what he finds there, man conceives of a natural law whose source at last is supernatural.

6. Law as the Correlation of Divine Sanctions

The divine sanctions themselves can be gathered together into a code. This can be done on the side of the cult. It can be done on the side of prophetic insights. In the Old Testament it is the cult which really becomes a code. Indeed, it becomes a number of codes. Technical Old Testament scholarship has done much to clarify the whole subject of the cult, and its expression in legislation in various stages. The book of Ezekiel represents a very late stage in this process. Here, in a sense, the prophetic words and the priestly cult meet and cross-fertilize each other.

Of course, this had happened before. The two movements crossed and recrossed and sometimes interlaced. The Deuteronomic Code, for instance, is enriched and sometimes mastered by many a prophetic insight.

The declaration of the word did not move toward codification as did the organization of the cult. Yet the great prophetic voices do represent truths and insights which belong to a corpus of consistent thought. There is such a thing as Old Testament theology, and the men who spoke what they claimed with such authenticity to be the word of God made a great contribution to it. The essential genius of that contribution lies in the conception of God as a living person, conscious and free, whose very character is an eternal goodness. The One God is righteous. And the one righteousness has its source in the character of the living God.

7. *The Law in the Heart*

So far we have been discussing law as an objective requirement, growing out of the very structure of man's nature as God made it, and also as the expression of the direct revelation of God's will to men. There remains to be considered the important matter of man's response to this law.

That human response to the law may be cold and formal and technical and external. The law calls forth two tragedies. There is the tragedy of those who violate the law. And there is the tragedy of those who keep the letter of the law and know nothing of its spirit. This formal response to the law leads to superficiality and externality on the part of the persons who come at last to play with forms of words and to miss genuine meanings. The prophets are all the while pouring out words of indignation against those who keep the cult and forget righteousness. And there is an increasing sense as time goes by that keeping the law must come to mean entering into the very spirit of the law and abiding by it.

The *locus classicus* in respect of this matter is, of course, the great passage in Jeremiah:

Behold, the days come, saith Jehovah, that I will make a new covenant with the house of Israel, and with the house of Judah: not according to the covenant that I made with their fathers in the day that I took them by the hand to bring them out of the land of Egypt; which my covenant they brake, although I was a husband unto them, saith Jehovah. But this is the covenant that I will make with the house of Israel after those days, saith Jehovah: I will put my law in their inward parts, and in their heart will I write it; and I will be their God, and they shall be my people.

Here the law ceases to be an external demand and becomes an inner compulsion. And here we have one of the profoundest passages in the Old Testament anticipating some of the deepest sayings of the New.

There is a sense, of course, in which we have left the realm of jurisprudence and the public practice of the law and have come to a new aspect of the law, namely, its relation to what we may call the psychology of a person and of a people. We cannot bring a man into court for his motives. Yet it is the motives which really count first, last, and all the time. And there is a truth about the whole matter which may be expressed by saying that the public practice of jurisprudence becomes dry and hard and ineffective unless the law written in the heart lies behind it. But this law written in the heart is itself the product of a deep and constant experience with a personal God who is righteousness alive. Everything we have said about the Great Person and His creative and sustaining relation to other persons fits in with this consummation of the law in a deep personal experience of devotion, not only to its specific sanctions, but to the very character and quality of that Divine Person from whom they spring. So devotion to the law becomes devotion to God, and devotion to God expresses itself in loyalty to the law.

Other profound and disturbing matters lie just beyond the area of the things we have been discussing. Does the law itself raise almost as many problems as it solves? Is the law a halfway house to something beyond itself? Is a very sincere man, trying with all his might to keep the law, entering upon a path full of strange experiences of curious complexity? Does the perfect law require more than any man can give in return?

The very conception of the law written in the heart is a part of a movement where loyalty is transcended by a devotion which, to be sure, includes the loyalty but moves far beyond it.

Is there something profoundly dangerous about the very attempt to keep the law so that at the end of the day you can look back with profound satisfaction on your achievement? Is there a moral process of obedience to law which leads to the depths of despair on the way to a great emancipation?

All these matters come to focus in great and classical writings in the New Testament, and in later chapters we shall be dealing with them. In the meantime we call attention to the fact that the personal interpretation of experience, for which this book contends, gives us all sorts of clues to the fashion in which law becomes a problem in a world of persons. That for which the law stands is a perennial part of life and must be retained at whatever cost. But the very ends supported by mighty legal sanctions can never be brought to full achievement until the battle for perfection leads on from a great struggle to a great trust.

It would be a mistake to suppose that these deeper aspects of experience were foreign to the religious life reflected in the Old Testament.

We shall soon be seeing how great problems come to solution and human experience comes to possess a quality of creative joy as the adventure with goodness comes to be a fellowship with a Perfectly Good Person. But all the subtle relationships of these experiences were worked out when the New Testament doctrine of the divine grace was enunciated. Life always moves out beyond the intellectual forms we have found for the expression of its meanings. And so the Old Testament saint was sometimes nearer to the Apostle Paul than has always been realized.

In the meantime the tragedies of the law, as well as the glories of the law, were being worked out to complete expression. The man of the cult had his battles with the prophet, and yet he was in spite of himself profoundly influenced by the prophetic insights. The great sanctions of the good life were seen in clearer and clearer perspective. And—this was the glory of Israel—they were always seen as the expression of the divine will and, even deeper than that, as the expression of the divine character. The Great, Perfectly Good Person was becoming more real to the men of Israel all the time.

It was, of course, a checkered story. There was apostasy dark and evil. There was the heresy which sees a part of the truth but so misses other truth that it betrays even the part which is held. There were all the curious human ways of going forward and going back—all the things which broke the hearts of the prophets and brought shame to the good men who expressed their devotion in the forms of the cult. But there was advance. There was a sharpened clarity of understanding. God was revealing Himself through all this experience. God Himself was the Great Lawgiver.

CHAPTER IX

The Battle with Doubt and the Lyrical Voices

M ATTHEW ARNOLD wistfully remembered the days of a faith which, it seemed to him, was fading from the consciousness of men:

> The sea of faith
> Was once, too, at the full, and round earth's shore
> Lay like the folds of a bright girdle furled.
> But now I only hear
> Its melancholy, long, withdrawing roar,
> Retreating, to the breath
> Of the night-wind, down the vast edges drear
> And naked shingles of the world.[1]

Sometimes, in a deeper mood of dejection, Arnold sees a leader of men:

> Still bent to make some port, he knows not where,
> Still standing for some false, impossible shore.[2]

Then, in full surrender to his thought of gloom, he writes:

> . . . amongst us one,
> Who most has suffered, takes dejectedly
> His seat upon the intellectual throne.[3]

Here you have the pessimism of the Victorian doubt expressed with complete intellectual distinction and a grace of form which in a way accentuates the despair within.

No doubt the documents of the Old Testament and the New present a great contrast to all this. They grow out of indubitable faith. They abound in stout affirmatives. They have the assurance of a great faith. But those records of living experience which we find in the Old Testament also tell the story of the struggle with doubt. And sometimes it becomes a very grim and desperate struggle.

1. Habakkuk

Principal Sir George Adam Smith described Habakkuk as *The Prophet as Sceptic.* In the little book which bears this prophet's name

[1] From "Dover Beach."
[2] From "A Summer Night."
[3] From "The Scholar-Gipsy."

the ways of God are a baffling problem. The word "why" is flung out with an almost heartbroken passion. There is black, bitter evil among his people. The very sight of it fills the prophet with a kind of impotent moral fury. What will God do about it? The reply comes swiftly: God will do something final and conclusive about it. He will send the Chaldeans to overcome the wicked people. But to the prophet the solution is in its way as tragic as the problem it solves. These mighty people who are to overcome his own evil people are themselves desperately wicked. So again the voice of the skeptic in the heart of the prophet cries out. He will take his stand upon his watchtower and see, if he can, what God is doing in the world. Again the answer comes with a certain moral decisiveness. These wicked peoples whom God uses to overthrow other wicked peoples have the seed of death in them. They are already condemned to death. And as the seed of death is in them, so the seed of life is in the righteous. A good man must learn to have faith in the integrity of his own soul. The righteous shall live by his faithfulness, if he is brave enough to have faith in it. To believe that evil has the seed of destruction in it is the negative part of the faith Habakkuk reaches through great struggle. To believe that goodness has the seed of life in it: that is the positive part of his victory over doubt and skepticism.

And at last right royally is this faith expressed:

> For though the fig-tree shall not flourish,
> Neither shall fruit be in the vines;
> The labor of the olive shall fail,
> And the fields shall yield no food;
> The flock shall be cut off from the fold,
> And there shall be no herd in the stalls:
> Yet I will rejoice in Jehovah,
> I will joy in the God of my salvation.
> Jehovah, the Lord, is my strength;
> And he maketh my feet like hinds' feet,
> And will make me to walk upon my high places.

It is a rather profoundly refreshing experience to read these glowing words of living faith after reading the phrases of distinguished pessimism written by Matthew Arnold. The great prophet knew the suffusing bewilderment of the fog. But he fought his way through the fog until the clear light came.

The Old Testament is a very cosmopolitan collection of literature, however. And there is a pessimistic doubt which at times descends to sheer cynicism to be found in the book of Ecclesiastes. The writing reports itself as the meditations of a great and wealthy king familiar to Israel. And often it reads like the philosophic musings of one who had been suffocated by magnificence. The poor who look with longing at the good things of this world are likely to overestimate the power to satisfy of that which they have never possessed. The irresponsible rich who have possessed everything are likely in their hours of disillusionment to underestimate the value of that which they have never rightly used. The cynical author of Ecclesiastes finds "vanity and a striving after wind" and "no profit under the sun." "And how doth the wise man die even as the fool! So I hated life." There are flashes of other moods: "He hath made everything beautiful in its time: also he hath set eternity in their heart." Sometimes there is a bit of shrewd sagacity: "Better is a poor and wise youth than an old and foolish king." Often there is a sentence which is the fruit of a bitter disillusionment: "The heart of fools is in the house of mirth." Sometimes wisdom is praised: "A man's wisdom maketh his face to shine." Then there is a bitter word of utter pessimism: "There is one event to the righteous and to the wicked." Always there is the theme song: Vanity! Vanity! There is a moment in the central Old Testament tradition: "Fear God, and keep his commandments." A strange book it is, without which the Old Testament would be incomplete. To read Ecclesiastes and the last chapter of Habakkuk together is itself a memorable experience.

2. Job

The magnificent book of Job is, of course, the great writing in the Old Testament about a man's struggle for faith as whole armies of doubt hurl themselves against the fortress of his soul.

Slowly and with difficulty the Old Testament people had reached the conviction that life has moral meaning. A mind which represents an eternal conscience presides over events. Goodness makes for happiness and prosperity. Evil makes for destruction and defeat and tragedy. All this because a Moral God is on the throne and rules the lives of men.

But once and again experience seems to contradict this bright and happy faith. The evil often come to great prosperity which sometimes they enjoy through many years. The good often suffer terrible adversity. How do you reconcile this with the moral view of history?

It is not enough to say—what is clearly true—that in a large way the principles do hold. Viewed over a large enough field, goodness does make for success and fullness of life. Viewed over a large enough field, evil does make for destruction and disintegration. But here are the exceptions vivid and dramatic and insistent. What can one say of them?

These questions are put with something like dramatic finality in the tale of a great sheik of the desert—we are not even sure that he was a man of Israel. He was good and he was godly. He was the best of men and he suffered the worst of fates. He loses his wealth. His flocks and herds are destroyed. His children are slain. And the desolate man is attacked by that dreadful disease leprosy. Even his wife in bitterness advises him to renounce God and die. His reply, sitting among the ashes, is memorable: "Shall we receive good at the hand of God, and shall we not receive evil?"

But though Job does not curse God, he does curse the day when he was born. His three friends Eliphaz, Bildad, and Zophar have heard of his calamity and have come to bemoan him and to comfort him. The best thing about their visit is that for seven days and seven nights they sit in friendly silence. Then Job in Oriental language curses the day of his birth with magnificent invective:

> Let the day perish wherein I was born,
> . . . .
> Let that day be darkness;
> Let not God from above seek for it,
> Neither let the light shine upon it.
> Let darkness and the shadow of death claim it for their own;
> . . . .
> Why died I not from the womb?
> Why did I not give up the ghost when my mother bare me?
> . . . .
> For now should I have lain down and been quiet;
> I should have slept; then had I been at rest,
> With kings and counsellors of the earth,
> . . . .
> There the wicked cease from troubling;
> And there the weary are at rest.

Eliphaz the Temanite is the first of the friends to speak. He wants to be friendly. But he is sure that Job must see that somehow God's justice has brought all these calamities upon him. Job must not try to judge God:

> Shall mortal man be more just than God?
> . . . .
> He taketh the wise in their own craftiness.

If Job will accept God's punishment, all will be well:

> Thou shalt be hid from the scourge of the tongue;
> Neither shalt thou be afraid of destruction when it cometh.

Job has all the sharp awareness of a great agony. He sees the subtle implication of his friend's words, and he cannot accept their implicit indictment. With a sad bitterness he declares: "To him that is ready to faint kindness should be showed from his friend." He is not afraid to come to the heart of the matter:

> Teach me, and I will hold my peace;
> And cause me to understand wherein I have erred.

And with a sincerity which is unmistakable he declares: "My cause is righteous." But it is not to men but to God that his real appeal is made:

> If I have sinned, what do I unto thee, O thou watcher of men?
> . . . .
> And why dost thou not pardon my transgression, and take away
> mine iniquity?

Bildad the Shuhite, the second of Job's friends, speaks. He is angered by Job's words. "Words . . . like a mighty wind," he calls them. Do they not reflect on God?

> Doth God pervert justice?
> Or doth the Almighty pervert righteousness?

"God will not cast away a perfect man," he declares.

Job does not contradict Bildad. Still the terrible problem remains:

> He will not suffer me to take my breath,
> But filleth me with bitterness.
> . . . .
> He is not a man, as I am, that I should answer him.

And with amazing daring he says: "There is no umpire betwixt us." Then he cries out in utter and tragic longing to God:

> Thy hands have framed me and fashioned me,
> . . . yet thou dost destroy me.
> Remember, I beseech thee, that thou hast fashioned me as clay;
> And wilt thou bring me into dust again?

Now Zophar the Naamathite speaks. By this time Job is an intellectual antagonist to be answered, not a friend to be comforted. "Should thy boastings make men hold their peace?" he asks. Like the other friends, he says—sometimes nobly—things which have their own truth but are not applicable to the present situation. "Canst thou by searching find out God?" he asks. "Vain man," he says, "is void of understanding, yea, man is born as a wild ass's colt." And he is looking at Job as he says:

> The eyes of the wicked shall fail,
> And they shall have no way to flee;
> And their hope shall be the giving up of the ghost.

Now it is Job's turn to be angry: "No doubt but ye are the people, and wisdom shall die with you," he hurls back.

But his argument is not with men whose "memorable sayings are proverbs of ashes."

> Surely I would speak to the Almighty,
> And I desire to reason with God.

He understands the tragedy of life:

> Man, that is born of a woman,
> Is of few days, and full of trouble.

A tree, when it falls, will sprout again—dare Job follow this analogy in a monologue really addressed to Someone who may be listening?

> Oh . . .
> That thou wouldest appoint me a set time, and remember me!

Suppose all does go wrong in this world. "If a man die, shall he live again?"—But the thought seems too daring.

> My transgression is sealed up in a bag,
> And thou fastenest up mine iniquity.

The friends, completely misunderstanding Job, are now on his trail, hot like hounds. Eliphaz speaks again with rebuke:

> Why doth thy heart carry thee away?
> And why do thine eyes flash?

Those burning eyes seem to him an attack on God. Wearily Job turns again upon his "miserable comforters." But his agony is too deep for controversy. "My days are past, my purposes are broken off." Bildad returns to the attack. "How long will ye hunt for words?" He pictures the evil man (all this for Job's good):

> And he shall have no name in the street.
> He shall be driven from light into darkness,
> And chased out of the world.

Job finds his brethren far from him and his acquaintances wholly estranged from him. Oh, that he could be sure God would hear!

> Oh that my words were now written!
> Oh that they were inscribed in a book!

Then there is a sudden deep act of faith. "As for me I know that my Redeemer liveth." After death, if not before, his great conversation with God will come to fruition.

Zophar speaks again—sure of the wickedness of Job. And Job confesses that he sees only falsehood in the words of his friends. They are not easily discouraged. Eliphaz speaks again—still missing the whole point of Job's need. A great moment of faith comes to the suffering man:

> But he knoweth the way that I take;
> When he hath tried me, I shall come forth as gold.

But baffling questions emerge. Bildad thinks he scents an advantage. "How then can man be just with God?" he asks.

> And the stars are not pure in his sight:
> How much less man, that is a worm!

Still Job goes on with his lonely quest:

> Where shall wisdom be found?
> And where is the place of understanding?

There is a sad, brilliant speech—it is no less—in which Job describes his old days of dignity and prosperity and power:

> I was eyes to the blind.
> . . . .
> I was a father to the needy.
> . . . .
> I smiled on them, when they had no confidence.

This was the day when

> The young men saw me and hid themselves,
> And the aged rose up and stood.

Then he was a great man.

> But now they that are younger
> than I have me in derision.
> . . . .
> Therefore is my harp turned to mourning,
> And my pipe into the voice of them that weep.
> . . . .
> Calamity from God is a terror to me.
> . . . .
> Oh that I had one to hear me!

At last the three friends are silent. In a strange fashion Job has now at least this victory. Stung by their silence, the young Elihu, son of Barachel, comes up. "I am full of words." Full of words he is, but not to much purpose. He answers when Job has not spoken. Following his own words, he "proceeds and says."

When he finishes, Job says not a word. Not with such a one is the great argument to be conducted.

Then God speaks. And Job, with strange, humble happiness welcoming the mighty voice, gladly lays his hand upon his own mouth to speak no more. God does not argue. In magnificent words the divine power is expressed. But as Job well understands, the point of the matter is that God is present and talking with him—sharing His glory with this loyal son.

Suddenly Job knows that this and this alone is what he needs. Not a discussion of suffering. Not a process of reasoning. But the presence of the friendly God. "I had heard of thee by the hearing of the ear," he cries; "but now mine eye seeth thee."

Now at last he can be satisfied, and in the glory of that friendly perfection he can repent "in dust and ashes." And in that very hour he realizes the satisfaction of knowing that he is indeed the friend of God. There is more to the book. But this is the heart of it. When life strikes us down, what we need is not a human argument but the vision of the living, friendly God and the sound of His voice speaking to us. No problem is solved on an impersonal level. Every problem is solved at the point of a personal meeting of man and God.

3. The Hero of the Book of Psalms

The collection of poems in the Hebrew book of Psalms is unique in the literature of the world. The singing gladness of it brings ancient joy to life in the modern world. The passionate pain of it makes the soreness of ancient wounds contemporary. The intimacy of it gives one the feeling of entering a room next to one's own and of touching a familiar hand. It sets the Old Testament law to music. It sets the Hebrew prophets to music. The practitioners of the cult and the servants of the moral voice meet in a great chorus of song. It is amazingly personal. People in general cannot feel. Abstract principles have no heartbeats. Everything must come to life in individual consciousness before it can burst into song. Thus the contention of this book that all experience is essentially individual comes to striking confirmation as we study the psalms. Even the Songs of the Pilgrimage are songs which individuals sing together as they journey to Jerusalem for the festal celebration.

The lyrics in this great collection come from many people and from various centuries. And these poems vibrating with keen emotion have a hero. That hero is not David, the messianic King. That hero is not Israel idealized as if the whole nation had become a person. That hero is Almighty God. Jehovah is the one tremendous Person of whom these lyrics sing. "They looked unto him, and were radiant." "In the name of our God we will set up our banners." "I love thee, O Jehovah, my strength."

This one golden thread binds all the psalms together. They never tire of the rapturous singing of the glory of the Divine Hero and

Friend, Lord and Master, King and God. The note of spiritual devotion has never been sounded more majestically, more gloriously, more sincerely than in these great poems torn from the hearts of men.

> Jehovah liveth; and blessed be my rock;
> And exalted be the God of my salvation.

Nature never speaks of itself. It speaks of God.

> The heavens declare the glory of God;
> And the firmament showeth his handiwork.

There is no antinomy between God and the world which He has made. "The earth is Jehovah's." Jerusalem is significant not for itself but because it is "the city of our God." Beautiful for elevation, its ultimate beauty is found in the fact that it is "the city of the great King." The man is a fool who has no God to sing about, and only a fool of fools can say in his heart, "There is no God." All the world is called upon to make one great and mighty sound of praise to God.

> Sing forth the glory of his name:
> Make his praise glorious.

The past has its true significance because God has been in it.

> Lord, thou hast been our dwelling-place
> In all generations.

The present has its significance because God works in it.

> Let the favor of the Lord our God be upon us.

The future has its significance in the fact that God will master it.

> He will judge the world with righteousness,
> And the peoples with his truth.

God is in the midst of life as a terror to evildoers.

> But the wicked and him that loveth violence his soul hateth.
> Upon the wicked he will rain snares;
> Fire and brimstone and burning wind shall be the portion
>   of their cup.

> Thou hast smitten all mine enemies upon the cheek bone;
> Thou hast broken the teeth of the wicked.

> Thou wilt destroy them that speak lies:
> Jehovah abhorreth the bloodthirsty and deceitful man.

He is the great God of all the battles for goodness.

God is gone up with a shout,
Jehovah with the sound of a trumpet.

For virile people alive in a tragic world he is the Divine Hero.

4. *The Individual Experiences of the Book of Psalms*

One late evening some years ago I was riding back from Jericho to Jerusalem in an automobile. Around one of the turns in the twisting road a little hill seemed to lean against the sky. And standing there silhouetted against the waning light stood a solitary shepherd surrounded by a small flock of sheep. There in the lonely strangeness of the falling night were the sheep. There with his staff in his hand stood the shepherd. It was an intimate little picture one could not well forget. And one could clearly understand how very long ago, on some such night, seeing some such scene, a lonely man with a sudden sense of the near and protecting presence of God broke into a night song:

Jehovah is my shepherd; I shall not want.
He maketh me to lie down in green pastures.

Again and again there is this most intimate and individual sense of God in the songs of the psalter.

For thou wilt light my lamp:
Jehovah my God will lighten my darkness.

Sometimes it is a cry for guidance.

Teach me thy way, O Jehovah;
And lead me in a plain path.

Bow down thine ear, O Jehovah, and answer me;
For I am poor and needy.

Sometimes there is the bright cry of deliverance from some ugly clutch of circumstance.

I waited patiently for Jehovah;
And he inclined unto me, and heard my cry.
He brought me up also out of a horrible pit, out
of the miry clay;
And he set my feet upon a rock.

In the seventy-third psalm we come upon a fascinating bit of autobiography telling the story of a man's battle with doubt. His feet were almost gone. His steps had well-nigh slipped. He looked at wicked men he knew, so arrogant and so prosperous. Their very eyes stood out with fatness. They were always at ease. They increased in riches. And they were evil within and without. It seemed as if the good man who contemplated all this had cleansed his heart in vain and washed his hands in innocency to no purpose. Then in God's sanctuary he considered the whole matter quietly. He saw the destruction of the wicked. He saw them utterly consumed with terrors. Then he was ashamed of his doubt, and he derided his fears. As long as he was sure of the friendship of God, what else mattered?

> I am continually with thee:
> Thou hast holden my right hand.
> Thou wilt guide me with thy counsel.

After all, he desired only God. His flesh and heart failed. "But God is the strength of my heart and my portion for ever." He is at last secure in God.

> It is good for me to draw near unto God:
> I have made the Lord Jehovah my refuge.

5. The Humanism of the Psalms

The book of Psalms is saturated with a sense of what we now call human values. The experiences it narrates are human experiences. When a writer of one of the psalms fails in insight, he calls himself a beast:

> So brutish was I, and ignorant;
> I was as a beast before thee.

> I am a worm, and no man.

> Be ye not as the horse, or as the mule, which
>   have no understanding.

He has sunk below the human and has only such thoughts of God as a beast might have.

The classical expression of the humanism implicit in all the psalms is found in the eighth of these great lyrics. After contemplating the greatness and mystery of the heavens, the poet suddenly senses the greatness of man:

> Thou hast made him but little lower than God,
> And crownest him with glory and honor.
> Thou makest him to have dominion over the works
>   of thy hands;
> Thou hast put all things under his feet:
> All sheep and oxen,
> Yea, and the beasts of the field,
> The birds of the heavens, and the fish of the sea,
> Whatsoever passeth through the paths of the seas.

Here is man master of nature, lord of a world which is below him, created by God to be a prince controlling the world of things and the world of beasts.

But this kingly man is created by God and sustained by God, and he is under the authority of the God who made him. The whole position becomes crystal clear as we see man over nature and under God. This is the true humanism gloriously free from the tendency to sink into the life of the beast which is below man or to try to be the God who is above him. Nowhere in the Old Testament is man's true position more clearly and definitively expressed.

But it is very important to see that this position so clearly set forth in the eighth psalm is assumed through the poems of the great collection, and, indeed, throughout the whole Old Testament. Man is not to sink into the world of things or beasts. He is to control them. Man is not to try to be God. He is to worship and obey Him. This is the view of man from which the Old Testament writings never deviate.

6. The Evangelical Note in the Psalms

Man cannot get along without God. It is God who reveals to him the true meaning and the true glory of life. It is in fellowship with God that he finds his chief joy. And when he plunges his life into treachery and evil and sensuality, it is God who is his mighty judge and yet also his mighty savior.

He begins the day with God.

> In the morning will I order my prayer unto thee,
>   and will keep watch.

He can sleep at night because he trusts in God.

> In peace will I both lay me down and sleep;
> For thou, Jehovah, alone makest me dwell in safety.

But this God with whom he has to do is a moral God. This is so constantly in the thought of all the writers of the psalms that we can go from one to another in dealing with the moral problem and the divine solution without doing injustice to any of them. They all think of God as full of wrath in the presence of unrighteousness. They all think of God as full of the grace of mercy for those who repent of their evil ways. Again and again the desperate sense of the tragedy of sin emerges:

> O Jehovah, rebuke me not in thine anger,
> Neither chasten me in thy hot displeasure.
> Have mercy upon me, O Jehovah.

> I will declare mine iniquity;
> I will be sorry for my sin.

> We have sinned with our fathers,
> We have committed iniquity, we have
>   done wickedly.
>
> . . . .
>
> They sang his praise.
> They soon forgat his works.
>
> My God, my God, why hast thou forsaken me?
>
> . . . .
>
> Thou art holy.
>
> Consider mine affliction and my travail;
> And forgive all my sins.

Then comes the cry of deliverance:

> Jehovah is my light and my salvation.
>
> Bless Jehovah, O my soul,
>
> . . . .
>
> Who forgiveth all thine iniquities.
>
> I will take the cup of salvation,
> And call upon the name of Jehovah.

In the psalms, then, God is seen most clearly as Judge and as Savior. Quite clearly He does not save men *in* their evil ways. He saves them as they turn from their evil ways. The joy of the man who in spite of his unworthiness—in fact, just because he feels his unworthiness and wants to be made worthy—has been allowed to become a friend of God, is one of the most characteristic things to be found in these poems of singing gladness. Here already we sense from before the day of the full evangel the joy of the forgiven.

7. *The Law Is Taught to Sing*

The songs of the law are among the most characteristic poems to be found in the whole collection. At the very beginning the "blessed man" is described as one whose "delight is in the law of Jehovah." And this note of gladness in God's law is recurrent. Law itself becomes lyrical in the psalter. The most conspicuous example of this is the series of alphabetical psalms, all put together as the 119th psalm. The series opens with praise of those who "walk in the law of Jehovah." A young man is to cleanse his way by taking heed to that word which gathers together the divine precepts. A man gladly claims: "I have kept thy testimonies." He has not taken the divine law lightly. "Teach me thy statutes" is the very cry of the poet's soul. He wants to go in the path of the divine commandments, "for therein do I delight." He hopes in the divine ordinances. He meditates on the divine statutes. God's statutes have been turned to music in the house of his pilgrimage. At midnight he will remember God's laws. He longs for the sort of God the very appropriation of the meaning of the divine statutes will give him. He wants really to understand God's laws. His delight in God's law has kept him steady in dark days. "Oh how love I thy law!" God's word is like a lamp in its immediate illumination. He is afraid of God's judgments; yet he loves his testimonies. When he feels small and despised, he knows that he has a certain dignity because he does not forget the divine precepts. He meets God in God's law. He finds God's tender mercies, even as he turns with loyalty to God's law. Great peace comes to those who love God's law. In God's law the poet finds his delight.

Such a sheer outburst of joy in the divine sanctions it can safely be said is unique in all literature. These poets have found something greater than themselves. They have found something mightier than themselves. They escape from their own littleness. They escape from their own smallness in the very glory of the law of God.

One needs only to call attention to how far all this is removed from that dislike of looking up which is characteristic of so many modern men. The man whose cosmos is all ego can never find such delight in a law which comes from Someone above himself. These men are gloriously emancipated from the obsession of self. They gladly look up. They rejoice, as Emerson might have put it, in "the manners of the sky."

All of this is because the law comes to them bright with the shining of the face of God, beautiful with the gleam of the eyes of God, splendid with the finality of the words of God. The law is not an abstract, impersonal thing. It glows with the quality of the Great Person from whom it comes. It is always a part of the adventure of living experience. It is full of the sense of the splendor of the divine grace.

It may be said, in the terms of a deeper evangelicalism, that these men sang of the glory of the God of the moral law without realizing the cost of fellowship with the God who is righteousness alive. They accepted the fact of grace without apprehending the cost of grace. This is indeed true. And surely it was necessary for it to be so. The long path of evangelical sorrow could be walked by men only when some of them had already by faith stood on the Delectable Mountains.

At all events here is a glorious phenomenon. In a world where so many men have hated discipline, these men loved discipline. They turned the divine sanctions into lyric poetry.

8. Social Insights of the Psalms

The writers of these lyrics are not without consciousness of what we would now call social problems.

> Deliver my soul from the wicked by thy sword;
>
> . . . .
>
> From men of the world, whose portion is in this life.

God is called upon to judge the poor and the fatherless to do justice to the afflicted and destitute, to rescue the poor and needy. There is far-reaching significance in the dramatic question:

> Shall the throne of wickedness have fellowship with thee,
> Which frameth mischief by statute?

There are real and downright curses in the 109th psalm. They are against the man who

> . . . remembered not to show kindness,
> But persecuted the poor and needy man.

The psalms are simply full of the stories of an inner devotion, but it would be far from true to suggest that they forget outer responsibility. Justice and good will and kindness to those whose life is difficult are part of the very character of that man whom the psalmists see becoming the friend of God. This awareness of the needs of others, this sense of responsibility for the poor and those for whom life is a difficult way, has the very genius of social passion. Something that comes to expression in the vision of Piers, the Plowman, something that speaks in the vigorous democracy of Hugh Latimer, something that calls from afar to Charles Kingsley and John Fredrick Denison Maurice, is speaking here.

9. The Tragedies of the Book of Psalms

As one goes over these many songs, one cannot avoid the sense that life is a tragic thing. There are breath-taking agonies, there are lonely bitternesses, there is national calamity, and there is individual sorrow. Sometimes we have to go through clouds and darkness to find God. But find Him we can. The tragedy is never meaningless tragedy. The woe is never pain without moral and spiritual meaning. Even in the valley of the shadow of death there is a Great Presence.

There is great comfort in all this. For the peace which comes from ignoring the pain grows very bitter at last. And the peace wrought out by the mastery of pain is a very glorious and beautiful thing. So somehow the God we meet in the valley of tragedy is more glorious than the God we meet on the tablelands of the untried.

10. The Triumphant Joy of the Psalms

You can always measure an age by its capacity to sing. You can always measure a nation by its capacity to sing. You can always find the secret meaning of a man's life if you ask whether sometimes he is so full of joy that he must burst into song. People write prose because they choose to do it. People write poetry because they must. And the greatest poetry is always personal. It does not falter into the grayness of dim abstraction; it glows with the sharp clarity of personal experience. You can only-pretend to love a thing by ascribing personal qualities to it. You can only really love a person. And you can only fully love the Perfect Person. He is all you would like to be. He is all you hope to be. He is the fulfillment of your rarest dreams.

All this comes to full expression in the book of Psalms. They are really songs of love to the Perfect Person. And in the light of that rare devotion the good men of that ancient day look like the Perfect One they so deeply love. Because they have loved the loving-kindness of God, their own lives are changed. They called. They know that God answered. So even when they go forth weeping, they come again with joy. Jehovah keeps their city. Their heart is fixed on God. So they must sing. They cannot sing enough. They sing at night. They sing in the morning. They are always singing. And their songs are full of ineffable joy.

11. The Hallelujah Chorus

The 146th psalm begins in Hebrew with the word "Hallelujah." It ends with the same word. So does the 147th. So does the 148th. So does the 149th. The last of the psalms begins and ends with Hallelujah, and it is one succession of calls for the praising of God. The psalter ends with the first Hallelujah Chorus.

We began this chapter with a wailing poet who saw the man who had suffered most, taking his seat dejectedly upon the intellectual throne. There may be a certain grim intellectual distinction, a certain dark sophisticated urbanity about such a position. But there is decadence and death in the pot.

Not here, O One nobler than Apollo, are haunts meet for Thee. There are sources of gladness and joy and creative energy and, mark it well, of truth untouched by distinguished pessimism. And the Hebrew psalter possesses all these sources of life and joy. It possesses these sources because to the writers of these sparkling, glowing, sunlit poems life is one long adventure with the living God. So the collection ends in a burst of choral song.

But the song it sets going in receptive hearts is more wonderful than the songs it records in an ancient script. As long as men have joy like this, they will not let this ancient music die. They will call it forth to express their own gladness, and they will write other music to tell the same great tale of joy. There is a straight line of continuity from the Hebrew psalter to the Hallelujah Chorus in Handel's *Messiah*.

The audience stands and listens as, wave upon wave, the choral melody pours forth. Tragedy is overcome. Death has become irrelevant. Life is eternally triumphant. God is on the throne. And living men have fellowship with the living God.

Then there comes the Great Amen. And then there is silence. And some men and women go back to dull and meaningless or evil living as if they had never heard. But it need not be so. The Hallelujah Chorus and the ancient gladness which anticipated its joy so long ago will survive when disillusionment and cynicism and treachery have said their last word and have fallen upon death.

CHAPTER X

Sermons on History

ARNOLD J. TOYNBEE'S monumental *A Study of History* is an attempt at historical synthesis on the widest possible scale. Six of the nine volumes have already been published, and the reading of these volumes is one of those stimulating experiences which come to a man not too often in a lifetime. There are questions which on a proper occasion we would raise about Dr. Toynbee's own work. Just now, however, we want to call attention to some of his observations in the introduction to the first volume which are relevant to our present purpose. He speaks of the "tendency for the potter to become the slave of his clay" [1] as an evident aberration. And he asks with almost stinging insight: "Why should we suppose that the scientific method of thought—a method which has been devised for thinking about Inanimate Nature—should be applicable to historical thought, which is a study of living creatures and indeed of human beings?" [2] All the meticulous implementing of technical scholarship is, of course, of immense importance in dealing with facts.

It is indeed possible so to write of human beings that they cease to be human and that the history ceases to be human history. But an impersonal fact has to be brought within personal experience before it has genuine significance for history. The historical writings of the Old Testament do not represent an attempt to understand the personal by translating it into impersonal terms. Indeed, the whole process is selective. It is carried on by men who have convictions about God and His ways with human beings and His ways with Israel. The chapters are really sermons on history chosen to tell a tale full of moral and spiritual meaning. That tale happens to be one of the defining and revealing stories in the higher life of man. What does not fit into it is ignored. What fits is emphasized. By this method you really get at the heart of the whole matter, and you do not reduce the whole story to mechanical dullness. You come to the discussion with a truth which gives you discrimination. It is rather a contrast to the type of writing which comes to every human experience with an untruth which so interprets it that it ceases to be human. And in this case it is the divinity which secures and maintains the humanity. We are not planning to make any complete inspection of the historical writings of the Old

[1] New York: Oxford University Press, 1934-39, I, 7.
[2] *Ibid.*

Testament. We do want to inspect some of the sermonic treatment of historical material in certain Old Testament books which gets at the very heart of the moral and spiritual meaning of history.

1. Samuel

The story of Samuel plunges you into an ancient Oriental type of life with a clear-eyed honesty in the recording of conditions which gives you that sense, so characteristic of the Old Testament narratives, that nothing unlovely is hidden. You enter a polygamous household where one wife has children and the other has none. The husband loves the childless wife, and the mother of his children taunts her cruelly. So there is tension and unhappiness enough. And at the place of worship in Shiloh, Hannah pours out her bitterness in prayer to Jehovah. Her prayer is answered, and erelong she brings her young son Samuel to be given to God as His servant at Shiloh. This place of worship was under the administration of the priest Eli, an old man pious but incapable of restraining his sons, who made the very ritual of worship serve their hot and lawless vices. Here the young Samuel served Jehovah and was trained by Eli. His clear eyes saw all the evil about him, but some grace of restraint kept him from personal contamination. And so the voice of God came to him with doom for Eli and his house. The tale is told with strangely gripping drama, and the picture of the child first hearing the voice of God and thinking he heard the voice of Eli has become one of the imperishable spiritual memories of the race. Eli received the bitter word with sad resignation. Time passed by. Samuel grew and God was with him.

At length a struggle with the Philistines came on. The people of Israel were defeated, the ark of the covenant of Jehovah was carried off, and the wicked sons of Eli were slain. The old man Eli, anxious for the ark which had been taken into battle, sat, earth upon his head and clothing rent, waiting for tidings of the fight. He listened with torn heart to the tale of the death of his sons, but when he heard that the ark of God was taken, the weary old man fell over and broke his neck. Samuel came to his golden hour, and, now for years an honest and de-voted judge, presided over the affairs of Israel. Continually you have living men under a living leader, receiving the judgment which they believe expresses the will of Jehovah. They are rude, vigorous people, and they need the strong hand of a strong man representing a God of moral strength. This they have in Samuel. You follow the very processes of the moral growth of a people. There is a fascinating folk tale of the ark which brought calamity to the worshipers of Dagon who had captured it, and of its return to its own land. You feel very near to a primitive people and their ways of life and worship. But you sense all the while the deeper and deeper moral meanings which are moving through their life. Samuel masters the Philistines and secures respite for his people. But most of all he makes them aware of the commands of God as they relate themselves to the everyday problems of the people.

For long years Samuel had a great and clean record: "Here I am: witness against me before Jehovah, and before his anointed: whose ox have I taken? or whose ass have I taken? or whom have I defrauded? whom have I oppressed? or of whose hand have I taken a ransom to blind mine eyes therewith? and I will restore it you. And they said, Thou hast not defrauded us, nor oppressed us, neither hast thou taken aught of any man's hand."

But Samuel's sons, like the sons of Eli, failed to follow their father. They "turned aside after lucre, and took bribes, and perverted justice."

2. Saul

The loose, more or less theocratic form of life for Israel was bound to come to an end. When the idea of a king was suggested to Samuel, he did not hide his distaste. And he believed that he was expressing the distaste of Jehovah, too. But the people got their king. And that king was Saul. God gave them the king with warning. But the people found that more closely knit life for which they were eager. They also found no end of the evil things associated with Oriental monarchy.

The story of the lad who went to find his father's asses and found a kingdom instead, of his tall and splendid figure, of his heroic quality, of his refusal to have revenge on those who had scorned him, when the day of victory came, of his military prowess and success, of his strange melancholy and of the shepherd lad who brought the good world back to him by his music, of this same lad who killed a giant with a little stone from his sling, of Saul's terrible jealousy, of his alienation from Samuel and his sense of being rejected by God, of his death with his son Jonathan in a great fight—all of this has the same tang and vigor as the tales of border warfare in Scotland. It is all refreshingly human. The God who is working in history deals with proud, sullen, easily angered men capable of great generosity, capable of great cruelty, and all of them capable of sensing the meaning of the divine voice. The very chords of human motives clashing, and various interpretations of the meaning of events, through which we see these ancient figures, give the stories an added verisimilitude. And somehow the tale of the witch of Endor and the shade of Samuel called up for the king who had lost his sense of the presence of God, gives a last touch of moral and spiritual realism to the story. No doubt a tale of a hypothetical revelation given in terms of mathematical definitiveness would be very different from this narrative of living men with their prejudices, their confusions, their angers, and their hates, and God moving in upon them to make them and their life His own. That would be dead revelation—if one can imagine such a thing. This is the living God approaching and mastering living men.

The life of Saul shows how a gifted and powerful man can use and misuse great opportunities. "Though thou wast little in thine own sight, wast thou not made the head of the tribes of Israel? . . . Wherefore then didst thou not obey the voice of Jehovah? . . . to obey is better than sacrifice." So Samuel cuts through the moral obfuscation of Saul's selfishness to a great principle. The conception of moral obedience dawns upon the unwilling mind of Saul. But that bright way is not the way for him.

3. David

Robert Browning's *Saul* really turns out to be a poem about David. And any attempt to tell the tale of Saul is sure to become a telling of the story of David, a story sometimes shining with light and sometimes heavy with a strange darkness.

The virile and far-seeing old Samuel presided at the choosing of David as he had made articulate the choosing of Saul. And the lad who had dreamed deep dreams as he was alone with nature and strengthened his arm for the fight with wild beasts now found himself in the midst of the bitter battles of the world of men. He had a good heart and a good head as well as a good arm. But wisely as he carried himself, he was bound to arouse jealousy. Cicero in one of his downright letters, which bring a breath of human actuality from his century to ours, speaks of those who might have retained his friendship by supporting him in a cause which was as much theirs as his, but they had estranged him by their jealousy. He adds with sharp point, "They are not so much pleased with the steadfastness of my public conduct as annoyed by its distinction." [3]

Saul tried to kill David. He drove him from the court. At last David became a leader of a band of outlaws, but presided over them with a kind of knightly generosity, always refusing to hurt the king. He and Jonathan formed one of those incredible yet actual friendships which are the glory of human annals. He had his own breath-taking adventures. And in good time he was ready for the kingdom. After Saul and Jonathan were killed, he wrote an elegy shot through with magnanimous feeling which has won its own immortality:

Thy glory, O Israel, is slain upon thy high places!

Tell it not in Gath,
Publish it not in the streets of Ashkelon;
Lest the daughters of the Philistines rejoice.

[3] *Cicero, The Letters to His Friends* (London: William Heinemann, Ltd.), pp. 34-35.

> The bow of Jonathan turned not back,
> And the sword of Saul returned not empty.
> Saul and Jonathan were lovely and pleasant in their lives,
> And in their death they were not divided.
>
> . . . .
>
> I am distressed for thee, my brother Jonathan:
> Very pleasant hast thou been unto me:
> Thy love to me was wonderful,
> Passing the love of women.

So David plunges into desperate war and enters upon a course of brilliant administration. His very success brings into his little kingdom the vices of Oriental courts. He captures the Jebusite stronghold and makes Jerusalem his capital. But something other than the glory of God is found there. There is hatred and jealousy and hot sensuality. David himself knows the deepest and most treacherous sinning and the most bitter repentance. His own family is torn by dissensions, and his heart fairly breaks in his cry for his false son. But through all these strange moral vicissitudes he remains God's man wanting God's will in his own life and in that of the kingdom. If his sins are tragic, he never hugs them to his bosom or claims that they are something other than they are. So the good God becomes to him the great reality, and his people see in his figure the outlines of the form of the messianic King.

4. Solomon

Alfred Noyes once wrote some ringing lines about King Solomon:

> When Salomon sailed from Ophir,
>   With Olliphants and gold,
> The kings went up, the kings went down,
> Trying to match King Salomon's crown,
> But Salomon sacked the sunset,
>   Wherever his black ships rolled.
> He rolled it up like a crimson cloth,
> And crammed it into his hold.
>
> Chorus: Salomon sacked the sunset!
>   Salomon sacked the sunset!
>   He rolled it up like a crimson cloth,
>   And crammed it into his hold.[4]

Solomon began by capturing the imagination of Israel. He was shrewd sagacity and magnificence packed into one. He went on by capturing the imagination of the East. He nearly became one of the heroes of *The Arabian Nights*. He ended by becoming an almost myth-

[4] From "Crimson Sails," *Collected Poems by Alfred Noyes*, III, 10. Reprinted by permission of the publishers, J. B. Lippincott Co. Copyright 1915 by Alfred Noyes.

ical figure representing the ultimate pomp and splendor of this world and something which came from another—a man who became a citizen of two worlds, of both of which he made the most until he was suffocated by magnificence.

He was a master of opulent luxury. He built a great house for himself. He built a greater house for God. And, according to the record, he was overawed by the glory of a God greater than all the splendor of magnificent houses: "But will God in very deed dwell on the earth? behold, heaven and the heaven of heavens cannot contain thee; how much less this house which I have builded! Yet have thou respect unto the prayer of thy servant, and to his supplication. . . . And of thy people Israel, when they shall pray toward this place: yea, hear thou in heaven thy dwelling-place; and when thou hearest, forgive." He is conscious that God teaches His people "the good way wherein they should walk," and from some deep place of his own personal experience of tragedy and struggle, he brings forth the knowledge that all the people of Israel "shall know every man the plague of his own heart."

Great words coming out of the experience of a great people and becoming articulate at a great moment are found in Solomon's prayer at the dedication of the temple.

But as years go on the magnificence devours the humble, pious king. The foreign wives in appalling number bring each one a particular technique for being disloyal to Jehovah. And Solomon surrenders to them all. His wisdom becomes more worldly. He becomes a kind of early corpulent Henry VIII who did not have to kill any of his wives because he could have them all. And so the inner glory fades in an outer pomp and circumstance. And at last the light goes out.

Did Solomon, when the day came for leaving his buildings and his wives, his treasures and his glittering jewels, have a last homesick vision of a moral and spiritual beauty he had bartered for the visibilities and the hot sensations of this glittering world? At all events his reign is part of that divine revelation where we learn that even a heaven-kissing wonder of material magnificence is not enough.

5. The Choice of Rehoboam

Round every corner of the life of which the Old Testament tells, we find a choice. In one way the Old Testament is a great literature of choices and of what happens after the choices are made. There are choices in the garden. There are choices in the sanctuary. There are choices in the army. There are choices in the field. There are choices in the palace. We are not surprised at this, for in a world of persons everything depends upon choices.

Rehoboam confronted a choice at the beginning of his reign. Would he make the people his friends? Would he try to make the people his slaves? The old men advised him to speak good words to the people. The fierce young bloods with whom he had grown up had proud eyes and unstable hearts. They put into his mouth the words: "My little finger is thicker than my father's loins. And now whereas my father did lade you with a heavy yoke, I will add to your yoke: my father chastised you with whips, but I will chastise you with scorpions."

Then men heard the fierce words from the Northern tribes: "What portion have we in David? neither have we inheritance in the son of Jesse." And then came the words of tragic finality: "To your tents, O Israel: now see to thine own house, David." So the kingdom was divided.

How the tragedy as well as the glory of choice comes out in these Old Testament documents! And when the choice of one affects the fate of many, how sternly the bells of destiny ring! The story is told in the tale of every king, though not always so dramatically as in the case of Rehoboam. The king did that which was good in the eyes of Jehovah. And this was a matter of choice. The king did that which was evil in the sight of Jehovah. And this, too, was a matter of choice. These royal architects of fate were always standing at the point of destiny when they said "Yes" or "No" to the great moral and spiritual demands of life.

And what of the people? There were those who kept alive the fire of goodness in secret in the days of bad kings. And there were those who kept the dark fires of evil burning secretly in the days of good kings. These, too, made choices. In the great sermons on history we are never allowed to forget that we live in a world of responsible persons.

6. Hezekiah

Kings come and kings go in the two little kingdoms. Great empires see in these small nations pawns in their mighty games of world conquest. Assyria has become a mighty power. And in the eighth century Assyria is in the background of almost every person's thought upon almost every subject.

So we came to the king Hezekiah. Looking back upon his reign, men thought of him as a reforming king. It was remarkable how much evil a king disloyal to the moral religion of Jehovah could do. And where once evil customs got established, they had a way of sticking. Even a good king would get rid of only part of them. The trend of Hezekiah's reign is sure even if we are not clear about details. He was not only a reformer. He was a good fighter. And he was a good ruler. That the mighty prophet Isaiah was about must have had not a little to do with the moral and spiritual quality of Hezekiah's reign. And we must think of Isaiah as in a way the head of a movement as well as a very powerful prophetic person. The time had passed when a great prophet had to stand quite alone—if, indeed, such a time had ever been.

The sickness of Hezekiah when he came to have a very vivid sense of the near friendliness of Jehovah, and his surrender to vanity when he showed his treasures to the embassy of congratulation from Babylon, are human touches not easily forgotten. But the high hour of his reign found Assyria headed straight for Jerusalem with no help and no hope —unless a little land could have a mightier God than a great empire of unlimited resources. Isaiah was adamant in his faith. The city trembled. The people scarcely breathed. The hosts of Sennacherib advanced. Isaiah's faith had a trumpet note in it. And Jerusalem did not fall. The Assyrian armies went away without their prey. This great episode left a tremendous impression on the mind, the imagination, and the conscience of the people.

These Old Testament tales have had a way of capturing the imagination of poets. Lord Byron found words which marched like soldiers when he wrote, in "The Destruction of Sennacherib," the familiar lines:

The Assyrian came down like the wolf on the fold,
And his cohorts were gleaming in purple and gold;
And the sheen of their spears was like stars on the sea,
When the blue wave rolls nightly on deep Galilee.

Like the leaves of the forest when Summer is green,
That host with their banners at sunset were seen:
Like the leaves of the forest when Autumn hath blown,
That host on the morrow lay withered and strown.

For substance of insight, if not perhaps in detailed statement of fact, Lord Byron was right. The blind might of Assyria had confronted a world of being beyond the seeing of its eyes. There were moral and spiritual issues at stake which Assyria could not understand. The God who is righteousness alive was doing a work, through the little hill kingdom whose royal city was Jerusalem, which could not be brought to an end.

7. Josiah

We have been getting glimpses of some of the experiences which certain historical books of the Old Testament set in the frame of what we have ventured to call sermons on history. We have been contented with a few typical examples and have made no attempt at exhaustive treatment. We have space for one more person whose adventure in being over God's people and under an ethical God has its own importance. Josiah seems to have been a reformer even more definitely than Hezekiah. He seems to have moved with caution, to have acted with decision, and to have secured definite and tangible results. There were always two tasks: the recovery of the cult of Jehovah in its true form, and the reformation of the moral life of the people in the light of the character of Jehovah. The two processes intertwined. It was when he was looking after the rehabilitation of the temple and so of the temple cult that the Book of the Law was discovered. This Deuteronomic Code came like a flash of lightning to the mind and the conscience of the people. There was a great repentance. There was a great turning to God. And for a period of years Josiah made the influence of the true worship of Jehovah, and the true practices of that good life which conformed to the character of God, a power in the land. In the queer twistings and turnings of world powers the little kingdom of Judah had a great opportunity for a time really to live a life of its own. And Josiah made the most of it.

Then came the invasion of Pharaoh Necho with an army whose purpose was to move on for a greater fight in the region of the Euphrates. Josiah decided to withstand the Egyptian army. He met the foe at Megiddo. And there Josiah was killed and his army was defeated. One finds all sorts of subtle implications in the whole tragic situation.

A good king fighting in a good cause had gone down to defeat. Did this mean that God had forsaken His people? Did this mean that God was unable to protect His people? Did this mean that God had ceased to be active in history?

Probably some men never recovered their faith. Probably some men sought costly comfort in one of the contemporary cults. The same problem which lies at the heart of the book of Job had emerged on a national scale.

In a moving address in New York City in 1944 Dr. Adam Burnet, the minister of St. Cuthbert's in Edinburgh, spoke of the problem confronting the Christian minister in Scotland in the darkest days of the war. He believed that the cause of his people was just. He hoped that victory would come to their arms. But he could not be sure that God might not have purposes which would be served by what might at the time be the tragic defeat of his own people. There is a place for a national cross in the divine plan. And who shall say God nay if He sends His nation as well as His Son to a cross? Most of those who heard Dr. Burnet must suddenly have confronted depths in the moral meaning of national life of which they had scarcely thought before.

What was a possibility to the Scottish preacher the year of Dunkirk became an actuality to the people of Josiah in the year of his defeat and death. The men of profoundest insight saw that they could have no easy rules to express the relations of God and men. Nations—even loyal nations—may have to go to the depths. There is an ultimate victory of light. There may be a temporary victory of darkness. The nation may have to become the suffering servant of God—a nation of sorrows and acquainted with grief. The experience of Judah in the days of Josiah was not forgotten by the author of the fifty-third chapter of Isaiah.

The picture of God's adventure with men enlarges and becomes more magnificent, more darkly glorious. And one of the final elements in the great panorama comes with this particular picture of the defeat and death of a good king. Even this God can make a part of His great and ultimately triumphant plan.

8. The Living Forces in History

The raw material of Old Testament history is clearly the raw material of life itself. Whatever the vicissitudes of the literary material, this vital quality remains. So the profoundest spirits of Israel regarded their own past. Thus they saw their own people. And thus they saw God moving in and through their life.

It is just these moral and spiritual memories of the past, poured through howsoever many minds and touched by whatever editorial hands, which have come to the men of later centuries and of other lands with a particular power because they come so deeply out of life to speak so directly to life.

The story is, of course, far richer and far more manifold than we have indicated. For we have endeavored to give only a few examples of the whole process. The wonderful thing about it all is that the deep meanings were available before the days of modern critical scholarship. A keen and understanding criticism always deepens a sense of their verity. And only a criticism so scholastic as to lose the sense of life in the study of words torn from living relationships, or a hard materialism of mind which has been incapable of responding to spiritual meanings, has robbed them of their power.

These Old Testament documents have to do with personal relationships. They never reveal abstract, ghostly principles fighting in the night of the mind. Nothing is real until it is real in the experience of a person. Nothing is good until it is good in the relations of living, intelligent beings. All this perfectly corresponds to that view of the universe and of experience on which we have been insisting in every page of this book. Clearly this interpretation is not enforced on the Old Testament from without. It is implicit in all of the materials contained in the Old Testament.

We have not said a great deal in this chapter about the worst days of the worst kings. That would only add to the vivid and dramatic way in which in the Old Testament moral meanings emerge as a part of history. We can always trace an evil thing back to the bad decision of some person who made the evil his good. These things are the very stuff of which history is made.

The real validation of all this lies in a realm deeper than technical criticism. It lies in the fashion in which we can relive these ancient struggles and remake these ancient choices. The form of our life may be different enough, but the essence remains unchanged. We too meet God every time we make a moral choice.

All this should make it abundantly clear, if it has not been clear from the beginning, that when you try to tell the history of human beings as if you were recounting the reacting of impersonal forces you are sure to go wrong.

The modern tendency to leave man out of his own history is a kind of world-wide writing of tales of the Prince of Denmark with Hamlet left out. The history of the dissecting room is always to be viewed in the light of the fact that you are dealing with dead organisms and not with living beings. You find out all sorts of interesting and, in their way, important things. But you miss that splendid quality which comes when life infuses all the organs with its own quickening energies.

More and more we must realize that we must be on our guard against two dangers in the study of the tale of man's life on this planet. We must watch always our tendency to personify that which has no conscious intelligence, as if history were a tale of abstract principles somehow dominating people. The number of contemporary books which put abstractions on the throne clad in the garments of living persons is most extraordinary. On the other hand, there is the tendency to emasculate human actions by trying to see them as the expression of impersonal laws rather than the outcome of intelligent decision. This is the reverse of the first danger of which we have spoken. The Old Testament is gloriously free from capitulation to either of these dangers. Indeed, we may go so far as to say that they did not exist for Old Testament writers. They saw living beings thinking and deciding and acting. Thus they touched the very actuality of life. To them the forces of history always have the force of a personal decision behind them.

This means, of course, that there is always a place for the individual flavor which is so attractive a part of the accounts of people which the writers of the Old Testament give. The schools of historical abstraction have a way of beginning with human beings and so thoroughly emasculating them as to remove every possibility of vital experience. When this tendency enters the field of religion, it soon follows that the interpretation of religion loses its compulsion and becomes as flat as if religion had never been a transforming power in the world. One must learn of religion, as of history, that you never explain a thing by explaining it away.

9. The Divine Meanings in History

Thomas Hardy, in a mood singularly uncharacteristic and perhaps for that reason all the more revealing, after he had heard "an aged thrush, frail, gaunt, and small . . . fling his soul upon the growing gloom" wrote:

> So little cause for carollings
>   Of such ecstatic sound
> Was written on terrestrial things
>   Afar or nigh around,
> That I could think there trembled through
>   His happy good-night air
> Some blessèd Hope, whereof he knew
>   And I was unaware.[5]

There is always the dull and heavy tragedy of those who view history and see no divine meaning in it. There is always the bitter misanthropy of those who view history and see in it no meaning at all. It is the glory of ethical religion, with a God who is moral good will alive marching through it, that perpetually it finds divine meanings in history. You cannot read the typical and rousing sermons on history in the Old Testament without becoming possessed of the thought that all history might be so read. And this may well ripen into the conviction that all history must be so read. Some men treat history in the fashion of a murderous bully who not only leaves his victim dead but beats his face flat so that all marks of individual quality are gone. There is nothing left by which you could recognize a human countenance. Some men see in history a tale of human lust and folly and treachery. Some men see in history impersonal forces playing at being persons. Some men see in history endless events but no meanings. And the men who put a soul into the world look at history and find God.

You do not have to possess a good world in order to find divine meanings in it. You do have to have a God who makes history His own battleground, the struggles of men His own arena, and His own majestic purposes the goal of human life.

The Old Testament has this immortal quality of enabling us to see God at work. This mighty smith who beats the materials of life into shape is not afraid of the bitter or the evil, the dull or the bad. He is not afraid of a world where man's freedom baffles Him at every turn and He must play the game with checkers which insist on moving from square to square without asking His permission at all. It is the wildest and most exciting game in all the universe, this game of the

---

[5] From "The Darkling Thrush," *Collected Poems of Thomas Hardy*. By permission of The Macmillan Co., publishers.

Great God with free men. Of course, it is possible to misread the tale. Of course, it is easier to trace the lines of confusion than the subtler lines of order. Of course, it is easier to see the footprints of the beasts than the tracks of God. But God has marched this way. And the understanding we find when we listen to the great voices which interpret the life of Israel may be applied to the whole puzzling panorama of human life. There is always the God of light striving to pierce the darkness. And there is always the possibility of turning one's steps toward the spots where God's light shines through.

It is not those who tell lies about the darkness who really help men to believe in the light. It is those who are not afraid to tell the truth about the darkness who can bring us to the most authentic experience of the light. The Old Testament writers are afraid of no ugly aspect of human life. They tell the truth. They tell the whole truth. They tell nothing but the truth about the men they love. And as the shadows play over the human stories you begin to see how great is the faith of these men who dare to tell the truth. The doubters tell falsehoods to keep this world from falling apart. The great believers are so sure of the triumphant light that they never fear to tell the truth about the shadows.

God is all the while making life more difficult. You must admit that. Wherever His light shines, the things of darkness are seen for what they are. He always comes putting weapons into our hands. And even better than that, He always comes giving us a cause for which to fight.

The traveler in Palestine muses over many an ancient fight as he visits the sites of battles whose names he has known from his childhood and whose very soil now responds to the presence of his feet. There is the tense struggle. There is the quick movement of the weapon. There is the gasp of death. And there is the victor's shout.

And none of it is meaningless. And all of it has more than human meaning. It is shot through with those divine meanings which the moral God is teaching His children in the busiest days of strife. And that meaning, He knows well, does not end with a single fight or a hundred fights. It goes beyond struggling bodies and struggling minds and struggling hearts. The blackness is in the valleys behind. The light is on the hills ahead. There is most light of all—strangely and tragically beautiful that it should be so—upon a hill called Golgotha. But in the Old Testament days that was hidden in the mists of the future.

CHAPTER XI

The Story of a Bridge

IN 1914, before the outbreak of the first World War, I was having my first experience of life in the British Isles, and London was revealing a fascination whose hold upon me was to grow with the years. One evening at his home Dr. J. E. Rattenbury waxed warm in praise of a Cambridge scholar, T. R. Glover, and especially of his book *The Conflict of Religions in the Early Roman Empire.* I was much impressed, and and after preaching my first sermon in England at the Ealing Congregational Church, of which the famous hymonologist the Rev. W. Garrett Hoder was minister, I bought a copy of the book by Dr. Glover of which Dr. Rattenbury had spoken so highly.

I suppose that anyone coming to this rich and ripe volume of ample scholarship with his mind full of the characteristic experiences and insights of the Old Testament would feel, as perhaps he had not felt before, how different was the world in which the Christian religion emerged from that in which the great characteristic Old Testament documents came to be. The wonder of the mind of Greece and the grasp of the power of Rome are outstanding features of the new situation. But more than this, much dramatic and influential thought and action had been poured into the alembic of history and had a share in the making of the world of assumptions and convictions to which Jesus spoke. Of course, it is possible to oversimplify the situation. The picture of four hundred silent years between the Old Testament and the New is clearly exaggerated and inaccurate. Critical scholarship has at least made it clear that much Old Testament material comes from this period. But it still remains true that in many, many ways the mind which is the background of the typical Old Testament utterances is one mind and the mind which is the background of the typical New Testament utterances is another. The great Old Testament insights and convictions maintained themselves in the new milieu, but with a difference.

There is a literature of the period which is extracanonical and which is of the greatest importance if we are to understand the changes which took place in the mental climate. Dr. R. H. Charles has put us all in his debt by his critical studies of these documents, and, to mention one other writer among many, Dr. William Fairweather, in his careful studies *The Background of the Gospels* and *The Background of the Epis-*

tles, has brought the significant materials in respect of the period within the reach of the man who wishes to read his New Testament intelligently.

It is not our purpose to make a detailed study of the matters which these and other scholars have subjected to minute scrutiny. But the fact that there was a bridge from one world to another, and that great old insights were carried over that bridge, gaining new insights on the way, is of importance for our argument.

1. The Exile

The central facts recorded in the later books of the Old Testament have to do with the death and resurrection of the nation. The Babylonian exile was the death. The return from the Exile was the resurrection. But the Exile seemed at the time to be more than the death of a nation. It seemed the death of a religion. The whole Semitic world thought that the fortunes of a deity were bound up with the fortunes of his people. If they were prosperous and successful, this proved that their deity was powerful. If they went down to defeat, their deity was defeated too. By this token, when Israel went into exile and the temple and the capital city were destroyed, Jehovah was completely discredited.

As a matter of fact, the deeper ethical history of Israel had already contradicted this position. Amos had declared that, just because Jehovah, who was righteousness alive, had known only Israel, he was all the more obligated by his own character to punish the sins of his people. The very fact of the Exile's coming to a rebellious, false, and apostate people might be the establishment of the judgment of God in history and not a proof of the weakness of Jehovah. The deeper spirits in Israel took this view. Their confidence in Jehovah survived the tragedy. God was not defeated by the defeat of Israel. His reign was established in the very tragedy which some men used to discredit Him.

2. The Return from Exile

The return from the Exile was in a way a political dramatization of the validity of the doctrine of repentance. The nation had sinned. It had been punished. It had been almost blotted out. It had repented. It had been forgiven. It had been given a second chance. Exiles returned. The capital city was once more enclosed within walls. The temple was rebuilt.

The tragedy of moral religion is always to be found in the seeming divorce between ideas and ideals and facts. It is a matter of central significance that the greatest tradition of ethical religion in the world is set in the midst of history. It is not a glory of impossible dreams. It is a series of magnificently ethical judgments. The prophet is set in the historical process. The priest is set in the historical process. The lawgiver is set in the historical process. There is a continual interaction between ideas and events. Or—to drop a figure which is apt to be misleading—living men having commerce with a Moral God and deciding for or against His commands find themselves thrust against the hard facts of a world controlled by the God whom they have chosen to spurn or have chosen to obey. All this is never more dramatically true than in the events of the Exile and the events of the restoration.

The Old Testament documents have a good deal to say about the witness of the pious remnant, almost trodden underfoot, when the whole current of events moves against them and they maintain in silence a faith which seems to be denied by the facts of life. But their hour comes. And it comes in two ways. First, the evil to which they refused to capitulate brings ruin to those who have surrendered to it. The majority, proud in their evil choice and complacent in their unethical prosperity, come to utter destruction at last. And the pious remnant have a sad satisfaction in witnessing the vindication of the moral law even at the expense of their own nation. The Exile is the execution of the death sentence on an unethical majority.

But this is not the last word. The minority—the pious remnant—has the seed of goodness in it; the seed of the future is in its possession. By the standards of the pious remnant the nation is judged. Because of the standards of the pious remnant the nation is given an opportunity of repentance. Because of the standards of the pious remnant the nation is given a second chance. The silent minority has become the controlling power when the great return takes place. Royalty is found not in numbers but in rightness. After the Exile the pious minority speaks with a masterful and controlling voice. And so it becomes the transformed majority.

3. The Resurrection of the Nation

Many people have said over softly certain lines of Rudyard Kipling. They are about one spot in the earth. The people who have recited them softly have usually had in mind some other spot than that which Kipling loved. In their minds they have put another name in the verses as they have said them over with quiet joy.

> God gives all men all earth to love,
>   But, since man's heart is small,
> Ordains for each one spot shall prove
>   Belovèd over all.
> Each to his choice, and I rejoice
>   The lot has fallen to me
> In a fair ground—in a fair ground—
>   Yea, Sussex by the sea! [1]

[1] From "Sussex," from *The Five Nations*, copyright 1903, 1931, by Rudyard Kipling, reprinted by permission of Mrs. Bambridge and Doubleday, Doran & Co., Inc.

The Jews who had returned to the land they had lost, who had "wept when they remembered Zion," found their nostalgia satisfied in a great and deepened loyalty never lost through the centuries. The resurrection of the people was in their own glorious hill country with the little city on the mountain, God's very special town in all the world. The old apostasies were rejected. Perhaps even more they faded away now quite robbed of meaning. The One God and the one moral code came to their true place at last. The Priestly Code was the ritualistic expression of the nation's deepest moral loyalties. It was not a substitute for them. The moral resurrection of the nation had come indeed.

But, as so often happens, the vanishing of old temptations brought new temptations. Men were not tempted to big apostasies. They were tempted to little loyalties. The scholasticism of the law came with Judaism. The petty faithfulness often took the place of the big understanding. And sometimes the very meaning of ethical religion, as centuries went by, became confused with a thousand minute moral performances which left the inner glory of the law unexpressed.

4. Persia

It was in the period of the Persian ascendency that the exiles were given an opportunity to return to their own land. The new power was a friendly power. And up to a point it was characterized by a friendly religion. This Zarathustrian religion is profoundly related to things taken across the bridge from the Old Testament period into the New. Its influence was made easier because of the happy contacts in many ways between the two peoples. As Dr. Fairweather reminds us "Both alike practised monotheism, abhorred idolatry, and valued morality; both alike cared for the poor, believed in the final destruction of evil, and laid stress upon a future judgment." [2]

The Jews carried away from Persia many fascinating beliefs about angels. And it seems clear that the belief in a rather shadowy afterlife not without similarities to the Greek Hades sharpened under Persian influence to a clear doctrine of immortality and of the resurrection of individual men and women. The assumptions of New Testament speakers and writers bear clear witness to the influence of the Persian beliefs at this point. The assumptions are not those of the typical Old Testament books. They are those which have come from Persia, perhaps to use one illustration, by way of the book of Daniel. The doctrine of the devil clearly owes something to Persia, too.

It seems clear that as Israel moved through larger and more cosmopolitan experiences by a kind of moral right of eminent domain, it appropriated that which corresponded to the deepest genius of its own quality as an ethical religion. All this, of course, merely fits in with the

[2] *The Background of the Gospels* (Edinburgh: T. & T. Clark), p. 45.

idea of revelation as something which comes through living experience.

If we may change the figure, we must admit that sometimes the good ship Israel came into port with barnacles attached to it. That, too, was a part of the living experience. And the getting rid of the barnacles was a part of the discipline of a living moral faith.

5. Babylon

The story is by no means so simple that you can tell it merely in terms of exile and return. Babylon was a very great and very ancient city full of wealth and full of learning, the home of great libraries and the seat of vast scholarship. In many ways as full and rich a life could be lived there as anywhere in the world. The Jews scarcely knew how versatile they were until they began to mix with men of power and position in the great world. When the Persians gave the Jews permission to return to their own land, perhaps fifty thousand altogether accepted the invitation. Many more remained behind. They had found wealth and security and power in their new home, and they did not return to Jerusalem. But, though the little mountain capital did not lure their feet, in an odd way it did dwell in their hearts. They kept the feasts and celebrated the rites of the cult of their own religion in a foreign land. And, as Hebrew ceased to be spoken in the homeland, the Babylonian scholars became the greatest masters of Hebrew in the world. Babylon and Jerusalem kept in close touch. Signals from hill to hill sent messages from one city to another. It was from Babylon that the scholars journeyed who brought an intellectual restoration to Jerusalem corresponding to the material restoration which was so important as a solid foundation for the loftier structure. Babylon became a brilliant Jewish literary center. Law and tradition, chronicle and historical interpretation flourished. At times Babylon seemed like the capital and Jerusalem a provincial center of Jewish intelligence.

So the Jews began to spread about that Eastern world. Everywhere they were men of property and power and political importance. And from these far-scattered Jews there came to Jerusalem all sorts of subtle influences. In the very days when in a unique sense Jerusalem became the center of an utterly devoted cult, it also felt the spice-laden air of a cosmopolitan civilization.

6. Alexandria

Alexander the Great flashed like a brilliant star in the ancient world. His conquering armies marched not many years to all their achievements before his untimely death. But everywhere he went he took Greek culture with him. And the Greek mind went on with its conquests long after the death of Alexander. It was, indeed, the Greek mind and not Alexander which conquered the ancient world.

It was the man of Macedon who founded the Egyptian city of Alexandria. It grew magnificently and erelong housed a population of over a million people. Here, as indeed to all those semi-Greek cities which sprang up in the wake of Alexander, the Jews came. They had made themselves familiar and masterful figures in all the cities where the generals of Alexander and their successors ruled. In Alexandria they had a place of singular distinction and power. Here the Jew met the grace and fascination and energy of the Greek culture. And so the process of the Hellenization of the Jews began. It flared out in writings full of trailing memories of Jerusalem and full, too, of trailing memories of Athens. The Old Testament was translated into Greek. And in this famous Septuagint the Hebrew prophets learned to speak in the tongue of Athens. By the time of Philo the attempt was made to build up a religious tradition whose spiritual foundation should be Hebrew and whose cultural tang should be Greek.

Echoes of all this found their way to Jerusalem. The Alexandrian interpretation of the old religion and the Babylonian met and exchanged ideas or contended on the streets of the Holy City. Winds from all the world were blowing lustily through the little mountain capital.

7. The Decadent Greeks

By the time Antiochus Epiphanes came to the Syrian throne in the second century B.C. it was clear that a decadent Hellenism would try to conquer what we might call a scholastic Judaism. With none of the restraint of a true Hellenism and with a completely barbarous passion Antiochus set about destroying that pure faith which had made Jerusalem a sacred city. It is one of the tragedies of history that the Greek spirit, as it was poured forth in the Dialogues of Plato, could not have met the Hebrew spirit in the passionate form in which it had come forth in the great eighth-century prophets. But Greece had passed its Indian summer and Israel had lost the first fine passion of prophetic insight when the mad Antiochus turned decadent Jews who were only too willing to do his bidding to the purpose of exterminating the religion of Israel. Antiochus was a savage who liked to play with the pomp and circumstance which he interpreted as the essence of the Greek spirit. Of course, Athens was drunk with hot Oriental wine before it entered the strange mind of Antiochus. In the climax of his activities against Jerusalem "an army, led by Apollonius, was sent against Jerusalem. Deceitfully on a sabbath-day that 'lord of pollutions' let loose his soldiers to plunder and slay in the defenceless city, which was then given to the flames. The sanctuary was laid waste. . . . The Temple was dedicated to Zeus Olympios, and in every township Jews were commanded to sacrifice to idols animals which they reckoned unclean, and then eat their flesh. . . . To all appearance Antiochus had achieved his object, and Jerusalem had become a pagan city." [3] It was a black hour. And there seemed to be no promise of light in the night sky.

8. The Great Patriots

Then came the glory of the House of Mattathias and one of the great periods of Jewish history. In a little village not many miles from Jerusalem, Mattathias the priest and his five sons refused to sacrifice upon the altar to pagan gods. And when an apostate Jew attempted to do what Mattathias and his sons had refused to do, the old priest in a sudden accession of moral wrath killed the Jew and the officer of Syria who was in charge of the enforcing of the evil demand. The standard of revolt was quickly raised, and multitudes followed Mattathias and his sons to the mountains prepared to resist unto death. Everywhere they destroyed altars devoted to pagan rites. Everywhere they restored Jewish worship. The old priest did not long survive the tense excitement of those stern days. But as he realized that he was dying, he committed the military enterprise to one of his five sons, Judas, who was, as it turned out, a military genius as well as a man of passionate faith in his nation's cause and of utter courage in fighting in its behalf. Judas won the surname Maccabaeus, and a hammer to the foe indeed he was. The name he won for himself became the name of the period. The first book of Maccabees tells the tale of superb achievement. Dr. Fairweather has a graphic chapter on "The History of the Maccabaean Struggle." And the fine little book *The Bridge Between the Testaments* by Henry Kendall Booth tells the tale in brief but compelling fashion. You see Judas defeat one army after another. You admire his strategy in the pass of Bethhoron. You watch him defeat a powerful army and behold his own fighting men entering Jerusalem in triumph, breaking down the pagan altar, restoring the rites of Jehovah, and founding that Feast of Lights to be kept in glad memory to this day. You see the inevitable interplay of religious and political motives, the disillusionment of the Hasidim ("the pious") and at last their turning from the support of the warriors, whose triumphs they valued only for the purposes of religion. Judas at last falls on the field of battle. Then his shrewd brother Jonathan and his wise brother Simon in turn succeed him. The Jewish battle is actually in process of being won. John Hyrcanus, the son of Simon, extends the newly won kingdom. It was in this period that the Jewish parties we find in the time of our Lord, especially the Pharisees and the Sadducees, emerged. On the death of John Hyrcanus the family kept its power. But many unpleasant things were happening, some indeed dreadful enough. In the first century before the Christian era the Sanhedrin—so important in the New Testament—was formed. And erelong, as descendants of the first great Maccabaeans fought for the

[3] *Ibid.*, pp. 102-3.

throne, the mighty empire of Rome—represented by Pompey—intervened. An epoch had come to an end.

The tale should be read and reread.

Dr. R. H. Charles's translation of the first book of Maccabees intersperses the historical narration with bits of poetry full of the passion of these fierce days:

> And there was great mourning in Israel in every place;
> And the rulers and elders groaned;
> Virgins and young men languished,
> And the beauty of the women faded away.[4]

> And, behold, our holy things, and our beauty, and our glory
>   have been laid waste,
> And the heathen have profaned them! To what purpose should
>   we continue to live? [5]

Then of Judas Maccabaeus:

> And his son Judas, who was called Maccabaeus, rose up
>   in his stead.
> And all his brethren helped him,
> And all they that clave unto his father,
> And they fought with gladness the battle of Israel.

> And he extended the glory of his people,
> And put on a breastplate as a giant,
> And girt on his weapons of war.

> He set battles in array,
> He protected the army with the sword
> And he was like a lion in his deeds.[6]

9. Rome

The independence of the Jewish state ended with the coming of Pompey. Long before, the handwriting might well have been seen upon the wall. The little city on the Tiber had become master of Italy and its power had begun to be felt with increasing finality all about the Mediterranean world. The Punic Wars told the long tale of Rome's struggle with Carthage in North Africa. With the power of Carthage finally broken at the Battle of Zama 202 B.C. and the end of Greek independence in 146 B.C., the power of Rome was firmly established in the Mediterranean world. All the world knows that the Romans were great organizers and great rulers. Dr. William Fairweather in his significant

---

[4] *The Apocrypha and Pseudepigrapha of the Old Testament in English* (New York: Oxford University Press, 1913), I, 69.

[5] *Ibid.*, p. 71.

[6] *Ibid.*, p. 75.

book *The Background of the Epistles* summarizes, as he sees them, the qualities of the civilization which Rome gave to the world. The student of the period comes gradually to have an intimate sense of the compelling might of Roman power entering every phase of life and administration, and of the subtle and pervasive influence of Greek intelligence.

When the Jewish state lost its independence, a clever and adroit man was fishing in troubled waters. Antipater the Idumaean, an unscrupulous politician, played with the waning power of the family of the Maccabees and above all played with whoever was powerful in Rome. He could be with Pompey. He could be with Caesar. And after his crafty and audacious career, his death found his son Herod seated on the throne under Rome. Herod the adroit, Herod the magnificent, the shrewd politician, the cruel murderer, who worshiped only power and those in power, became in a strange black way Herod the Great. With the end of his evil, powerful career, we are on the edge of New Testament days.

The little city and the little land among the hills were different enough from what they had been in the earlier days reflected in the typical books of the Old Testament. Roman soldiers were everywhere. Buildings after the Roman pattern with something of the Greek spirit stood out before the eye. Greek games, Greek and Roman costumes, played their part in the life of many men. And Greek ideas subtly suffused men's thought. The ancient religion of the Moral God was alive too—potently alive in the midst of all this confusion.

10. The Fresh Insights

That something from this maelstrom of ideas and events was gathered up into the stream of ethical religion is undoubtedly true. And the sense of the process of discrimination and rejection and appropriation represents some of the subtlest matters in the history of the living experience of revelation.

The extracanonical writing of the period is deeply related to the whole process. This writing can be studied in the massive volumes of Dr. Charles, and as one reads his translations it is important to remember that once and again he is reading words which were familiar to Jesus, and thoughts which became a part of the background of his teaching.

One watches the play of the Jewish mind with fascinated interest as one sees it in certain passages of the book of Enoch:

And I saw till the sheep came to a goodly place, and a pleasant and glorious land, and I saw till those sheep were satisfied; and that house stood amongst them in the pleasant land.

And sometimes their eyes were opened, and sometimes blinded, till another sheep arose and led them and brought them all back, and their eyes were opened.[7]

The Wisdom of Solomon describes the very qualities which give to wisdom moral and spiritual dignity:

> For there is in her a spirit quick of understanding, holy,
> Alone in kind, manifold,
> Subtil, freely moving,
> Clear in utterance, unpolluted,
> Distinct, that cannot be harmed,
> Loving what is good, keen, unhindered,
> Beneficent, loving toward man,
> Steadfast, sure, free from care,
> All-powerful, all-surveying.
>
> . . . .
>
> For she is a breath of the power of God.
>
> . . . .
>
> But she reacheth from one end of the world to the other
>   with full strength,
> And ordereth all things well.[8]

The Wisdom of Jesus ben Sirach (Ecclesiasticus) speaks with urbane, shrewd wisdom of friendship:

> Gentle speech multiplieth friends,
>   And kindly words those that give greeting.
> Let those that are at peace with thee be many,
>   But thy confidant one in a thousand.
> If thou makest a friend test him,
>   And be not in haste to trust him.
> For there is a friend (who is so) according to occasion,
>   And continueth not in the day of affliction;
> And there is a friend that turneth to an enemy,
>   And he revealeth strife to thy reproach.
> And there is a friend who is a table-friend,
>   But he is not to be found in the day of affliction.
> When thou art in prosperity he will be like thee,
>   And will lord it over thy servants.
> If evil overtake thee he will turn against thee,
>   And will hide himself from thee.
> Separate thyself from thine enemies,
>   And be on thy guard against thy friends
> A faithful friend is a strong defence,
>
> . . . .
>
> And he that findeth him findeth a treasure.[9]

[7] Ibid., II, 253-54.   [8] Ibid., I, 546, 547, 548.   [9] Ibid., I, 334-35.

The introduction to the praise of the fathers and princes and leaders of Israel has a form which is familiar to lovers of good literature. The less known translation of Charles deserves attention:

> Let me now hymn the praises of men of piety,
> Of our fathers in their generations.
> No little glory did the Most High allot them,
> And they were great from the days of old:
> (Men) who wielded dominion over the earth in their royalty,
> And men of renown in their might;
> Counsellors in their discernment,
> And all-seeing in their prophetic (power);
> Princes of nations in their statesmanship,
> And (trusted) leaders in their penetration;
> Clever of speech in their (scribal) instruction,
> And speakers of wise sayings in their tradition;
> Devisers of psalms according to rule,
> And authors of proverbs in books;
> Men of resource and supported with strength,
> And living at ease in their dwelling-places:
> All these were honoured in their generation,
> And in their days had glory.
> Some of them there are who have left a name,
> That men might tell of their praise:
> And some of them there are who have no memorial,
> So that there was an end of them when they came to their end;
> They were as though they had not been,
> And their children after them.
> Nevertheless these were men of piety,
> And their good fortune shall not come to an end;
> With their seed their prosperity remaineth sure,
> And their inheritance to their children's children.
> In their covenant their seed abideth,
> And their children's children for their sakes;
> Their memory abideth for ever,
> And their righteousness shall not be forgotten;
> Their bodies were buried in peace,
> But their name liveth unto all generations.
> The assembly recounteth their wisdom,
> And the congregation declareth their praise.[10]

All the while you are conscious of new ideas, new experiences, new aspects of culture. The world is widening, and the Jew looks with infinitely curious eyes upon this larger world. As far as it is the world of the Greek mind, there is the possibility of complete surrender. This can mean the repudiation of the clean, pure Jewish faith and become the way of the apostate. There is the way of defiance. This may mean

[10] *Ibid.*, I, 479-82.

loyalty to a tradition which so hardens that it has no real response to the manifold experiences of life. There is the way of that loyalty to the Jewish past which is so confident of itself that it moves with discrimination among the offerings of the new culture, accepting and rejecting, often very much attracted by the new but always possessing a standard by which to judge it. But, of course, ideas and beliefs and hopes and fears were coming in from far larger areas than that represented by Greek ways of thought and life. The Jew was literally hurled into contact with every culture and every world power. His quick mind moved through all these experiences with amazing versatility and skill. And so at last the Jewish mind of the time of our Lord was made. The important thing for us to see is that all this experience was a part of the divine revelation. It was all an adventure with God as well as with men. And this subtle divine guidance was not absent when the belief in personal immortality was gladly accepted. And it was not absent when something of the Greek urbanity entered into the stern Hebrew ethic. And it was not absent when Jews who might have become conventional and bigoted votaries of a formal law became men full of warm human feeling, based upon a deeper feeling of the glory and splendor of the Moral God. If there was a bridge between the Old Testament and the New, God Himself was on the bridge.

11. Casually Accepted Beliefs

During all this period there were casually accepted beliefs thrown up from the varied experiences of the passing years which were to be tested and thrown off. They came on the borders of the experience of a great people. When they got into the clear light of criticism, they were not good enough and they faded away. The systematic hierarchies of spirits went beyond the reality of revelation, though many a pious Jew doubtless quite literally accepted them. But deepening experience would tell the tale. For experience itself has a way of becoming criticism.

The hard and fast literalists have always had a difficult time with those elements in the Scriptures which represent this process. They want a mathematics of inspiration and a mathematics of authority. They must be told quite bluntly that they can have neither.

You meet the truths of religion as you meet living human beings. And, as with human beings, the experience of intimacy is the great test. There is the central aura of friendship shining with glowing light. There is no doubt here. There is only authentic love and deeply justified devotion. At the periphery there is a difference. Here nothing is so clear. Nothing is so sure. There are things about the best of friends which do not belong to the central authenticity of friendship. This, you learn, is true of their relation to you. And if you watch the process with sharp intelligence, you soon begin to suspect that this is true of your relation to them.

As the truths of religion come to you through manifold revealing experiences, you have the same apprehensions. There is a great center of blazing light. Here everything is certain. Here there is no doubt. And here is the basis of your assurance.

But the experiences of relative men in a relative world contain much that does not belong to this region of blazing light. On the periphery there is much to be inspected with the most critical understanding. And there is something to be rejected.

The people who are so much annoyed by the honest confusions at the periphery that they will not accept the glowing certainties at the center make great trouble for themselves and, when they can, great doubt and bewilderment for their friends.

The men who gladly accept a living experience of a living religion can escape this confusion.

12. The New Imperial World

The coming and the going of world empires at last taught the Jew that there is such a thing as a world empire. The great writing of the period of the bridge is full of this sense of world movements, world tragedies, world victories, a world religion, and a God for the world. Life has become imperial in its outlook. When we come to consider the writings of Paul, we shall see how deeply important all this is. And even sooner we shall see, when we consider the temptations of Jesus, that a false imperial dream was one of them.

The quality of a new age is indeed upon us; the winds of a new age are blowing upon us when we actually cross the bridge. For it is not a space bridge. It is a time bridge. And the new land is the land of a new day.

Of course, we have been able to do little more than hint at the varied meanings which this adventure with God, which became revelation, brought to men. But we have said enough to make the sheer vitality of the process clear. The principles involved begin to stand out. Or, to put it more adequately, we see the persons and we see the Great Person and we begin to understand what happens when they meet. All this had massive vividness as we confronted the great experience reflected in the canonical Old Testament writings. And in a lesser way it is relevant to the experiences of the intertestamental period and to the literature in which these experiences are expressed.

CHAPTER XII

The Human Life Divine

A WELL-KNOWN public man in America in times of self-revelation used to tell a dramatic tale of the critical moment in his life. He had felt the lure of the gold rush to Alaska and, like many another adventurer, went forth hoping to make his personal fortune. He was caught in a blizzard and, struggling through snow and wind, finally was completely lost. Some grim central strength of character kept him struggling on. He wanted to fight the fierce and cutting cold to the very end. He wanted to die on his feet. Then suddenly he was amazed to see before him in the Alaskan wilderness a white cross. At once he felt that he knew what had happened. He was beginning to have illusions in that treacherous land of driving snow. Filled with panic, he turned and ran, with no sense of direction except to escape that illusion of a white cross. Then his character reasserted itself. He would fight the fantasy. He would conquer it. If he went right up to the cross and found nothing, his sanity and his perspective would be restored. He forced himself to move forward through the driving snow. But again the sight of the cross filled him with panic, and again he turned and ran. So he played tragically with his own fierce fears until at last he gathered enough resolution to go on right up to the white illusion. And when he came to it, he fell against its hardness. The snow dropped away. And there it stood, an actual cross. At once his mind cleared and he knew what had happened. He had run against the cross marking the grave of a missionary who had died in Alaska and had been buried here long ago. He stood looking at the cross and thinking of the man buried under it. What devotion the man of Galilee had commanded! How men had loved Him and lived for Him and died for Him century after century in land after land! Nobody could really escape Him. The gold hunter could not escape Him. He could not even freeze to death in the wastes of Alaska without being forced to confront that strange man who died upon a cross. It was a staggering experience. The adventurer confronted reality in the midst of the freezing cold as he had never done before. And he confronted the Inescapable Person who had been served by the lonely missionary who lay buried beneath the cross. Then the unbelievable happened, and the man who, hunting gold, found a more precious metal was rescued and came back to live a different life because of an hour in the presence of an icy cross in that far northern land.

1. The Portrait of Christ in the Gospels

Christianity is always doing something to men which, though it may seem less dramatic, is quite like the experience of the gold hunter in Alaska. They meet the Inescapable Person, and then everything is changed. A person meets a Person. This is the tale of the Christian religion in the world, age after age and country after country. And we can easily see how it all fits in with that analysis of human experience as a series of personal adventures which is the theme of this volume. We meet this Person as He walks through the pages of the four Gospels. And something final happens when He walks right out of the Gospels into our own lives. We must read the Gospels if we are to come to any genuine apprehension of their quality with precisely this sense of the passing centuries during which men of many lands in various continents have found the Inescapable Person here. And we must let this Person speak to us by means of the whole body of writing in the four Gospels just as He has spoken to men in all the Christian centuries. We shall have something to say later about the relation of all this to the closest literary criticism of the documents in which we find the portrait of this Mighty Figure. But in the meantime twenty centuries of Christian history make a claim which we cannot ignore. These are the documents which in the fierce battle for life survived because they presented a Person the world cannot allow to die. And we must let the very words which have spoken to men through the long and checkered and majestic history of the Church speak to us in their very fullness. Twenty centuries of transformed lives have a right to come to us with a great claim. They have a right to insist that we shall not confront an emasculated Christ in the supreme crisis of our lives. The commerce between this Mighty Figure and battle-scarred men in all the ages represents something in its own way thoroughly commanding. Human need has found in this many-sided portrait a satisfaction which it has found nowhere else. This mighty mark of authenticity which the ages have set upon the Christ of the Gospels must never be forgotten. The portrait is completely commanding. It is entirely final.

Once Sir William Robertson Nicoll gave to an important editorial in the *British Weekly* the title "The Bones of Elisha." He told how, according to an Old Testament story, a dead man was buried in the sepulcher of Elisha. And as soon as his body touched the bones of Elisha, he revived and stood on his feet. Sir William said he would like to bring the discussion to the test of the bones of Elisha. And he proceeded to quote from Dr. Robert William Dale, not very long dead. Dr. Dale was a prince of preachers, using the good old English speech with a certain royal urbanity and at times with a shining splendor. He was a keen thinker and a powerful theologian. His little book *The Living Christ and the Four Gospels* deals with principles which have a perennial significance. As he beheld the critical armies advancing, he desired to find a basis for assurance in respect of the deepest matters of the Christian religion, which criticism could not touch. He was quite ready to give every technical scholar his day in court—indeed, if necessary, to give him many days. But it was unthinkable to Dr. Dale that anything so massive and finally significant for man as the Christian religion should hang suspended in every generation from a set of syllogisms created with infinite versatility and diversity by successive groups of technical scholars.

He laid down these principles in dealing with the whole matter. First, the portrait of Christ in the Gospels is self-authenticating. Whoever were the authors of the Gospels, whatever were the conditions of the writing, there the portrait stands. It is the supreme literary miracle of history. And in its own right it compels the judgment and commands the acceptance of men. That immediate intellectual and moral and spiritual effect cuts right through all critical processes to an unquestionable center of reality.

Dr. Dale's second principle may be expressed in this fashion. When a man accepts the Christ of the Gospels and puts Him in command of his life, the Great Person ceases to be a figure in a series of books and becomes a living fact of personal experience. He ceases to be the Christ of history and becomes the most Intimate Companion of the soul. Now you find Him at the very center of your own life. And He is there to command and to reign. This immediate personal experience is utterly decisive. Like the blind man who said, "Whereas I was blind, now I see," you have come to a direct contact through spiritual sight which cannot be questioned.

Dr. Dale's third principle had to do with the social confirmation of personal experience. This contact of the individual with the living Christ has been repeated by countless men and women of the most varied countries and languages and races through all the centuries since Jesus lived in the world. And this social authentication of individual experience becomes at last a thing of perfectly overwhelming power. Dr. Dale set forth his principles with a wealth of illustration and an aptitude in argument which carried conviction to many able young men who were following with keen interest every movement in the marching of the critical armies. The principles themselves are just as important today as when they were first uttered. They really represent a focusing to a sharp point of intellectual apprehension of the method which by a happy instinct, which may perhaps be described better as divine guidance, the Church has followed.

2. *Vital Perfection*

We are all familiar with the dramatic question of Sidney Lanier as to what possible fault can be found with the crystal Christ.

The very question forms a natural introduction to a discussion of the sense of perfection which has come to men of every century as they have contemplated the figure at the center of the Gospels. Sometimes they have been clearly conscious of this overwhelming impression. Sometimes it has been a subtle part of an apprehension mediated through the thought forms of various centuries. But always it has been there. And it is important from the very start to change the emphasis from that of Sidney Lanier's question, though we must remember that it is our Lord's question too, for with infinite daring He asks: "Which of you convicteth me of sin?" This freedom from stain is of overwhelming importance. But we must go on to see that the perfection of Jesus lies essentially in what He has included even more than in that from which He has turned away. It is a rich and ample thing. It is a vital perfection. You feel that He is more alive than any other person you have ever known. You feel that He is more virile than all the men you have ever met. This sense of stinging and vibrant vitality is a part of the impression He makes constantly upon men.

The pale Galilean of Swinburne's Julian the Apostate is not at all found in the Gospels. He is a product of a diseased imagination not capable of apprehending the sheer magnificence of the vitality which characterized this One Great Figure walking in the ways of men. The principle is a very far-reaching one and deserves the closest inspection. Every "Thou shalt not" in the New Testament is the prelude to a greater "Thou shalt." As you see the meaning of the discipline of an athlete when the silken movement of his muscles in the decisive moment of a race reveals a co-ordination in all the forces of his body which fills you with a sort of amazed delight, so the perfection of the New Testament Figure is not the cold perfection of endless negatives. It is the warm and glowing perfection of tremendous affirmations in action. All the restraint is for the sake of a positive and forthright living. It was this which made Him so appealing to sinners. They were suddenly aware that all that they had mistakenly tried to find in decadent vices He had gloriously found in imperial virtues. All of this in a sense constitutes the miracle of the four Gospels. For they are a literary miracle answering in their own fashion to the miracle of the life which they portray. And as we discover the way in which that subtle power which is Christian consciousness quite rightly seized upon those things to be retained and quite rightly apprehended what should be left out, we begin to discover that there was a wonderful social authorship in the forming of the New Testament canon at this point of the Gospel records. We may even come to understand what a man means when he says that in a sense Christian consciousness was the author of the four Gospels.

3. The Compelling Person

Only once in history has a figure appeared who had a complete right to use with its amplest meaning the first personal pronoun "I." He knew that this was so. Indeed, He asserted that this was so: "It hath been said by them of old time, . . . but *I* say unto you." A study of Jesus' consciousness of His own significance is an inevitable part of a serious consideration of the Gospels. With all His gracious and understanding nearness to people, He walked among men conscious that He belonged to a class which contained only one person. He did not strain after this position. He did not assert it violently as if to reassure Himself. He accepted it as the background of everything which He said and everything which He did. He was casual about it with the magnificent casualness of complete assurance.

The effect of this upon other people was constant. The experience of meeting Jesus was unlike the experience a man had ever had or would ever have in meeting another person. There was a compulsion about Jesus as if He knew more about you than you would ever know about yourself and perceived the inner meaning of your life with indubitable certainty. Rough, hard-headed, and hard-handed men felt the power of Jesus the moment He spoke to them: "Come ye after me, and I will make you to become fishers of men." Had anyone else in all the world ever seen the strange unrest at the heart of a fisherman? An angry crowd would push Him off a cliff. He walks past the sullen faces unharmed and by some strange majesty of bearing maintains His own safety. He whips the money-changers from the temple with totally inadequate material weapons. He really whips the money-changers with the piercing flash of His eye. He really whips them with the awful power of His personality.

There is the same story in the Synoptics and in the Fourth Gospel. Critical problems will have their own day in court. But this complete composite portrait which has come as a gift to the Christian Church of all ages must be seen for just what it is as a totality. There is a famous old story to the effect that in a moment of self-conscious egotism Dante once cried out, "When I am present who is absent, and when I am absent who remains?" You read the story with a certain distaste even when you connect it with the very great powers of Dante. You feel that it is rather an understatement of the exact truth when it is applied to Jesus.

He is always in command of every situation of which He is a part. Even when the days of suffering and death come, He moves through them as one who deliberately accepts their agony and not as One upon whom the tragedy has been forced. Men do the most incredible things at His suggestion. "We toiled all night, and took nothing: but at thy word I will let down the net." And, what is perhaps most astonishing, this masterful personal power moves right through the books which tell of His words and of His deeds. If a scholar can for a moment get far enough from verbal analysis to see the Person and to feel His quality, he will begin to see that this is the real miracle of the Gospels. A transcendent Person lives in them. All your scholarship is futile and barren unless it takes account of this and makes room for it and leaves it untouched. The Great Person must dominate the scholar. The scholar must not emasculate the Great Person.

Men met this Person. He met men. It all fits perfectly that frame of interpretation on which this book is built. It is always truth given through personality. And unless you feel the compulsion of the personality, you miss the real quality of the truth.

4. The Words

Words have the inevitable stamp of personality upon them. If there were no persons, there would be no words. When there are words, there are persons. Speech is not a characteristic of the subhuman. It is gloriously characteristic of the human. It rises to the height of the divine. It is the mental currency of a world of persons.

So we turn to the words of Jesus with the keenest sense that here we shall find a part at least of His secret. We are met at once by pithy sayings. They are the sort of sayings which stick like burrs in men's minds. "Ask, and it shall be given you." So simple a form of words and yet what awful assumption that the speaker has a right to make promises for the ultimate universe. The simpler the saying, the more profound the implicit authority. The God of the sparrows is much more the God of men, declares Jesus. In the most quiet and unhesitating fashion He assumes that He has the right to tell men what God is like.

Soon we come upon the mighty paradoxes of Jesus. I have always felt that in a sense a course in Gilbert Chesterton is the best possible introduction to the study of the Gospels. The partly Oriental delight in heightened statement is characteristic of Jesus. When a noble loyalty becomes first a hard convention, then a heavy burden which you cannot carry if you are also to bear the burdens of the Kingdom, He speaks out bluntly: You must be ready to hate your father and your mother at the high behest of the supreme loyalty. But He is not depreciating these earthly loyalties. One of the greatest things He has to say of God is that He is the Heavenly Father. In the swift vitality of keen conversation, one minute He throws a conception away. It does not serve His purpose. The next, He picks it up and uses it to express the very character of God.

There are the astonishing answers to questions which on the surface turn the point of an argument but always move beyond the verbal victory to a deeper meaning. Rome had mastered a people with a deep sense of national integrity when it conquered the Jews. They hated the authority to which they were forced to submit. Was it lawful to pay tribute to Caesar? If you used a coin with Caesar's image on it, you had already become a part of the vast organization which, whatever its tyrannies, had given a certain peace and order to the world. "Render unto Caesar the things that are Caesar's, and unto God the things that are God's." There is the immediate authority necessary for the practical ongoing of life. There is the ultimate authority, the final master of destiny. Render unto each what is due to it.

There were the parables of which in one of His most daring paradoxes Jesus declared that He used them so that men would not understand what He was saying. There was in truth something judicial about them. If you were a person beginning to long for moral and spiritual understanding, they allured you and drew you on. If you were a person whose life was already being set in ways of selfishness and evil, by a sound perception you instinctively disliked them.

There were values worth any sacrifice. The pearl of great price took away the attractiveness of a lesser jewel. And it is interesting to note what fascination money and its use had for Jesus. He tested men in one story by their power to make good investments. The coin of the realm could be ugly and betraying metal, but it could be used for such noble purposes that the coin itself was transfigured. However, organic figures of speech appealed to Jesus rather more deeply. There was good seed. But it was curiously limited by the kind of ground which received it. You are the soil, He was always seeming to say. What kind of ground are you giving to the truth? Life had some engrossing adventures it was easy to miss. There was the joy of finding the lost. Lost coins, lost sheep, lost people made an immediate appeal to the imagination of Jesus. He had an instant sympathy for the man who had missed his chance and the woman who had lost her way. His perfection was never of that fragile quality which fears contact with imperfection. After all, you were never hurt by the mere physical presence of evil. It was the evil to which you responded which was dangerous. And if you responded to evil, there was already evil in your own heart. But the amazing thing about a man is precisely that he can create a good which did not exist until he lived. And he can create an evil which would not have existed but for him. So out of the inner life of men comes forth evil and good.

There is the series of utterances which must summarize much public teaching of Jesus and which strike very characteristic notes of His teaching. True felicity is not found in the pompous visibilities of life. The sense of spiritual poverty may lead to a great enrichment. Those who do not try to escape life's agonies but accept them may find a comfort which comes only to honest souls. Those who have lost sight of self in a feeling of the greatness of life have already entered into a great inheritance. The passionate desire for righteousness is the beginning of its possession. The capacity to give mercy is the greatest claim on mercy for oneself. Singleness of purpose which casts out all duplicities is the road to the Kingdom of God. Those who sow seeds of peace where seeds of discord have been sown before are God's children. When you care enough for righteousness to suffer for it, the Kingdom of God is already yours. There is an order of suffering because of loyalty to the good which has the promise of great reward in it. If you are glad for the sake of that which has no seed of gladness in it, you are miserable indeed. If you bear wounds for the sake of the goodness which would bless mankind, you already begin to have a foretaste of the great happiness which is to be yours.

The friends of Christ who really belong to Him are to save the world from decay. They are to provide illumination for mankind. They are to make it easier for other men to believe in God.

There is a real continuity between the teaching of Jesus and the noble spiritual past of His people. He comes to bring that deepest meaning of their history to fulfillment and not to destroy it. But His very fulfillment sometimes revolutionizes old teachings. What complete moral victory do you have if you refrain from murder but keep murderous anger in your heart, if you refrain from deeds of lust but live with a lustful mind? Loyalty to God and to goodness is a downright thing. It demands complete and decisive faithfulness. Love of the sort God inspires finds something to love in unlovely people. It detects the unsuspected good as well as the hidden evil.

The good man is not a playwright parading his good deeds. He is as reluctant to admit his good deeds as evil men are to admit their vices. His prayers are not elaborate. There are the simple human needs he takes to God. There is the request for power to meet the deep obligation to God and to men, and the sad and honest prayer for forgiveness. The good man is a man of undivided life. He cares so much for eternal things that the temporal things fall into proper perspective. In all these words everything is deepened. The inner takes the place of the outer. The eternal dominates the temporal. The Great Teacher is building a house for men's minds which will not fall when storms come.

5. The Great Insights

When the words of Socrates fell on the ears of Xenophon, there was one set of memories. When they fell on the ears of Plato, there was another. In the Fourth Gospel you have memories full of the deepest understanding. That Christian consciousness which has been the deep-

est fact in the history of the Church at once claimed these insights as
its own. And ever since they have been a part of the complete interpretation of the life of the Great Person. Here you see His teaching passed
through a mind of amazing responsiveness to the very quality of the
mind of Jesus. And in a new way you appreciate the vitality of His
teaching. How He loves what we would now call biological figures!
He is bread satisfying men's hunger. He is water satisfying men's thirst.
He is the light of the world. He is the way, the truth, and the life. He is
the way from men to God. He is the way from God to men. He is one
with God, and He has made Himself one with men. He would have a
unity among the men who love Him like that perfect moral harmony
which binds Him to God. But He is more than living truth. He is living moral victory. "Be of good cheer; I have overcome the world." So
He gives men peace in the midst of tempest, and He admits them to that
fellowship of love which is His own Kingdom. They must grow as they
do battle with life and with truth. It will be better for them not to depend upon His physical presence. So He will go away, but a Divine
Presence will be with them as they suffer as He has suffered and conquer in His name.

6. The Deeds and the Life

The Gospels do not present a figure who in a literal sense is merely a
figure of speech. He is a Person who is alive. He wins His moral authority through personal struggle and victory. His first deeds are
achievements on the arena of His own life. He is hungry beyond endurance and refuses to use His power to give Himself an advantage
over hungry men who have no such resources. He sees a world to be
won and refuses the external mastery of an Alexander, for those who
really belong to His Kingdom must be those of gladly surrendered
hearts. For the recalcitrant He makes it clear enough in utterance after
utterance that there is to be the hard argument of irresistible strength.
But His Kingdom is to be a Kingdom of willing allegiance. He wears
the thin texture of His nerves to the very edge of endurance in spiritual
ecstasy and knows the temptation of casting away all normal relationships—a temptation which the most gifted men of the world have
known so well. The leap from the temple has sudden baffling allurement. But He walks amid the live wires of His mutinous nerves a con-
queror, completely steady, completely sane, completely sound. His
whole life until the final "It is finished" was full of moral and spiritual
struggle and of moral and spiritual victory. He wove the garment of
His perfection with sweat and tears.

He used His mighty powers lavishly for others. He did it, too, with
a certain wistful hesitation. He loved to make sick folk well. But He
knew the danger of being considered a great magician. And only by the

force of His own character did He prevent the people from acclaiming Him a prince of unearthly powers available for the purposes of their very earthly life. But He was the great physician, the great master of the forces of life. Death itself fled at His presence, the storm was stilled at His word; He could feed the body as well as the soul. And all this power He dispersed with a loving heart and a desperate sense of the importance that it should not be misunderstood. For something other than a material drama of omnipotence had He come to the world. And yet the very power which He refused to misuse was a part of what He brought to the world. He was a master in the realm of facts as well as in the realm of ideas and ideals. But His perfection was not merely the perfection of abstinence. It was the still integration of bewildering powers into a perfect unity achieved under the one great purpose of moral love. So by life and words and deeds He mastered men. And when multitudes misunderstood Him and began to turn from Him, the disciples were ready for the test: "Would ye also go away?" Peter, the spokesman as always, was ready with the reply: "To whom shall we go? thou hast the words of eternal life."

Day by day and month by month the impression deepened. At last it became imperative that a word be found big enough to contain Him. He Himself precipitated the discussion at Caesarea Philippi. "Who do men say? . . . Who say ye that I am?" And again with a flash like inspiration Peter flung back, "Thou art the Christ, the Son of the living God." Whatever the lack of dialectical skill which characterized the mind of Peter, it was clear that only the word God was capacious enough for this Great Person.

7. The Great Invitation and the Great Divide

The paradox of the work of the Great Person in history lies in the fact that He brought the great invitation and led men to the great divide. Nothing is more important for a comprehension of the genius of the Christian gospel than an apprehension of the distinctions which arise at this point. As we have seen, the first effort of Jesus was to secure a company of men and women joined to Him by ties of willing allegiance. One cannot make a kingdom of the spirit which consists of cowering slaves. A tyrant can create a totalitarian state of enforced obedience. He cannot create a free state. He cannot create a church. Those in the Kingdom of God have said "Yes" when they might have said "No." Their loyalty is the loyalty of love. It is not produced by force. It is the perpetual and joyous commitment of willing hearts. So the gospel is first of all a great invitation. "Come unto me, all ye that labor and are heavy laden, and I will give you rest." And the love which seeks men will go to astonishing lengths to break their hard hearts and to secure free and glad acceptance. It will go a second mile when one is asked. It will give the cloak when the coat is asked. At the stage of invitation, instead of resisting evil it will buffet it by deeds of love. And it will go—its Master did go—to the whole length of the Cross. Christianity is the religion of the great invitation. It is the religion of love on the Cross opening its arms and calling men to come.

Now at various times men have been tempted not only to set forth the great invitation but to conclude that it is the whole of the Christian religion. They have declared that if the sun of the divine love is allowed to shine long enough, it will melt the hardest ice of resistance. They have declared that if we bring to men the smile of God, no one will resist it forever.

This, however, is very clearly not the view of Jesus as He speaks in the Gospels. Indeed, the gospel which He brings offers men the great invitation, but it brings them to the great divide. Jesus never doubted that men could say "No" to the love of God. He never doubted that men would say "No" to the invitation of God. Man in his freedom could make evil his good. Man could and some men would confront the self-giving love of God utterly unmoved. So Jesus was always stating the great invitation with qualifications. At the great feast there was the man without the wedding garment who had to be cast out. In the party which went to meet the wedding procession there were five foolish virgins with no oil in their lamps. The doors were shut, and they were left without. There was the city so evil that an army had to be sent to destroy it. Then there was the grand and terrible picture of the great adjudication when those on the left who had made evil their good were shut out from the divine felicity forever. The sheer might of God was to restrain recalcitrant evil in the ultimate universe. The whole Christian message sees love on the Cross and judgment on the Throne. It has only doom for those who say "No" to the love of God.

Of course, all this has tremendous relevance for the human world where we live. If God must use His majestic might to restrain recalcitrant evil in the ultimate universe, we cannot expect the outbreak of this very soul of evil in the relative human world of which we are a part to be conquered by the smile of love. In time as in eternity Christianity must recognize both principles. It must speak in the voice of love on the Cross. It must also speak in the voice of judgment on the Throne. It must offer men the great invitation. It must bring them to the great divide. It must never forget that its voice is to be the voice not of sentimental gregariousness but of moral love. And moral love must at times confront the outbreaks of utter moral evil in the world, as an army with banners. Sentimental men and women have tried too casually to banish the Christian soldier from the hosts of God. St. George in shining armor still confronts the dragon.

But the other side of the paradox, too, must be kept in emphasis.

Wistfully, tenderly, at infinite sacrifice, the great invitation is presented. The whole wonder of the word "Come" must be exhausted before men hear the word "Go." And the hand lifted in judgment when the word "Depart" is spoken has the mark of a nail in it. So far has moral love gone before pronouncing sentence.

8. The Personal Experience Back of the Gospels

The Gospels are always full of the sound of human voices. And above all there is the sound of the Great Voice. Jesus is always meeting people. He is living among them. He is talking to them. He is seeing them. He is giving Himself to them. And they are giving themselves to Him. That personal experience which we have found to be basal in all thought and action is perpetually in evidence here. And all of it is poured into the vessels where the material for the four Gospels is found. It is secreted personal experience. And it is as precisely this that it is divided and judged by the processes of experience itself. All the many-sidedness set forth by Dr. Ernest F. Scott in that book of rich and varied learning *The Varieties of New Testament Religion* are easily accounted for by the richness, the many-sidedness, and the constantly personal quality of the whole process. Such an adventure in analysis as is carried out with constant and eager good will by Dr. Frederick C. Grant in *The Earliest Gospel* can easily be related as a matter of principle, if not in matters of detail, with the whole process of contact with Jesus and the gaining of these personal experiences which a clear and unconfused study of the whole situation discloses. Such a book as Dr. Clarence Tucker Craig's *The Beginning of Christianity* must, of course, with all its knowledge and understanding, meet many tests. But it is to be said without hesitation that it moves in that world of personal experience where all clear and dependable thinking must be done. Every attempt to get back of impersonal literary problems to living personal experiences is at least in that endeavor moving in the right direction.

9. The Criticism of Christian Experience

We begin to see, then, that the four Gospels came to exist through the ample and manifold personal experiences of various people with Jesus Christ. And all the while something which we may call Christian experience was being established. It was a more rich and varied thing than we have sometimes supposed. And it was the basis of the Gospel records. But more than this, Christian experience was the final judge as to what was to find a place in these records. It was the experience of many individuals. And as traditions came up for acceptance or rejection it was all the while saying: "Yes, this is right—this fits—this must have a place." Or it was saying: "No, this is wrong—it does not fit—it has no right to a place." So the canon was established. This may be said not only for the Gospels but for all the New Testament books. You can say it in various ways. You can say that the invisible spirit of God present in His Church was the guide, the judge, in a certain sense the author, of the Gospels. Or you can just say that they are the product of Christian experience. The "thumbs up" or the "thumbs down" of classical Christian experience is always the most important—and in the long run, it turns out, the final—matter in New Testament criticism.

The various movements in technical New Testament criticism have been confronted by too great a hostility on the part of their foes and too sanguine an expectation on the part of their friends. You have to watch for the impersonal rationalism which decides problems negatively before the facts are really studied. There is always a lunatic fringe carrying any principle to extremes from which the sane and the sober minded draw back. And almost always there is the vain assumption that a particular set of critical instruments may change the essential characteristics of the Christian faith. Even the friendly scholar is likely to chuckle over the omniscience with which some practitioners of form criticism tell us what Jesus could have said and what was quite indubitably the contribution of an editor. The Christian faith does not stand or fall in connection with the meticulous and patient processes of analysis of even very good scholars. In the long run they are judged by classical Christianity. And by it they stand or fall.

But for all that every scholar must have his hearing. Every movement must have its hearing. And it always will turn out that something precious has been added to our understanding even by what we may be tempted to call the more rationalistic processes of criticism. But when this has been said, it remains true that the New Testament is the creation of living Christian experience, and living Christian experience is its final judge.

To put it in another way, from the men in whose souls the Christian fire burns today to the men who talked with Jesus there is a person to person series of contacts moving through the centuries. This gives the Protestant his equivalent of the Latin conception of the authority of the Church. And by this authority of Christian experience the whole of the Gospels, and the whole of the New Testament, has a right to speak and must be heard. This is the result of the criticism of Christian experience whose judgment is final for the contents of the Christian faith. It is a matter of living personal relations perpetually renewed. It is the only kind of authority able to secure and maintain indubitable authenticity in a personal world.

10. The Human Life Divine

So the Great Person walked among men. So He spoke words which could not be forgotten. So He wrought deeds, the memory of which cannot be allowed to fade away. So He lived a life which found words for the telling of the tale of it, which make the literary miracle of a divinely human book to tell the story of a Divinely Human Person.

He was a real man. The thousand revealing terms of speech and qualities of life which have been captured by the memory of the Gospels tell us this with unquestionable certainty. He is on our side of the gulf separating the infinite and the finite. There is no make-believe or noble deception about His nearness to us. He is bone of our bone and flesh of our flesh.

But this Person who crossed the gulf separating time from eternity came from the eternal world. In Him eternity breaks into time. In Him the infinite becomes the finite. In Him God becomes a man. The Word became flesh and dwelt among us.

Here as ever the central matters are parts of the personal experience. The God-man is not the fastening together of two impossibilities by the external nexus of men's words. He is one of us. He is God come among us. What we see in Him is the very quality of the Divine Character—the very actuality of the divine life made real under the conditions of human living. So His life is in very truth the human life divine. The God who had spoken in the prophets is now the God who has come in His Son. And although His earthly form is not within our vision, He Himself is with us now and forever more.

CHAPTER XIII

Religion as Redemption

PRINCIPAL Peter T. Forsyth was probably the most brilliant master of theological dialectic in the British Isles during the first quarter of the twentieth century. His irony was so coruscating, his paradoxes were so daring, and his style so redolent of explosive epigrams, that pedestrian thinkers were likely to find themselves first annoyed and then repulsed. But under all the pyrotechnics a first-class mind was at work, and an intelligence set against all forms of mental dishonesty and moral obfuscation. There was something very solid about this mind although it played like quicksilver. And back of the solid mental qualities there was a person who knew the Great Evangel as a matter of individual experience. Forsyth was always a little more than shy about talking of the critical time in his own life when he ceased to be the eager and flashing advocate of a liberalism which had traveled everywhere and had sounded no depths and when he became a convinced evangelical using every power of an extraordinarily sensitive and penetrating mind to establish the evangelical position. But the results of that time of crisis were clear enough in all his afterlife. When he coined the phrase "the cruciality of the Cross," some men who were shrewder in analyzing an etymology than in apprehending an insight criticized the phrase with much gusto. What he was really saying was that the fact that the Cross had led to the existence of the word "crucial" is the most important fact about the Christian religion. He belonged to that great company of men throughout the centuries to whom the Cross has been the Christian religion. To him Christianity was essentially the Great Redemption.

1. Ideas Connected with Religion as Redemption

The study of religion is inevitably approached by means of implicit presuppositions on the part of the thinker. It is possible to write a gregarious and sentimental interpretation of religions on the basis of the assumption that they are all equally true. It is possible to make a study of religions on the basis of the assumption that one must take the life from every religious idea before it is ready for use in a scientific study of religion. It is possible to approach the study of religions on the basis of the assumption that one has no assumptions, and that is the most dangerous assumption of all. It is possible to write voluminously in such a fashion as to manifest a genius for missing the significant and

176

dignifying the irrelevant. It is, on the other hand, possible to discover the genius of the one defining ethical religion and to see everything else in its shining light.

When one enters upon a study of religion as redemption, it is particularly easy to lose one's way. There is no end of sacrifice and blood-letting in ethnic cults, there is no end of magical formulas of appeasement of angry gods, there is no end of rites sometimes cruel, sometimes sensual, all of which have significance but all of which may be studied in such a way as to clutter up the intelligence.

We do not propose in this chapter to approach ethical religion through a study of unethical rites, now and then lighted with a sense of wistful ethical longing. We propose to go right to the supreme ethical religion and to contemplate its classical form in evangelical experience. No doubt the fierce light which falls upon evangelical religion is capable of shining out and illuminating many dark places. At all events we do not propose to study the circumference to find the meaning of the center. We propose to study the center and to attempt to find a meaning which goes out to the circumference. All instincts immature, all purposes unsure, all the varied experiments and false turnings in the strange and checkered history of the religions of the world, no doubt can be understood so that they may be turned to very important uses. It might even be possible to create a vast dialectic of the false and by a process of elimination to move ever nearer to an approximation of the true. If it were possible to have a collection of the biographies of all the cripples in the world, it would no doubt throw valuable light on the uses of legs. But the study of one sound human organism is rather more rewarding. So we shall not stop for a study of human sacrifice and its relation to religions of redemption, or of baths in the blood of bulls and their relation to men's thought of cleansing, or of all the vast paraphernalia of confusion through which men have tried to find their way. This sort of study is, of course, legitimate enough and may be very rewarding indeed. But if we look out over all these regions of human experiment from the vantage ground of the classical religion of redemption, the rewards will be greatest of all. When there come to what seems to be an untutored clod thoughts of destiny and God, the experience is never to be treated lightly or casually. But the full sunshine of understanding has certain advantages all its own.

It is also important to remember that a great conception is never to be judged by its history. It is rather to be judged by its consummation. The important matter is not that from which it comes. It is that to which it leads. A process is to be judged in the light of its completion. There are many false starts. And often they are valuable only in pointing out ways to be avoided. The clue is to be found in the good conclusion. Even the false starts are seen in a new perspective when viewed in the light of the genuine consummation. There is, of course, a type of pathological mind which is restless in the presence of the true unless it has been fertilized by the false. It would find heaven inconclusive unless it had had a try at hell. The cult of trying all the possibilities has a certain spacious plausibility. But the garments of urbane open-mindedness cover a good deal which is not very capable of standing up to critical inspection. One does not need to try all the diseases in order to be ready to vote for health.

Logan Pearsall Smith has a very naughty tale in the *Trivia* of a parish clergyman who became so much interested in certain naturalistic forms of religion that he shocked his congregation by a seasonal festival with symbols rather remote from a decent civilization. The clergyman ended conveniently in a house of detention for the mildly mad. Sometimes the wisdom of the children of this world is sharper than that of some of those who regard themselves as sons of light.

2. The Classical Form of Christian Experience

One can, of course, begin by going right to the New Testament. There one will find various types of Christian experience. There preeminently one will find evangelical Christian experience. One will find Paul.

But there is another way to approach the whole matter. One can begin with evangelical experience as a phenomenon in the life of the Christian Church. One can see it in these large relations. One can make some historical studies in different centuries. Then one can go back and confront Paul in the light of the vast ramifications of evangelical experience. In a sense one can allow the Christian centuries to shed their light on Paul. And at last one can see the Pauline experience and the Pauline theology in the perspective of the whole history of Christian experience of this type in the Church. And so we shall see the tale of the adventures of human persons with the God of moral love in what may turn out to be the clearest possible way.

Let us take John Bunyan. The Bedford tinker is an amazing person in the life of seventeenth-century England. None of the cool and clear urbanity of a period when English society guided by Charles II was going to school to France is reflected in his writing. None of the sometimes succulently sweet qualities moving out from the German pietism of the seventeenth century upon the world is found in his writing. He is a very sturdy Englishman of the people. Something of the England of Hugh Latimer has got into his blood. He has a crisp and downright speech. He has a mind clear and keen. He has an imagination at times all aglow with spiritual light. He does battle for his soul. He is in the

conflict between darkness and light. He is mastered by the things of the
spirit. But that mastery is a very practical thing such as can come to a
real man in a real world of experience. He knows torturing unrest. He
finds ineffable peace. He puts the tale of it into *Pilgrim's Progress,* and
indeed into other books as well. *Pilgrim's Progress* is in a sense his own
spiritual autobiography. But it is literally the spiritual autobiography
of millions of other Christians who in its pages become articulate. That
Pilgrim's Progress helped to create the type of experience it described,
there can be no doubt. But millions of people do not rush at a type
of experience just because it is described in a book. Christian was just
what his name implies, a typical Christian in the great tradition.

The great moral and spiritual realities became supremely masterful
to Christian. The city which had a right to be became more real than
the city in which he lived. His town had the seed of death in it. He set
off to find the city which could not be destroyed. He journeyed bearing
a heavy burden on his back. Directed by Evangelist, he came to a Cross.
And as he gazed at the Cross, the burden rolled away.

Bunyan knew nothing of the processes of training through which a
Jewish boy passed. He knew little enough of Levitical law, and in a
sense his interest was even less than his knowledge. He was not trying
to imitate an experience described by someone else in the terms of an
alien culture. Everything he wrote has a fiercely firsthand quality. It
has all the authenticity of the immediate.

He too, like Christian, had carried a heavy burden. He too, like
Christian, had carried that burden to the Cross. And he too, like Christian, had found that at the Cross the burden rolled away.

Since the time of Bunyan no end of pseudo evangelicals have used
the vocabulary of this glowing speech with little awareness of realities
back of the words. And there are a good many people of quiet dignity
and restraint whom the pseudo evangelicals have robbed of the evangel.
We must endeavor to get back to the first fine rapture, not merely in
the seventeenth century, but in every century when the evangel has
become so real that it has set religion to music, the music of a great and
triumphant gladness.

Shall we try to find some ways in which the central truth of the
matter can be expressed?

You must be your true self. But you cannot be your true self without
God. The fire of God is a dangerous thing. It brings heat and light. But
it easily becomes conflagration. What if the fire without which you cannot live were to destroy you? You are only a piece of a person without
God. But you cannot get to God. And how will God come to you in ways
which will bring satisfaction without bringing destruction? There is
that strange man of Nazareth. He hides the divine glory a little so that

it does not destroy. But it always shines in His face, is glorious in His words and majestic in His life. And even He reveals a glory which may well smite you to the earth. His perfections stab and smite even when He means them to be only friendly. You cannot do·without them. What can you possibly do with them? Then you see Him despised and rejected of men. You see Him suffering upon the Cross. You stand by while He dies. You know that He dies for you and for men like you. And in His death He has made God real without making Him a destroying fire. Perfection on the Cross heals men. Perfection on the Cross re-creates men. Death on the Cross produces life in men who see it for what it is and who make it their own.

Suppose we put it in another way. A man cannot live without his ideals. They are the stars in his sky. But how can he live with them? They become so engrossing. They become so commanding. They terrify. A man is haunted by moral dreams which betray him even as they glorify him. The very conscience which is a nexus joining him to God is a revealer showing his utter moral incapacity, his inevitable moral failure. He cannot be saved without his conscience. But the sad, bitter honesty of his conscience makes salvation impossible. God the Perfect only confirms the verdict. But the suffering God making His own perfection the servant of pain for the imperfect changes everything. If perfect goodness can suffer for the unworthy, making its imperfection a burden which the Perfect God gladly bears in an agony with the joy of saving at the heart of it, then we can see why the burden rolls away at the Cross.

Let us make one more trial. On the impersonal level there is no repentance, and there is no salvation. Moral facts are there. We can only declare them. Immoral facts are there. We can only let them work out their effect by a moral chemistry which is inevitable and irresistible. But on the level of personal relationships that is possible which could not happen on the level of mere hard, objective facts. A sinful person may love goodness in great agony. A good person may love a sinner for his capacity to love the goodness he has betrayed. The Perfect Person in a great deed of suffering agony and death may change the whole world of moral relationships and open the gates to a new life of transformed purposes, transformed motives, renewed life. Persons can do what abstract laws can never do. The death of Christ upon the Cross is the greatest personal event of history.

Whatever else may come into the mind of a man who attempts to follow such processes of analysis as these, one thing is sure. If he knows something of the history of Christian experience, he will be aware that he is nearing the place where the Shekinah shines. He is hearing the notes which belong to the classical type of Christian experience.

3. Some Historical Examples

Let us then make the appeal to history. Of course, volumes and volumes would be necessary for an adequate treatment of this appeal. We must get such content as we may from a few examples.

Suppose we look in upon Dr. Alexander Whyte. Many would say he was the greatest Scottish preacher of his time. He was soundly trained in the humanities. And he loved their sweet reasonableness with a great and surpassing devotion. He would have understood Paul Shorey's word about the passionate pursuit of their passionless perfection. But rich and profound as was his culture, it was not here that his soul dwelt. The sense of owing everything to the Christ who called him from the Cross was literally the defining matter in his life. And he believed with all his heart that it ought to be the defining matter in the lives of all men. He preached it with a quivering vitality which searched the conscience of Scotland and made the Christian religion a new and commanding thing in the lives of multitudes of people. He saw Christian history in the light of it. And year by year he published the series of volumes on the Evangelical Succession in which he called many able men to come to Edinburgh to interpret the central matters in evangelical religion through a study of evangelical leaders from Paul down through the centuries. None of this represents the compulsion of an alien religious culture imposing upon men a format of the conscience and the soul foreign to the real meaning of their lives. To Whyte, and to the men he gloriously interpreted, this sense of religion as redemption through the Cross of Christ was so deep and real that it would well seem that he himself must have seen and proclaimed it if no one else had seen and proclaimed it before.

Suppose we think of Bishop Lancelot Andrewes, the saint and scholar of the currupt court of James I, whose *Private Devotions* are among the priceless documents of the life man lives in conscious relation to God. Andrewes was a man of superb intellectual powers. The wily Francis Bacon, whose intellectual energies were so much more vital than the moral forces of his character, was proud to submit the subtlest products of his thought and learning to Lancelot Andrewes. The life of the Bishop in the court of James was an amazing study of sparkling white against a very dark background. He was also an outstanding man among the learned figures of Europe, and when he entertained one of the greatest of European scholars it was as when prince meets prince. So with ample intellectual distinction he moved among the men of the great world and was himself a notable part of the pomp and circumstance of his time. But it is in his *Private Devotions* that his soul is revealed. Here you see the humble penitent beating his breast in the presence of the white glory of the Holy God. Here you see the devout

evangelical Christian personally accepting and constantly renewing his
loyal appropriation of the great redemption. Looking back from his
own century, Alexander Whyte finds in Lancelot Andrewes an evangelical Christian after his own heart.

Let us turn to General William Booth. Perhaps it is only through
Vachel Lindsay's wholly astonishing poem that the sophisticated are
really able to see him for something of what he was. Here you do not
have the noble humanism of Whyte or the distinguished gentility of
Lancelot Andrewes. But you do have precisely the same sense of the
Christian as a man who owes everything to the Cross of Christ. You
can imagine Booth and Whyte and Andrewes meeting on some high-
land of fellowship in the afterlife, very little interested in many things
which had seemed important in their human world but eternally aflame
with love to the Divine Person whose death upon the Cross opened the
gates of new life to them. Booth made articulate to the last and the
lowest and the least the same gospel of redemption which was the living
passion of Andrewes and of Whyte.

Let us think of Robert E. Lee, the royal knight of a genuine Southern
chivalry. If we had no other way of knowing what the South at its best
was like, it would be enough to know Robert E. Lee. A great and in-
corruptible gentleman, a military genius whose equal America has not
produced, a man who wore the garments of an authentic nobility, he
was at the center of everything else a man of the great redemption. He
did not wear the heart of his religion on his sleeve. But no one who
has had any true contact with the literature in which Lee actually lives
doubts that he was another of the great company of those who felt that
they owed everything to the great deed accomplished by the Son of God
upon the Cross.

When we begin to count these beads, of course, the experience is
endless. The hall of fame for men of faith in the eleventh chapter of
Hebrews suggests another great list of men of the Christian redemption.
John Wesley, the precise little Oxford scholar whose heart was strangely
warmed, would have a place all his own. And he would speak for millions of others: miners whose tears wiped the black coal dust from their
faces, men as seraphic as Fletcher of Madeley, and pioneer proclaimers
of the Cross like Francis Asbury. Martin Luther would walk into the
company, his rich peasant face and his keen scholar's eye glowing with
the peace of the great redemption. And with him would come a vast
company of men and women who bear his name in order that they may
express the sense of the fashion in which they learned to bear the name
of the Christ of the Cross. Augustine, the hot-blooded, sharp-minded
North African who ruled the intelligence of Europe for a thousand
years, would call from his *Confessions* and the stately tomes of his
theology in the unmistakable tones of a man who, moving through all

the ways of an intricate theology, comes to the great peace of a vast simplicity in the presence of the Cross of Christ, always a man of the great redemption.

We are saying that the only way to approach the New Testament interpretation of a Cross-centered Christianity is through the vast and overwhelming testimony of the mighty men of Christian history.

4. The Reverse Approach to Paul Through Twenty Centuries of Christian Experience

The man who knows the vast and overwhelming history of evangelical piety in the Christian Church is ready in the light of it to see with clear eyes all the New Testament writings and especially the writings of Paul.

One sees at once the advantage of this approach. Nobody would be studying the Pauline theology if the tracks of Paul were not found all over the world. The study of the whole body of evangelical life and action through the passing centuries gives one just the proper clues for understanding the interpretation of evangelical religion in the New Testament. For first of all we must understand that, whatever the varieties of thought and expression in the writings of the New Testament, they speak with one voice in the presence of the Cross. All the Gospels tell the tale of Calvary with a wealth of detail and a fullness of emphasis which clearly say that everything else leads up to this, and this is the most important matter of all.

It is sound Synoptic doctrine that Jesus taught the disciples the necessity of His death. It is sound Synoptic doctrine that in instituting the Lord's Supper, Jesus said: "This is my blood of the covenant, which is poured out for many unto remission of sins." The Fourth Gospel puts the Cross in the central place: "And I, if I be lifted up from the earth, will draw all men unto myself." "The good shepherd layeth down his life for the sheep."

Indeed, a close and careful study of the New Testament writings makes it abundantly clear that there was a universal sense in the early Church of the significance of the Cross.

In a sense all the separate rays of evangelical consciousness are focused in the white light of the teaching of Paul. And when we come to Paul's experience from a study of Wesley and Luther and Augustine, it is clear that we are dealing with precisely the same type of experience in the life of a different man and a different age. We have misunderstood some things Paul said because we have thought that he said them as a Jew when as a matter of fact he said them as a human being. All that he says of the Old Testament law and the necessity of its being transcended by the divine grace is deeply related to that law which becomes too much for any man who tries to realize a complete ideal or to do perfectly the will of God. This doctrine of freedom through the grace of God which is set forth so passionately in the Epistle to the Galatians is a word to all mankind, for all need the same freedom. The doctrine of a righteousness of faith set forth with such elaborate dialectic in the Epistle to the Romans is for all mankind. Only if this were true could the deep and penetrating evangelical experience of twenty centuries have come to be what it has become. And nothing could be clearer from Paul's own writings than the fact that it is autobiography first and doctrine second.

Nothing could be crasser than Matthew Arnold's suggestion that Paul Judaizes when he speaks of those high matters. The whole weight of the experience of evangelical Christianity is against Arnold and with Paul.

And the heart of it all as the story of Paul's own experience is clear enough. He took his religion seriously. He took the Old Testament revelation as a great moral demand. All this he must do if he would earn the peace of God, if he would be justified by deeds. He had possession of a magnificently complete moral revelation. And this made the tragedy even more acute. The more he knew the less he could do. The law of God made him a slave to a task he could not perform. And his very earnestness became a heartbreaking tragedy. But what Paul saw was that this is an essentially human experience. It happened to him not because he was a Jew but because he was a human being. Every man of every culture and civilization and even of every religion finds when he tries to live with an earnestness as passionate as that of Paul that life asks more of him than he can do. He is a slave to a demand he cannot fulfill. And what Paul discovers with a burst of joy which never leaves him to his life's end is that he is not expected to earn peace by slavery to a hard demand. He is to receive peace as a gift of God through the Christ who died for Him on the Cross. Not what he does for God but what Christ has done for him is the central matter. And by a noble paradox the moment he ceases to be the slave of moral demand and becomes the son of a great moral freedom he keeps the law in its inner meaning as he never could do in his days of meticulous observation. This freedom of a living trust in the Christ of the Cross is the freedom he commends to the Galatians. This righteousness of a great trust which finds goodness in what God gives to you and not in what you do for Him, and yet enables you as a free son to do for Him what you never could do as a slave dragging the chains, is the very essence of the Epistle to the Romans. Every evangelical Christian about whom you know in all the centuries of Christian biography is its interpreter. The one place where no Christian has a right to go wrong is in the interpretation of Paul. Of course, the scholar who has never had an evangelical experience is sure to go wrong. He is like a grammarian who has never been in love trying painfully to interpret Elizabeth Barrett Browning's "Sonnets from the Portuguese."

5. The Pauline Theology and Classical Christianity

Paul has had many friends. He has had many foes. And he has survived both his friends and his foes. He has had to triumph in spite of the misunderstandings of his friends and the hostility of his foes. And his power—this we must well understand—has come from the fact that he has spoken so deeply to men that the sheer cut of his insight has mastered them. It can all be said best when we declare that classical Christianity is Pauline. This becomes clear as we read the words of Tertullian, and feel the quality of the leadership of Gregory the Great, and watch the impact of Bernard of Clairvaux upon the twelfth century. We find the same note in the piety of St. Francis of Assisi in the thirteenth century. It is deep in the thought of Wycliffe in the fourteenth century. We cannot understand Huss without it in the fifteenth century. It is at the root of the theology of John Calvin. It is central in the thought of John Knox. It is central in Anglican piety as it becomes conscious of the meaning of its own life. Lutheran and Reformed theology and the religious experience which that theology crystallizes are united here. The Clapham group in England could not have existed without the Pauline type of religion. The modern missionary movement bloomed on the plant which came from its seeds. The Methodist revival set the Pauline doctrine of the Cross singing in men's hearts. The Salvation Army taught it to use drums and tamborines. Men felt that they owed everything to the Christ of the Cross. They gave themselves to Him in a great leaping act of faith, trusting their past, their present, and their future to His grace. It was Paul who made the experience theology. And nobody has ever been able to give good account of it intellectually except on the Pauline basis. It is classical Christianity.

6. "Other Sheep"

To be sure, there are other sheep who do not belong to this evangelical flock. But they do belong to the fold of Christ. And there is one Shepherd. I remember once having a vigorous conversation with my friend and teacher Dr. Olin A. Curtis, who was a very stout evangelical if there ever was one, and who was also a man of cosmopolitan intellectual interests. We were talking of a very great Scottish preacher who rendered deep and lasting service to the Christian Church. "You must admit," I remember saying, "that he was not an evangelical." Dr. Curtis' eyes flashed in a way that was rather characteristic of him, and he turned upon me with some impatience. "Surely you have not known me all these years," he said, "without understanding that of course I recognize the possibility of the moral equivalent of an evangelical experience."

There you have it. The experience which centers in the Cross is classical Christianity. But there are types of Christian experience which in their own way are true though they are not classical. You find indubitable evidence of this in the Epistle of James in the New Testament. You find it in mood, if not always in sharp discrimination, in some of the Greek fathers. You find it in Abelard. You find it in Erasmus. You find it in Zwingli. You find it in some of the moods of some of the Cambridge Platonists. And so one might go on and on. If a man has made the doing of the will of Christ his central loyalty, he is a true Christian even if he has not had an evangelical experience. But this is not saying that he is a productive Christian in the same powerful and creative sense which has characterized the great evangelicals. Wherever in all the long story of the Church evangelicals have been in the place of supreme influence, the Church has prospered and its influence upon the world has been transforming. Wherever their influence has waned, the Church has tended to become arid and unproductive.

7. Great Christians Who Were Not Evangelicals

The spectacle of Luther and Zwingli meeting for conference about great matters and parting in disagreement is not very edifying, but it is most significant. Not only do we see the profounder moral and spiritual quality of Luther, but we also see that, more than Luther knew, Zwingli was a man of profound sincerity, a loyal Christian, ready to give his life for that in which he believed. When Bernard of Clairvaux pursues Abelard like an avenging fury, we feel, if we know the whole life of Bernard, what a grand and imperial person he was and how deep was his sense of the profoundest meaning of the Christian religion. But Abelard, fragile and all too human, surely has a heart which belongs to Christ. Surely he has his place in the one flock. And where everyone owes everything to the grace of Christ, surely it is not scornfully to be held against him that he owed so much to the divine forgiveness.

The century of Wesley saw the spectacle of many a stately latitudinarian who was earnest and sincere and committed to the doing of the will of God even though he quite missed the secret of the great evangel.

The nineteenth century, which beheld such sturdy evangelicals in Dr. Spurgeon and Dr. Dale and Cardinal Newman and many another, also saw figures of great impressiveness as Christian leaders who walked outside the evangelical tradition. Charles Kingsley was a stout Christian, but he would have felt ill at ease in the presence of John Bunyan. George Macdonald knew everything about Scotland except the heart of the evangelical tradition. Matthew Arnold was in his way a loyal Christian, but the classical Christian tradition was a closed book to him.

Twentieth-century America has mighty evangelical preachers. But it has also men of eminent power and influence who have never come within sight of the deeper meaning of the Cross. They do a good work in a good way. And they leave the deepest word of all to be said by other men.

8. The Soft Substitutes

One cannot speak urbanely, however, about all the substitutes for evangelical Christianity. There are men who have never faced moral problems seriously and who have never really understood the deadliness of making evil one's good, whose soft and sentimental influence has gone like a poison through the Christian Church. They have never understood that the love of God is moral love, and the love of which they speak is not the love of the New Testament. As far as they are concerned, the religion of the great redemption has been succeeded by the religion of the great gregariousness. Nearly all the obsessions which come in our time from taking a part of Christianity for the whole take the form of seeing Christianity without the stern integrity of its doctrine of sin. Men live in a world whose great defect, as they see it, is bad judgment. And as they see it, what that world needs is intellectual illumination. But intellectual illumination can never take the place of moral transformation. So all the soft substitutes for the honest realism of the religion of the great redemption bring blight to the Church which they profess to serve. The gospel of moral love is scarcely served by the apostles of unethical sentimentality.

9. The Modern Experience of Redemption

We have been claiming that the very structure of human nature and the very processes of personal human experience so relate themselves to the facts and the sanctions of ethical religion as to give the evangelical position an authenticity only appreciated when approached through the deepest vitalities of experience itself. The message of the Cross speaks to men as does no other message. Throughout Church history, in defiance of human complacency and on the wrecks of human folly and failure, it has maintained itself with a sort of imperial power.

It must be said frankly, however, that the modern man meets all this in the midst of certain very grave difficulties. The world in which we live has been much more engaged in mastering the forces of nature than in achieving human control on the level of personal discipline. It is expert in the presence of things. It is confused in the presence of persons. Even the scientist in the laboratory is likely to be so busy with the impersonal mathematics of the things he is studying and classifying and controlling that he forgets his own free mind doing the controlling. Not only so, but over vast areas the attempts to interpret personal experiences in impersonal terms have run riot. So we have had a psychology which has been engaged merely with the physiological accompaniments of mental action. And we have had a left-wing sociology which has reduced social relationships to impersonal and largely abstract social forces. In all this the free man has lost the sense of his own importance.

All of this has produced the modern debacle. Man has not made a success of interpreting life and acting in life in the terms of mathematical formulas rather than in the terms of free personal choices. The rebellion of man in the presence of the tyranny of things is the most important matter in contemporary life. The modern man is learning that, even where he has good formulas, a free man must use them. He cannot think merely in terms of the automobile and forget the driver. He cannot think merely in terms of the airship and forget the pilot. The so-called social forces all depend at last on free human choices. Even the totalitarian state depends on the free choices of the tyrant. He must be free even if he masters a world of slaves. And he must be overthrown by those who reassert the rights of all free men. For the very sake of society a new cult of the individual would be necessary. But, even deeper than this, the free individual making good choices is the finally significant matter in the world.

It is in the light of such facts as these that the great historical interpretation of religion as the redemption of the individual gets a new hearing. Man is driven in upon himself whenever he really exercises critical intelligence. And when he faces the moral meaning of life, classical Christianity gets a stupendous and glorious hearing.

For a man can attain individual co-ordination in this or in any age only through the grace of God. Life is too big for him. He cannot meet it alone. Only a man with the help of God can find harmony and peace and power. But when a man faces the true meaning of his own life, he finds more than inner incapacity which must be supplemented by the divine power; he finds inner treachery which must be met by the divine forgiveness. As soon as he is brave enough to refuse to hide behind his environment and to face his own capacity to create both good and evil, he lives in a new world. And when he honestly faces the fact that he has used that capacity to create evil, he has come to the place where he can hear the Divine Word speaking from the Cross with an actual sense of its authenticity. The experience of personal repentance, the experience of personal pardon through the grace of God offered in Jesus Christ, the experience of power through a divine fellowship—these become the supreme facts of his life. And he, the new man in Christ, approaches all social problems and all social tragedies and all social tasks with a new equipment. It is at this point that the modern man can turn from frustration and confusion and failure to achievement and creative life and intellectual understanding and moral and spiritual victory. So in the new terms of the new life of the new day he rediscovers the great evangel.

CHAPTER XIV

Religion as Apocalypse

A POET who cared for William Blake once wrote the following lines:

> He came to the desert of London town,
>   Gray miles long;
> He wandered up and he wandered down,
>   Singing a quiet song.
>
> He came to the desert of London town,
>   Mirk miles broad;
> He wandered up and he wandered down,
>   Ever alone with God.

There were so many enigmas about Blake that it would be a brave man who would suggest that one approach apocalyptic writing through his fascinating visions. Since no one really understands Blake, it might be argued, why use one mystery to unravel another? The situation is not quite as bad as that, however, though confessedly it is difficult enough. There was no doubt a touch of the charlatan about Blake. But there was much that had nothing to do with the charlatan. And there was sometimes the essence of wisdom. Yet he was a man who approached truth by seeing it rather than by thinking about it. Phillips Brooks once defined preaching as truth given through personality. William Blake might have defined poetry—his kind of poetry—as truth given through the imagination. To him the invisible was more real than the visible. The eternal was more magnificently present than the temporal. He brushed aside the shrewd materialisms of a day engrossed with the pursuit of things as a man might brush away a fly which had lighted upon his face. So in Blake we do see a modern man having the type of experience out of which apocalyptic writing comes. He lifted the flag of his brave invisible world in the presence of all the hard visibilities and quite casually declared, *This is the real.* It is the casualness which is so instantly impressive. Blake knows the whole value of being so sure that he does not need to argue. He proclaims. This, too, is the mood of apocalyptic. But the central point is this: There is so much that is obviously true, said with a certain royal splendor, that you soon come to understand that you must take him seriously. He lives not because of his oddities and eccentricities but because of his central insights.

And really, when you stop to think of it, for precisely the same reason the classical apocalyptic writings, Daniel and the book of Revelation, made their place secure in the canon of the Old Testament and the canon of the New. You can almost see the knitted eyebrows and the shaking heads. "Surely this will never do." Then a page is turned, and there is a royal sentence flowing from the very heart of reality itself. "Surely this will do. Surely this must do."

It is all a matter of central experience of personal meanings personally appropriated. And again it all fits in with the central contention of this book, that consciousness dealing with living relationships between persons is the main matter in existence. For the writer of apocalyptic literature never loses himself in impersonal abstractions. His very imagery is always richly personal.

1. The Conditions of the Rise of Apocalyptic Literature

Speaking broadly, apocalypse always arises in a time when the world of facts is set in battle array against the world of ideals, and quite obviously the world of ideals is being defeated. Right is on the scaffold. Wrong is on the throne. It is not even safe to speak frankly of the great things in which one believes in the presence of the triumphant powers of evil. Those who have kept their souls pure are a remnant. They are invisible to the naked eye. And when they speak to each other it must be in symbols whose sharp general meaning is clear enough to them but will be incomprehensible to their foes. So the stage is set for the apocalyptic writer and for his works. He is not an idle and luxurious dreamer tempted to fall into a mood of ennui and scarcely able to rouse his dull mind to a state of keen interest in anything whatever. He is not like the rich author of the book of Ecclesiastes who has possessed the body of everything and has lost the soul of everything, and who cries "All is vanity" because he has kept only that which fire destroys and has allowed to escape everything which fire cannot touch.

The writer of an apocalypse has seen everything which he cares about trampled underfoot. And suddenly it has become unbelievably precious. You see the value of the thing you are about to lose. So men in oppressed European lands and soldiers on battlefields all around the world have suddenly become aware of the utter value of things which they had all too easily taken for granted. The apocalyptic writing is always dramatic. And the drama is not something which the writer invents. It is something he finds in the tragedy which is unfolding all around him. He simply must appeal from visible facts to invisible facts if he is to go on living. It is this central definiteness in all his thought and struggle which must be kept in mind as we read his writing. It means everything to him, and it must mean everything to us. He picks his figures and his symbols with an almost wild lawlessness. He is not at all ill at ease if you show him that he has been incoherent in his use of figures. A figure is seen in the sharp light for a moment, and behold, you have seen one aspect of truth. Is truth a rich and manifold thing? Very well, just be patient. Soon another figure will be seen in the full light of dramatic presentation and another aspect of truth will become clear. It will all be nonsense to you if you have no experience which parallels that of the writer. But if you can match his experiences you will begin to play with his symbols as if you yourself had invented them. This is the reason that whenever there is a crisis in the life of a nation or of the world and evil seems to be set securely on the throne, there is always a new interest in apocalypse. Living experience gives the key and the locks begin to open.

2. *Sense of Complete Frustration in the Presence of Evil Powers*

"Careless seems the Great Avenger." That is always the background of apocalypse. In the days of Antiochus Epiphanes, a brilliant and lawless and triumphant paganism seemed about to blot out the Jewish faith. It was a decadent Greece which was on the throne. But there was all the fascination of belief in this life and this world given a certain dignity by the Greek past. It was a kind of barbarous primitiveness made distinguished by Greek garments. The shattering victories of Alexander had made a great impression upon mankind. And when his generals divided and organized the world, that too seemed to belong to an order of irresistible fact. And Antiochus Epiphanes, with his mad and glittering intelligence, may at times have seemed more like a portent of nature than a man. A sense of dark and heavy frustration settled upon the people who inherited the Jewish faith. There is something not unlike hysteria which runs through these dark and terrible days. And when the book of Daniel comes it is as if the blackness of time is confronted by the light of eternity.

At a later time, when Rome definitely sets itself against the new faith which is spreading about the world, there is the same sense of awful finality. In the most impressive way Rome belonged to the world of fact. Rome was the master of the world. And with a certain gesture of inspired generosity Rome had made a place for little faiths in the great empire. If the small faith of your small land was precious to you, Rome was quite ready to have you keep it under the all-inclusive and absolute splendor of the emperor worship. But Rome had no room for a moral God who would judge Roman emperors. Rome had no room for a moral religion at whose bar the empire itself would be judged. So the new faith almost in swaddling clothes confronted the great empire clad in the armor which centuries of triumph had made possible. What could this little faith of a little and timid people hiding about the world do against the might of imperial Rome? Again the experience of frustration came heavily upon many minds and many hearts. The facts all pointed one way. Truth and right pointed another.

Then through the bitter silence came the voices which speak in the book of Revelation. Here was something more imperial than Rome.

Here was something greater than the power of the emperor seated on his throne in the city of the seven hills. Here was an invisible throne which judged all visible thrones. Here was the stark reality of eternity against the passing shadows of time which seemed so mighty while they lasted, but which were so impotent in the presence of the living God and the mighty instruments of His will.

If you are to realize the depth of gloom in which the new voices were heard, you must witness the drama of broken homes, you must see the scythe of death mowing down the Christians, you must apprehend the vast and awful strength of the empire which had said in effect, "O Christ, you shall not be." The Christians had been driven into hiding. From the depths they had cried unto God. And the spectacle of those who could not stand the strain but surrendered the purest faith which had ever been offered to mankind was a shame never to be forgotten. Suffering became intense. It became too intense. Often it became psychopathic. Indeed, you can say that at times apocalyptic writing represents the use of the psychopathic as an instrument for the discovery of truth. Of course, the mind staggers if this sort of thing is carried too far. But even then, as Robert Browning has reminded us in that startling poem "Childe Roland to the Dark Tower Came," some central insight may be maintained and expressed. By a miracle of passionate vision the worst turns to be the best in the great Apocalypse.

3. The Faith of the Hopeless Minority

When we confront a man who obviously has nothing and suddenly discovers that he has everything, it is a dramatic experience. The throne of the Caesars rested solidly upon the crushed-out dreams of men who supposed that they could judge Rome. But the writer of the New Testament Apocalypse sees a throne mightier than the throne of Rome. A rainbow of perpetual and glorious expectation gleams around it. Great and glorious words are spoken of the Mighty Presence upon the throne: "Holy, holy, holy, is the Lord God, the Almighty, who was and who is and who is to come." The hopeless minority appeal from the thrones on earth to the throne in heaven. And on that throne they find a friend. Those who would crush them are created beings like themselves. Their royal friend is the Creator of all things. His will plunged them into being, and so they are safe with a great inner safety. Suspicious eyes follow them, but there are other friendly eyes "before and behind" seeing for God and missing nothing. The very thought of these endless good eyes used for God and for His persecuted people somehow brings exhaustless comfort. The throne stands for power and understanding. The power that made the world is the protection of those who suffer for their faith in God. Faith literally repudiates a tragic and an evil environment and replaces it by an environment of moral and spiritual glory seen by the soul alone. Anybody can despair, crushed by the hard and ugly visibilities of the world. Anybody can be a cynic. Only a hero can see the throne with the rainbow of hope about it.

This is the faith which sustains the hopeless minority, so that it is not really hopeless after all. For democracy itself breaks down when the majority becomes a tyrannical beast. Yet that vast majority temporarily may possess a crushing power. But the vision filling the eyes of the faithful minority is more powerful than all the energies at the disposal of the brutal majority. It is more powerful because God is the object of that vision. Quality and not quantity counts here. But quality in a genuine sense becomes a power only when it is united to the character and to the strength of God. This power of direct vision to give the righteous minority all the sense of victory which the majority claims for itself is one of the most remarkable things about apocalyptic writing.

But this faith is also a living witness. That which has a right to be cannot be silenced. That which has no right to be vainly claims the throne of the world. The power of the minority to live by an invisible conviction and to witness to that conviction by life and death changes something in the very hard structure of events. The majority which is wrong has the seed of disintegration in it. The minority which suffers for righteousness has connections with reality which the world does not understand. The invisible throne seen by the eyes of faith is mightier than all the thrones of the world.

4. The Appeal from the Acts of Men to the Acts of God

In a world crisis great thoughts are good, but they are never enough. One must have more than great thoughts. One must have great actions. And when men are incapable of these actions, they must be acts of God. In the characteristic situations out of which apocalyptic writing comes men reach an impasse. They can do nothing. Then God breaks in upon the scene. He acts with tremendous finality. He proves Himself not only to be a great ideal but also to be a power in history. By means of all sorts of vivid and brilliant and bizarre symbols, this action of God in history is expressed. It comes as an incredible relief to those men and women of good will who cherish the eternal loyalties in an evil world. The world is always saying to them: "You are dreamers of vain dreams. There is nothing in reality which corresponds to your beliefs. You live in a world which has no substance. The world of facts will always beat down your world of vague and impractical loveliness." Then God acts. It is the hard materialisms which go down. It is the thrones of wickedness which fall. It is the things of the spirit which prove triumphant on the very field of history. So in the world of action comes a mighty clarification of the problem of the meaning of life. The loyal minority is vindicated. The disloyal majority falls into the very frustration and tragedy to which it had tried to condemn that minority of men and women who clung to ways of good. So "they that are wise shall shine as the brightness of the firmament." Thus it may be said that one book of the New Testament tells of the acts of the Apostles, while another is the symbolical, lyrical song of the acts of God. The rider of the white horse

is arrayed in a garment sprinkled with blood: and his name is called The Word of God. And the armies which are in heaven followed him upon white horses, clothed in fine linen, white and pure. And out of his mouth proceedeth a sharp sword, that with it he should smite the nations: and he shall rule them with a rod of iron: and he treadeth the winepress of the fierceness of the wrath of God, the Almighty. And he hath on his garment and on his thigh a name written, KING OF KINGS, AND LORD OF LORDS.

5. Mysterious Symbolisms Whose Central Message Is Obvious to the Oppressed

The presence of almost endless mysterious symbols is a characteristic of apocalyptic writing. Sometimes the symbol is a scarcely veiled promise of divine help. Thus Daniel is represented as saying:

I lifted up mine eyes, and looked, and, behold, a man clothed in linen, whose loins were girded with pure gold of Uphaz: his body also was like the beryl, and his face as the appearance of lightning, and his eyes as flaming torches, and his arms and his feet like unto burnished brass, and the voice of his words like the voice of a multitude. . . . Then said he unto me, Fear not, Daniel; for from the first day that thou didst set thy heart to understand, and to humble thyself before thy God, thy words were heard.

Sometimes the symbols become complicated, as in Daniel's vision of the four beasts. There is often a sudden sense of clarification, as when after the vision of the beasts there comes

one like unto a son of man. . . . And there was given him dominion, and glory, and a kingdom, that all the peoples, nations, and languages should serve him: his dominion is an everlasting dominion, which shall not pass away, and his kingdom that which shall not be destroyed.

So the sense of the beast transcended and mastered by the man comes to us with indubitable clarity. There is a power which goes down beastward. There is a power which goes up manward. It is the one like unto the son of man through whom God can do His work.

The symbols may be as subtle as the seven seals in the book of Revelation which only the Lamb can open, and the prancing horses of terror which come forth as seal after seal is opened. Or the imagery may become more involved as in the case of the seven angels and their seven trumpets. But always there is evil judged and overthrown and cast out, and always there is good protected. Sometimes the very vagueness must have been a comfort to the reader. For, while there was vagueness in respect of the method of deliverance, there was no vagueness about the fact of deliverance or the source of deliverance in powers commissioned and sent forth by the living God.

As a matter of fact, the moment one ceases trying to find a detailed map of the future in the book of Revelation and begins to read it with the awareness of human tragedy and divine power which were the central matters to its first readers, everything begins to clear in an astonishing fashion. When one treats it as he might treat a book of spiritual crossword puzzles, he is sure to go wrong.

6. Apocalyptic Writing as a Literature of Consolation

The Apocalypse brings consolation to those in sore need of encouragement. They have seen all their hopes turn to disappointment, and all their expectations have fallen in futility at their feet. They have looked bleak and hard despair squarely in the face. The Apocalypse comes with an almost unbelievable relief. It is their conquerers who stand in slippery places. They themselves stand on a rock. The all-powerful God holds their cause in His mind and in His heart. Therefore they need not fear. Their dead are held safe under the altar of God, and they will have rich reward for their suffering for righteousness. In the book of Revelation no individual is lost in the vision of some ultimate goal afar off. All the individuals of every period are part of the ultimate plan which sweeps beyond death so that mortality itself becomes irrelevant. No soul is ever lost from the sight of God. The richness of comfort which such thoughts as these brought to men in an age of persecution can scarcely be overestimated.

The city of triumphant evil might seem the one powerful city in the world. Rome itself had seemed to become such a city. And, hidden under the name of Babylon, it is described, characterized, and seen plunging to its doom.

The words flash like vivid fire. There is no doubt of the fact that the writer finds the deepest comfort to himself and seeks to give the deepest comfort to his readers as he pictures the fate of the unrighteous city. He cares enough for goodness to rejoice in the thought that evil is to be defeated, is indeed already defeated in the fact that the God of moral love is against it. There is in the New Testament Apocalypse none of the sort of tenderness which gently presses the evil to its heart, watchful lest the dark and bad thing should be hurt. And the knowledge that when men deliberately and with full purpose make evil their good you must include them in your condemnation of evil is very clear in the analysis of moral situations to be found in the book of Revelation. The understanding that the man who has made evil his good has the seed of death in him is a very comforting sort of understanding. The assurance that the city which has made evil its good has the seed of death in it is a very comforting sort of assurance. The knowledge that the empire which has made evil its good has the seed of death in it is a very comforting sort of knowledge. There is no genuine consolation if evil is not cast from the throne. The consolation the New Testament Apocalypse offers is never the comfort which comes to those who surrender to evil. It is the comfort which comes to those who, resisting unto death, know that God holds their cause in His heart and will bring it to victory.

7. Apocalyptic Writing as a Literature of Triumphant Hope

The book of Revelation reeks with tragedy. Yet its pages are full of outbursts of triumphant song:

> Great and marvellous are thy works, O Lord God, the Almighty; righteous and true are thy ways, thou King of the ages. Who shall not fear, O Lord, and glorify thy name? for thou only art holy; for all the nations shall come and worship before thee; for thy righteous acts have been made manifest.

> After these things I heard as it were a great voice of a great multitude in heaven, saying, Hallelujah; Salvation, and glory, and power, belong to our God: for true and righteous are his judgments.

> And I heard as it were the voice of a great multitude, and as the voice of many waters, and as the voice of mighty thunders, saying, Hallelujah: for the Lord our God, the Almighty, reigneth.

> And I saw a new heaven and a new earth. . . . And I saw the holy city, new Jerusalem, coming down out of heaven from God, made ready as a bride adorned for her husband. And I heard a great voice out of the throne saying, Behold, the tabernacle of God is with men, and he shall dwell with them, and they shall be his peoples, and God himself shall be with them, and be their God: and he shall wipe away every tear from their eyes; and death shall be no more; neither shall there be mourning, nor crying, nor pain, any more.

So in the complete achievement of God's mighty acts of deliverance the New Testament Apocalypse finds the basis for a finally triumphant hope. And the holding of this hope in the midst of defeat and sorrow and tragedy and death is the very genius of apocalyptic writing.

8. *Apocalypse as a Philosophy of History*

Both the book of Daniel and the book of Revelation contain the elements of a philosophy of history. In each case the fundamental clues are the same, but the New Testament writing is shot through with the sense of the redemption wrought by Jesus Christ and of its significance for the world.

The author of the book of Daniel is sure that God presides over the coming and the going of the kingdoms. In imagination he projects himself backward and sees them coming and going. They are arrogant and proud and have a hot sense of security. But they come only as God allows them to come. And they go at the hour when in God's plan they should go. To use language coming from a later period, we may say that history is not a tale told by an idiot, signifying nothing. It is a tale of events wrought out under the mighty lordship of the God of righteousness. The main outlines are clear enough. And often the detailed references are clear, too.

To the New Testament Apocalypse, too, God is not only involved in history; he is the Master of history; in a tremendous sense—allowing for man's freedom—he may be said to be the Author of history. Read history apart from God and you are sure to misread it. Read history with a sense of the God of moral love on the throne and you are sure to read it aright. For God always has the last word.

In history evil is seen trying to pretend that it is something which it is not. In history—God sees to that—evil is sooner or later revealed to be just what it is. And in history evil is at last overthrown and good is triumphant. Many ideas are played with. For many a century the conception of the thousand-year reign of the saints will probably bewilder scholars who happen also to be thinkers. The least that can be said of it is that the author uses a conception he found floating about to express his complete assurance that there would be relative and dramatic triumph of good in history even apart from and before the ultimate consummation.

The life of man belongs to God. It is not lived apart from God. It finds God's judgment in history as well as at the consummation of history. Evil is given its day. It is given its hour of seeming triumph. It is given its hour of brilliant duplicity. Then inevitably under God's mighty hand it is seen in its true and essential quality and goes straight to the doom which it deserves. If evil has the seed of death in it, goodness has the seed of life in it. And God is the great gardener who brings the good seed to abundant fruitage.

In the book of Revelation men and nations are seen in the light of the choices they have made. They are not seen making the choices. You do not see the seed deciding what sort of seed it will be. That, of course, is a part and a very important part of the whole story. You can view history as choices are being made. That is a legitimate and important way to study history. You can view history after the choices have been made. That also is a legitimate and important way to study history. And it is the way of the book of Revelation.

The central word the great apocalyptic writers have to say about the life of man in the world is this: You cannot write history and leave God out. Many persons come on the stage of history. They say their words and do their deeds. But the greatest person who appears in history is the Person who is above history. He is indeed the Alpha and the Omega. He presides over the processes of events. He brings down the curtain on the play of time. He lifts it again for the drama of eternity.

9. Modern European Theology and the Apocalyptic Mood

The Christian world is divided into hostile camps in respect of certain movements in modern European theology. When you name the name of Sören Kierkegaard and remind men of his passionate sense of moral values and the strange spiritual light which sometimes shines in his eye, the faces of some men who listen glow with happy response, the faces of some men are drawn in baffled perplexity, and the faces of others sharpen with definite hostility. When you mention the name of Berdyaev and refer to his caustic and effective analysis of a decadent civilization, some men will turn toward you as men turn from darkness to the light. Others will turn away in bewilderment and distaste. When you mention the name of Karl Barth, some men will at once declare that now we are to consider real Christianity. Others will say quite bluntly: "If this is Christianity, we have never been Christians." It ought to be clear enough that if we can see the profound historic kinships of these thinkers, we can come to understand them better and to have an appreciation not obsessed by subservience and not defeated by hostility. We want to make the suggestion that their deepest roots are to be found in apocalyptic writing. There is the same sense of a human tragedy completely beyond man's resources. There is the same sense of the solution of the problem of human frustration not through human acts but through the acts of God. And while the writing may be dialectical rather than symbolic, the roots are finally the same as those of apocalyptic writing.

It is true that apocalyptic writing begins with a concrete crisis in history. It may seem at first that the movements of European theology of which we are speaking begin with a human crisis so profound that it includes every century and every age. But surely Kierkegaard and Berdyaev and Barth are all colored by the quality of the crisis of the age in which they find themselves. It is true, however, that it is the human city per se and not any particular city of any particular time which is Barth's

City of Destruction. Even so the kinship is very deep. The movement of Barth's thought includes a dialectic of complete human frustration, an inevitable and utterly final crisis, then the coming of the divine word and the consummation of the divine act. And in broad outline this represents the direction and points the thought of contemporary European theology. In a way you may say that its crisis is even more apocalyptic than that of the apocalyptic writings. It is clear enough that if Karl Barth had been writing the book of Daniel there would have been no figure like a son of man. He would have been afraid of conceding so much to humanity—even in symbolism. And in the letters to the seven churches in the New Testament Apocalypse there is a sense of the value of human struggle and victory before which Karl Barth would draw back. But with all that, the apocalyptic writing sees a moral crisis which can be met only by an act of God. And modern European theology sees a moral crisis which can be met only by acts of God. There are indeed kinships which are very profound.

In the apocalyptic writings, however, you always have the group—the remnant of good will—who are on the side of God and for whose sake God must act. There is a tendency in Barth so to reduce man, so to emphasize his incapacity and futility and treachery and evil, that when God finally speaks and acts there is nothing in man to which God can appeal, and so by a special miracle God must create the responsiveness and the response in each person who does respond. Clearly this is going too far. And with all the splendid realism which European theology has brought to its anthropology, so that serious-minded men have ceased to look at humanity through the sentimentally tinted glasses of an optimistic utopian humanitarianism, it remains true that you cannot destroy a man and then resurrect him for purposes of salvation. You cannot destroy humanity and then make it the object of the grace of God.

There is an exquisite human sense running through the book of Revelation which the Barthian might well make his own. There is the sense of the value of separate human persons. "I will give him a white stone, and upon the stone a new name written, which no one knoweth but he that receiveth it." Human personality is so sacred a thing that the man who turns to the light will have at the central citadel of his personality a secret meaning known only to him and to God forever.

10. The Permanent Significance of the Apocalyptic Elements in the Christian Religion

It is not surprising that Jesus, much of whose teaching took quite other forms, appropriated the apocalyptic approach and made it the vehicle for significant teaching. He made His own the sense of terrible crisis. He made His own the secure sense of the necessity of a divine act.

He associated Himself with that divine act: "Ye shall see the Son of man sitting at the right hand of Power, and coming with the clouds of heaven." And in His own interpretation of ultimate meanings and ultimate events He put tremendous emphasis on the faithfulness and the faithlessness of men. Clearly to Him, back of the apocalyptic judgment there was always the human choice. Christianity, of course, has made a part of its most classic form this sense of the great divide, the human choices, the mighty act of God in overthrowing evil, and the decisive act of judgment of our Lord Himself.

We need not be troubled by the fact that the pictures we find in apocalyptic writing are all foreshortened. The great persons are there. The great truths are there. The great acts are there. But the whole picture is seen in one flash, and its relation to events in time must always be considered in the light of this fact.

There are the aspects of Christian truth which are reached best in other forms of experience than those which lie back of apocalyptic writing. God leads His children in green pastures and by still waters as well as through the valley of the shadow of death. And the harvest song of the green pastures is as truly a part of ethical religion as the passionate cry of faith in death valley.

But the experience out of which apocalyptic comes is true human experience. It may almost be said it is the profoundest human experience. The hour comes when a man must attain the moral courage of a triumphant faith or be a spiritual coward forever. It is not a normal experience any more than it is a normal experience for a man to risk his life in a sudden crisis. But you learn a great deal you never knew before about a man in such an hour. It may be said that you learn the most important things you can know about him.

That there are psychopathic elements in the great experiences at the heart of a moral crisis no one could deny successfully. But when you call the theologians who emphasize these things psychopathic theologians, while you do call attention to a danger, you by no means speak entirely in detraction. There is a road from the heart of any experience which is not entirely evil to a new understanding of the character of God. This is true—in a way it is particularly true—of psychopathic experiences. A little book called *The Golden Complex* once made the point that many a man the world came to value moved from an inferiority complex out to greatness. Life is more than the elucidation of logical formulas, and experiences least responsive to logic may have meaning of which even the logician must ultimately take account. Christianity is, after all, the religion which offers salvation to sinners. And, judged by any standard, sin is a psychopathic experience. It is a preoccupation with that which has no right to be. It is an obsession with that which does not belong to health. When you come to think of it, the existence over large areas in pseudo triumph of that which has no right to be, makes necessary the great acts of God in history. A conception of Christianity which has no place for the cry, "God, be merciful to me a sinner," has ceased to be Christian. The perspective of the sinner who in utter moral honesty has faced the meaning of his sin, and of himself as the man who liked it and wanted it and put it in a place of power in his life, is a tragic thing, but it is very important for the true understanding of the nature of Christianity itself.

Contemporary fiction sometimes seems completely taken up with a study of the abnormal. That often its purpose is less than noble and its technique is full of flaws, we shall not deny. But we must say frankly that, when over large areas the abnormal becomes the real, we must deal with the abnormal in order to make the actual the normal. And this is just what Christianity does.

There will never come a time in the human story when Christians will cease to learn from men whose outlook on life is essentially apocalyptic. Not merely in occasional instances but in human life at its heart there is frustration and folly and tragedy. And all this can be met only by acts of God. That it has been met by acts of God is the assertion of the whole New Testament. It is the assertion of Christianity in its classical form. The human debacle and the divine acts do make up essential matters in man's experience of his own life, of his experience with men, and of his final and transforming meeting with God. Granted that apocalyptic writing probably has more elements which are temporary and are transcended than any other writing which has been the vehicle of revelation, it remains true that it has been and is a vehicle of revelation. If we read the book of Revelation today with any sort of understanding, it speaks to something at the very center of our lives.

CHAPTER XV

The Queen of the Sciences

SIR Arthur Eddington would doubtless have accepted the definition of science as the measuring of the measurable aspects of existence by means of instruments of precision or their equivalent. This conception of science is sharp and clear, and much may be said for it. It makes science the supreme expression of the potentialities of mathematics. There is a pattern of impersonal mathematical relationships in the world. These science discovers, charts, classifies, and uses.

1. Science as Measurement

Of course, with such a conception of science we must say at once that the area of reality is larger than the area of science. For reality includes the measurer as well as the measurable. And the central characteristic of the measurer is the fact that he cannot be measured. His free intelligence discovers uniformities. It analyzes their relationships. It uses them for its own purposes. And it does all this because it transcends the realm of impersonal uniformities which it studies. All those disciplines which deal with the activities of free intelligence transcend the scientific formulas. With this conception, the humanistic studies belong to a realm which transcends mechanical measurement and therefore cannot be reduced to the terms of scientific formulas. Art and ethics and religion have to do with the experiences of free intelligence in respect of the beautiful, the good, and the Eternal Person. They have aspects which can be related to science considered as measurement, but they transcend it at every point of characteristic significance. But it is also true that the scientist who is a free intelligence inspecting and classifying uniformities transcends the uniformities which he classifies. Science deals with the measurable but is the achievement of a free person who can measure just because he possesses powers which cannot be measured. In this sense the history of science is a humanistic story. It is the tale of free men dealing with the uniform aspects of their world.

When all this is seen clearly, there is an honest distribution of labor, and much good results. It must be confessed, however, that trouble is likely to begin almost at once. The scientist is likely to become so engrossed with the uniformities which he studies that he forgets the free intelligence without which no such study would be possible. Then he is likely to try to reduce all those aspects of existence which cannot be measured to the control of measurement. So all the pseudo sciences emerge. For the pseudo sciences are precisely those which attempt to reduce to measurable terms those aspects of existence which by their very nature cannot be measured. In this way psychology becomes a branch of physiology, the study of the social adjustments of men becomes an abstract analysis of impersonal relations, history becomes a study of conscious mechanical reactions, literary criticism becomes philology and a study of human experiences from which everything human has been abstracted, ethics becomes a study of abstract principles quite apart from free human choices, philosophy becomes the claim that the subhuman includes all reality, and theology a series of figures of speech by which impersonal conceptions are given a spurious personal value. All this, of course, represents the emasculation of the human. And it leaves hanging in the air the activities of the free intelligence without which even this misinterpretation of the human would be impossible. It would be unfair to the clear-minded scientists who have done the most brilliant work in relating science to the humanistic aspects of experience to hold them responsible for the vagaries of pseudo science. Men like Sir James Jeans have seen clearly enough that when one attempts to get at reality either human or divine, one must go from a mathematical formula to a mathematician.

2. The Larger Conception of Science

It is always of the utmost importance in all thinking that we clearly define our terms. If we divide reality into free intelligence and the uniform aspects of existence with which free intelligence deals, and call the measuring of the uniform aspects of existence science, clearly theology belongs to the side of free intelligence. It is not the queen of the sciences. It is not science at all. It does, however, belong to the side of life which makes science possible, namely, to free intelligence analyzing its own experiences.

There is, however, another conception of science. According to this conception, the task of science is the orderly setting forth of the truth as it comes from *all* departments of life and thought. This conception is large enough to include the relative free intelligence of man and the perfect free intelligence of God, with the patterns of dependable uniformity which God has made possible for men. This includes the science which catalogues the measurable but transcends it and includes the free intelligence which does the measuring. It is with this conception that you can call theology not only a science but very especially the queen of the sciences.

Here, of course, you have to be on your guard all the while against one danger. You may talk and speak a great deal of science, slipping from one meaning into another so casually that finally you do it quite unconsciously. Then the conception of science as the classification of the uniformities of the subhuman may return to plague you and to confuse all your thought. There is really no method which is free from danger. The only safety lies in going back to your definitions constantly and in thinking clearly whatever the cost.

We shall, then, for the purposes of the argument of this chapter, think of science as the orderly setting forth of what we know of reality. If the ultimate reality is the Perfect Conscious Person who is the Creator and the Preserver of the world and of men, we see that theology is indeed the final science, the veritable queen of the sciences.

The justification of this position may be attempted in three ways. The first has to do with a facing of the ultimate problems of the theory of thought and knowledge and of existence itself and a close process of dialectic which eventuates in the conclusion that a world of persons has been created and sustained by a Perfect Person who gives them uniform patterns of experience and large and significant areas of responsible freedom. The place of theology in such a world is inevitably central and supreme.

The second dialectic for the authentication of theology proceeds from a study of ethical religion as it reaches its consummation as revelation through human experience in the Old Testament and the New. Here you move through stage after stage in the history of religion, standing at length in the presence of Jesus Christ and all His impact upon human life and history. Here, too, you come at last to the God whose face we see in the face of Jesus Christ, and once more theology comes to sit grandly upon the throne.

There is a third dialectic for the authentication of theology. This begins frankly with the uniformities which form the proper subject of the investigation of science as measurement. At once it sees that there is no measurement without a measurer. There is no science without the scientist. And in the free intelligence of the scientist you have met the analyzing and controlling mind which transcends the world of uniformities and yet without which the uniformities themselves could never be studied. You have to accept the freedom of the scientist. You meet free spiritual intelligence in all his activities. But if free intelligence is necessary for the study of the uniformities of nature, the step is easy to the free intelligence which created and maintains these uniformities. This is the path of cogent dialectic, if not precisely from science to God, much more fundamentally a process moving from the scientist to God. Anybody who has ever fully and critically considered all the aspects of the work of a scientist in a laboratory ought not to find it hard to believe in God. In fact, he has entered upon a process of thought which, if followed to its logical conclusion, makes such a belief inevitable. In man the world of free intelligence and the uniformities controlled by intelligence meet in a relative way. In God the world of free intelligence and the uniformities created and sustained by the free intelligence of the Perfect Person have their conclusive and final meeting. But it is clear at once that while the Perfect Person of free intelligence can make and sustain impersonal patterns of uniformity, He can have fellowship only with persons who have free intelligence in some way like His own. God and that free person, the scientist, belong to the same order. The scientist is made in God's image. But the free intelligence which the scientist has used for the study of nature, the artist has used in respect of beauty, the moralist has used in respect of the good, and the everyday man has used for a thousand decisions. This world of the relations of free persons has a reality all of its own. Here men meet each other. And here they have that finally significant experience which is their meeting with God. The Perfect Person has the keys to all the experiences of persons. So once again and quite inevitably we come to theology. And if we use the word science now to express the orderly setting forth of the results of the study of reality, with the reality of persons and of personal experiences in the place which actually belongs to them, theology stands in undisputed royalty the queen of the sciences.

3. Theology the Keystone of the Arch

That men in our time find it easier to think of things than of persons, that they find it easier to think of the subhuman than of the human, not to say of the divine, ought not to astonish us. We are witnessing the complete breakdown personally, politically, socially, morally, and spiritually of that materialistic synthesis which saw everything in the terms of things and sensations and could not rise to the level of personal responsibility for free choices which decided the fate of the individual, the family, the city, the state, and the nation. Clearly we must repudiate the philosophy which has betrayed us. Clearly we must find a philosophy which will set us free.

No end of stately tomes have been written which have interpreted the human in subhuman terms. And many are the discussions which have interpreted the human without reference to the divine. The common characteristic of all of these is that at last they have broken down completely. They have broken down intellectually. They have broken down practically. The wreckage all about us belongs to a world which has interpreted the human in the terms of the subhuman and has never seen the human in the light of the divine. The haughty materialisms have had their day and have wrought tremendously in the life of the world. And they have turned the human hopes to frustration and the human desires to despair. By these things men cannot live. By these things men cannot even come to a good death. Everything falls apart in complete ruin without the Great Person. Everything fits together and is seen in true perspective if we have the Great Person of moral love, the Creator and the Sustainer of the world and man. So theology becomes indeed the keystone of the arch of existence.

Everything significant in the life of man comes to a point in his use of his freedom. When he is a man of good will and wants above everything else to use his freedom wisely, he needs standards upon which he can depend, and knowledge which will not fail him in any crisis. He needs to hear God speak. He needs a sure word of revelation. Here his need is answered by the voice of ethical religion in the world consummating in the supreme words in the Old Testament. Here, too, theology as the interpretation of the God who has spoken is the keystone of the arch of human life.

But man has misused his freedom. Knowing the good, he has done the evil. He has chosen his own gratification rather than the good of his fellow men. He has chosen to be a god worshiping himself rather than an obedient and loving worshiper of the living God. So he has wrecked his life. And in the ruins something has been left which called for God. Something has been left which cried for salvation. When man has made this cry his deepest voice, the cry has been answered. Indeed, it was really answered before man began to call. God the Revealer has been a great divine resource to man. God the Redeemer has met his utmost need. God the Redeemer has solved his ugliest, most bitter problems. Here, too, in tragic glory theology becomes the keystone of the arch.

But the man caught in the slippery ways of his own selfishness may refuse to cry for help. He may make evil his good. He may make evil his god. He may himself become his own god of evil. This man and the group of men to whom he deliberately and permanently attaches himself must meet the God of moral love as a judge. The stability of the moral universe rests at last on the judgment as well as on the salvation of God. And here, too, theology becomes the keystone of the arch.

It is seen in this fashion that theology will restore that moral understanding which the modern man has so strangely lost. Here are the materials by means of which civilization itself may be rebuilt. The casual thinkers who have believed that they could build a church without a theology—without this theology—have seen their work come only to disintegration. The very half truths which they have held have only given a temporary plausibility to their betrayal of themselves and of their followers.

The men who have supposed that they could build a world without a theology—without this theology—have moved with great pomp and circumstance, they have come to great places of power, and they have seen their work disintegrate before their faces. Theology has been winning many victories in the contemporary world. They have been the victories which have come when theology has been repudiated with scorn and in that very hour the processes of decay have set in. They have been the victories which have come as the world which has cast out theology has been reduced to moral and social despair. This negative argument represents the most tremendous dialectic worked out on the field of history in our time. We have cast theology from the throne, and the world has fallen into chaos. When we restore theology to the throne once more, there will be genuine hope for civilization. Here again, to go back to our original figure, theology is the keystone of the arch.

4. Exegetical Theology

Ethical religion in its final form comes to us in two great collections of sacred literature. They are found in the Old Testament and the New of the Christian Bible. Centuries of use for purposes of religion have had their inevitable effect upon the study of these documents. The large impact of writings coming out of human experience and speaking directly to human experience is, of course, the matter of central importance in respect of these documents. But the human mind has a curious tendency to go back from the personal to the mechanical, from living experience to processes of impersonal logic. Thus the books which were dependably sacred in a living sense came to be considered sacred in a hard mathematical sense. And so theories of verbal inspiration have run riot in the processes of biblical interpretation. The inevitable breakdown of all such theories when used by scholars who faced the facts candidly has led to the complete discrediting of that whole approach. But there are still a surprising number of scholars who deny verbal inspiration in one breath and construct word studies in the next quite as if the theory of verbal inspiration were true. And there are others who despise the theory of verbal inspiration in the main and yet, when they find assertions which fit into their favorite preconceptions, fall back upon it with great enthusiasm. That a movement of biblical thought may come to final and classical expression in a brilliantly conclusive sentence is, of course, true. But the true scholar is always on his guard in the presence of isolated sentences and isolated words.

Nevertheless, there is such a thing as exegetical theology. It is perpetually asking the question: Just what does this word mean? It is also perpetually asking the question: Just what does this sentence mean? And it brings every resource of knowledge of language and grammar and literary history to bear upon the answers to these questions. It makes the most microscopic study of all the words and sentences of the Old Testament and the New. The ample knowledge of Hebrew and cognate languages, of Greek and Aramaic, and especially, through the papyri, of colloquial Greek as it was spoken in the time when the New

Testament writings took form, is of great importance for this study. There is always, of course, the danger of overestimating the importance of the tiny fragment which is being considered with such meticulous care. There is the danger of not seeing the forest on account of preoccupation with particular trees. There is danger of not seeing the oak through preoccupation with the acorns. But, for all that, the painstaking scholar whose preoccupation is with the particular sentence and the particular word will always have his place in theological studies. He cannot be bowed out of court.

5. Biblical Theology

We are using the term "biblical theology" just now to designate that biblical study which, not content with the inspection of particular sentences and particular words, attempts to discover the important teachings of particular books, of particular authors, of the whole Old Testament, of the whole New Testament, or, finally, of the whole Bible.

Here the scholar is obviously upon sounder and more dependable ground. He follows processes of thought through a book, through the utterances of a specific writer, and at last sees their importance as they are commanding features in the landscape of the whole Old Testament and the New. If a thing is said once, it may be quite incidental, even unimportant; if it is part of the warp and woof of the most powerful writings in the Old Testament or the New or both, it has achieved a certain masterful authenticity. The assembling of the prophetic teachings about God and man and sin and deliverance is a great theological task. The assembling of the essential ideas of the whole Old Testament on these great themes is an inevitable element in the building of a secure theological structure. The theology implicit and explicit in the Synoptics, in the Fourth Gospel, in the Pauline writings, and in other parts of the New Testament is of the most definite importance. And when a synthesis of these teachings is made so that we confront the New Testament conceptions of God, man, sin, Christ, the Cross, and Redemption, we have something quite at the basis of classical Christian theology. When the central teachings of the Old and New Testaments are built into a great synthesis of biblical teaching, we are ready for the highest tasks of theological thought.

6. Philosophical Theology

The complete mental account taken of the truths of the Christian religion by a theologian in any century will set them forth in the frame of a philosophical system which commands the confidence of the writer. We may call the product systematic theology. Perhaps it is better to call it philosophical theology. Here we come upon the climax of the attempt to see the Christian religion steadily and to see it whole. The theological frame may be that of Aristotle, as in the consummate work to be found in the *Summa* of St. Thomas Aquinas. It may be found in Hegel, as in some of the most characteristic forms of Scottish theology. But always the philosophical frame is used to give coherence and consistency to the synthesis of theological truth. Here, too, one must be on one's guard. The philosophy may serve a very noble purpose. It may also betray. The tendency to substitute abstract principles for concrete realities which is so characteristic an element in the Hegelian philosophy has betrayed many an earnest theologian.

It is the conviction of the author of this book that a philosophical system built about the insights of personal idealism will offer to the Christian religion the soundest frame for an adequate presentation of Christian truth. It keeps forever before our minds the experiences of living men and the living God. And it does not tempt us to interpret personal experiences in impersonal terms. Nothing that is relevant to Christianity as the religion of moral love is left out. Everything that is important in the experiences of living men with each other and with the living God is retained.

7. *The Greek Theology*

Christian theology first came to life in the atmosphere of Greek intelligence. Men like Origen, Clement, Athanasius, Basil, and the two Gregories each brought to the interpretation of the Christian religion the heart of a Christian and the mind of a Greek. To the Greek theologian everything else revolved around the fact that in Jesus Christ, God had become man. The word had become flesh and dwelt among us. Greek theology was the theology of the Incarnation.

The Greek Christian thinkers had tremendous confidence that the human mind was made to be responsive to Christian truth and that Christian truth could be made compelling to the human mind. And this truth was important. Understanding it and accepting it was a very vital part of the experience which made a man a Christian. It was not that any first-class Greek theologian would have said that formal acceptance of Christian truth could be a substitute for the honest doing of the will of God as it had been revealed in Jesus Christ. The Greek never put the two things over against each other in that way at all. If you knew and accepted with all your mind and heart the fact that God had become man in Jesus Christ, you had the most compelling reasons for giving yourself to Him completely and for doing His will with the utmost loyalty.

The battles of the Greek thinkers are of perennial importance. Only those who have failed to understand them have spoken slightingly of their significance. When Athanasius and Arius came to royal battle about the nature of the Christian faith, the matter in contention was precisely the question as to whether Christianity was big enough and final enough to become the religion of the whole world. Only the religion of the Incarnation could become a world religion. No wonder that Athanasius said: "Our all is at stake."

But the Incarnation was not a means by which man could complacently find his way into the life of the Deity and worship himself. It was a unique event. It was just that uniqueness for which Athanasius contended. It was in this quite unique sense that Christ was of one substance with God. The Greeks sometimes used loose phrases about our participating in the divine nature through Christ. But no one reading them carefully can possibly say that by this they meant that man became divine. The distinction between the moral nature which we can share and the metaphysical essence of Deity which we cannot share was not for a moment lost by the great Greek theologians. God had come to us in Jesus Christ that by means of Him we might truly worship God, and not that we might become guilty of the idolatry of self-worship. It was the faith of the Greek theologian that through Jesus Christ man could enter into harmonious relations with God. It was never his belief that man could become God.

8. The Latin Theology

Historical generalizations which are exclusive and antithetical are apt to be dangerous. But in a sense we may say that Greek theology approached the Christian religion through the intelligence while Latin theology approached it through the world of action. The tragedies of the world of action profoundly impressed the Latin mind. And this world of evil action in which man had so deeply entangled himself was one of which the Latin Christian could never cease thinking even for a moment. Evil from which a man must be delivered loomed large in all Latin thought. So while the Greek emphasized the Incarnation, the Latin emphasized the Cross. The doctrine of sin was to receive searching analysis by the Latin. Men like Tertullian had a tremendous experience of personal deliverance. And this became fundamental in their theology. To Augustine, with his experience of personal salvation through the grace of God in Christ, Christian theology became his own spiritual autobiography writ large over Africa and Asia and Europe.

With the Latin there was always the fear that man would think that he had redeemed himself. So at last even his decision was regarded as an act of the Almighty rather than his own. The instinct away from human complacency was nobly right. The belief regarding the complete devouring of human freedom by the divine grace was a testimony to the essential rightness of the Latin heart rather than to the clearness of the Latin mind. We surely do not dishonor God when we insist that enough liberty be left in man to enable him to accept the divine redemption by his own free act. But at the center this Latin insistence on the sovereign grace of God possessed something the Christian religion could not discard. The mighty redemption wrought by the One who died upon the Cross received its true place in the Latin theology.

9. The Intellect and the Will

The battle between Thomas Aquinas and Duns Scotus was another of the struggles about things which eternally matter. An old popular putting of the dispute reduces it to two questions: "Does God will a thing because it is true? Does a thing become true because God wills it?" Is the ultimate standard the nature of God which is eternal truth or the will of God which decides what must be true? Put in this form, it is surely not too hard to see that God's nature is fundamental and that He always wills what agrees with His fundamental nature. So St. Thomas strikes the profounder note. But the controversy and its everlasting reopening have been by no means in vain. The will must not be forgotten. The place of the will must be asserted. It is the glory of God that there is no battle between His intelligence which sees the nature of reality and His will which asserts it. It is the recurring tragedy of man that there is a tense and tragic battle between the insights of his mind and the affirmations of his will. The Christian experience of redemption makes the will one with the deepest affirmations of the mind.

10. The Reformation Takes Theological Forms

Put in the bluntest and sharpest form, one may say that the theologians of the Reformation, both Lutheran and Reformed, believed that the Latin theology had given to the Church a place which belonged only to God. They asserted the sovereignty of God over against the sovereignty of the Church. This practical aim must never be forgotten when one reads the most emphatic statements of Protestant theologians of the sixteenth and the seventeenth centuries. They had not only the constant Christian motive of guarding against human complacency. They had also the motive of guarding against ecclesiastical autocracy. To be sure, they put the authority of the Bible over against the authority of the Church. But their final refuge was the sovereignty of God. And the constant emphasis on the relation of the individual to God put a new accent both upon the right of private judgment in respect of biblical questions and upon the direct nexus between the individual and God in the experience of the divine grace. To be sure, there was a sense of corporate relationships in both the Lutheran and Reformed theologies. But the sovereign God speaking through the Scriptures to the individual mind chosen and enlightened by His own grace was central in the theology of the Reformation. The tension which might have become intense was eased by the fact that the theologian always wrote as one of the number made the object of the divine grace. He never fairly faced the problem of those who were passed by. And belief in the sovereign God speaking through the sovereign word of revelation to men freely chosen by God's own grace made possible a mighty corpus of thought by whose means to confront the claims of the sovereign Church.

11. The Theology of Fulfillment

Theology, however, goes beyond the intellectual and practical exigencies which are so constant and so insistent. The sense of the Christian religion as the fulfillment of the deepest requirements of human nature would not be silenced. The Cambridge Platonists saw the reason of man as the candle of the Lord. And the sense of Christianity as essentially the fulfillment of human nature was given classical expression in the work of the great Danish theologian Bishop Martensen. He saw in the Incarnation the very flower of the meaning of human life. For one only understands human nature when one has seen that it is capable of so receiving and responding to the impress of divine nature that God Himself can enter into it. This approach to the realities of the Christian religion has flashed out in great thinking and in great preaching. In the United States of America, Phillips Brooks's most characteristic sermon was preached on the text, "Son of man, stand upon thy feet, and I will speak with thee." That all the Christian message cannot be put into the theology of fulfillment is clear enough. That no complete Christian theology can exclude the theology of fulfillment ought to be equally clear.

12. The Theology of Crisis

It was not an accident that in the personal battle of Kierkegaard the theology of fulfillment and the theology of dramatic tragedy met in terrible conflict. And in Europe since that day many men—conspicuously Karl Barth—have sought to put the theology of crisis on the throne. Berdyaev would see the crisis boldly written in political and cultural history as he writes of the end of the age. To Barth the contrast is so sharp that human nature is seen as utterly corrupt and destined to the most absolute frustration. The crisis is so sharp that there is not enough goodness left in man to see or to apprehend the divine word when it is spoken except by a sort of special miracle of grace. All this is understandable enough as a psychological reaction from a confident and complacent pseudo liberalism. As a final position of Christian theology it is simply impossible. Man continues to bear the signature of God—half effaced, to be sure, but still there. The discontent with the sin to which he gives himself remains. The nostalgia for a goodness and a beauty he has never achieved haunts his dreams. His mind is capable of apprehen-

THE QUEEN OF THE SCIENCES

sion and still remains the candle of the Lord. Until a man by a final personal act has made evil his good, there is something in him to which God can speak and which can respond to God's voice.

13. The Theology of Social Action

Both in England and in the United States the vigorous pragmatic quality of characteristic minds has led to what may, by courtesy at least, be called the theology of social action. We say "by courtesy" because so often the theological sanctions are valued only as they can be used to further social programs and are not seen to have any ultimate validity in themselves. Since the days of Kingsley and Maurice in England, and Rauschenbusch and Josiah Strong and Shailer Mathews in America, social Christianity has always had vital and commanding leaders. Such a thinker as Reinhold Niebuhr attempts to unite the deeper insights of European theology in respect of human frustration with the moral indignation and moral struggle of the social prophet.

14. The Great Synthesis

The more one studies the whole situation, the more it is clear that we are being betrayed, not by thinkers who are committed to falsehood, but by thinkers who have mistaken the part of truth they have seen for the whole truth. Classical Christianity will come upon days of new power when the great synthesis is achieved. We shall owe to the European theology of crisis, with its insistent going back to Augustine and Paul, a complete deliverance from that superficial optimism which supposes that man can do without God. Man *is* doomed to frustration apart from the grace of God in Christ mediated through the Cross. The theology of fulfillment will also make its essential contribution. The Genesis story which sees God making man in His own image and, after making man, seeing everything He has made as *very good* has permanent significance. Sin is a departure from the human. Salvation is a restoration of the human. All that God intended in creation is made possible by the divine grace in spite of the dark tragedy of human selfishness and treachery. Man's deepest cry is always for the God of moral love, and never is this more true than in the hour when he realizes the fashion in which he has betrayed his own manhood.

This man of the grace of God is one of a company of men of the grace of God. They cannot refuse to face their social responsibilities. They cannot evade the social tasks which the God of moral love puts upon them. No wrong is safe which a Christian or a company of Christians can overthrow. No right is without a voice as long as the voice of the Christian is heard in the land.

When theology is placed in the frame of a clear personal philosophy full of the sense of living men and of the living God, it is seen that ultimate significance is always found in individuals. Every social action is the action of individual men. It has no significance without them. Only an individual who is right can be trusted with social rights. And the individual is made right by the grace of God. He may also be made wrong by his own evil choice. He may be and has been a part of a corporate life of evil, consisting of the life of the company of men who have definitely and finally made evil their good. This is the last tragedy of human freedom. In time and in eternity it must be met by force. In the great adjudication, God says "Go" as well as "Come." God is indeed a God of *moral* love, and the adjective is as important as the noun.

> There came a day when thought was clear and sure
> And light effulgent played upon the mind,
> When rock-ribbed logic made the end secure
> And inspiration truth to truth could bind;
> When words obedient to their master's call
> Came forth forgetting their wild lawless ways,
> To make thought true and so the mind enthrall,
> To make thought lovely as a poet's lays.
> The Christian thinker of embattled brain
> Saw man above the nature which he rules
> But under God whose right it is to reign,
> And won the ripest wisdom of the schools;
> Then looked to Christ imperial and alone,
> Love on the cross and judgment on the throne.

CHAPTER XVI

Thy Sons, O Greece

COMPETENT thinkers have reminded us often that the Hebrew-Christian tradition and the humanistic tradition originating in Greece have produced civilization. In any definitive discussion of the meaning of human experience full place must be given to the humanistic impulse from the time of its Greek origin. To this we now turn.

Robert Browning tells a delightful story of how a group of captive Athenians found everything changed when it was discovered that one of them could repeat plays of Euripides. Even their captors were servants of the Greek mind.[1] There is something symbolic about the tale, for, in a sense, as far as men are civilized they are Greek, and the sons of Greece became the masters of the world's mind even when they were slaves. We have already met with Greece as we have followed the story of ethical religion and its consummation in Christian sanctions. A decadent Greece met a decadent Israel in the second century B.C. in the time of Antiochus Epiphanes. The Christian religion even in the first century A.D. felt the presence of Greek forms of thought and a little later frankly accepted Greek frames for its sanctions. There has always been a Greek theology attempting to make itself heard, and sometimes making itself heard very powerfully through the centuries of Christian thought. And even Latin theology depends structurally for its intellectual patterns upon the Greek mind.

As we study the significance of human experience, however, we must have a more direct commerce with Greek culture. We must see something of what it was, for and in itself, and so something of what it poured into the life of civilization, or, to put it in sharper words, how it became civilization.

1. The Living Process

The modern scholar is confronted by what at first seem to be strange inconsistencies in Greek culture. The primitive survivals are constantly appearing in the midst of a restrained and distinguished civilization. Some noble thinkers have been disconcerted by these primitive survivals and the place they were given in a more mature Greek life. Some of the lesser breed of scholars without the law of understanding have tried to foul the Greek nest by interpreting even Plato in the terms of

[1] "Balaustion's Adventure."

that out of which Greek life came and away from which it was moving, rather than by that which gave it distinguished and characteristic quality and ultimate power. The clue to the whole story is to see it as a living process. In an incredibly brief period a group of barbarous people became the most civilized men and women the world had ever seen. It was all a matter of living persons grasping and acting upon clear and discriminating apprehensions. And just because the movement was one in actual life and not in impersonal logic, there were odd confusions and inconsistencies enough. For a time things which did not at all belong together flourished side by side. One must discover the real movement and have a dependable sense of direction if he is to understand it all. It is the goal to which it is moving which is important. And once seen as an experience of living men moving away from barbarity to disciplined civilization, the tale can be read with some genuine grasp of its meaning. This very quality of understanding gives a fine human sanity to the scholar who is making the investigation. He receives with full appreciation the great and almost unbelievable insights of the most commanding Greeks. He sees with happy appreciation, too, how these insights became part of the warp and woof of Greek life itself. And he is not too much disconcerted by the clinging barbarities which are seen around so many corners of Greek thought and action. He has a suspicion that a civilized scholar studying our life twenty-five hundred years from now may find more to disconcert and confuse him than we find in the study of fifth-century Athens.

There are, of course, deep mysteries in all the supreme aspects of history. What restless spirit of moral discontent led the people of Israel to be able to respond to the lofty summons of the eighth-century prophets? What subtle sense of human relations and of the understanding of human beings led the Romans to master the world through the forms of law after conquering the world by force? What was the source of the qualities which caused the human mind to flower as it did in fifth- and fourth-century Athens? These questions we can never answer fully. But we can see that it happened in each case as living men confronted and dealt with actual situations. They found their insights in life. They did not bring them to life. And if in the case of Israel it is clearer than in the others that the Great Person who is Master of the world was moving toward men in revelation as they responded with quivering eagerness, it is no doubt true that in some genuine sense the same thing was happening in respect of the deepest insights of Greece and Rome.

We must be prepared, too, for the fact that certain Greeks in every period were taking the journey back to the primitive and not forward to the truly civilized, just as during every century of the life of Israel there were all too many people who were taking the road back toward that from which God was saving Israel. The sense of the defining quality must be preserved in the presence of other qualities. And the other qualities represent forces which resent civilization and which would overthrow it if they could.

2. *The Mingling of Primitive and Civilized Life*

The reader of Gilbert Murray's brilliant study of Aristophanes sees Greek comedy against a background in which the barbarities of a lawless nature worship have a frank and unhesitating expression. The god Dionysus and the fertility cults are very much alive in the Greek imagination even in the great days of Athens. So in the plays of Aristophanes we have the most exquisitely beautiful lyrics, the most cutting and effective social and literary criticism, the coarsest buffoonery, and at times a vivid enough sense of the biological energies. There are, to be sure, most redeeming features in the writings of Aristophanes. The hot vices never flourish in an atmosphere of mirth. And the plays of Aristophanes are saturated with laughter, sometimes gay, sometimes scornful, always antiseptic. There is never in Aristophanes the sophisticated cult of the unclean which appears in many modern writers. There are urbane passages of subtle viciousness in the writings of W. Somerset Maugham or Logan Pearsall Smith which would have made Aristophanes very angry. There is in Aristophanes the honesty of the barnyard but never the inverted sacrament of brutal sensuality such as appeared in particularly corrupt perversion in the catacombs of Paris.

The Platonic Socrates lives in a world with many primitive survivals. He does not ignore them. He sees them quite clearly. He writes of them quite frankly. At times he seems to accept some of them. But at the long last of his discussions he always transcends them. And in a way he transcends them all the more effectively because he treats them so honestly. He never closes doors upon aspects of human experience which he is afraid to face. He keeps all the doors open. He lets in the sunlight everywhere. He keeps the great winds blowing through all experience. The *Symposium* is a particularly effective example of this process. Love is the subject of discussion. And with no hesitations or evasions the lower experiences for which that word has been used are discussed. But with Socrates guiding the discussion one simply cannot remain on that level. The whole dialogue is an experience in moral and intellectual mountain climbing. And at last one emerges on the heights with the miasmic swamps left far behind. Gradually one becomes aware that the insights of moral and spiritual understanding have a more gripping power just because the discussion has avoided nothing and evaded nothing. The brilliant young Athenians who hung on the words of Socrates were fairly swept off their feet by his utter intellectual and moral honesty. And it was Alcibiades, the most unscrupulous of them all, who said that only Socrates had ever been able to make him feel ashamed.

So we can see that the mixture of primitive and civilized life among the Greeks of the great period, while it had its subtle dangers and even its dark evil, was capable of being turned to good account morally and spiritually. This was actually done by the best of the Greek thinkers and by numberless quiet people who made no claim to immortality but did know what it meant to exercise moral discrimination and to turn from darkness to light.

3. The Direct Gaze at Nature

Perhaps the defining characteristic of the best Greek minds was the direct gaze. There is something disarming about its simplicity. There is something most discriminating about the way in which it shuts out many things in order to see one thing clearly. But it is never an empty mind which achieves this direct gaze. It is always a mind which has learned to look for something before it begins to look. In later centuries this having something for which to look was called a working hypothesis. No such complicated mental analysis lay back of the Greek use of the intelligence. But from the first there was a sense of coherence and a sense that things work together, a sense of definitiveness and a sense of harmony.

The worship of the empty mind is a rather modern cult. It is called being objective. And it must inspire the mocking laughter of the gods of intelligence. You might look forever and you would never see meaning unless you brought a sense of meaning with your looking. This the Greek understood well enough. When Thales saw in water the solid, the liquid, the subtle mist, and concluded that water was the ultimate principle, he was combining the sharpest observation with a sense of relationships which guided his speculations. When the Eleatics investigated solidities and called them the ultimate actualities, they were combining observation with a sense of something for which to look, in this case a definite and dependable basis for experience. When Heraclitus and his followers studied every form of physical change and saw in change itself the ultimate actuality, they were combining the direct gaze with the directed mind.

Yet the direct gaze itself proved that both the Eleatics and Heraclitus were right but that each was incompletely right. By the combined use of the direct gaze and discriminating intelligence Democritus and the reconcilers found the solidity in unchanging atoms and the change in the constantly new relations of these atoms. So the ideas of substance and change sharpened and gained in clarity.

But the sense of orderly relationship, of correlation, of co-ordination, was all the while at work as an assumption back of all thought with the Greek. And this gave his gaze at nature a significance of very far-reaching character.

The direct gaze at nature had the same quality as it became the sort of experience which at last crystallizes into poetry. The Greek looked straight at nature. And he saw with sharp clarity what he saw. But here, too, there was a profound sense of harmony. And this sense of orderly actuality in nature became a happy sense of beauty. The Greek was not a Wordsworthian before the days of Wordsworth. He did not create a mystical pantheism as he looked at nature. His sense of distinctions was too sharp for that. And the indubitable sharpness and concreteness of natural objects in Greek poetry have all the appeal of this direct gaze. Indeed, the pantheon of the Greek gods and goddesses is profoundly related to this sense of the actuality of separate things. It is as if the Greek is so afraid that concrete objects will lose their sharp individuality that he makes them divine. There is something as sharp as a good photograph even about his nature myths.

4. The Direct Gaze at Man

In the dialogue *Phaedrus* the Platonic Socrates says: "I am a lover of knowledge, and the men who dwell in the city are my teachers, and not the trees or the country." It is easy to find evidence that Socrates loved nature as did all the Greeks. But with a sure insight he saw that one could learn more from studying the mind of man at work than from all the observations of the uniformities of nature.

The Sophists, too, were most keenly interested in the way the mind works. All too often they desired to study the way the mind works and the processes of argument in order to achieve some selfish end. They, or at least many of them, sought not truth but power. They set forth what may be called a politician's view of the human mind at work. Socrates was often confused with the Sophists. But where the end of so many Sophists was political, the purpose of Socrates was intellectual and ethical. He wanted to find the truth about the action of the human mind in order that he might further the good life for man.

The conversations of Socrates are a singularly adequate representation of the Greek mind applying the straight gaze to the processes of human thought and argument. Socrates has a genius for brushing aside the irrelevant. He sticks to a point with a bulldog grip. He sees the outcome of the implicit assumptions of the man with whom he is speaking more immediately and truly than does this man himself. And relentlessly he pushes the man to follow the logic of his own position. So perpetually he forces pompous assertiveness to recognize its own folly. His seemingly simple questions are deadly. The process is called Socratic irony. And repeatedly it has been used by caustic and brilliant teachers in dealing with pupils strong enough to take its medicine. The mind, so Socrates believes, is indubitably an instrument for the finding of truth. It may, however, be used to build a road to the palace of error.

So the Socratic conversations are in effect a criticism of man's use of his own mind. The unexamined life is to Socrates most tragic and futile. The examined life may in turn become the good life. Thus Socrates becomes the great apostle of critical intelligence. It is not in the study of the processes of nature that you find the defining truth about life. It is in the study of the free mind of man accepting this and rejecting that, in the study of the intelligent use of mental freedom, that you come to grips with what really matters. The moment Socrates found the word νοῦς in studying the teachings of Greek thinkers, he was greatly excited. For to him the great question was: "What are you doing with your mind?" But he soon discovered that he was putting into the word "mind" more than had been put into it before. Sometimes he seemed to love the negative approach. The first step toward knowledge was to recognize the areas of one's ignorance. The oracle had called him the wisest of mankind because he knew how ignorant he was. But Socrates always tore down in order to build up. His negative was always on the way to a great positive. Despite that confusion of virtue with knowledge which was the greatest defect in his thinking, he knew, and no one knew better, that at last everything comes to be a matter of loyalty to the best one knows. The final teaching of Socrates is to be found not in one of his conversations so much as his choice of faithfulness when he knew that faithfulness would mean death. Socrates drinking the hemlock put the keystone into the arch of his philosophy. He had found truth by which to live while he was allowed to live. And he had found truth for which it was worth while to die if that was the alternative. So the most ironic, provocative, and brilliantly belligerent Greek found satisfaction in a great loyalty at last. The straight gaze at man found men thinking. It found them accepting and rejecting. It found them acting on the basis of thought. It found them living in a world where you must find something to which you can be loyal, you must find something on which you can depend.

It is not strange that Socrates was so impressed by the betraying power of falsehood that he made knowledge of the truth the equivalent of virtue. Here he was tragically wrong. But even here there is an element of truth which must always be preserved. It is tragic, even in practical effect, to be wrong intellectually. One cannot be loyal to a truth one cannot see. Sincerity is never a substitute for contact with reality. A sincere fool will always create confusion. A sincere man of ability caught in the coils of inadequate thinking may betray a generation. Socratic devotion to the truth was no unimportant matter. And Socrates incessantly pursuing men to find how they use their minds is a great portent. For the direct gaze at man as he uses his freedom to think and to act is the central matter in the study of human experience.

Aristotle and men of like mind reduced the study of human intelligence in action to the laws of formal logic. And most of this work was done once and for all. Aristotle found in nature a logic corresponding to the logic implicit in his own mind. And in studying that logic in nature he became in a sense the first of the world's great scientists. But even here he brought something from the direct gaze at the mind of man. He sought for evidences of reason in nature, and he did not seek in vain. But there would have been no quest had he not brought human reason to the task.

5. The Dangerous Gift of Abstraction: the Good, the Beautiful, and the True

It is possible to consider relationships apart from the objects which have the relationships. It is possible to consider qualities apart from the objects which possess the qualities. All this belongs to the great and dangerous art of abstraction. As a brilliant intellectual shorthand it is one of the most useful arts in the world. As a method of considering the essential elements of an idea apart from the other qualities which may be combined with it in any specific instance, it is a most important instrument of thought. There is always the danger, however, that the abstraction may come to be considered to have a reality of its own apart from the living situation of which it is a part. And in this way abstraction becomes one of the most dangerous and betraying forms of human thought.

The most brilliant form of abstract reasoning in which the process reaches a level of scientific precision and importance is the science of mathematics. Here Pythagoras achieved an eminent, not to say preeminent, position. The mathematician, as we now know, analyzes the impersonal logical relationships implicit in the mind itself and sets them forth as an abstract objective science. It is the very apotheosis of the sense of structure. The result is impersonal, but it is always, as a science, the product of the action of free personal intelligence. It becomes a complete analysis of the possibilities of numbers, of the relationships of planes and solids and moving bodies, and of the possible relationships of forms which could by no means exist except as hypothetical considerations existing in and for the mind. Whatever may be said of the fourth dimension, when one has reached the seventh one has passed the borderlines of reality. This sense of the orderly relations of a structure, which is an abstract creation of the mind and which not only reflects the logic implicit in the mind but may have no end of reference to a logic explicit in things, is the great achievement of mathematics. Of course, the Pythagoreans were pioneers and much of this science belongs to a later period. But their spade work was far more fundamental and important than anything done by later mathematicians in the sense that all later work has been based upon their insights.

Naturally enough, the exhilaration over the possibilities discovered in the world of mathematical relations led to a certain amount of confusion in the earliest periods. There is an attempt to see magical values in numbers and a certain subtle mysticism of numerical relations in the Pythagoreans which has to be watched.

In the world of mathematics the Greek achievement is another example of the direct gaze. You get the conception of abstract relationships. You eliminate everything else. You look straight at your abstract world. You analyze what you find. And the science of mathematics is created.

The discovery that these abstract and impersonal relationships, which are a part of the very frame of personal experience, have an objective reference and can be used in connection with all the uniformities of the physical world was the very birth of the physical sciences. For the physical sciences investigate the natural world in the light of mathematical relationships. Here, of course, the big things were done after the Greeks on the foundations which the Greeks laid. And here again, as we have seen, there was always the danger of the mistake made by those who, having discovered that some reality is measurable, come to the conclusion that all reality is measurable and that that which cannot be subjected to the laws of impersonal measurement is unreal. This, of course, would give us mathematics without the mathematicians, which would reduce the whole position to absurdity. It would also leave out the free moving mind of the scientist. In this case we would need a laboratory which would itself secrete impersonal formulas. But even then there would be no one left to understand them. Alas, the attempt to interpret personal experiences in impersonal terms is always with us. In a sense it is the real "Decline of the West."

Plato had the profoundest connection with the Pythagoreans, and he was completely fascinated by what he saw. Applying their abstractions to the stars, he found in the sky a glorified geometry.

But these same principles of abstraction applied to qualities give us a remarkable opportunity to study adjectives without their nouns or, if you like, to turn the adjectives into abstract nouns. From the good man you can go on to study goodness. From the beautiful object you can go on to study beauty. From the man who makes clear and honest statements you can go on to study the truth. There are great advantages in such processes of analysis. You get rid of much that is adventitious. You get rid of much that is irrelevant. You see the great qualities in themselves for just what they are. Nobody understood this better than Plato. His world of ideas was a world of glorified abstractions. The idea of the true mastered his mind. The idea of the good mastered his conscience. The idea of the beautiful mastered his imagination. That he was a very great literary artist as well as a thinker of superb genius made the product of his thought all the more wonderful when it was set forth in written form. That there were menacing dangers as well as magnificent possibilities in the sort of use of abstraction involved in his use of ideas will become clear as we go on.

6. The Living Faith in the Ideal

By a brilliant use of abstraction Plato isolated the great principles which give ultimate meaning to life, and he set them forth with compelling power and poetic beauty. But the very process of abstraction made the analysis a judgment of the actual in the name of the ideal. These glorious principles did not actually reign—or only reigned, as it seemed, sporadically and spasmodically in the life of men. Were they, then, as fragile as the stuff of a dream? Did they belong to the world of the imagination rather than to the world of the actual? There were several possible answers to such questions. One was the ironic answer of a devastating criticism of the actual in the name of the ideal—of what is, in the name of what ought to be—without seeking any metaphysical basis for the criterion. One was the cynical answer that the real is in essence a contradiction of the ideal, and a surrender to the ugly real for the sake of practical success. One was a great act of faith which affirmed that the ideal forms are real and everything else has only a deceptive reality. The ideal beauty has a right to be. Therefore, it is. The ideal truth has a right to be. Therefore, it is. We live in a world of illusion and confusion. But in the world of ultimate reality, the true, the good, and the beautiful are on the throne. This act of faith in an invisible ideal was the basis of the Platonic doctrine of ideas. The perfect forms were not mere abstractions. They were the ultimate realities. What you saw and felt and heard was only real as it participated in the quality of these perfect ideas. You could always challenge the ugly visibility by lifting the flag of the invisible beauty. And so with every one of the great ideas. This became a living faith with Plato. It re-enforced his confidence when he confronted the ugly facts of life. No doubt it comforted him when he tried to be a philosopher for a king and came upon catastrophe. Thus Platonism became more than a philosophy. It became a religion. You lived by your faith in what you could not see. By fascinating myth and by exquisitely persuasive speech, Plato set forth this glorious appeal from that which has no right to be, but is, to that which has a right to be but whose reality you can apprehend only by faith.

No wonder Platonism became a schoolmaster leading Greeks to Christ as the law was a schoolmaster leading Jews to Christ. On the philosophic side Paul could scarcely ask a better preparation for his own message than a profound study of Plato. The faith in the metaphysical reality of that which has the moral right to be is one of the cornerstones of a Christian civilization.

7. The Halfway Houses: the Things Which Seem Better than Gods; the Virtues Which Have Fruits Without Roots

All the while a fascinating polytheism was flourishing as a religion of bright and alluring tales and a haunting traditional ritual. But the gods were in many ways a bad, sad lot. They were guilty of all the vices to which men surrendered. They decided through whim and caprice. And they sometimes seemed to have immortality only for purposes of perpetual lust. A brilliant materialistic philosophy of things, with endless forces but no gods, at least put an end to all this. So Epicurus reasoned, and so the Epicureans declared. You lived for the satisfactions you might find in life. And these were surest and most dependable in a life of moderation, neither very hot nor very cold. You looked at the facts of the material world quietly. They were the ultimate facts. You lived calmly, avoiding all extremes, in the felicity of walking gently in an even way. Only a halfway house this. A deliverance from gods of caprice, yes. But what if you journeyed on until you found a god with a character?

Nature itself moved with a stern impersonal order. It was all determined and fitted into one harmonious whole. Why not live according to nature and find a law of virtue like its own immutable laws? So reasoned the Stoics, and so once and again right gloriously they produced the fruits of righteousness. Their morals were, of course, better than their philosophy. For in a completely determined universe, how could you decide to make the orderliness of nature the law of your own life? A halfway house again. For there is a moral order to which you can decide to conform, but you are a free man when you make the decision. And it is this moral freedom which gives meaning to your life.

Men lived in these halfway houses in Rome. They have lived in these halfway houses in every century since. The urbane, materialistic man of the world has always inclined to be an Epicurean. The man who could not live without a commanding moral purpose, whatever his metaphysic, has been inclined to be a Stoic. And beyond the halfway houses there has always been the home of the mind and the soul.

8. The Deliverance from Abstraction

The great Greek tragedians lived in a world of actual men and women confronting actual situations. And they dealt with very concrete gods with actual ways of experience. In Euripides we see the Greek ashamed of his deities. There is a downrightness in his implicit and sometimes explicit criticism which is fairly startling. In Aeschylus and

Sophocles the great gods tend to possess a grandeur far apart from that ascribed to them by many Greek myths. And in many Greek writers there is a tendency to see one mind and one high moral purpose in the divine and to say God when speaking of this ultimate moral reality.

All this moves in the direction of the concrete and of an antiseptic criticism and away from the realm of abstraction. How was Plato affected by all this, and how was he related to it?

As we have seen, he made his brilliant moral and intellectual analysis through a process of effective abstraction. Then by a great act of faith he made his abstractions real. He made them the ultimate reality.

But Plato was a true Greek, and the direct gaze did not fail him here. For if you looked at his brilliant abstractions with complete honesty, they remained abstractions even when you called them real. How could you give them dependable and permanent reality? There was only one way. Plato's own ideas were real because he held them in his mind. If the ultimate ideas of the good, the beautiful, and the true were held in the mind of a great, eternal conscious intelligence and made operative through his perpetual power, then they would be real indeed. Ideas are real only in the mind of a person who holds them. The ultimate ideas are real because they exist first in the mind of God. To this position Plato came in the *Laws*. It represented a genuine deliverance from the fallacy of the abstract, and it represented the highest achievement of Greek thought. So Plato moved from a world of glorified figures of speech to a world of living persons.

But the fallacy of assuming that abstractions are real apart from living persons has remained to haunt and to confuse the mind of man. Philosophy has been confused by it. Theology has been betrayed by it. The study of human relations has been befogged through its obfuscations. Even Christian theologians have used the word God as if it were only a convenient term for a set of abstract and impersonal principles. But Greek thought at its best moved from ultimate principles to the ultimate conscious, living intelligence. So Plato came to his most shining hour.

9. Athens and Jerusalem

It has always been too easy for a man to say, "I belong to Athens; I do not belong to Jerusalem," or to say, "I belong to Jerusalem; I do not belong to Athens." There are, of course, differences enough. In a sense, at its best Athens represents man marching Godward. And in its defining meaning, of course, Jerusalem represents God marching manward. And when the two roads converge, as converge they must, it is true that Jerusalem is able to speak words Athens has never been able to utter because Jerusalem has seen and known things beyond the mind of Athens. But in a very profound sense the two cities belong together.

And if it is true that Athens will come upon frustration at last unless it receives the insights of Jerusalem, we must also be honest enough to say that Jerusalem with all its glory needs something which only Athens can give.

"Now there were certain Greeks among those that went up to worship at the feast: these therefore came to Philip, who was of Bethsaida of Galilee, and asked him, saying, Sir, we would see Jesus. Philip cometh and telleth Andrew: Andrew cometh, and Philip, and they tell Jesus. And Jesus answereth them, saying, The hour is come that the Son of man should be glorified."

Greece was all unconsciously creating intellectual forms and even moral and spiritual apprehensions which would prepare Greek minds to receive and interpret the Christian religion and to train the Latin minds which were to carry the interpretation into deeper regions of tragic insight.

The comprehensiveness of the mind of Origen and the passionate insight of Athanasius reveal the Greek mind and the Christian facts and insights at home together. But the matter is much deeper and broader than one might understand even after a patient and profound study of the Greek theologians.

It was in Greece that man emerged. The cult of man might end in self-worship. This would mean the development of the type of humanism which dehumanizes man. But the man who emerged in Athens was a creature of free intelligence capable of seeing that his resources were inadequate even for the completion of his own life. He was capable of being loyal to that which was beyond himself and that which was above him. The very critical quality of his humanism, as its thoughts come to fruition in Plato, inevitably leads beyond the human. Man finds the meaning of his life as he looks up. He participates in something he did not originate and without which he would lose his humanity. So the central line of Greek development leads not to the worship of humanity by humanity but to the quest for God.

But the Greek sense of the human puts man clearly above the thing and above the beast. He may choose to surrender his birthright. He may become a thing. He may become a beast. But that free intelligence which is his essential characteristic is destined to be lord over that which is below and the voluntary servant of that which is above. This is the consummation of the thought of Athens. And it is in profoundest accord with the deepest insights of Jerusalem.

The Greek belief in the human was not the deification of the human. It was the critical inspection of the human, and it found in man just what were his real and essential possessions. Here the direct gaze served the Greek well. For it enabled him to tell the truth even about himself.

The large and many-sided investigation of human possibilities and powers by the Greek mind had a far-reaching significance for Christianity. For, once the Christian religion had solved man's central problems, he could appropriate all that versatile and agile-minded Greeks had discovered and make it a part of his own great corpus of thought and life.

There are contemporary interpretations of the Christian religion which have missed the secret of Athens and have also missed the secret of Jerusalem. This emasculated Christianity which has lost the vital energies of Greek culture and the profound experience of moral transformation so essential to that evangelical faith which comes from Jerusalem is a sad substitute for the splendidly human, surgically evangelical religion which is classical Christianity. And oddly, yet perhaps naturally enough, this curious product which bears the Christian name is betrayed by that very apotheosis of abstraction which tempted the Greeks themselves. The mighty commerce of the living God with living men is lost in a barren abstractness which can find itself no better name than a way of life. It is a very empty road until there walks there the One who said, "I am the way"; and in Him the sense of the living God which comes from Jerusalem and of living men which comes from Athens becomes actual for the living men who walk the earth today. The direct gaze is only satisfied when it meets God in Christ. Here all figures of speech become a Great Figure in life and above life, Master and Friend and Lord and Savior of men.

CHAPTER XVII

Critics of Many Lands

THE inspection of human experience must include some consideration of what man has thought of his own experience. He has expressed his apprehension of the meaning of his own life in many a volume in many a literature. He has expressed it in that writing which is a criticism of literature. He has expressed it very especially in that writing which is a criticism of life. And if he has been a wise man he has understood perfectly well that an authentic criticism of literature always includes a criticism of life. We happen to live in days of inner confusion and outer chaos. The quest for significance and for dependable standards in such a time is of the very greatest importance. This is particularly true because in days when civilization itself is falling apart there are subtly persuasive voices lifted in praise of chaos.

1. The Voice of the Critic

Of course, the critic himself may be an unreliable guide except as a photographer of moral and spiritual confusion. Oscar Cargill's *Intellectual America,* as we have had reason to remark before in these studies, deals principally with those who thought that sensations have all the rights of ideas and biological processes all the qualities of spiritual emancipation. It is an account of those who have become experts in that which is unlovely and of bad report. It reflects the preoccupations of those who deal with that which corrupts the imagination and disintegrates the moral fiber. The genealogy of decadent ideas is traced with brilliant finesse. The erotic takes the place of that which is full of clean health. The decadent takes the place of that which is truly creative. But the rosary of evil whose beads the author is able to count gives a startling sense of the depths to which we have sunk. There is even more cause for pessimism to be found in this volume of Oscar Cargill than in the brutalities of the second World War. The war is at least a conflict. The contemporary mind is too often contented with adventures in slime without having any battle at all.

We turn, then, for a quick look at some of the critics of the ages of man's civilized life to see what they had to say about man.

2. Through the Eyes of Aristotle

When Aristotle turns from the study of nature to the study of man, he finds man a part of a society. This is what he means by calling him a political animal. And in the life of men together we come upon the state. Aristotle takes a high line at once. "A state exists for the sake of the good life and not for the sake of life only." Aristotle studies the forms of state organization with which men have been familiar. "There is also a doubt as to what is to be the supreme power in the state:—Is it the multitude? Or the wealthy? Or the good? Or the one best man? Or a prince?" He always keeps in mind certain standards. "Then ought the good to rule and to have supreme power." Yet he recognizes the rights of the multitude and the place which must be given to them. He sees the evils possible in a democracy and, like other great Greek thinkers, he sees the menace of the mass when the mass is wrong. He is frank enough about what he calls "the wickedness of human nature," but he is not without hope of a good life in a good state.

Aristotle presses more closely to the heart of the problems of the individual person in the *Nicomachean Ethics*. He finds that eudaemonia which is the object of human life in the activity of the rational faculty. "The function then of man is an activity of the soul in accordance with reason." "And the Good for man is an activity of the soul in accordance with goodness." Man is to use his rational faculty to choose the good. Here we come upon the doctrine of the golden mean. In every problem which man with his free mind confronts there are extremes to be spurned and there is a central course to be followed.

In his *Poetics* Aristotle is less the mere clear thinker and plunges into the heat of the tragedy of life. His doctrine of catharsis has been the object of debate for centuries. If we subject the discussion to the test of experience, it is not too difficult to come to the heart of it. Tragedy bursts upon a man and almost breaks him. But when he reads or sees the production of a great tragedy which may be like his very own, it suddenly becomes possible for him to see his tragedy as a part of the human lot. His own pain is no longer the ugly isolation of a private grief. It is a part of the human lot. So his sense of loneliness departs. He can bear his share of the human burden. The great act of catharsis has been wrought.

There are always two elements in tragedy. There is the great principle which is timeless. There is the particular example which is concrete and individual. The principle is changeless and eternal. The particular example may be different from every other in its individual quality. So the tragedy is classic, as we would say, in the principle it illustrates and has all the freshness and originality of individual experience in the particular story it tells.

We see Aristotle, then, finding man with a free mind able to choose the central path amid contending extremes, able to create a society for the good life in which the mass of men give power to the best, and able to see individual experiences in the light of eternal principles and individual agonies in the light of the common lot.

3. Longinus and the Great Soul

The famous treatise *On the Sublime,* which bears the name of Longinus, has won the praise of critics of every succeeding age. Sometimes they praise it for good reasons. Sometimes they praise it for reasons less good. But they always sense its very great excellence and power. You actually come to its central insight in Longinus' conception of the sublime as the echo of a great soul. Loveliness must have a basis in character. And character at a peak of moral excellence is the basis of the sublime.

It is noteworthy that historical criticism in its central movement recognizes again and again the moral responsibility of the artist and of the critic. According to Aristophanes the literary artist must be judged at last by the power of his work to make a good citizen. The cult of moral irresponsibility in art was not a Greek cult. When Plato criticizes the literary artist as making an imitation of an imitation, he is fearing the tendency of art to get away from that intellectual and moral and spiritual reality in which the good life consists. He judges the artist finally by his power to contribute to the excellent life. So when Longinus sees the sublime as the echo of a great soul, he is in the central stream of classical criticism.

4. Cicero and the Battle Between Appetite and Reason

Cicero is in the midst of the very movement of Roman life. And he does much to control that movement. He exposes the conspiracy of Catiline. He struggles for the free life in the days of increasing tyranny. He is a clear thinker, a superb man of letters, and, in his own way, a philosopher. In *De officiis* he comes to the center of his own thought about human life. He finds man in a state of tension. He finds man in the midst of a battle. It is the battle between appetite and reason. And in that battle reason has a right to be victorious. Cicero would have liked to believe that all the polished urbanity of his persuasive speaking and writing was at the service of the rational. It was his object to lend his abilities to the triumph of reason.

The Roman as well as the Greek sees man as a responsible agent of thought and action, choosing between contending powers which would rule his life. It is he himself who can put reason on the throne over appetite. Cicero would have been very scornful could he have confronted the modern cult of surrender to impulse. He would have seen in that great surrender the beginning of the end of civilization.

5. Quintilian Directs the Man with a Voice

The *Institutio Oratoria* of Quintilian belongs to the same great tradition. Quintilian lives in a world where the power of speech is everywhere recognized. He writes a book to make the speaker powerful and effective. Sometimes he drops to a level of not very lovely expediency. But on the whole he sees the power of speech as the characteristic of a being made for life at good levels and to be used for purposes of the establishment of good. He is not studying the uniformities of nature to find the secret of life in the level below the personal. He is discussing the voice as the vehicle of the controlling mind for the direction of life. The appeal is always to good intelligence. The implicit assumptions are always those of free intelligence. In discussing the making and the equipment of the orator, Quintilian is really discussing the making and the equipment of the civilized man.

6. Lucian Scorns His World

The literary phenomenon which bears the name of Lucian is of very great importance. This master of ironic writing is an ancestor of Erasmus, of Voltaire, of Dean Swift, and of all the wielders of the corrosive pen. He owes something to the Socratic irony. He owes something to the misanthropy of Diogenes. He owes something to the antiseptic mirth of Aristophanes. But he is his own man thinking his own thoughts and expressing them in his own ways.

It is easy to think of Lucian as no more than the master of scornful and cynical laughter. And this beyond the peradventure of a doubt he is. But his bitter irony in the presence of evil is doubly scornful because of his love of the good. And his biting thrust of satire in the presence of falsehood has its last cutting edge because of his love of truth. His method is negative. His purpose is positive. So in his own inverted way he is always pleading for dependable standards. His scorn is a form of loyalty to the good in the presence of that which denies it. And when he comes to brief and yet adequate self-revelation, what he wants for himself and for mankind is a plain and reliable map of life. The true sons of Lucian have been on the side of civilization in the great battles of the world.

7. Boethius Confronts Tragedy

To come to a place of glittering power in the state, then to be the object of unjust suspicion and to endure imprisonment, torture, and violent death, was the experience of Boethius. He was a Christian. He

232   THE MEANING OF HUMAN EXPERIENCE

had his own theological interests. And he possessed a philosophic type of mind. Much of the classical heritage passed through him to the Middle Ages. And in his hour of tragedy he found the great principles of reason to which he was devoted a powerful support.

The meeting of Chirtian loyalty and philosophical urbanity in Boethius forms a fascinating combination. If our source materials were more adequate, it would be an illuminating study. At least it is clear that his *Consolation of Philosophy* was one of the most popular books of the Middle Ages. And it was Christian men with whom it was popular. They saw no reason why the quiet and reassuring words of a gentle and understanding philosophy should not be received and appropriated by men who inherited the Christian tradition. Reason was not to give up the battle in an irrational world. And even when true reason was flouted and cast down, its loyal servants were to accept suffering and death rather than to depart from its behests. The quiet possession of the truth was something which could establish a man confronting the ugliest onslaughts of evil. And the Middle Ages saw this as something that could be made a part of the Christian tradition and not as something apart from that tradition.

8. Thomas Aquinas Finds Reason in Theology

We must take a look at a great theologian of the Middle Ages and of all time. Thomas Aquinas set forth the Christian revelation in the forms of orderly thought. He believed in man's reason. He believed that there are truths man's reason can reach without revelation. He believed that there are truths which can come to man only through divine revelation. But he believed that the higher truths, once revealed, can be apprehended and classified by man's reason. And he used the thought forms of Aristotle as a frame for his great *Summa*. One sees at once that he is a part of the great classical tradition about the powers of the human mind. He fits neatly into it his truths from loftier regions. But he believes that man's mind is so essentially made for the truth that when God speaks, His word quickly finds a home in the full corpus of true human thought.

All this is different enough from the conception that man's mind is so essentially corrupt that it is not made for God's truth nor is it capable of responding to it except through what in almost every case amounts to a miracle of divine grace. Thomas Aquinas may be said to fit the deepest insights of the Latin theology and the deepest insights of the Greek theology into one corpus of thought, putting it all into a frame provided by classical philosophy in its noblest appreciation of the powers of the human mind.

9. *Pico della Mirandola Finds the Dignity of Man*

The famous oration on the *Dignity of Man* by Pico della Mirandola has a place all its own in man's estimate of himself and of his experiences. Pico played about a bit with a curious and often pseudo mysticism which has to be subjected to very critical inspection. But when he put forth his sharpest thoughts about man he was on very solid ground indeed. He saw man living between two worlds—one above him and one beneath him. By the sentence of his intellect he could make his own the quality of life and the insights of the world above him. By the sentence of his own decision he could sink to the world below him. So man stood poised between alternatives. So man must make the great decision. And herein lay the dignity of man.

10. *Francis Bacon Turns to Nature and Misunderstands Human Values*

Francis Bacon, it must be confessed, is very much out of the great tradition. He writes magnificently. He is even capable of a royal splendor of phrase and a many-colored pageantry of the imagination. And he can use the vocabulary of leaders of the mind and guides of the soul whose positions he never really makes his own. In all his genuinely characteristic processes of thought his mind is taken up with the control of nature through the understanding of its uniformities rather than with the control of human nature by great acts of intellectual and moral choice. He is one of the first great prophets of preoccupation with the subhuman. It is part of the essential irony of his life that the failure of moral self-control in the name of great standards of right living led to his own downfall and disgrace. But he is an almost regal portent of the way in which men were to go wrong. The man who is so busy understanding things that he forgets the essential characteristics of men will always find grist for his mill in the writings of Francis Bacon. And a world which follows him in his preoccupation with the subhuman may be expected, like him, to meet the hour of moral demand with blind eyes and to come to the hour of the great human choice without understanding.

11. *Dryden Comes to His Throne*

The seventeenth century is often more significant in what it assumes than in what it declares. For the seventeenth century inherits a classical tradition which has not been confused by alien lights. Men are much more likely to go wrong in their lives than in their thinking. They have not yet found a philosophy to justify moral deterioration. So when Dryden is a glittering literary figure he wears with the utmost dignity the robes of the great tradition. Sometimes there are suggestions of a critical thought which, in being correct, has forgotten to be vital. But there are flashes enough of living light. The flag which floats high and serene will go through many a bloody field in days to come. But there it stands and under its banner men write a prose of Augustan dignity and flowing power and a poetry which turns ancient sanctions to contemporary beauty.

12. France Attains a Fine Certainty

The classical period found superb expression in France as well as in England. And to this day the cult of the depreciation of Boileau has never succeeded in clouding completely his sense of man's significance. France had its hidden tragedies. And it may be possible to say that the splendid urbanity of its seventeenth-century writing was obtained by ignoring as well as by looking frankly at the real. But it would be hard to overestimate the significance of the fact that the men who mastered the mind of France in the seventeenth century believed that there is a royal way of life and there is a royal way of speech. Something of crystal clarity entered French thought and something of controlled vitality entered French writing which is not to be disparaged, is not to be forgotten, and is to be prized as long as men prize civilization itself.

Of course, one must have unhesitating loyalty to clearly held standards to get this product of fine clarity and high urbanity. Men had not then come to believe that the liberty of the pigsty is better than the controlled dignity of the royal audience chamber. And it was a part of a very deep human tragedy that when men turned with hot anger from the misuse of royal power, they turned from what was lofty and worthy in the regime which they repudiated as well as from what was unjust and tyrannical. Democracy is most unlovely when it attacks what has true quality in order to get rid of what is actually evil. The solution, of course, is to be found in a democracy which attains and practices the aristocratic virtues without being betrayed by the aristocratic vices. One may put the formula in a phrase and sharpen it into an epigram. But to turn the description into an actual achievement is difficult indeed. As one thinks of these things in connection with the seventeenth century, he sees long shadows cast backward from days which followed.

13. The Coffee House Becomes Articulate

The Queen Anne period retains a kind of deathless fascination. And at the heart of the Queen Anne period is the Coffee House. Here Addison, with the voice of a very fine gentleman, and Dick Steele, with a speech all full of gentle humanity, so gaily and persuasively made vice a thing at which it was necessary to laugh and virtue a thing of all happy grace, that they changed the manners of London and made goodness fashionable. The perusal of the old pages of the *Spectator* makes one think long, long thoughts. The London to which these men belonged had passed through the debaucheries of the Restoration. It had its own deep dark secrets. Perhaps that was a part of the story. Perhaps it was very weary and very lonely after its nights of wild lawlessness. In any event the assured step of an honest gentleman walking into the coffee house made a great difference. And his quiet voice, too sure to be hotly assertive, presided at the birth of a new society.

If one is to understand at all what happened, one must have a feeling for the assumptions which lay back of the words and the writing. The classical tradition still gave men a sense that humanity ought to be a very noble thing. There was still a belief that the resasonable—meaning by reasonable that which commended itself to the reason and not that which responded to the need of plausible compromise—had the right of way. For centuries the classical tradition had been filling even men's subconscious thought with a sense of the gracious charm of gentle ways of life. The coffee house quite easily and happily assumed this tradition and set it forth as something men already believed rather than something which they were asked to accept. So the genius of a more gracious habit of life came to London and to England with the aroma of a cup of coffee.

14. Dean Swift Castigates

Dean Swift seems always to be angry. He looks life straight in the eye. He dislikes it. More than that, he hates it. He holds it up to corrosive scorn. He is always wielding his whip. He is always lashing that which belongs to the realm of darkness and would flee from the light. Indeed, he not only lashes the evil, he lets the light in. But it is the light of swift and revealing lightning followed by the crack of thunder which somehow indicates how deadly the light has been.

An adequate psychology of moral hate has never been written. When the task is attempted Dean Swift will provide certain inevitable and necessary materials. For his hatred is the reverse side of a great and hidden love. Only one who loves the good can lash out so frightfully against the evil. There is a sense, of course, in which sentimental and gregarious goodness is not really goodness at all. You cannot love truth without hating falsehood. You cannot love loyalty without hating treachery. You cannot love beauty without hating ugliness. Gregarious and sentimental affection is all the while kissing the evil in fear of a too belligerent assertion of the good. In a war where great moral issues are at stake it is likely to be so busy being generous to its enemies that it becomes incapable of being just to its friends. Dean Swift's moral wrath is very terrible and very corrosive. But it has much to teach us. If we take virtue seriously, we must hate the lie which corrupts the soul. Because he saw this, Dean Swift belongs to the great tradition.

15. Dr. Johnson Pontificates

Dr. Johnson was full of curious eccentricities in loyalty to a great center. The eccentricities give him a certain human fascination. And he was more fortunate than most men in finding a Boswell who was quite willing to efface himself in order to make his hero live. But it is the central loyalties of Dr. Johnson which make him an Olympian figure. He often expressed them with magnificent rudeness. But men sensed in him something more than sincerity. They sensed a relation to the permanent which abides in the midst of the passing. And so in his own way he became a king because he believed in kingliness.

The man who is free to do anything but has no standards is not really free at all because in his world nothing is actually worth doing. Dr. Johnson moved among imperatives, and so he had, and he gave to others, the sense that life was full of meaning. The anarchist never knows what to do with his freedom. Dr. Johnson found a real freedom *in* law and never sought a pseudo freedom *from* law.

16. Burke Beholds Sublimity

When Burke delivered his memorable speeches in the House of Commons, men did not always realize that they were listening to one of the immortals. But he gives to his whole period a certain richly tapestried dignity. He never takes men's minds down in order to make them comfortable. He always takes men's minds up in order that they may dwell upon the heights and see far vistas. He believes in a great and historic order. He sees the majesty of the great tradition. He fears nothing more than the disintegration of ancient sanctions and the falling apart of a venerable and noble tradition. So he becomes the most brilliant critic of the French Revolution. The radical democrats were willing to cast out all the good of the ancient regime in order to get rid of its appalling evils. Burke was no doubt willing to be patient with evils which called loudly for correction in order to save the world from the sheer breakdown which would come if the great structure of civilization fell to the ground. He did not say everything which needed to be said. He did say many things which very much needed to be said. But in these days when we are so much more keen about overthrowing the evil than about maintaining the good, his sense of the sublime structure of orderly civilized life is very much needed.

17. Sainte-Beuve Writes Royally

Sainte-Beuve had the imagination of a humanist and the intellectual frame of a hard determinist. On one side he represents the same materialistic determinism as Taine. On the other he represents the rich and understanding entering into men's experience of French humanism at its best. The *Causeries du Lundi* are a sort of school in the practice of humanistic criticism. They clothe the experiences of men as one might put on a perfectly fitting garment. And they find endless firm and sure and understanding phrases to express this apprehension of the meaning of all sorts of experiences. It is as if civilization turned keen and searching eyes upon its own long and manifold tale of conscious life. The paradox of Sainte-Beuve is that he all the while implicitly assumes as a critic the freedom he denies as a deterministic philosopher. But it is as a critic that he will live. In every one of his essays he enables you to look out on the world through the eyes of men very different from yourself. For in him a cosmopolitan sympathy becomes a cosmopolitan understanding.

18. Carlyle's Clouds and Darkness and Flashing Light

One may say without meaning to be irreverent that in one respect Thomas Carlyle represents the Old Testament conception of the loftiest figure of whom we may think. Clouds and darkness were all around him, and he gives you a mysterious sense of the sweeping winds that move through eternity. Then there are flashes of revealing light.

An age which has reduced life to mathematics will find it difficult to understand Carlyle, just as he would have scorned the age which found in existence nothing more than automatic mathematical formulas. He despised shams as few men have despised them. He believed in sincerity with an awful faith. He worshiped his heroes with a loyalty which sometimes forgave them too much. But above the clutter of convention, and breaking the clanking chains of impersonal existence, he saw the majestic man in full-orbed power and had some sense of the mightier majesty behind him.

19. Matthew Arnold Remembers the Best That Has Been Thought and Said in the World

The Oxford which saw a singularly well-dressed and distinguished young man who was the son of the great master of Rugby walk through its quadrangles was much impressed. And in due season this coiner of memorable phrases which captured memorable insights won his place in the critical world. He was not the believer in sweetly singing an idle day. He believed in high thought and high seriousness. He distrusted loud voices. He believed in sweet reasonableness. He wanted to conserve and to appreciate the best that had been thought and said in the world. Sometimes he had splendid insights which he never worked out into the structure of his thinking, as when he said, "Man must begin, know this, where nature ends." This was because he did not have a real corpus of understanding. He was a man of thoughts rather than of thought, as he himself said of Emerson; and, though he would have

been glad to make real what he said of Sophocles and to have been able
to see life steadily and to see it whole, he never quite rose from the power
which makes for righteousness to the Great and Eternal Person who has
made and sustains the world and man.

20. Ruskin Teaches Beauty to Face Social Responsibility

John Ruskin was essentially an artist. He loved beauty more than he
loved anything else. He saw very clearly, and he perfectly understood
the mathematical aspects of beauty as well as its deeper moral and spiritual significance. But most of all he believed that we cannot have
beauty in art apart from the presence of beauty in life. And so, from
being an art critic, he set about being a social reformer. He commanded
words for social purposes as Charles Kingsley and Frederick Denison
Maurice never commanded them. And when he turned art criticism to
social analysis and a call for better living conditions and a better life
for all men, the artist became the prophet with a fire not unlike that
of the Old Testament.

21. Saintsbury, the Hedonist

George Saintsbury in the long run will be remembered as a landmark
of the time when literary criticism lost its way. He was a man of immense erudition, as a perusal of the three volumes of his monumental
History of Criticism will show. But he cared for literature only because
of its pleasure-giving qualities. And he saw in criticism only an estimate
of literary products in the light of their capacity to give pleasure. So he
became the great apostle of literary hedonism. So he became the typical
Epicurean in literary criticism. The fashion in which he has to deal
with the great critics of the ages, who have characteristically insisted
on a criticism of life as a part of literary criticism, would be amusing
if it did not possess a touch of tragedy. But Professor Saintsbury never
loses confidence in his own position even when it almost seems that all
the regiment of critics is out of step and only he is in step. It is to be
said in all honesty that he polarized the judgment of many men who
ought to have been too wise to be betrayed by his hedonism. But often
his own *History of Criticism* gives the materials for the correction of
his Epicurean obsession if one reads that history with sharp intelligence.

22. Physics and Biology Rampant

The criticism which was a by-product of French materialism set the
stage for a criticism based on the subhuman and forgetting that free
intelligence which is the essentially human. And with the immense
activity in physics and biology it was inevitable that there would be in
literature schools of writers who saw men as puppets moved by invisible wires, and as animals, the meaning of whose life was exhausted

in the energies which were a defining part of their physical organism. This sort of thing was often done with great distinction and power. But it always led to a betrayal of the human, and both as literature and as criticism it used human powers for the glorifying of that which is below the human.

23. The Freudians Inspire Literary Criticism

We have already referred to Oscar Cargill's *Intellectual America*, a characteristic example of the type of criticism in which Freud takes the place which belongs to Aristotle. As a history of decadent literary movements the work is superb. And no one can read it or the typical books which it discusses without realizing the place of the subconscious in literature. The "stream of consciousness" literature is a literature of obsession. But it has something to be obsessed about. Even when this has been admitted, however, the central human interest will always be with the free mind of man controlling the stream of the subconscious and not with the subconscious overflowing and submerging the free mind of man.

24. The Social Radicals Have Their Day in Court

It is a long call from the hedonism of Professor Saintsbury to the social radicalism of Professor Parrington or the communistic criticism of Bernard Smith. But criticism in our time and the period immediately before it has rather rounded the compass. There is much that is good about the literature of social indignation. And there is much that is good about the criticism of social indignation. But it is—for all its contributions—apart from the central stream. And it has one great and ugly defect. It is so busy creating indignation with the present social order, for the purpose of getting dynamite ready to blow it up, that it can never tell the truth about its good aspects. The account of American life reflected in Parrington's criticism, in spite of all its elements of truth, again and again becomes a travesty of the actuality. Both the literature and the criticism of social indignation have the heat of fever rather than the warmth of health. They are always superficial both in their preoccupation with environment and in their underestimate of the power and the significance of the person.

25. Humanism Becomes Mighty in Irving Babbitt

One can find an indication of the actual power of the criticism of Irving Babbitt in the way in which the critics of the flux become apoplectic and profane at the very mention of his name. It is as if they feel instinctively that they do not dare to treat him fairly. The characteristic references to Babbitt in contemporary hostile criticism are written hastily in hot impatience and are not the product of thorough study of his writings and patient and complete appraisal of his position.

This is partly explained by the fact that Babbitt thought and declared that contemporary thinking had gone wrong on first principles. This traveling on false trails was largely the product of a romanticism which moved out from Jean Jacques Rousseau. Babbitt's brilliant and conclusive analysis in the famous volume *Rousseau and Romanticism* will go down as one of the supreme critical achievements of the century which saw its publication. Over against the philosophy of impulse, Babbitt put the philosophy of discipline. He was not the foe of the rich fecundity of the life of impulse. But he did believe that impulses must be mastered and controlled in the light of dependable principles. Over against the world of vital impulse he put the rational control of vitality. The critics of his *frein vital* have usually remembered the *frein* and have forgotten the *vital*. With a wealth of erudition of fairly breathtaking quality he criticized the surrender to lawless impulse which is the outstanding characteristic of the contemporary world. The subhuman world of mechanical interaction and biological impulse must be mastered by critical intelligence on the human level for the sake of the survival of civilization itself. Indeed, Bacon's preoccupation with the uniformities of nature to the exclusion of the critical choices of men was in its way as menacing to the good life as the lawless romanticism of Rousseau. Babbitt always faced the vast product of the human mind in the manifold writings which he knew so well with a keen scent for those permanent values in loyalty to which life finds its true meaning. In this apprehension of quality in contrast to mere quantity, he felt that the final test of democracy was its power to practice the aristocratic virtues. To be creative was to see eternal values come to the fullness of vital expression. No critic of the mental and moral and spiritual anarchy of our time spoke with a more commanding voice. He made his chair at Harvard a veritable throne. And no one of his critics was able to meet him on his own level either of knowledge or of intellectual power.

26. Humanism Becomes Christian in Paul Elmer More

The spiritual pilgrimage of Paul Elmer Moore as revealed in his many volumes of distinguished and discriminating writing has a significance for the student of the meaning of human experience which will be increasingly clear as the years go by. This cool and clear-minded friend of Babbitt, with an unsuspected spiritual fire burning at the center of his personality, spent much of his life in an ample study of the great literature of the world, engrossed with the enterprise of finding its meaning. In a way, his *Shelburne Essays* are at the peak of American literary criticism. Like Babbitt, he saw that one can never explain the human by means of the subhuman. And the characteristic human quality he found in intelligence choosing between alternatives in the light of standards. The ripest intellectual and moral and spiritual experience of the race had a right to claim the allegiance of the human mind. He became an eager Platonist, finding the source of the real as apprehended by men in a realm above the human. He had tried to be contented with a secular humanism. He tried to be contented with a humanism corresponding to the earlier insights of Plato. Then in the *Laws* he found a clue in the belief in a great conscious intelligence. Here the ideas had their reality. They were not abstractions hanging in thin air. But if there is a great conscious person in whom truth and goodness and beauty live, must he not speak to the men whom he has made with an intelligence in some way corresponding to his own? The answer took him beyond Plato to the moral and spiritual voices of the Old Testament. As he reread the prophetic writings, he became convinced that God had indeed spoken. The traveling now became swift and perilous and full of mental adventure. God had spoken. Did he dare to ask the question: Had God come? He did ask it, and he found the answer in the New Testament and the Greek Fathers whose insights were expressed at Nicaea and Chalcedon. The answer was the Word made flesh. The answer was the Incarnation. Toward the end of his life he put another question: Had God allowed the passionate pain of man's tragedy to pierce His own heart? And he found himself able to write at the end of his long pilgrimage of the Lamb of God that taketh away the sins of the world.

27. *Evangelical Humanism*

There is one more step. The humanistic pilgrim must come to full consciousness of the meaning of the Cross. When humanism itself becomes evangelical, Athens and Jerusalem truly meet. The man who follows the world-wide lines of the inspection of the human, will come at last upon two great needs. One is the need for fulfillment. The other is the need for antiseptic surgery. And following the line of this chapter we can see in another fashion how right was the insight of the Greek theology, that the incompleteness of the human is brought to fulfillment through the completeness of God. The Incarnation is the symbol and the actuality of the great fulfillment.

But the broken, tragic life of man requires more. And not only theology, but that criticisim which in literature sees a profound reflection of life and its deepest demands, must come to stand at last on Mount Calvary. The call for the great evangel is written at the very heart of the profoundest literature of the world. And the criticism which follows literature to these tragic depths must itself call for the Cross.

CHAPTER XVIII

Fiction Finds Truth and Falsehood

CURIOUSLY enough, fiction is one of the most perfect means of telling the truth about people and also one of the most effective means of decorating falsehood and of telling plausible lies. With the telling of tales something very delightful begins to happen to man. The ancient bard brought multitudes of invisible people with him when he came. And to many persons of sensitive imagination he must have seemed to leave life empty when he went away. These people who may or may not have lived in the actual world but now were very much alive in the mind of the storyteller, came also to be splendidly alive to those who listened. The man who knew how to tell tales with simple, graphic power was sure of a welcome everywhere. The charm of the well-told story early captured the interest of man, and it has never lost its hold.

1. Escape

From the beginning life has had aspects of sordidness and dullness and monotony and heavy meaninglessness. And often it has settled into bleak hardness. The tale well told has been for an hour an almost magical escape. When we read the ancient stories, we think of their charm, their glamour, their subtle beauty. We forget almost always the light shining in lusterless eyes, the quick beating of hearts which had almost forgotten the joy of a great expectation, the dull sky of the weary mind before the bright light the imagination kindles began to shine. But just because fiction was so often a method of escape from dullness and heavy routine and even tragedy, it was often tempted to seem to promise what it could not give. Cinderella must have set numberless maidens watching for princes who never came. But, whatever the other effects of the story, what was the delight of the forgotten and the ignored as they heard the tales of rich compensation! The romances of escape often assumed that the change which would bring happiness was merely a change in circumstances. Rarely did the listeners realize how little happiness the most brilliant material gifts can bring to those who can hold gold in their hands but do not have golden hearts. The rubbing of Aladdin's lamp suggests a gambler's philosophy. Indeed, the vast and bewildering number of tales of magic all too often suggested escape without meeting the conditions of escape, of prosperity without paying the price of prosperity. To be sure, as Sir William Robertson

Nicoll used to insist, stories like the *Arabian Nights* often contained no end of wisdom apart from their paraphernalia of magic. We cannot dispose of a literary genre by a formula, not even a magical formula. But the audience of the tale is very important if we are to understand the tale itself. And the army of the discontented ready to follow any pied piper of the imagination who would lead them into ways of escape, though the escape would be but for an hour, must never be forgotten by those who follow the telling of tales through the centuries of human experience.

2. Adventure

Life has always been an adventure. Often it has been a very difficult adventure. Sometimes it has been an almost impossible adventure. And sometimes it has broken in complete frustration and tragedy at last. When the stakes were high and the conditions difficult, the adventure became gloriously and happily exciting.

So inevitably the tale of adventure became one of the great forms of storytelling. It was a tale of endurance. It was a tale of the quick mind and the agile body. It was a tale of the man who knew how to grasp success from the jaws of failure. Old legends of many lands were full of the stuff of adventure. Hercules went forth in many countries and in many ages for more than seven labors. Knights and men of knightly spirit fought bravely before and after the days of Arthur and the Round Table. The matter of Britain and the matter of France were filled with brave struggle against terrible odds. The Teutonic legends were full of heroes. There was a curious mingling of the authentic and the magical. The mystery of life was full of the tragically unexpected. But it had, too, the gloriously happy unexpected. And men in many ages were haunted by a belief that a magical formula or a magical object could be a substitute for ability and character or at least the servant and rewarder of ability and character. The sense that a glad surprise might lie waiting around any corner of life has kept men's courage up, sometimes by all too artificial a stimulant. And the men who have ceased to believe in the glad surprise have fallen into terrible cynicism.

But the real heart of stories of adventure has always been the courage and the quickness of the mind and the agility of movement of the hero. To take great risks and to win by sheer power of character and virtue of mind has been something men have always deeply admired and something which has greatly thrilled them. So saga after saga of heroic feats has grown up. Something of the finest of human life has been recorded in the tale of the hero. And the narrative itself has helped to keep heroism alive. There has always been more than a basis in fact. From the siege of Troy to the invasion of Europe by the Allies in 1944 the great struggles of men have been full of the stuff of which heroic tales are made. Heroism is not, of course, only a matter of war. The hero of civil life may be as daring as the soldier. The man who risks his life to win new truth for science, the man who risks his life to save others in an epidemic, the man who risks his life in journeys of exploration, these and many others in their turn offer materials to the tellers of tales of adventure.

3. Vicarious Satisfaction

It is one of the rather delightful things about human nature that men love to read stories in which other men do the things they themselves would like to do or say the things they themselves would like to say or possess the prosperity which they themselves would like to possess. These vicarious satisfactions are alluring and may become dangerous. To spend one's life in lotus-eating, daydreaming, one's imagination fed by glamorous tales, is to miss the personal opportunity which for every man is the center of the significance of the great adventure. Professor William James used to say that it was dangerous to have an emotion without straightway going forth to do something about it. The man of vicarious experience may easily be a man who tries to enjoy all the emotions of a rich life without having any of the actual experiences of which these emotions are a by-product. On the other hand, nothing so quickens the imagination, enlarges the sympathy, and expands the area of the action of intelligence, as just vicarious experience. There is a sense in which one can define an educated man as a man who is capable of learning from vicarious experience. The centuries are his servants, and all human life is his slave.

At all events, in curiously adequate fashion, fiction offers vicarious experience to human beings. Walter Pater's *Marius the Epicurean* is better than a course in the philosophy of the subtlest and most gracious form of hedonism. Many a reader will tell you what varied aspects of experience became real for him in Goethe's *Wilhelm Meister*. It is not always a work of great intellectual distinction which achieves this result. Mrs. Charles's *Chronicles of the Schönberg-Cotta Family* reproduces the very spiritual nuances of the Reformation in Germany. The expanding of the areas of personal sympathy and understanding is a great matter. And millions of readers of fiction have had this experience scarcely knowing what was happening to them.

Of course, the brilliant teller of tales may foul the nest he is describing. He may tell part of the truth in such a way as to achieve a complete falsehood. By letting the light fall here and the shadows there he may create something quite foreign to the life whose essential quality it is his responsibility as an artist to reflect. The reader and the critic must be on guard all the time against these possibilities of deception. But the artist may use all his powers for the ascertaining and the conveying of truth. And then the vicarious experience he makes possible is essential to the life of a civilized man.

4. By the Light of a Thousand Campfires

For untold centuries stories have been told by campfires. There has been the weariness at the end of the day. There has been the kindling of the fire and the preparation of food. There has been the curious comfort by the fire which followed, with the stars overhead and the wind whispering through the trees. There memory has begun to work, and the tales of the hunter and the fighter and the memories of the tribe have been passed along while eyes keen with interest and faces glowing with sympathy have stood out in the light of the bright flames, or become shadowy beside the slowly burning embers. So the great tales which became part of the folklore of the race were told. So the traditions which grew into mythologies were formed. The very wisdom and ripened experience of centuries got into these tales. The brooding sense of tragedy which haunted a whole nation became imperishable in a story. The sense of mystery and of the elusive quality of many experiences found haunting words for the telling. Here, too, the picture could be foreshortened. The story could be told in such a fashion as to become a finely wrought instrument of deception. Men's prejudices as well as their understanding have crystallized into a tale. There is always the necessity of analysis. There is always the necessity of testing. There is always the choice which the stories themselves make necessary between rival interpretations. So the mind of man wakes and grows. So the understanding of man deepens and becomes capable of more significant apprehensions. For the campfire is a school as well as the place of an evening's hour of rest.

And the campfire is a part of the heritage of highly civilized people. It goes with the pioneer as he enters upon the enterprises of exploration, and the settler as he goes about the tasks involved in making the desert blossom as a rose. The old civilization which sends out the discoverer and the settler lives in tales of the campfire. Sometimes the nostalgia of loneliness makes the tale of far-off towns more full of that which satisfies than are the towns themselves. Sometimes the perspective of the silence under the stars gives an acuteness to judgments which has its own importance. All in all, the tales wrought out of memory in the light of campfires have been part of the mental treasures of the race.

5. By the Lamps of a Thousand Libraries

Memory becomes a transcendent thing in the libraries of the world. Men who have been dead for centuries exercise the right of the franchise through their books. They refuse to be inarticulate because of the accident of death. The garnered tales of all the lands and of all the ages find their way into the palaces of books. Every experience which has been rich with the gratification of desire or lonely with a quality of longing finds its way to the heart of a tale. And the tale finds its way to the shelf of a library. Dr. Caleb Winchester not too critically described literature as that writing which has power permanently to appeal to the emotions. If literature is much more than this, it includes this, and the stories in the great libraries of the world are there partly because they meet this test.

The men who read in the libraries are often solitary men. They seek in the centuries what the century has not given them. And by participation in the thoughts and actions and the emotions of the race they make up for something which has been denied to them in a hard and difficult world. If they could choose, many frequenters of great libraries would be in the midst of brilliant pleasures, but when other doors are closed they enter the palaces of books. Without the insight of loneliness many of the great books of the world would never have been written. Especially the literature which bares the heart to the reader is likely to be the product of a mind whose understanding comes from a struggle to get along without that which life has refused to give. It would be a tragic thing if men and women became so satisfied with the experiences of the passing hours and days that the libraries were forsaken.

Gradually this home of books, which includes the great tales of the world, becomes a place of testing. The fires of the library are invisible. But in these fires the pure gold survives, and many a fallacy and many a deception is burned to ashes. The test is not complete, however. The evil has its own secrets of survival. The lie which betrays the soul manages to keep alive in many a library.

6. By the Fireplaces of a Thousand Homes

The seat by the fireplace in a man's home is the most intimate place in all the world. The great narratives of the world make possible the most wide-ranging experiences going from continent to continent and from century to century. As Emily Dickinson says:

> There is no frigate like a book
> To take us lands away.

So the man sitting by his own hearthfire opens doors of imagination and brings the whole world of human experience within his reach. All the while unsuspected aspects of his own personality are called forth by the books he reads. Emerson reminded us that what a small boy in a corner reads of a king is true of himself.

By the fireplace the great tales of the mythologies of the world tell themselves over again. Athena is once more clear intelligence. Apollo is once more light and heat. Zeus is once more Olympic and far-flung power. Thor again wields his hammer. Odin is again the mysterious source of life. The tree Yggdrasil grows again with all its infinite number of human leaves.

The old, old tales of human love tell themselves in manifold fashions. Arthur is splendidly above the imagination of Guinevere, and Lancelot, hot and impetuous and flashing with his brave sword, sweeps her away in a passion of surrender, until she learns at last that

> We needs must love the highest when we see it,
> Not Lancelot, nor another.

Dan Chaucer is teller of tales as well as poet when he unwinds the stories of his good women. The deeds men did for love in the days when knighthood was in flower are told over and over again by the fireside. The spirit of a nation and a race is put into revealing fiction as when George Macdonald writes *What's Mine's Mine, Sir Gibbie, Donal Grant,* and all the rest. Sir William Robertson Nicoll used to say that no one had put so much of Scotland into books.

The adventure of a man in a society alien to his training, and speaking to something in his own mind which he did not know he possessed, is told in novels like Charles Kingsley's *Hypatia* where Philammon suddenly confronts a new world and must forsooth find out what it means. George Sand can combine phantasy and reality in a wholly amazing fashion in a tale where a young musician senses the meaning of his life and tries his wings.

The depths of the soul can be torn away and brought to the light of day by the great Russians. And the diseases of the soul may be subjected to subtle and sympathetic scrutiny by a writer like Dostoyevsky, who reverses the process Peter the Great desired for the opening of a window toward the West and actually opens a window toward the East.

The reader by the fire is seeking books which speak to him. If they are books whose distinction the world has recognized, well and good. But his democratic vote is cast for that which comes sharp and direct to his own mind. And so the book as yet unrecognized, the writer as yet uncrowned, find a place. And sometimes the book never to find a great place has its own meaning for the man by the fireplace. He accepts it and makes it his own, perhaps with a more eager affection because it will never have many friends.

He listens by the fire to taletellers of infinite sophistication. Henry James, who lost one country without finding another, has something to say to him. Virginia Woolf allures him by her distinguished force, yet causes him to withdraw as he comes to feel that somehow she missed more than she saw, and that what she missed was of very great importance. George Meredith gives him Diana of the Crossways and many another person as a fascinating acquaintance, if not always as a friend.

The corner by the fire at last comes to be associated with thoughts which have come from all the world, thoughts clear in the brightness of human eyes and shining in the eagerness of human faces. The man by the fire may lead a busy and even a somewhat mechanical life in our highly organized world. But the home of his mind is with his books. I used to know a worker in a great establishment for locomotives who would come to his house black with the marks of his toil, but would soon emerge from his bath remade in appearance and would go into an incredibly good library for something that was a great deal more than a bath for his mind.

The reader is continually himself being tested. His sense of actuality, his sense of truth, his sense of essential meanings, must be kept keenly active all the time. His "thumbs up" and "thumbs down" as he reads tells something about the book. It tells everything about himself. The reader is always on a battleground when ideas are contending for the possession of his mind. He must decide when to let the portcullis fall.

7. The Isolated Reader Who Finds a Society in Books

John Ruskin was much impressed by the fact that you can meet any person you desire to know if he lives in a book. And by the same token you can refuse to meet any person you do not desire to know if he lives in a book. The age in which you live may limit you. The social milieu of which you are a part may tragically limit your range of social experience. But in the great fiction of the world you have the freedom of the centuries and the mastery of your own age. All the doors are open. You can keep them open or you can close them as you choose.

The social limitation may come about in all sorts of ways. A member of a distinguished and sophisticated society who knows all the passwords of a brilliant circle may be so shut off from the roots of human vitality in the common life as to be dying at the top. Abraham Lincoln knew American life as Henry Adams never knew it. On the other hand, the very conditions of living shut out from the rich tradition of human culture many a man who is capable of a thorough and understanding response. A man who spends most of the working hours of the day in the depths of a mine may miss more than physical sunlight. But perhaps most of all the comfortable members of a prosperous society, which has confused the owning of pretentious houses and automobiles of the latest model for a full life, exist in a state of cultural and social malnutrition rather difficult adequately to describe. The world of manufacture, transportation, and salesmanship has tended to produce men and women a good deal like the blind fish of Mammoth Cave. The difficulty with the complacent members of these groups is that in their abject practical materialism they go through life without the knowledge that they are missing anything. They need some equivalent of Stevenson's sin which stabs a man wide awake.

But, whatever the cause of the socially closed doors, in the great fiction of the world the isolated reader can find a good society if he can realize his need of finding it, and can appreciate what it offers. He can live over again the experiences which have come to very great men and women as they appear in historical novels. And often the social aptness and understanding of the work of fiction does not depend upon its meticulous accuracy in factual details. Sir Walter Scott took liberties with facts, but he could capture the very quality of life of a period in which he was interested. Thackeray could picture a corrupt society at the point of its corruption in *Vanity Fair* and in respect of a certain idealism which could live graciously in spite of the decadence in *Henry Esmond*. Bulwer-Lytton could enable the reader to live over again an old political situation in Italy in *Rienzi,* and could accomplish something more than a tour de force in *The Last Days of Pompeii.* Mrs. Humphry Ward had qualities of perceptiveness not always credited to her, and the ruling class which she knew so well come to life in her pages. Mrs. Edith Wharton wrote with a literary distinction which has its own claim upon the reader. But her eyes were clear. And if she did not picture a good society, at least she gave a good picture of the society she portrayed.

The assumptions, the watchwords, the ways of thinking, and the ways of living of every type of society have been made immortal in adequate fiction. Boccaccio's *Decameron* is the description of a social group and of an era done on a large canvas.

There is in all this, of course, often an inverted picture of the good society through the portrayal of the bad. But the elements of the good society have a way of being present as in some of the great portraits of Thackeray. And in a way the good society consists of men and women of good will battling against the untoward elements of a wicked world. It certainly does not consist in the elusive dwellers in a utopia which exists only in the imagination of a novelist. Bulwer-Lytton's *The Coming Race* and Bellamy's *Looking Backward* are significant as social documents rather than as examples of that literary art which enters into the secrets of living in the actual world.

8. Fiction Heightens and Dramatizes Life

A shrewd soldier once described the practical experience of war as being like a dull Sunday afternoon followed by an explosion. In a way life is like that. Only the climax is not always an explosion. Sometimes it consists in walking through the gates of a lovely garden. Fiction quite characteristically picks out the heightened moments of good or evil and dramatizes them effectively. The constant reader of novels must be on his guard at this point. He may come to demand that life itself always maintain concert pitch. But life is not always at concert pitch. Indeed, there are often years of such slow and sluggish movement that the meaning itself may seem to be lost. But sooner or later events sharpen into clear and indubitable meaning and persons meet their critical hour.

The great literary artist has a sense for the human crisis. Victor Hugo could not possibly miss the night of battle when Jean Valjean contends for his soul or the hour when he appears at the court where an innocent man is about to be condemned and says: "I am Jean Valjean." Nathaniel Hawthorne could not possibly miss the scarlet letter burned upon Dimmesdale's breast. Charles Dickens could not possibly miss Sydney Carton's going to the guillotine to save a friend for a good life in England.

But the drama is often the hidden drama of the soul. A smooth and urbane face is offered to the world, but the fox is gnawing at the vitals. Diana of the Crossways carries herself with complete and easy poise as her world is falling apart. Mrs. Wharton's Lily Bart moves like a queen when the play which is her life comes upon its hour of dissolution and tragedy. The perception of what goes on behind the steady eye and the seemingly placid countenance is full of importance to the true artist as he tells the tales of human beings. Powerful short stories put into cameo form these tremendous insights. The curtain lifts for a moment and you look into a human soul.

9. Fiction Photographs Human Life

The cult of the photographer has always been an interesting aspect of the novel. Sometimes such tales have been called novels of manners. Jane Austen was a supreme master in this field. The impeccable precision of her portraits is a thing at which men never cease to marvel. Anthony Trollope had his own skill in this kind of writing. The Barsetshire novels give you a feeling that you must have been in the cathedral. You must have known the members of the chapter and the people who live about the cathedral and worship there. And especially you must have known the Bishop's wife. No literary map of England would be complete without Barsetshire.

In America, William Dean Howells was an exponent of fiction as a kind of literary photography telling unimportant things about unimportant people in such a way as to create a sense of significance. Silas Lapham did not rise very high. But there he is. Silas to the life. And only in rare moods when you suspect that you are being too critical does the thought come to you that perhaps there were things about Silas which William Dean Howells did not know.

The five towns live in the literary photography of Arnold Bennett. It is all very detailed, very patient, very thoroughgoing. And what it does, it does very well indeed.

Long before the days of the modern literary photographers, Henry Fielding knew very well the secrets of accurate picturing. What a healthy young animal Tom Jones is! And in certain ways how much potential goodness there is in him. A young man of his type drawn to the life. And the old squire represents something like the portraiture of genius. Fielding was determined to deal with people whom he had met in his England. There are heights he did not reach. There are depths he did not probe. But, reacting against the sentimental manufacture of tears, he did write of a real world. He did not desire the reputation of Richardson as one who set Europe weeping. The curtain goes up, and you see not a play but the very people with whom you were talking on the street only yesterday.

10. Fiction Brings Back Golden Memories

John Galsworthy had his own secrets of bitter irony, and his distinguished style could achieve the cutting edge of a corrosive satire. But I like to remember him as the author of the tale of the two makers of shoes who could not surrender to the methods of the machine and kept their flag of sound and perfect craftsmanship flying to the tragic end. With all his irony Galsworthy had a way with golden memories. The *Forsyte Saga* is full of solid and dependable stuff of a type of character we should not like to see perish from the earth. There were many secrets which the Forsytes did not know. And some of them were the very greatest secrets of all. But they were in their own fashion made of sterling material, and the reader joins John Galsworthy in remembering them with a certain nostalgia.

Willa Cather is a realist. But she sees the things she perceives honestly and at least now and then, and in some of her books continuously, with a golden light falling upon them. *Death Comes for the Archbishop* is full of the primitive ways of primitive people, and much that belongs to the world of darkness is not far away. But the central light falls upon something it is good to remember and good to love. When she writes of Old Montreal, there is the same quality of golden memory. Realism can never be quite sordid when handled by such a pen.

11. Fiction Brings Back Memories That Corrode and Burn

When you think of the novel as the sword of the apostle of social indignation, probably if you are a Frenchman the name of Zola comes to your mind at once, and if you are an Englishman you think of Charles Dickens.

The apostle of social indignation is really a lawyer with a brief. He tells the truth. But he does not tell all the truth. He tells the particular truth which is relevant to his winning of his case. Social wrongs of a concrete type had a way of going down before the pungent pen of Charles Dickens. He could pronounce the sentence of death on a social institution with a single book. It was his happy secret to tell the story of the wrongs of the poor and the underprivileged in such a fashion as to leave them with their human dignity intact. Life was always in some way good to Dickens even under the most sordid circumstances. So you had at least the suggestion of a song in your heart as you tried to make it better.

Many of the novelists of social indignation in their entirely undisciplined wrath reduce man to a clod. And then they shout with almost fiendish glee: "See what you have done to him!" No doubt the literature with the smell of brimstone on it serves a useful purpose. But it is singularly fragmentary, and in one way it is singularly false.

In America the contrast between Edward Eggleston's *Hoosier Schoolmaster* and the contemporary novel of social wrath is sharp enough. It needs to be borne clearly in mind that the contemporary writers have one hot and impetuous desire—the desire to hit and to hit hard. Our American heritage has been neither so bleak nor so treacherously selfish as they would have us believe. When they are afraid of the memory of every flower which grew on old fences, lest it help to make us contented with evils which characterized the old life, one can understand their impetuous wrath. But what they write is social propaganda. Only in a modified sense is it art. And only in a very modified sense is it life.

12. Fiction Criticizes Life

Sinclair Lewis doubtless would like to be remembered as a keen and ruthless critic of a crass and essentially vulgar life. He learned from Whitman how to catalogue, and from other masters how to put a cut at the heart of a paragraph, at the end of a sentence, or on the tip of a phrase. But in a curious way he likes the things he fights and feels a lure in the things he lashes. At times one feels rather definitely that he has surrendered to the vulgarity which he castigates.

It can scarcely be denied that the whole tone of American life has been lowered by those who, in process of making their novels into social criticism, have literally packed their minds with unlovely images, their thoughts with ignoble conceptions, and their vocabularies with words caught up from the gutter. You actually become like what you think about, and one hesitates to picture what the readers of the literature of moral surrender which poses, and not without moments of sincerity, as social criticism will actually be like when they come back from their long journeys in the dark underworld of contemporary life. There has been a realism which could indicate the evil without becoming evil.

There has been a criticism which could fight slime without becoming slimy. But that is not the characteristic of much of the outstanding fiction which would attempt to do for our day what Juvenal did for his.

13. Fiction Records the Adventures of the Soul

Old ecclesiastical stories of miracles and of the ways of the spiritual life such as we come upon constantly in the Venerable Bede introduce us to a type of tale in which truth and fiction combine oddly and the sense of spiritual values is very profound. The Middle Ages has many such stories. Perhaps the legend of St. Christopher is the best of them all. The gladiator who carried the Christ Child over the tempestuous stream on the dark and stormy night and then saw the sudden flash of a divine glory is part of the spiritual treasure of the race. And the golden legend of the monk for whom the shining presence waited while he fed the poor at the convent gate is worth its weight in something more precious than gold.

The modern tale of spiritual adventures is often a strange and inverted thing, a light on the edge of black darkness. The Russian novelists have a way of illuminating the life of the soul as it walks amid the shadows.

Many of the characters of Hugh Walpole are pursued by something so insistent that it in turn becomes their own pursuit. And in tales like *The Cathedral* the soul at last comes to its own. There is a pseudo spirituality like that of Maugham in *The Razor's Edge* which reveals unconsciously a good deal of desperate hunger but never finds the right fruit.

Any man who has had firsthand contact with the cure of souls knows that at the point of spiritual quest and spiritual satisfaction and especially at the point of God's quest for the human soul, life has been much richer than its record in fiction. There has been something truer and deeper than one can find in any *Magic Mountain*. Sometimes one feels that the supreme failure of Christianity in our time has been precisely its missing the opportunity to put into adequate literary form the tale of triumphant Christian experience in the twentieth century.

14. Fiction as the Voice of the Body

But if the novelists in our time have not been conspicuously successful in telling the story of the soul, they have been very successful indeed in telling the tale of the body. Indeed, a good deal of contemporary fiction is little more than self-conscious biology taking the form of literary art. Sometimes the story is told with a vast air of discovery and emancipation, as if nobody knew that men had bodies until the cult of physical sensation became rampant in our time. Sometimes it is hot with the mere energy which comes from the type of imagination which cannot rise to ideas and looks at spiritual experiences from afar but is very much at home in analyzing all the expressions of the biological urges. Sometimes it takes the form of that pseudo mysticism of the body to which we have already referred. The clichés of contemporary criticism usually describe such books as very beautiful and very daring. The daring to the point of audacity is evident enough. The beauty is not so clear.

That sense that it is the very nature of the material to express the volitions of the intelligence and to wear the livery of the spiritual is sure to come to its own in a nobler fiction in days to come.

15. Fiction Gives Life to Great Hopes

In a time of hard and brutal realism like our own the optimisms are likely to be implicit rather than explicit. The quest for hope is clear enough in the heavy and bluntly disheveled writing of Thomas Wolfe. And once and again there is the air of another world in which we can breathe more freely, a clear atmosphere where one can expect the birds to sing. Anne Sedgwick's *Little French Girl* possesses this implicit optimism. And something very deep and full of good human expectation is trying to get itself expressed in Dorothy Canfield's *The Brimming Cup*. But in the main contemporary fiction has a subtler art for our despairs than for our hopes.

16. Fiction Interprets Life

When fiction actually tries to come to grips with life, we often find ourselves confronted by a world where there is no moral freedom or spiritual expectation and where puppets with no real chance move according to the pattern of an impersonal necessity. Thomas Hardy is a very especial priest of this cult. And it has many, many votaries.

George Meredith tried to tell the tale of life so that it had a meaning other than frustration. Then the impersonal physics practically submerged the personal life even in fiction. One of these days the new physics will get a hearing in the novel. And there are deeper sources than this for an interpretation of life which is more than the distinguished account of the doom of man. The thinker familiar with the corpus of thought connected with classical Christianity sees fairly breath-taking possibilities here.

17. Fiction and the Rights of the Soul

In almost haphazard fashion we have touched upon some of the aspects of this great field belonging to the teller of tales. It is packed with materials of the utmost significance. It tells no end about the things which disrupt life and break down personality. It is haunted by high dreams which sometimes turn into noble realization. Positively and negatively it is the useful servant of the interpreter of life. And always it looks in moments of awareness to heights it has never climbed and has a sense of vistas it has never quite made its own.

CHAPTER XIX

Poetry Opens and Closes Its Eyes

UNLESS we are so obsessed by pseudo democracy that we are afraid to give special significance to anyone lest he should tower above the non-entities who combine to make the democratic society, we need have no hesitation in saying that the poet is a royal person and that he has a royal role to play. He has a richer experience of life than other men, and he knows how to express that experience in words of haunting loveliness. The harmonies into which he weaves his words express something which he has found in life itself. He has a keen eye for the actual, but he also captures illusive hopes and impalpable dreams. The ideal itself is given reality in his golden words.

1. Homer

As we look upon some of the achievements of poetry in expressing significant qualities of human nature and possibilities of human achievement, we shall follow the custom of this volume and make no attempt at what would be in any fashion a complete survey. Rather, we shall turn to a number of significant poets and see something of what human life has meant to them, and the quality of its interpretation in their writings.

Homer was more than a poet. He wrote what was in a sense the Bible of the Greeks. Here they saw life in the pattern for which they cared most. Here was life in what they were glad to believe was its true meaning. Much of the very stuff of which the Greek mind was made is found in the *Iliad* and the *Odyssey*. The style itself is a part of the power of these epics. It is direct. It speaks at once to the eye. It is full of colors clearly seen. It has a certain elevation, a certain quiet dignity as of one who watches even small things from the heights. It has a singular beauty. Its adjectives combine musical sound with a portraiture which speaks to the visual imagination. The reader feels that he lives in a magnificent world, not without its dark mystery, but for all that full of high thoughts and brave deeds.

And the casual fashion in which the gods come and go somehow does not take away the quality of verisimilitude from the writing. They themselves are brilliant and glittering Greeks, and their very human qualities become part of the story the poet has to tell. There are problems here which later poets will have to consider. But Homer takes the gods as he finds them. He takes people as he finds them, too. And he does not tell lies about his heroes to make them more splendid. Achilles sulks. Agamemnon is sometimes strangely petty for a brave king. Odysseus is too wily for the character which ought to go with wisdom. But all these people are seen for just what they are. Some of them, like Hector, walk splendidly through the pages of the epic. All have moments of something not unlike magnificence. You live the life of these fighting men with them. And all the while a sense of loveliness beyond their life hovers over you. And a sense of human dignity comes to you which will lead you to ask many questions which Homer cannot answer.

2. The Greek Tragedians

Heavy shadows have fallen upon human life by the time you sit in the theater listening to the plays of Aeschylus, Sophocles, and Euripides. You see evil flashing in human eyes and breaking out in wicked deeds. And then you see how this evil works its way through life after life. You see a poison get into the blood of a family. And you watch that poison run riot. The tales are told with a breath-taking yet reserved intensity. They are never mere tales of horror. There are moral processes at work, and the poets try to interpret for you these moral processes. There are glorious flashes of insight, as when Antigone appeals from human laws to a law eternal in the heavens. Olympus itself is the home of a more searching conscience and a deeper sense of moral values than in the time of Homer. And there are ways through tragedy to peace which come to the consciousness of the spectator of the play with a healing balm.

There are great solidities in the moral consciousness of Aeschylus and Sophocles. Euripides breaks in with ceaseless and insistent questioning. He is impatient with the good which is not good enough. He has a conscience even for Olympus. And by that conscience many a god is condemned. He sees in all the old tales what has never been seen in them before. Life has a new drama, tragedy a new sharpness as he interprets the ways of these strange human beings. The conservative Athenians are angry because he asks questions they do not know how to answer. Socrates attending all his plays thinks long, long thoughts. But in truth there is faith in his insurgency. He will not be contented with inadequate answers to life's ultimate questions. And he will not have the questioners silenced. All this because he is reaching for an intellectual and moral satisfaction deeper than Greece has ever known.

3. Vergil

In a sense Rome itself is the hero of Vergil's epic. At least it is true that the Rome which is to be lives in the imagination of Aeneas as does nothing else. Danger cannot baffle him. Human love cannot restrain him. He must do the great thing he came to the world to do. He must found the city which will make a new place in the world for the civilized man. Great standards emerge in *The Aeneid*. And they are standards to which a mighty hero must be loyal. The most tremendous thing about Aeneas is that he has discovered in life something greater than himself. But a very especial characteristic of the writing of Vergil is the constant sympathy for and understanding of aspects of human life apart from the great drive of the central moral drama. One sees very clearly what Aeneas gives up for the sake of the Rome which is to be. The loveliness and the delightfulness of that which is surrendered are never underestimated. As Vergil so clearly perceived, for many reasons there are tears in things. And always when a man leaves a dear human joy for a great cause these tears fall most tenderly and yet with austere firmness on his countenance. Civilization has a right to its regal city. The city has a right to command its heroes. Civilization is a costly thing. But however great the cost, it is never too great. So Vergil tells us in what Tennyson thought was the mightiest measure ever bent to the purposes of a poet's pen.

4. Dante

Dante did not write the *Divine Comedy* in Latin, the language of scholars. He wrote it in Italian, the language of common men in his native land. And he made a language glorious at the very moment when he wrote an immortal poem. At once we must say that in majestic sweep and searching insight and lovely singing sentences, it is the greatest Christian poem which has ever been written. Some of the intellectual forms have an almost mechanical interrelation. The moral and the spiritual and the material are scarcely related in a fashion the Christian consciousness can finally accept. But after all qualifications have been made, the poem stands like Mont Blanc, the queen of the Alps, glorious in the sunlight against the sky. The insights outnumber the expressions of confusion of thought a thousand to one. Great standards of moral and spiritual excellence are seen with a kind of eternal clearness. Judgment is sharp and unhesitating and deeply ethical. The glory of moral love shines with an effable brightness. The meaning of discipline is told in imperishable speech. And there is at last the rose of love and fire gloriously blooming and burning forever.

The very synthesis of Aristotle and Christian theology and human sympathy and understanding and intimate knowledge of the ways of men is found here. Vergil speaks for the ancient classical world. Beatrice speaks for the Christian insights apprehended by clear intelligence. And Dante with his quicksilverlike brain and his burning heart translates it all into poetry which will not die.

5. Chaucer

We breathe sharply as we turn from Dante to Chaucer. Dante, like the bush which Moses saw, is burning with an eternal fire but is not consumed. Chaucer is a man of the world—suave, urbane, adroitly accustomed to the ways of courts, not too much shocked by men's treachery or women's folly, capable of appreciating goodness and nobility but very much at home in his not too good world. In Dante men come to judgment. In Chaucer they come in for description without too much judgment. Or if judgment, the shrewd, oblique judgment of a diplomat and not the judgment of the flash of lightning from heaven which illuminates the true nature of the soul.

The fourteenth century becomes articulate in the *Canterbury Tales*. And if we put the tales of these very human pilgrims against the larger background of a deeper understanding, we may find there even more perhaps than that of which Chaucer himself was aware. The classic civility gives charm to all he says. And we move along the road from London to the cathedral city where Thomas à Becket was murdered with a sense that centuries are irrelevant and fourteenth-century highways are indeed our own.

6. Spenser

To say that poets know Spenser better than most people know any poets is to say no more than what is quite true. His gift of music has transformed many another voice which is better known to us than his own. Lonely in Ireland, he lived in a world full of allegorical figures and made his *Faerie Queene* a more gracious person than the marvelous woman of the Tudors who turned her very limitations to greatness to match the marvel of an age when everything quickened to a new vitality. We try to overhear the talk when Sir Walter Raleigh visits him and persuades him to take the light and beauty he has caught in a net of words and to present it to the queen.

The senses have their rights and more in the writings of Spenser. But the great virtues have rights which must not be denied. He wrote a marvelous song for a wedding. But his best wedding song was the nuptials of body and spirit when the body is shot through by spiritual splendor and the spirit majestically commands the physical and turns it to its own purposes.

> For of the soule the bodie forme doth take;
> For soule is forme, and doth the bodie make.

7. Shakespeare

Up from Stratford to London town went a lad of keen intelligence and vivid imagination all compact. He did not know it at first—unless his imagination, too, was prophetic. But he was made for the hour, and the hour was made for him. England's past came to life in his mind, and he gave his countrymen a land of the spirit to love. The human past came to life in his mind. He could not even read Plutarch without seeing the men of whom he wrote with an understanding vividness which Plutarch himself never compassed. The raw and the real stuff of human life was all alive in him, and as he wrote, nothing missed him, nothing escaped him. Everything called itself by its own right, true name. He could climb to heights and think the thoughts of the great of the earth. He could walk the ways of common men and overhear not only their speech but their thoughts. His moral insights were as sharp and as unhesitating as those of Puritanism. His sense of the stately pageantry of the Church carried a touch of the royal purple of an ancient tradition. And withal he was a son of the Renaissance, feeling its fire and creative energy burning in his blood. It was a shrewd practicality which sent him back the first citizen of Stratford. But he had put a singing ethereal grace into words of great loveliness and a sense of the mystery of life into words which cannot be forgotten, even as he had felt the cutting edge of the bitterest tragedy and put that too into words. Like Ben Jonson, we too love him short of idolatry.

8. Marlowe

The very incarnation of the most sumptuous and limitless dreams of his age, Christopher Marlowe died in a tavern brawl. Even patient research finds it hard to get at the actualities of his life. His connection with the intelligence service of his period, his place among the wits, his cultivation of brilliant skeptical minds—all these things suggest regions where there is much argument. But the argument is a little beside the mark. We know well enough the Marlowe who described the passion for gold in *The Jew of Malta,* the passion for power in *Tamburlaine,* and the passion for lawless knowledge in *Dr. Faustus.* The scorning of limits, and thereby the very scorning of the law of measure, points the way to the heart of the strange and exotic mind of Marlowe. His imagination was spacious, his power over words an opulent possession. He always tells us more than he knows because he does not know how to turn what he knows to disciplined uses.

9. O Rare Ben Jonson

Ben Jonson, who carried the marks of his physical encounter with law to the grave, was at heart a classicist who usually expressed his love of the good by writing with a corrosive satire about the evil of the human species. *Sejanus* is a remarkable study of decadence in the Roman Empire. But it is of more than Rome that Ben Jonson is thinking. The more laughable practice of deception in a disintegrating society is subjected to ironic narrative in *Volpone*. The double-minded ways of the men and women on the streets of the towns men have built stand sardonically revealed the *Bartholomew Fair*. There is rough and energetic speech. And under the surface there is the clear organization coming from loyalty to classical formulas. Before you have finished with Ben Jonson, you know a good deal about that from which men must be saved when they are saved from themselves.

10. John Donne

To be the libertine poet of the gayest London, to be a man whose life is almost broken by complete faithfulness to one great love, to be an intellectual who treats words with something little less than cruelty in making them the servants of powerful ideas, to be a great and compelling preacher making the sermon a thing of explosive moral force and the loftiest spiritual aspiration, to be the distinguished dean of St. Paul's Cathedral with a personal flare for walking nobly in high position which answers to the quality of the great church itself—to do all this and to be all this in one life is rather compassing the round of the clock. And all this may be said of John Donne.

He will be seen always in contrast with that placid and gracious figure Bishop Lancelot Andrewes, who with the deadly integrity of a saint repented of sins which to a man of the world must always seem unimportant, and put his repentance into that immortal classic of the inner life, *The Private Devotions of Lancelot Andrewes*. The very abject repentance of Andrewes moves in a realm beyond the reach of the everyday blood-and-flesh man who walks the earth. But John Donne is bone of that man's bone and flesh of that man's flesh. He sinned with a vivid profusion of sinning. He repented with an honest and blunt sincerity. And he told the truth about the ashes which remain on the tongue after years of lawless indulgence. Because added to this he possessed an intellect of first-class power to penetrate the truth of things, and poetic gifts of a rare and decisive quality to express what he saw and felt, his impact upon men was great and deep.

11. Other Metaphysical Poets

There was a still depth to the spiritual contemplation of Vaughan, who "saw eternity the other night." Herbert made the temple a place with a hierarchy of spiritual experiences. In the metaphysical poets Christianity took something from Platonism and at times something from Neoplatonism. And always and in all ways it found the world of spiritual experience more real than the world of intense physical sensation. The material, too, the metaphysical poets knew was to be subjected to the rule of the spirit. But in men like Vaughan and Herbert the quiet, brooding apprehension of the spiritual was likely to take the place of everything else and to give their lines an ethereal loveliness.

12. Alexander Pope

The curious cripple who seemed to hold his body together by various fastenings had a mind clear and cold and hard and wrote couplets where every thought became a cameo and every sentence crystallized in quick antithesis a process of mental activity which might have been expanded into a paragraph or a chapter. In one way the poet of a deft and polite worldliness, in another Pope was the would-be interpreter of a crisp and brilliant secular philosophy. When he was dealing with great matters he usually seemed wiser than he was. He missed the very point of critical understanding, for instance, when he said:

> Presume not God to scan;
> The proper study of mankind is man.

He never understood that God and man are so related as perfect and relative intelligence that you cannot understand one without the other. He brought expression to a shining polish, and he could give an artificial and half-laughing dignity to that which was less than trivial, as in *The Rape of the Lock*. He could be bitterly cruel, as in his famous characterization of Addison, and his temper is subtly caught in his characteristic work, *The Dunciad*.

13. John Keats

The lad who turned the tap to supply drinks for a public house and whose mind haunted regions of imperishable beauty is such a study as this odd human world often presents. His taste belonged to Attica even when his body was busy about tasks which belonged to something less than the ordinary routine of life. The spirit of beauty moveth where it listeth. And not perversely but with a sure sense of fitness it settled upon the soul of John Keats. When you think of Lord Chesterfield writing subtle and sophisticated letters for the education of a son who refused to be educated, and the winds from regions of imperishable loveliness settling upon the soul of Keats as he went about menial tasks, you think thoughts which may have the genius of democracy in them. The aristocracy of taste may miss spacious mansions and come to dwell in places remote from marble halls. In a sense the aesthetic tension had the place in the experience of Keats which ordinarily belongs to a more direct moral tension. He had to fight for his world of beauty. Perhaps too casually he assumed that the things about which he cared belonged to those who possessed them only by his gift of imagination. And his own physical organism with its early decay was not made to be the organ of the Greek sense of physical well-being. But he lifted his flag where it floated high. And when he died so young, the flag was still floating.

14. Shelley

Perhaps when you were a little child if you lived on a farm you played with other children in the cheerful morning hours. You can remember a morning when the other children seemed singularly obdurate. They would not play the games you wanted to play. They would not let you be the person you wanted to be in the games which they did play. So, full of childish anger, you left them and sat under a tree where you could make a world of your own. You invented a farm and a company of children who always played the games you wanted to play and let you have the part you liked to have. So you passed the time quite pleasantly until the dinner bell rang. Then you forgot all about the morning's disappointment and joined the other children at the noonday meal.

Once there was a gifted lad who had this experience. But he became so busy with his fascinating world of phantasy that he did not hear the dinner bell when it rang. So he never came back but lived all his life in an unreal world. His name was Percy Bysshe Shelley.

It was a strange life that he lived. And it was poetry of a strange, illusive exquisiteness that he wrote. Like so many of those who avoid the very standards which give permanent significance to life, he was quite ready to be a moral teacher and, condemning the universe which did not correspond to the pattern of his phantasy, to destroy God and then remake Him after the fashion of his heart's desire. He became a Prometheus whose imagination at least was unbound. He was determined to have the heavenly music even if he did not belong to the heavenly choir. And he at least won citizenship in fairyland if he never succeeded in storming the battlements of the New Jerusalem.

15. Lord Byron

Lord Byron was always in curious fashion the physical symbol of himself. With the face of Apollo, he carried about what was in more than a literal sense a cloven foot. And so the midnight beauty of his mysterious face haunted his generation. It was by the cutting power of the angry rhyme that he first woke to find himself famous. *English Bards and Scotch Reviewers* came straight from a gifted, wrathful mind armed with a pen which could pierce like a sword. He could write with a certain romantic sincerity of all the nostalgic emotions of one who regretted what was lost and longed for what could never be regained.

> O could I feel as once I felt—
> O could I weep as once I wept,
> O'er many a vanished scene.

He could paint black pictures of ultimate frustration, as in "Darkness," and he could apply his irony to even larger areas, as in *Don Juan*. He responded with quite simple honesty to the call for courage. One likes best to remember him as he wrote:

> The mountains look on Marathon—
> And Marathon looks on the sea;
> And musing there an hour alone,
> I dreamed that Greece might still be free.

And for that dream he gave his life.

16. Wordsworth

Dove Cottage tells the story of Wordsworth. It is simple and bare and set in a frame of great natural beauty. No wonder that sophisticated people, tired of the artificialities of a conventional society, have gone like pilgrims to the little house in the lake country, finding there a shrine of noble honesty and solid, direct simplicity. The journey from Pope to Wordsworth surely may seem to be a journey well worth taking.

The tale is not so conclusive, however, as worshipful Wordsworthians have often tried to make out. And with no desire to depreciate the revelation of beauty in his greatest lines or the significance of his cult of the direct and honest word, one can venture to call attention to something in his nature worship which was essentially false. It is not true that one impulse from the vernal wood is more significant than Socrates, who was surely one of the sages. And the more one studies the mysticism of Wordsworth, the more one finds something suspect in it. The call of pantheistic monism was in a way in his blood, and that is always a bad call to which to listen.

17. Browning

It is easy to go wrong in dealing with Robert Browning. Paul Elmer More never had much that was good to say about Browning, and he had much to say that was not good at all. Much of his criticism had its own importance and its own relevance. But the man who knows Browning well is likely to feel that the most important things about Browning somehow escaped More's keen and clear intelligence. Browning treated style with a certain grand lawlessness terrible enough to a man with great refinement of apprehension in these matters. He could say things which seemed the product of a rootless mind. And he could make pronouncements which seemed odd enough from a man who was essentially on the side of the angels. But on the side of the angels Robert Browning indubitably was. His greatest poem *The Ring and the Book* is one long and splendid tribute to the essential meaning of personality: "Life's business being just the terrible choice." He loved to give evil its day in court. But at the end of the day, as in "Fifine at the Fair," it was always clear that evil had failed to make good its case. He always confronted Christianity with a fresh and original mind but with absolutely no prejudices against the Christian facts or truths or sanctions. "Saul" is a brief and glorious saga of the soul showing the necessity of the Incarnation. "A Death in the Desert" faces the fact and the glory of Christ. "Colombe's Birthday" shows that the great day of life is the day when you choose to be born into a world of great and imperishable values. Browning did not always make his connections clear and sure. But if you take all of him you will get less of evil and more of good than in most poets who wrote anything like as much as he. And you will have a veritable shower bath in life itself. Even when he plunges into the darkness like Paracelsus, he presses his lamp close to his bosom.

18. Tennyson

Tennyson has nothing like the intellectual range of Browning. He is a master of impeccable and many-stringed music. He holds a mirror up to the mind of the age and thinks its doubts after it, so that he becomes its father confessor by an almost inevitable process of understanding. He, too, sees the center of all human meanings in the "Strong Son of God, immortal Love." He has a sense of the past full of a shimmering beauty which Sir Walter Scott would have loved. And his *Idylls of the King* falls under clouds only to be kept safely for a brighter day. The conclusion of much that is ultimate in human life still rests with the words of Guinevere already quoted:

> We needs must love the highest when we see it,
> Not Lancelot, nor another.

He could capture the very idiom of the Northern Farmer, but he could capture his mind as well as his vocabulary. In an age when the machine was claiming new territory for its rule every day, he turned English words to such loveliness as even the greatest masters of English words have rarely attained. He still had a quite authentic sense of the unseen when men were surrendering to the reign of the visible.

> Sunset and evening star,
> And one clear call for me!

—the words rang out as the fogs were settling upon the nineteenth century.

19. Goethe

An epoch lives in the life of Goethe. He was a German who wanted to make the urbanity of the French indigenous to the Teutonic mind. He was a man whose roots were in the German forests but who always had a nostalgia for the clear and cool intelligence of the classic mind. Out of such tensions magnificent writing comes. And so it was with the great German. It was inevitable that he would be allured by the Faustian legend. And his tale of the man who refused to accept human limitations because though a creature he wanted to know and to act like a god, has a place all its own in the interpretation of the particular form of sinning whose imperial ambitions seem so gallant and splendid, and which contains seeds of such incredible evil. If contemporary Germany had read Faust with understanding, we might live in a different world.

20. Longfellow

Sometimes it seems that Longfellow must perish condemned by the ennui of those who can survive only in an atmosphere of impropriety subtly veiled in urbane speech or impropriety rampant in brutal and muddy phrases. But his quiet and unpretentious understanding expressed in words which, if they do not have the music of the spheres, do at least have the music of a serene mind is not destined to be forgotten. *Evangeline* will read better in a hundred years than it reads today. The sense of the beauty of loyalty does not die out of human life. And *Hiawatha,* if it does not have the particular penchant expressed by the *Golden Bough,* may have compassed simple insights which the author of the *Golden Bough* did not take time to apprehend.

21. Lowell

Those who despise what they call the genteel tradition have only scornful words for James Russell Lowell. But this attempt to damn by a phrase must itself be subjected to the sharp criticism of the sound mind. The men to whom sensations take the place of ideas, and biological experiences take the place of spiritual insights, will always be baffled in the presence of that moral intelligence which lives in the light of distinctions not within the range of those who make humanity a collection of conscious beasts. And those who live on subhuman levels have no refuge in the presence of the higher values except in profanity.

Lowell lived in an age when men had a little less taste for unsavory images than characterizes those to whom surrender to a lustful imagination seems to represent the ultimate human emancipation. He knew the vocabulary of the shrewd everyday Yankee and turned it to good account in *The Biglow Papers.* He knew a man when he saw one. And he wrote words about Abraham Lincoln which will not die. He was not without a sense of the claims of the last and the lowest and the least. And *The Vision of Sir Launfal* is not about something concerning which men read only to forget. If he did not fight in conflicts which belong to a later day, he was a right good warrior in the battles of his own time.

And these fights have not ceased to have meaning. If we lost the ground they won, they would have to be fought over again.

22. *Whitman*

America was sure to produce at least one poet whose central characteristic was a gregarious and lusty vitality. Whitman liked everything. He liked everybody. He liked every experience. He had no reticence. He had no restraint. He was inclined to say that everything was as good as everything else. And he was inclined to say that everybody was as important as everybody else. So writing, with him, was sure to become a glorified catalogue with bursting adjectives. As he grew older he came to have questions. And he came to have doubts. His final doubts are more important than his uncritical assertions. Life consists of a good deal more than *Leaves of Grass*. Whitman sometimes saw this. One cannot forget *O Captain! My Captain!* It is not strange that to those to whom virtue had become a sham his robust naturalism seemed a virtue.

23. *Hardy*

Hardy tried to set mathematical materialism to music. *The Dynasts* is a tale of human puppets pulled by invisible wires. At times he is weary in the midst of his conscious machines, and we wonder if we shall hear the voice of a free person. But the pattern of impersonal, interwoven events is too much for him. So he becomes the poet laureate of slaves who have become conscious of their chains but cannot change their fate.

24. *D. H. Lawrence*

The grinding out of impersonal laws is really all you hear in the poetry of Hardy. The throb of biological impulses is all you hear in the poetry of D. H. Lawrence. The cult of the body has now become a religion. Vital physical impulses make up the whole of life. The coiling grace of a serpent is almost the ultimate beauty. You are nearer to the final disillusionment and frustration than you know. The music of the spheres is forgotten. You have only the throb of the glands.

25. *Robert Bridges*

One wants very much to find a *Testament of Beauty* when one emerges from the hot darkness of D. H. Lawrence. And Robert Bridges comes with a civilized mind speaking of many things which must not be forgotten. His style has been molded by much hard discipline. His thoughts have been formed by earnest consideration of many serious matters. If the basis of his assertions is sometimes insecure, and if he sometimes feels the call of that which does not really belong to man's peace and power, one knows all the while that he is a serious man who loves high beauty and is trying to find his way through the fogs to a place where the steady light is shining.

26. Edwin Arlington Robinson

The quiet cynic who is haunted by a beauty he cannot quite forget comes to his own in the poetry of Edwin Arlington Robinson. He is master of a good craftsmanship. He can make portraits you will always remember. And he can cause you to ask questions you would very much like to ignore. Sophistication has made him afraid of simple faith. He never quite achieves the direct gaze. And so he becomes the poet of those to whom an old and simple and beautiful world has become impossible and who play with a gentle cynicism sharpening sometimes into bitterness and always haunted by something never quite said. The world of their inner hopes is always "powerless to be born."

27. T. S. Eliot

Possessing a sensitive, responsive mind and a keen apprehension of contemporary life, a listener to all the mixed voices the subconscious hurls above the level of our awareness, T. S. Eliot became the very portrait painter of *Waste Land,* an expert in its confusion and futility. Then voices from another level spoke to him. The most characteristic product of the new awareness was *Murder in the Cathedral.* And Eliot seemed to have journeyed from Waste Land to some true home of the soul. Then as the voices of Venusberg and the voices of the Pilgrims do battle in Wagner, the fight was on again and no Pilgrim's Chorus sounded triumphantly on the air. Is Waste Land to have the last word after all?

28. Robert Frost

There is no such complicated storm and stress in Robert Frost as in T. S. Eliot. Such tensions are not quite characteristic of life north of Boston. He knows well the New England type of whom one may say:

> He was a cold and austere man;
> His thin and scraggy roots were all
> Above the timber line. No warmth from rich
>   well-watered soil
> Low-lying, holding still the sun's bright
>   burning in its depths,
> Had upward crept into his sharp clear countenance.
> Yet you had to own his face had caught
> A wintry beauty from the heights.

Bare, clear, honest words about bare, clear, honest men are written by Frost. And if he more than transcends the New Englander of whom we have spoken, he still speaks for a New England in which that which has ceased to speak as conscience still remains in power as mastering and controlling taste.

29. Decadent Poetry

From the right and from the left the hosts of the decadent poets come sweeping in upon us. Often they are masters of a superb technique. They have phrases all alive with boiling energy. They have words with a blunt and bitter actuality. They have powers of expression which once and again we feel to be quite adequate for the thing they have to say. But very soon we feel that there is something the matter. The fire is conflagration. It is not the glowing warmth and the bright light of the bush which is burning but not consumed. The vitality all too often suggests the busy activity of worms. The eyes of the poets have a touch of madness. And after the voices there is not fulfillment but the exhaustion of hope. At last we feel that for all the brilliancy there is only one verdict we can pronounce:

> Better is silence than those spurts of flame
> Thrusting volcanic speech to mad eruption
> From the depths of a disordered mind,
> A will unleashed from all control,
> A heart whose palpitations have no rhythm of rich health
> But only the dark flutterings that end in death.

30. Finding One's Way

A dangerous and glorious gift the poets possess. So much depends upon what they choose to see and what they choose to tell. The greatest poets have seen the whole picture. And they have had the divine gift of a right perspective. One is inclined in the dilemma of our time to go back to Edmund Spenser. He understood the rights of the body without forgetting the rights of the soul. He always knew who must command and who must obey.

And there is Milton—blind but seeing many things. We know now the confused ways in which his mind sometimes moved. But at his best how clearly he saw that there is a great corpus of thought in which everything finds its place and is seen in its true significance. How nobly he declared the place of the Lord and Master of all thought as overlord of the world of understanding as well as the world of action. How plainly he portrayed that fight and mastery in the heart of human life without which there could have been no *Paradise Regained*. How unhesitatingly he declared that the temple of evil must be brought low even though blind eyes make it difficult for strong hands to find the supporting pillars.

There is always Dante, who saw everything summed up in that moral love which is alive forever in the life of God. Soldiers of freedom march into the ancient city of Florence as these words are being written. The old monuments are safe. The new hope walks the streets. Dante's town rightly combines ancient memories with resurrected expectations.

Then there are the poets to come. If the pages of this book have made anything clear, it is that there is a perfect wealth of Christian knowledge and experience waiting for a poet great enough to grasp the mighty harp and to sing the glorious song.

CHAPTER XX

Biography Hides and Tells Its Secrets

W E have seen something of the sort of material that fiction and poetry offer to the student of human experience. It may seem that there are more byways than highways and that the highways themselves sometimes lead to the City of the Dreadful Night rather than to the City of the Glorious Day. There is much truth in such an observation as this but not the whole truth. The roads of deception have their own significance for the critical student. And every byway has something important to tell when it is studied with intelligence. Indeed, as one studies the great fiction of the world, gradually a corpus of thought begins to appear. Some principles have the power to guide and enrich and ennoble life. Some principles by an inevitable process bring decay and death. The same results are even more clearly evident in the great poetry of the world. Slowly and with complete finality there is a verdict against some principles and some ways of life. Gradually and inevitably there is a verdict in favor of permanent principles which are good for the life of men. Literature is, indeed, a vast laboratory whose experiments come at last to an increased knowledge of what is really good and beautiful and true.

When we turn from the study of descriptions and interpretations of life by literary artists to the study of actual men and women who have walked this earth, we may seem to strike at once a note of sharper reality. These men are the veritable stuff of humanity. They felt the needs and the urges of the life of man. They worked and slept. They ate and drank. They felt the pull of impulse and the gracious drawing power of high ideals. They sensed the compulsion of that which has a right to be. They conducted processes of thought. They reached critical decisions. And after making what impact they could on the lives of other men and women they came upon death. Surely they are the genuine source material for the study of humanity.

All this is true, though we must not forget that a great writer of fiction or a great poet may see farther into the life of man than even a great biographer, and there are imaginary persons dropped from the pens of great writers more significant for the understanding of humanity than multitudes of actual human beings.

1. How Much Can We Know About Particular People?

There are other questions we must meet as we attempt to make the study of concrete individuals the basis of a further understanding of human beings. There is the question: How much can we really know about particular people? At first it may seem an idle query. Of course, we can know what is important about any person who has made a real impact upon the life of mankind and has left a record of his deeds behind him. But can we? Was the record made honestly and with the desire to tell the truth? Were all the facts which are involved in a dependable judgment clearly and unequivocally stated? In all the cases where a knowledge of motives is important, how can we be sure that we have probed back of the deed to the reasons for its doing? Men who have asked such questions have often been led to qualify very much our assurance that we can really know individual people who have lived in the past with any completeness or with an adequacy. Our speech about men of the past, they may be inclined to say, is a little light, edging the darkness of a cloud beyond which the mind of man cannot penetrate.

But actually the working of the minds of men upon the materials remaining to give us access to significant lives, has a way of being fairly shrewd and often genuinely wise. The light may not always be clear. But we are by no means in the dark. And sometimes the light is completely revealing. We know all that we need to know about Socrates as he drank the fatal hemlock. And so we have given him his sure place among the greatest of mankind.

2. How Much Can Particular People Know About Themselves?

There is a second important question: How much can particular people know about themselves? The first answer may be that of course they can know everything that there is to know. They are the spectators and the guides of their own thoughts. They preside over their own decisions. They follow through their purposes to the end of life. These plausible answers will not quite successfully meet critical scrutiny. Every man wants to appear well in his own eyes. And so even congenital liars probably tell themselves more falsehoods than they ever tell other people. The story of a man's life which in imagination he writes for his own perusal, and for his own perusal alone, is often a most partial and sometimes a most misleading tale. Even the memoirs of great generals have to be read with a shrewd watchfulness. A man is always his own lawyer with a deep concern for his brief. Sometimes he deliberately falsifies the record if he can. More often he instinctively places facts and events in just the light which will make the best impression through memory and, if he tells the story to others, the happiest impression upon their minds. There are differences, of course. Some men have a gift of almost devastating honesty. And some men so fear falsehood that they are afraid to tell the whole truth about good aspects of their own lives. In all sorts of ways one has to watch a man's knowledge of himself.

But despite handicaps and confusing elements in the situation you can learn an astonishing amount from men's estimate of themselves. Their vanities and their subtle posings often become fairly obvious. So you can get at the truth back of the endeavor to paint the picture as the eye likes the look. There may be depths you cannot probe. There will be a good many matters regarding which you can be comfortably sure.

3. Can We Know a Man's Secret?

The ultimate question, of course, has to do with our ability to probe a man's life to the center, to know and to tell his secret. And here the answer is that sometimes we can and sometimes we cannot. Actually quite often the real meaning of a man's life is so clear that it seems inappropriate to call it a secret. The fine, clear manhood of Robert E. Lee stands forth so that he who runs may read. The purposes of David Livingstone are not at all hidden from anyone who studies the life of that great missionary and explorer. But in many cases a man seems to be a different man in different periods of his life. And sometimes he seems to fail completely in achieving unity of purpose. There are also men whose deeds appear to contradict each other and to cancel each other out. We must move through this realm circumspectly enough. But unless we make it a point to magnify difficulties we shall have to admit that in numberless cases, and these the most important, we can say: This was the man, and this was what life meant to him.

4. Through the Civilized Eyes of Plutarch

Plutarch was interested in great men. He loved to study them. He loved to gather materials concerning them. He loved to write about them. He loved to contrast Romans and Greeks. And in his writings these great people live as individuals in the mose remarkable way. He may not give us a philosophy of history. But he does give us a clear and graphic picture of an individual confronting his world.

In telling about all these great people, unconsciously Plutarch tells us a great deal about himself. We behold a gracious, just, and benevolent man, entirely civilized, a good person to know and a good guide through the manifold ways of men. And he reveals, too, the quality of the best Greco-Roman life at the end of the first century A.D. There was a day when all well-read young men had perused Plutarch's *Lives*. It would be well to have that day return. The things these biographies assume, the things they care about, the things they see with quietly glowing eyes, belong to the excellent life for man.

Plutarch was also a moralist and a writer on many themes. Here again he reflected the thoughts and the attitudes of the well-bred man of his period. We look right through a window into the mind of the gentleman of his time. And a happy sort of mind it is to know and to understand. Over against the angry cult of the despisers of men with the bitter and corrosive descriptions of those who rejoice in depicting the evils of life, it is well to put the writings of this open-eyed, sound-hearted person. He has crystallized the quality of the cultivated intelligence of a thousand men of his world. Unconsciously he has written the biographies of men whose names he has never heard.

5. Through the Spacious Eyes of Macaulay

We have already made some reference to the writings of Lord Macaulay. It is rather the fashion now to depreciate the work of the great stylist who knew how to capture the paradoxical elements of a man's character in a brilliant antithesis and to put the drama of his life in the many-colored pageantry of a rich literary brocade. But it is good to read of powerful men of a stalwart breed who made the culture, established the political forms, and enlarged the scope of a great empire. The men were big enough for the sweeping phrases used to describe them. Whatever else you say of Lord Macaulay, you have to admit that his intelligence is at work every minute. And he knows how to tell what he has seen in men's lives and what he has thought about their motives in keen-edged, well-rounded speech. No doubt he loved pomp and circumstance in words. But there are some deeds which cannot be described adequately in language of cynical depreciation. The building of an empire comes to a time when its deeds must be celebrated by an emperor of words.

Macaulay was by no means lacking in knowledge of the motives which moved men! And he could analyze a situation in a fashion which leaves little to be desired. He set forth the ideals and achievements of a certain type of Englishman—and a very powerful and important type at that—with something like finality. Sometimes we do not see that his amplitude of words came in part from fullness of thought. And sometimes we do not see that a dislike of generously full and periodic writing may come from a smallness of mind. There is a literary penuriousness which is the characteristic of intellectual penury. At all events, without claiming too much for Macaulay, we may say that there are rooms we shall never enter if we are unwilling to pass through his spacious doors. And there are men who refuse to be captured by a style less masterfully opulent than his own.

6. The Sensitive Plate of Sainte-Beuve

The seventeenth- and eighteenth-century *Portraits* of Sainte-Beuve are a part of the essential experience of every cultivated man. That curious man of letters, who buried himself for days with the materials which would enable him to re-create a person or the quality of a period and put forth the product of his feat of vicarious experience in writing as miraculous as his insight and understanding, and then made up for his concentration by a license we should like to forget; who had a hard materialistic philosophy which he transcended every time he set about describing a human being; who could probe as skillfully as a surgeon, or could bring to bloom again dead flowers of beauty as though he had been a gardener of the Resurrection, deserves our own closest and most thorough study. No doubt there are ugly and shabby things he never sees in the stately men and women who pass through the purple corridors of his mind. But he sees all these people for what they wanted to be and liked to believe that they were. One scarcely sees a man when his face is dripping with the ugly ink of satire or swelling from the bludgeoning blows of insulting truth. Sainte-Beuve brings to his characters the rare gift of understanding sympathy. And we see something which has passed from the earth because it was inadequate at the one point where it ought to have survived because of its adequacy. The grand monarch once again makes his regal gestures. Statesmen and ecclesiastics and men of letters move to the rhythm of a clear intelligence which only a mind of the most delicate perceptiveness could understand or portray. For what he tells we may thank Sainte-Beuve with all our hearts. For what we must find without his telling perhaps we shall not be grateful to anyone, but it is a part of the whole picture of the centuries Sainte-Beuve knows best and of which he writes with clairvoyant apprehension.

7. The Biographical Detective Appears in Gamaliel Bradford

This man of letters who judged the world from an invalid's chair will be an increasingly interesting figure as years go on. The American mind—perhaps particularly the mind of New England—came to one of its characteristic expressions in his writing. As he read of the great and fascinating men and women who have walked this earth, he did in imagination with them all the things his physical handicaps made it impossible for him actually to do. And what pleasure he derived from judging them with his shrewd and meticulous and somewhat cynical methods, the reader can surmise and sometimes see clearly. He was tremendously impressed by the difficulty of his task. He read untold pages of source material to find a revealing sentence or a revealing deed. This he pounced upon as a detective who arrests a criminal after a long chase. Indeed he was an intellectual detective pursuing furtive motives to their lair. Perhaps it is not unfair to say that his blade works a little more effectively when he is uncovering a hidden vanity than when he is uncovering a hidden excellence. His conscience is rather more effective in its effort not to miss the well-covered weakness than in the effort at all costs to find the virtue the world might miss. He writes of all sorts of people. Glorious women of the French salons who always have the perfect word and the perfect gesture allure his imagination. Men of religion from St. Francis of Assisi to Dwight L. Moody exercise a constant fascination upon his mind. Men of action like the Union and Confederate generals in the War between the States call forth his efforts to understand and to appraise. Men of letters and scientists offer grist to his mill. The men tragically weakened by some all but fatal flaw call for his most careful inspection. He writes of wives and enters with unalloyed delight into'the study of what wives have meant to husbands, and husbands have° meant to wives. His very titles reveal him, *Bare Souls, Damaged Souls, The Quick and the Dead*. When we have finished reading his many volumes of what he loved to call "psychographs" we know a very great deal about many people. And we know more than he ever meant to reveal about Gamaliel Bradford.

8. The Perceptive Analysis of Gilbert Chesterton

That mighty wielder of paradox Gilbert Chesterton was—if he happened to be interpreting the right person—a master of the biographer's art. His book about Robert Louis Stevenson was one of his least successful efforts. But when it came to writing of Dickens and Browning and St. Francis of Assisi and St. Thomas Aquinas, his talents shone. He could follow the loving humanity of Dickens with his capacity to capture the hearts of the poor. He could walk through every maze of Browning's thought with keen delight, matching mind with mind. And he understood the little brother of Assisi as that prophet of austerity with the shining eyes could never have hoped to be understood. St. Francis always used his heart as a substitute for his mind. But Chesterton also understood Thomas Aquinas, who subjected his heart-throbs to the analysis of his mind without doing injustice to his heart. Chesterton has keen enough eyes, but he is quite without the cynical disillusionment one has to watch in Gamaliel Bradford. He believes in life. He believes in God. He believes in Christianity. For all his tantalizing paradoxes, he is the servant of the intelligence which affirms and not of the frustration which denies.

9. The Heroes

There is much to learn from the writers about people. But we must turn to the people themselves. And let us begin with the heroes. Man's first battles were with an intractable nature and with hostile men. These conflicts required the utmost endurance, the utmost self-control, and a complete capacity to act quickly and adequately in a crisis. So the first great man was the hero. And the hero is still a great man.

Sometimes we see the quick movement of his strong hand, the strength of his stout heart, and then all is darkness again. All that we know about the hero is his heroism. Sometimes he is pictured on a large canvas—as is Moses in the Old Testament—leading a confused and not too tractable people to great goals almost in spite of themselves. We see him ready himself to be blotted out of God's book of remembrance if only they can remain. The hero stories of all lands are inspired by sturdy and powerful men about whom doubtless gather many heroic tales so that the story in its final form is in a sense the saga of a nation's courage or a race's bravery. From the Spartan to the Roman and on through the medieval knight to the soldier at Guadalcanal the great story goes on. It is the epic of the virility of humanity.

Sometimes we see the hero in ample relations, with many loyalties. Robert E. Lee is a Virginian. And this he never forgets. He is a gentleman. And he is loyal to a gentleman's code without thinking too much about it. He is a soldier. And he knows what is required of a soldier when he obeys in the ranks and when he commands as a general in full authority. The soldier's reputation never suffers from him. He is a great Christian, and the unobtrusiveness of his loyalty to Christian sanctions must never be allowed to confuse one as to its firmness. He is a great man in many fashions, and each in its turn makes its stern demand for self-abnegation and for heroism. The men of the South who love him most are to be excused for saying that he wore the white flower of a blameless life. Few men in this fallibly human world have come nearer to deserving that tribute.

10. The Saints

Next to the heroes come the saints. When Athanasius wrote the life of St. Anthony, he was working in a pattern which was to become very popular. The Venerable Bede studded the pages of his ecclesiastical history with tales of saints and sainthood. When Farrar wrote his *Lives of the Fathers,* he did not miss the saints, but he discussed much which cannot be classified under the category of sainthood. Some men stand each alone in his age. Whether it is Gibbon with his polished scorn or the English ecclesiastic who is writing of Athanasius, the great Alexandrian stands like a lofty mountain against the sky. Gibbon with unwonted enthusiasm suggests that he would have adorned the office of emperor. He is a great Christian bishop—as great in exile as in the occupancy of his high office. When the bishop is a saint and the saint is a bishop, we have come upon a notable day for the Church and a good day for the world.

Ever since Sabatier made Francis of Assisi a saint for Protestants as wall as for members of the Latin communion, the little brother who founded the Franciscan Order has been the outstanding example of sainthood of all the years which have followed the apostolic age. He loved nature and men and God. This love gave grace and splendor to his austerities and made the ascetic sing like a troubadour. He was as gallant as any knight who ever appeared in a joust, and his gallantry was the expression of a divine love which gave a new tenderness to all human affection. Burning with physical vitality he could leap into the snow to cool his hot body, but his best solution of the problem of the blazing heat of him was to burn for God. He found a passion for the Christ of the Cross which destroyed all other passion, but it left him with a heart singing with human kindness. He taught asceticism how to be so happy in what it loved that it forgot what it suffered. And he made self-denial a vast affirmation of the goodness of God and the goodness of life.

11. The Statesman

It may well seem that the statesman is a man who writes the history of a country rather than a man whose biography we can write. But his power to be a statesman often has odd relations to his personal quality. When Solon succeeded in having his code accepted and then became a voluntary exile so that the laws could be seen apart from any personal ambition of his, he did something which throws a clear and revealing light upon the man himself. When Cicero, whose own life had its dubious aspects, stood firm by the principles of the Roman Republic, commanding at long last the respect of the young Augustus, the path of whose large ambition made him Cicero's relentless foe, he did something which lets you look through a window into his own soul.

Dante's *De monarchia* is the work of a statesman, but the Dante who wrote the *Divine Comedy* is in it. And the Dante who lived an exile from the city he loved, and who longed for an order where all political and spiritual authority would express noble sanctions for the good of a world-wide state, is seen peering through pages of stately exposition.

The elder Pitt, who put a moral sense into the public life of a nation debauched by the shrewd and unethical practicality of Walpole, can never be understood as a statesman until one has entered into the meaning of his life as a man.

The tale of the younger Pitt is the biography of a glorious person as well as the history of a country. He put the thrill of his own quality into every characteristic action as the guide of a nation's destinies.

The Gladstone who could make the figures of a budget fascinating and gave the liberal party a new idealism did not by accident exert such a power that when he died Sir William Robertson Nicoll could say of him that he kept the soul alive in England. He did not live one life as a man and another life as a statesman. He suffused his work as a statesman with the quality of his character as a man.

Abraham Lincoln for all time made biography and statecraft not two tales but one epic of a great life. The Gettysburg Address and the Second Inaugural are red with the lifeblood of a man as well as rich with the noblest quality of a nation's spirit.

In Woodrow Wilson somehow the Westminster Assembly got into the chair of the president of the United States. With all the commanding power of his intellectual distinction, with all the large sweep of his scholarship, with all his shrewd gift for action, which not even the failure of the League of Nations can quite hide, the man with the Reformed theology in his blood is there continually.

And with the quicksilverlike motion of the perhaps too great political sagacity of Franklin Roosevelt, there is never far from the surface the profound human understanding of the man who conquered infantile paralysis and who has dipped his mind in pools of understanding. When all the intense hostilities of those who distrusted the politician, and even felt that they could not trust the man, have been forgotten, and when even his great achievements in international affairs have become part of the common heritage of the nation, the man who fought a difficult personal battle and won, and who never forgot the other men who were fighting difficult battles and with tragic eagerness wanted also to win, will have a distinct place in the heart of the Republic.

12. The Thinkers

There are those who would say that you must forget yourself in order to think. Perhaps it is better to say that you must remember that the typical human qualities are alive in you and must be kept alive in all your mental investigation if your thought is to have true vitality and permanent wisdom. The men who are only inventors of impersonal formulas do not survive as representative of the great thinkers of the world.

No one can really understand Plato who does not see in his doctrine of ideas his own biography writ large. He made his problem a human problem, and so he projected his thought into the farthest regions.

Epictetus gave Stoicism a form which can be understood only when you remember that he was a slave and was propounding a philosophy which would make a slave so superior to his slavery that he was actually the monarch of his own soul.

Spinoza worked out a philosophy of reality which would have made Spinoza himself impossible, but it was his free and spiritual loyalty to a determined order that made his monistic theories shine with a moral beauty and a spiritual charm which they had no right to claim as their own.

Francis Bacon is an illusive and arresting figure as you watch him moving in his dubious and darkly bright way through the complicated life of his time. But the man who had studied things more than he had ever studied the deep moral sources of the personal life, the man who had studied the ways of shrewd flattery, by means of which he could get men to do what he wanted them to do, more than he had studied the straight appeal of an honest mind to an honest mind, was just the kind of man who would find this sort of thinking easy. The more you know of Bacon the man, the more you understand why he betrayed the mind of Europe, to the degree that Europe followed him. His biography gives no end of clues to his philosophy.

When Kant at Königsberg served as a clock by the regular timing of his walk, or as an old man still loved the glory of the night sky and the splendor of the moral law, a man moved in the ways of men whose inner life is the very best explanation of the particular genius of the *Critique of Practical Reason* and the *Critique of Judgment*. He did not always guide the world which came to him to learn how to think in the fashion which meant the most effective pursuit of truth. But he did have a sense of values which must never be forgotten and an apprehension of the ways of the mind with experience which must always be taken seriously by critical students of human experience.

13. The Scientists

The personal life of the scientist is a matter with an interest of its own. Some of the story we know quite well. Galileo's adventures with the Inquisition and his silence, which was not quite silence, reveal something fundamental regarding man's attempt to crush the free and inquiring mind. The Franciscan Roger Bacon, with the inductive method in an ecclesiastical background, gives us other aspects of the same tale. The men who founded the Society for the Advancement of Science in the time of Charles II have their own revelation of human stuff to make to us. The Vulcanists and the Neptunists were men as well as scientific theorists. Charles Darwin with his twenty years of observations and Alfred Russel Wallace with his flash of swift generalization, and their gallant fairness each to the other, represent something of which scientists may be proud. The heroes who risked life and health for the discovery of scientific truths have their great importance. The honest facing of truth in the physical and biological regions by men who made a code of their open-mindedness in these respects must be included in our account of man's putting of truth before personal preference. The effect of men's preoccupation with the uniformities of nature on their sense of the adventures of the free mind and the play of the imagination must be included, too.

14. The Preachers

When Phillips Brooks described preaching as the giving of truth through personality, he struck just the right note. This is precisely what preaching was when Amos threw his explosive words into the minds of the worshipers at Bethel. It is precisely what preaching was when Jeremiah turned many years of suffering for God into the power to speak for God with increasing and authentic compulsion. It was the genius of preaching when all that Jesus was, subtly suffused and made potent every sentence which He spoke. It was this which made Paul an arresting figure whenever he addressed men in his Greco-Roman world. The man with the blazing eyes, whose capacity to speak with the tongues of men and of angels put a touch of anxious watchfulness into one phrase of the thirteenth chapter of First Corinthians, the man who carried the human world in his heart so that in a sense all living men were alive in his imagination, was because of all this one of the greatest preachers in the Christian Church. Chrysostom made preaching imperial because every word he spoke first of all came to life in his own mind and moved with quick energy in his own heart. Bernard of Clairvaux with almost irresistible power could call men to make the great surrender and live for God alone because he had made that surrender himself. Kings and knights came to his monastery to spend a night and, captured by some impalpable excellence and peace which glowed in the very face of Bernard, remained his companions in the holy way for the rest of their lives. Wycliffe always fought and won a personal battle in thinking and in living before he put a truth in burning words which made even a scholastic treatise a sermon. Huss made certain ideas splendid, not because he originated them, but because he was ready to die for them, and, seen in the light of the fire which consumed his body, they were revealed to be worthy of commanding the loyalty of his soul. Luther was Everyman confronting characteristic battles of the spirit of man; in him Everyman found the way of faith, and so when he spoke Everyman listened. The downright English yeoman who became articulate in all the sermons of Hugh Latimer went right on speaking until this sturdy man of men uttered his last word. John Knox carried into the pulpit the steellike purpose which as a galley slave looking up at the distant heights of St. Andrews made him feel that he had a great work to do. Edinburgh was always conscious of the man who spoke the truth as well as of the truth which the man spoke when John Knox preached. John Donne, as we have seen, brought the whole subtle mind of him, and the whole tension of the battle of his spirit and his body, into the pulpit of St. Paul's Cathedral.

Richard Baxter brought an opulent mind with the sympathies of an ample personality to the proclamation of the gospel in the days of the Commonwealth. Jeremy Taylor was a person with the afterglow of the Renaissance upon him before he brought that glow to his golden words when he adorned the gospel with a royal rhetoric. Whitefield standing at the top of the stairs and holding a candle as he spoke his last word for Christ in the new world to which he had journeyed so many times was somehow a typical figure. In the old world with Lord Chesterfield in the congregation and in the new with the Master of the Wilderness so near, there was always a glow of light when he spoke—a little candle burning in every word and at last a great radiance suffusing the whole sermon. The light had been burning in his own soul before it glowed in the shining sentences which came from his lips as he preached.

Sir William Robertson Nicoll liked to feel that there had been many princes in the pulpit in his time, and he wrote a book about them. One finds the great human and personal quality—autobiography frankly revealed or implicitly expressed in all of them. Spurgeon exercised a fascination quite inadequately explained when we have studied his ideas. It was the way the ideas met in the man, and the way the man incarnated the ideas, which counted. Newman followed what he believed to be a most kindly light to Rome, and the story of his pilgrimage became the tale of numbers of the ablest young men in England. Dale, who made the voice of a spacious nonconformist chapel more commanding than the words uttered from bishops' thrones, and in whose large mind and conscience the Church and the city met, can best be approached through the biography by his son. Then his books—sermons turned into books—speak with their full power.

The Church always grows strong when mighty preachers give truth through their own personality. It always grows weak, whatever its organization, whatever the beauty of its glorious ritual, whatever its social services, unless there stands in the pulpit the man who speaks for God.

15. The Reformers

Wilberforce was an example of the reformer at his very best. The biography by Professor Coupland lets him live and speak and act for us today as he lived and spoke and acted when he walked the earth. He was a devoted evangelical Christian. He was a gifted orator. He was a man of all the social graces, whose charm Madame de Staël instantly felt. He was the friend of the younger Pitt. He became the conscience of the House of Commons. And he was the great and successful fighter against the slave trade. Not even the ferocity of the Napoleonic Wars could stifle his passionate thought and action. The moment men had a little freedom from the necessity of fighting Napoleon, there he was with his moral battle against slavery. And when Napoleon came to defeat at long last, he was ready to bring the slave trade to its Waterloo.

Wendell Phillips' statue stands on Boston Common. Perhaps few think much today about the years when that trumpet-toned voice of a patrician with a conscience spoke out so that the Boston which did not want to hear what he had to say was forced to listen. But his personality, his powerful advocacy, his literal incarnation of the moral voice, are a part of the ethical history of the Republic. And the willing sacrifices he made for a great cause make his public service autobiography.

The play *Harriet,* so brilliantly staged, brought to the imagination of many men and women the very quality of the days of America's greatest moral battle. And the "little woman" whom Abraham Lincoln so whimsically addressed lived once more in her oddly gifted family, with her absent-minded professor, with her contemporaries, and with her social conscience. At the crisis of the play the reformer meets the test when her principles make demands upon her own family. Is she willing to have her own son fight for the cause of which she had so eloquently written?

In truth the biography of the reformer always captures the very genius of the reform.

16. The Women

Sainte-Beuve wrote with marvelous understanding about women. Gamaliel Bradford followed their ways with his alert, observant eyes and recorded them with his pointed, sometimes malicious, pen. Of Frances E. Willard, for instance, he could never think without annoyance. It is diverting to ask what Frances E. Willard would have thought of him. Countless novels have tried to follow the manifold fashions of women's thought and action. Chivalry idealized woman. The Church of the Middle Ages saw all women with eyes made tender by gazing upon the Mother of its Lord. Women themselves, sometimes with loud shouting and sometimes in the most patient and disciplined writing, have attempted to interpret themselves to the world. The student of human experience, in so far as it is the experience of women, is indebted to all of these and to many more. He is indebted most of all to the women he has known.

When Elizabeth Barrett Browning shyly put her *Sonnets from the Portuguese* into the hands of Robert Browning, she made a gesture beautifully revealing. There are no skills to be denied to those women who can attain them. There is no wisdom to be denied to those women who can master it. Increasingly they are the comrades of men in the tasks of life. But the woman with the sonnets standing beside the man for whom the sonnets were written is a symbol of something which is a permanent part of the structure of human life.

The mother of the Gracchi reminds us that motherhood has come to flower in pagan as in Christian culture. And always in moments of supreme quality and of supreme demand motherhood has been self-sacrifice alive.

17. The Men

All the while we are feeling our need of the biographies which have never been written. All the while we are feeling our need of the stories which have never been told. There are the men on all the farms. There are the men in all the mines. There are the men in all the factories. There are the men who make up the vast processes of production and transportation and salesmanship. There are the masses of the underprivileged. There are the strange hosts of the vagrants.

None of these have been without voices speaking for them or from them. Old literatures had to do principally with the joys and sorrows, the hopes and fears, the fruitions and the tragedies of the highly placed. When Richardson wrote *Pamela* and set all Europe weeping over the experiences of a servant girl, something new happened. There has been the literature of emotional exploitation. And as we have seen, there has been the literature of social indignation. There has been the literature of portrayal. Josiah Flint's *Tramping with Tramps* set a new pattern. Jacob Riis's *How the Other Half Lives* was the beginning of a vast body of writing. And in one way or another bits of the biography of those belonging to the great inarticulate groups are found in all this writing. But at best it leaves much to be desired. The Welsh miners have found a method of expressing themselves in glorious singing. But there is all too little of that writing which is simply writing with understanding of those who have had least to say for themselves. Neither the writing of social indignation, useful as it is, nor the writing of emotional exploitation, though bits of truth come through it, is quite what we need. There are quiet victories, and pleasant compensations, and good fellowships, and great heroisms belonging to the company of inarticulate men of which we know all too little. Personal friendships and personal observations without condescension may give us much. One day the masses of men may reach a level of simple and direct biographical writing which will give us something of quite inestimable value.

18. The Valley of Decision

The percipient writer who called the world a vale of soul making might well have called it a valley of decision. The net impression we get from a study of human biography, gather our materials as we may, can indeed be summed up in the phrase, "Multitudes, multitudes in the valley of decision!"

All this confirms from the vast laboratory of human thought and action everything we have said about the free mind of man. The focal point in every human story finds a person confronting alternatives and making a significant decision. The decision is always in the light of standards. Men repudiate them theoretically only to return to them practically. Even a working hypothesis is a temporary principle. And the temporary principle is always used as a method of finding a permanent principle. Sometimes men's principles are implicit. But they are pivotal for their decisions. And the repudiation of principles in the name of endless experiment, with no goal except the excitement of the experiment itself, is based upon the principle that the psychological experience of experiment is more important than the permanent principles to which experiments might lead. Or if the possible existence of permanent principles is denied, then the denial itself is made on the basis of a worshipful acceptance of chaos.

However we look at it, biography is the story of human choices in the light of standards. It is the story of what man has done with his freedom. Or to put it more adequately, it is the story of what endless numbers of men have done with their freedom. And if the study is carried on with critical intelligence, it will be seen that we always have implicit in human experience the sense of something dependable enough to be the basis for a decision and the possession of freedom enough to make the act of choice authentic and unforced.

Certain other things become clear. There must be a truth we can find, or the quest is meaningless. There must be a good we can apprehend, or life itself becomes a tale told by an idiot, signifying nothing. Treachery is the essential of the betrayal of the human cause. It poisons all human relations. And as men must live together, selfishness, too, is the betrayal of humanity. We must give to others as much as we expect to receive from them in order to make society tolerable. So one may go on and on. And all these insights coming from a close inspection of the human story of numberless individuals increasingly become a corpus of sanctions necessary to the ongoing of human life itself. In the light of these sanctions the individual must live. He betrays them at his peril and the peril of the human world. He accepts and obeys them for the sake of the good life, for himself and for his kind.

CHAPTER XXI

History and the Christian Sanctions

THE reader of the six volumes of Arnold Toynbee's *A Study of History* which have already been published is confronted, as we have already seen, by an incredible mass of erudition. One gets the feeling that Professor Toynbee has read every monograph in every language on every historical subject. There are insights so piercing and full of understanding that they are worth the price of the six volumes. The material gathered together is of the utmost value. But the big pattern is singularly artificial and unreal, and arguments are sometimes built by emphasizing superficial likenesses and ignoring essential differences. The critical reader is inclined to change the familiar lines and say vast learning is a dangerous thing. Yet it is not the learning which is at fault. It is not the learning which leads Professor Toynbee to pour brilliant scorn on the apathetic fallacy of treating persons as if they were things, only to fall himself into the fallacy of using impersonal formulas to explain the vast movements of personal activity. It is only that he remains a son of his own brilliant materialistic age even when he tries to break his chains. And the way in which he uses biblical quotations with amazing facility yet in such a fashion as to turn them shrewdly from their central meaning, reveals his lack of that last quality of a great historian, desperate faithfulness in dealing with his sources. In marshaling facts he is a scholar of genuine trustworthiness. In dealing with living experience his mind slips.

But at least Professor Toynbee represents a step on the journey away from the hard mechanism of Oswald Spengler and his ilk. The author of *The Decline of the West* was once described by Irving Babbitt as a charlatan of genius. It is good to escape from his unrelieved impersonal mathematics. But Arnold Toynbee lives in a halfway house. He knows, at least at times, from what he would escape. But he does not know with any security in just what the freedom of history consists.

Of course, history can be used clearly and plausibly to prove anything. It has been used with a parade of scholarship to prove almost everything. The man to whom the Christian corpus of interpretation has become commanding knows full well the danger of attempting to force history into the molds of any interpretation. But he has more than a suspicion that, if Christianity holds the secret of the goal of history, it may furnish many definitive clues for the understanding of history. It may make clear the reason for the breakup of many a pretentious historical movement. It may throw a new light on the quality of every historic movement at the point where that movement touched the deeper meaning of human life or destiny.

1. The Breakdown of the Older States

Our oldest historical memories are mingled with an echo of crashing timbers. The history of many a land could borrow a title from Gibbon and be called *The Decline and Fall*. The empire is a tremendous expression of power. So it was in the Valley of the Nile. So it was in the Valley of the Euphrates. And whenever the noun power is without qualifying adjectives which express secrets of moral vitality, the noun itself begins to disintegrate. These great empires of the ancient world knew all the potency of mighty force. There was more than that. Babylon tells of many other things in the Code of Hammurabi. Assyria had great gifts of organization. Egypt had the golden glow of Ikhnaton. But the seed of life in each case failed to come to full and fructifying energy. As empires of unethical power, these states went down. The sword must always represent something beyond the sword if it is to continue powerful. It is in this bare and definitive sense that they who take to the sword must perish by the sword. To use the sword to defend the rights of man and to put a wall of might around the garden of civilization is quite another matter. The debacle in the older states came when the noun cast aside all the adjectives and only unrelieved power remained an active force. But in another sense something did remain from Babylonia and Egypt and Assyria. The good adjectives were waiting to be picked up by other lands.

Persia seemed a genuine advance. Its life possessed a sharper sense of moral values. The religion of Zarathustra, with its mighty struggle between light and darkness, poured into its people qualities not belonging to older states. But when Persia tried to crush Greece, men whose hearts still belonged to a world of tyranny were fighting men whose hearts were free. It was not by numbers that the Greeks repulsed Persia. The Greek spirit was something which would enable one man to put ten thousand men to flight. And the Persia which was not strong enough for Greece was not able to resist Alexander the Great. One may say that it possessed good but was not good enough. Its face was turned toward the past of power and not toward the future of freedom. Alexander was attempting to spread the Greek spirit by a tyrant's methods. This amazing pupil of Aristotle captured something from the Greeks with which he infused his armies. But it was Greek culture which he loved and not Greek freedom in which he believed. Again we may say: Good but not good enough. Another spirit would have been needed to weld his empire together when he died. But the good as well as the evil survived. Something of the grace of Greece touched remote parts of the earth. The debacle was not an unqualified tragedy.

As we appraise these ancient powers and their fall, we can see a mighty series of experiments through trial and error. It is not without significance that we can say that the absence of what would later be called Christian sanctions was involved in the whole process. In a strange negative way these catastrophes prophesied the coming of that which these far-off men and states did not know.

2. The Debacle in Greece

We have seen something of the greatness and glory of Greece. In Athens the human mind came to flower as it had never bloomed before. Ideas full of power to enrich the life of man became the possession of the Greeks. They began to study and to understand the ways of nature. They became masters in the analysis of the ways of the mind of man. They turned from things to thoughts and from thoughts to thinkers. They established a tradition of free men forming a state. They knew something of the wonder of spiritual beauty.

Yet Athens fell. The Greek states wasted their substance in internecine warfare. And at length Greece lost its independence. There was much intellectual energy and moral force and political understanding and spiritual power. And life had many gracious satisfactions. But for all that the debacle came. We remember that Greek freedom was founded on slavery. We remember that Athens in the day of its power became unscrupulously tyrannical. We remember that the excesses of the nature religions were never far away, and it was very easy even for a brilliant Greek to be mastered by his body rather than controlled by his mind. At all events Greece failed in the long last to produce that moral fiber which resists attack. This it had done when confronted by Persia. This it failed to do when confronted by Rome. It was good— very good indeed. But it was not good enough. So the end came.

But what glorious things were left behind. The world was never to be the same. Athens in chains remained the monarch of man's minds.

Thornton Wilder, in his distinguished and revealing little tale *The Woman of Andros,* tells something of the magnificence and something of the limitations of the Greek spirit. And as his little tale comes faltering toward its end, he remembers that just about the time of the story a little child was born in a land edging on another part of the Great Sea. Even upon Greece that child was to pronounce judgment.

3. The Debacle in Rome

Greece knew how men could live separately with brilliant individual intelligence. Rome knew how men could live together in a great empire. The sense of human solidarity was deep in the consciousness of Rome. The Pax Romana became the most splendid political achievement in the establishment of order in the ancient world. The Roman was an autocrat. He ruled by force. But he made his rule full of meaning and of opportunity for those whom he ruled. Assyria had represented pure, naked force. Persia had moved in the direction of a sense of something to be given to those its satraps ruled. Rome came to have an amazing sense of social responsibility. The Roman government was perpetually benefiting those under its sway. The Roman roads made travel easy and safe all about the empire. The Mediterranean was made a sea safe for commerce. Order and law were established over vast areas. Roman citizenship was extended. Local cities and local provinces were given their own rights and a genuine opportunity to live a life of their own as a part of the great empire. Law was codified and given far-reaching effectiveness. The world became one as it had never been one before. Many a man all about the vast areas of the empire had reason to be grateful for the Roman peace and the Roman law and the rights he could claim under Roman rule. The Apostle Paul proudly made the most of his Roman citizenship, and the Roman peace and the Roman roads made his great career of evangelism possible.

But Rome's religious gregariousness had the seed of moral decay in it. Religions came in from the East whose genius, to use a truimph of understatement, was biological rather than ethical. Even the physical virility of the Roman was eaten into by wild and lawless cults. The accounts of Roman decadence bring a sickening order of decay across the centuries.

And Roman government, despite famous good and great emperors and many faithful and wise administrators, became hopelessly corrupt. The throne itself was sold to the highest bidder. And the naked power of the army became the supreme arbiter of the Roman world. The army itself lost the old Roman qualities, and the sturdy manhood of soldiers of conquered lands was used to make up for the decadent quality of the soldiers of Roman blood. Peculation and bribery suffused the empire. The law of force was modified by the law of greed. Bad administration led to bad economic conditions, and the empire was bleeding at its heart. So at last the unspoiled strength of barbarism conquered the effete civility of Rome. The inner weakness led to outer tragedy, and the great debacle came.

Again, while much was lost, much remained; and much would be one day recovered. But of Rome also we must say that, while it brought much good to the world, it was not good enough. It could corrupt the barbarians; it could not tame them. And it could not give them virtues it had ceased to possess.

4. The Debacle in the Middle Ages

It was the Christian Church which tamed the barbarians. It was the Christian Church which handed an ennobled classical tradition on to the Europe which was to be. The penitence in respect of the excesses of the pagan world and the establishment of a higher, cleaner code was like a Lenten repentance for a whole continent. The Church took the Roman organization as a pattern for a great ecclesiastical order. The idea of a Christian world mastered men's minds. It was given superb expression in Dante's *De monarchia*. Life became suffused with a new tenderness and a new sense of the stewardship of the strong for the weak. The house of religion became the friend of the poor, the home of an earnest agriculture, and a center of noble learning. Greek philosophy was used by a kind of right of eminent domain to give a framework for theology. And theology itself turned stones to its purposes in the magnificent Gothic cathedrals, as it had made religion imperial in the Byzantine temple of worship. Europe knew such oneness as had never been its experience before. The Christian Empire which included the growing secular states had a spiritual basis the Roman Empire had never known. Multitudes of men lived for eternity as men of an older day had lived for the world of time. And in the case of Bernard of Clairvaux a saint was more powerful than any monarch or any pope.

But alas, this is not the whole story. The repentance of evil all too often took the form of the repudiation of life itself. The ascetic became the Christian hero. And the high ecclesiastic was frequently the slave of the very world he tried to master. When he tried to be a citizen of two worlds, all too often the world of the flesh had a greater share in him than the world of the spirit. The vices of the old decadent civilization returned to be the vices of the Church. Supernatural authority was claimed for a lordship having all too little to do with the Kingdom of Heaven. So in spite of commanding and majestic figures like Gregory the Great, Gregory the Seventh, and Innocent III, decay took possession of the Church.

And the world of warring princes was not saved even by the high ideals of knighthood or by the grace of chivalry. There were knights of the noblest quality, and there were gentlemen of the rarest chivalry, but decay was entering into the very organism of Europe. So the inner debacle came to the Church. And the inner decay became an outer scandal. The Babylonian captivity of the popes at Avignon and the great schism revealed to the world the inner cancer. Amid forms of imperial power the ecclesiastical organism was torn with deadly fever.

Of the medieval synthesis we must say that it was great and good. But as a practical achievement it was not good enough. It was not Christianity that failed. It was the Church which did not become thoroughly Christian. And the Christian sanctions which have no more tenderness for a decadent church than for a decadent world judged the Church. For now a Christian conscience existed in Europe. The last strange glory of the Church was the fact that it produced its severest critics from within its own life.

5. The Debacle in the Renaissance

The Church had repented of the vices of a decadent classicism. The Renaissance repented of the otherworldliness of an ascetic church. A profounder study of the Renaissance than Berdyaev has ever made will make it abundantly clear that if in sheer reaction from human evil the Church allows too little dignity to man there will be a wrathful reaction and man will claim too much for himself. The revival of learning had given Europe a new sense of the splendid achievements of man. The memory of Attica became a golden inspiration. The classical world rose from its ashes to assert its own essential dignity. Some men misinterpret the Renaissance by saying that it contained much good but this good was all present or at least implicit in the Middle Ages. Some men misinterpret the Renaissance by saying that it contained much that was energetic and vigorous but that its very genius was betraying and evil. Some men have put the contrast all too bluntly by saying that in its worship of God the Middle Ages forgot man, while in its worship of man the Renaissance forgot God.

As a matter of fact, however, the Renaissance at its best brought something very splendid to the world. There was a hearty and joyous belief in life and a confidence in the possibilities of man which opened glorious vistas of hope and became the basis of notable and far-reaching achievement. The springtime flowers bloomed with a new loveliness when you possessed eyes which actually could see their beauty. The world about you took on new meaning when you looked upon it as a good home for man and not as something to be distrusted and hated. The forces of nature revealed their secrets to you when you approached a study of the natural world with a sense that somehow it was made to be understood and used by man just as he was made to understand and use it. The sense of a commanding energy in man and a human kingliness yet to be expressed all spoke to something very deep and very real in the human spirit. And when, as was the case with the Florentine Platonists, all this was connected with a great world of spiritual reality beyond and above man and ready to express itself through man, the possibilities were very great indeed.

But once more we must sadly confess that this was not the whole story. For from the beginning there was a tendency to think of man as a conscious body rather than as the spiritual master of his body. The repentant ascetic is always tempted to become a voluptuary. From distrusting and despising the body he is likely to move to the opposite extreme and to surrender entirely to the body and the world of sensation. That there is another possibility, namely, that of viewing the body as the happy and responsive servant of the life of the mind and the spirit, having its own rights and having its own place and its own pleasures but always under a higher overlordship, quite failed to come within the ken of many a Renaissance man of tremendous vitality who came to regard the lusts of the body as more important than the kingliness of the mind or the splendor of the spirit. So by another door the old pagan vices came in again. There was vice. There was abnormal vice. There was sadic cruelty. The art of poisoning became a highly regarded skill among some Renaissance men.

But the root of the evil which led to the final debacle was even deeper than the worship of the material and the cult of the body. The very sense of man's power, the very sense of man's tremendous potencies, led to a mood of self-assertion which repudiated with scornful distaste the thought of any authority to which man must submit. The Christian who realized the implications of his position saw man over nature and under God. At his worst moments of self-adulation the Renaissance man was determined to be his own god. His only worship was self-worship. So by his cult of the body uncontrolled he sank to the subhuman, and by his Faustian repudiation of human limitations he became mad with his lawless self-assertion in a world where there was no room for God. In every way he repudiated the true human position. And the debacle was dark and tragic and terrible indeed. There was great and glorious good. There was bitter and loathsome evil. So of the Renaissance, too, we must say that it was good. But it was not good enough. Indeed, at its worst it was the creature of poisonous uncleanness. The man who belonged to the debacle made the fatal mistake of thinking that he had to become a pagan in order to be truly human. And he taught even paganism new secrets of rebellion. For he followed Prometheus in his defiance without the moral justification which led Prometheus to defy Zeus. Indeed, he invented a world which did not even have a pagan pantheon. For he lived in a universe from which man had banished God.

All this is dark and evil enough. But it must never lead us to forget the good which belonged to the Renaissance and which, had the Renaissance become Christian, might have brought untold blessing to the world. It is only a very dignified creature who can sin as the Renaissance man sinned at last. Only a creature made in God's image can be jealous of God. The man whom God made in His image cannot make that good gift of God evil without a blasphemy of his own. It was not in uplifting the flag of man's dignity that the Renaissance man did evil. It was in failing to see that man holds his dignity in glad allegiance to the God in whose image he is made.

6. *The Debacle in the Reformation*

The Reformation was a moral movement. It was in part a repentance for the ethical lapses of the Middle Ages. It was a religious movement. It claimed a direct relation between the soul and God which was more fundamental than any ecclesiastical decision. It was an intellectual movement. It put the mind of the individual Christian in direct contact with the Scriptures and placed squarely upon his shoulders the responsibility of interpretation. It was a political movement. It expressed the revolt of national governments in the presence of extranational authority and the flowing of wealth from the nations to an international center of ecclesiastical authority. That with the progress of these varied movements one sees the beginning of the modern world is a claim which very correct and competent men would make with much assurance. Or, if they did not put the matter quite so boldly, they would claim that the Reformation gave the Renaissance a conscience and a soul and so saved the best of it for the centuries which were to follow. Of course, one must not forget the Council of Trent and the Counter Reformation. The Latin Church itself examined its life and moved forward with a deeper assertion of moral and spiritual sanctions. That the Reformation did answer to something very deep in the mind and the conscience of multitudes of men can scarcely be denied. The Protestant Revolt was not a revolt against the Church as such. It was a revolt against the decadence which had depleted the moral and spiritual life of the Church, the clarity of its intellectual processes, and the quality of its political relationships. In a sense it was the Renaissance turned passionately Christian.

But again one must admit sadly that this was not the whole story. Indeed, for all the men like Calvin who moved from a scholarly humanism to evangelical Christianity and retained their humanistic intelligence—if one may call it so—as a part of their equipment as evangelical theologians, there were others who forgot their clear intelligence in their repentance of the abysmal depths of human evil. The break between Erasmus and Luther is no doubt a sad story from whichever side one sees it. One wishes that Erasmus could have had something of Luther's depth of moral and spiritual experience, and that Luther could have had something which his cool humanistic culture gave to Erasmus. The day came when in certain ways the Old Church seemed nearer the true insights of the Renaissance than did some followers of Luther. Melanchthon represents an attitude one remembers with deep appreciation. The abysmal repentance which uplifts the grace of God in such a fashion as almost to deny human freedom, by a curious twist is likely to lead to a certain type of antinomianism. Luther's advice "Sin boldly" may be so interpreted as to have very dangerous connotations.

Then the frequent subservience of the Lutheran Church to the secular state was full of danger to the Christian life of a nation. Luther's apologetic attitude toward the bigamy of Philip of Hesse and the spectacle of Henry VIII as head of the English Church and the treatment of the houses of religion and their wealth in England have always been hard to associate with the idea of Reformation.

The Middle Ages had known a scholasticism when the living spirit was lost in endless splitting of words, and Protestantism came upon a Protestant scholasticism scarcely less arid.

One has to admit that the golden gates which opened often led into something very different from the happy gardens of God. The Reformation had its own debacle. And it is sad enough to contemplate its ravages. If the full spiritual afflatus of the Reformation in its best hours could have been preserved in Europe, we should live in a different world today.

Something gracious and good was left. The Reformation churches, state and free, Lutheran and Reformed, have done a great work in the world. And if they have fallen sometimes into moral and spiritual confusion which radical thinkers might believe calls for a new reformation of the reformed, we must sadly admit how frequently institutions and cultures have come upon just such regrettable sinking below the level of their best meaning. The Reformation was good. It was very good indeed at its high moments. But it was not good enough. If we are dealing with Christian sanctions, not even the Reformation can refuse to submit itself to judgment.

7. The Debacle in the Enlightenment

Men wearied of ecclesiastical leadership, both that coming from the Old Church and that coming from the new churches. So once more man tried the experiment of building the structures of his own life. So comes the Enlightenment. One can see its influence spreading out in the deism of England, with its absent god and its self-sufficient man, and in the Encyclopedists in France, who made all knowledge, except the most important knowledge of all, their province.

Perhaps the most incisive way of approaching the debacle in the Enlightenment is to say that with all its cool and secular urbanity it was the precursor of the excesses of the French Revolution. It is a deep and importtant truth that Enlightenment is never able to prevent the reign of terror. It has its own contribution to make to the ongoing of human life. But it is not sufficient for the meeting of the human problems. Once again we must say: It was good. But it was not good enough. So the debacle came.

8. The Debacle of the French Revolution

Many wrongs led at last to political eruption. The reign of autocracy was succeeded by the assertion of the rights of man. The new wine of freedom began breaking the old bottles, and tyrants trembled all over Europe. There was wild jubilation, and in France utopia, it seemed, would cease to be a dream and would become an actuality. But the rule of reason turned into the rule of the mob. And as the underprivileged came to power, the mob became a tyrant. The wild dreams went down in tragedy in the midst of strange and lawless faces with the light of hell in their eyes. France found order at last, but it was under the military despotism of Napoleon, and that in turn was followed by the triumph of reaction and the period of Metternich in Europe. When we think of the Old Regime and all the evil that was overthrown, when we think of the excellent purposes which inspired many of the revolutionists, we must say that in so far forth the Revolution was good. When we think of its excesses and lawlessness and anarchy, we must say that it was not good enough. In fact, we must say that it turned many evils loose upon the world. And with Madame Roland we must cry: "O Liberty, what crimes are committed in thy name!"

But here again if all was not gain, surely all was not loss. In truth Europe has never been the same since the fall of the Bastille. We have learned that the human problem is much more complicated than we had supposed. We have learned that there are demonic forces with which we must reckon. But reaction has never quite had its way even in the era of Metternich. And we are not able to forget the rights of man.

9. The Debacle in the Society of Science

As time went on science became more than a technique for investigating the uniformities of the natural world. It became a philosophy of life. And men began to think of a society dominated by scientific sanctions. The science whose principles were to dominate human society was that intellectual discipline which measured everything which could be measured by instruments of precision or their equivalent. Principles of measurement began to be applied to society, and a materialistic sociology was forthcoming. Principles of measurement began to be applied to literature, and a glorified study of words took the place of literary criticism as a corpus of deathless laws to be applied to literary production. In every direction the human was interpreted in terms of the subhuman. Men began to dream of a society of comfortable bodies instead of a society of free minds. The impersonal uniformities of mathematical science were to form the pattern of a new society.

During all this period man obtained such control of nature as he had never achieved before. And he did it, one must be reminded again, by using powers not accounted for by the formulas of mechanical science. He came to understand how to master and use impersonal forces. But his impersonal society was more and more hard and arid. In all directions the humanities began to have their revenge. Even before the analysis was clear and the criticism was complete, the spirit of man began to rebel against the clanking chains of an emancipation which did not emancipate and a freedom which only meant accepting a place in an impersonal order where liberty itself perished.

The world of thought dominated by this sort of science made many and great and lasting contributions to human welfare. And by its coherence on a level lower than that of free intelligence it did at least suggest the repudiation of any philosophy of chaos and the securing of some sort of dependable social order. It was good. In some ways it was very good. But it was not at all good enough. So the debacle of what had seemed a messianic hope for man inevitably came.

10. The Debacle of the Society of Social Blueprints

In a way the society of pseudo science inevitably led to the dream of a society of social blueprints. And this society did at least come to exist on paper. There were reams of paper. And if millions of fluttering blueprints lifted by the wind which blew in through manifold windows could have made a new world, the new world would have been made. The dialectical materialism of Karl Marx cleared the way by a brilliant negative analysis. He attempted to make a great blueprint of the inevitable historical movement of social forces leading to the disintegration of the old society. He never attempted to make a blueprint of the new.

The makers of blueprint utopias were found, however, on every hand. That their thought was merely empty and idle no one would attempt to say. The vast amount of blueprint social thought threw light on many problems, and it at least led to the asking of many relevant questions even when it was unable to provide adequate answers. But actual social experiments, especially the vast experiment in Soviet Russia, kept facing facts not provided for by the blueprints. The story of the ongoing of the Union of Soviet Socialist Republics has been a tale of constant adjustment to the actualities of social situations at the expense of loyalty to blueprint solutions. There is now genuine reason for hope that Russia will at last have incorporated so much of dependable social and economic experience that it will take its place in a Europe which is not afraid to break with the past, but which knows that its roots must be nourished by the whole body of human experience. At all events the blueprint has been seen by many critical minds to be just what it is, namely, another attempt to apply mathematical formulas to the free life of man. These formulas have their place. But they must be mastered and controlled by free intelligence.

11. The Debacle in the Society of the Machine Age

The Machine Age has not knocked at our doors. It has burst into our houses unannounced. It has entered our inner chambers. It has pervaded every aspect of our experience. It is only when we stop to think of it that we realize how thoroughly our lives are dominated by relationships which the machine makes inevitable. The telephone is an institution which takes an increasingly important place in all our organization of production and transportation and salesmanship. And it has become in itself a social institution. The radio brings us the news of the world almost as soon as the events of which it tells have transpired. The cinematograph brings us plays which have all the appeal of the legitimate stage and in which the same actors can be seen at the same time in a hundred cities. All our manufacturing is a tale of endless machines and mechanical devices. Even the farmer would be at a complete loss as to how to carry on without the contribution of machinery to his cultivation of the soil. The production of books is the work of elaborate mechanical processes. The great ocean liner and the streamlined passenger train depend upon mechanical processes. The machine has given man a new world in which to live.

That much convenience and comfort has come to man through all these mechanical agencies we should all gladly admit. That they have made possible much that is good for man we should be ready to declare. But Samuel Butler's angry repudiation of machines and the Machine Age does not seem so completely unintelligent as it did seem when it was written. That the world has been made a tragic place in quite a new sense no one would deny who has studied the ruthless ravages of mechanical warfare. We begin to see that the cult of more and better machines has its own dangers unless a good master and a good controller is found for the machines. The robot bombs bringing havoc to southern England were terrible enough in themselves, but as a symbol of what machines in the hands of ruthless men may do in future wars they were even more menacing.

Such a book as Lewis Mumford's *Technics and Civilization* unconsciously makes clear to the critical reader how barren and arid is the life of a world where technics have a greater place than the purposes for which the technics are used. Romain Rolland's *The Revolt of the Machines* was more than a clever piece of writing. Here we are in the presence of a force menacing and terrifying if in the use of the wrong hands controlled by the wrong minds. The messianic cult of the machine went down amid the atrocities of Nazi armies as they crushed the very life out of so much of Europe.

But we must not forget that the machine may be the instrument of good. It depends upon who controls it. It depends upon the purpose for which it is used. The main matter in respect of the automobile is the character of the driver. The main matter in respect of all machines in all the world is the matter of the character of those who control their use. We see clearly enough now that we cannot afford to have Hitler controlling the supremely powerful machines of the world.

At first Christianity may not seem to have much to do with machinery. But the moment you think of the controllers of the machines, the importance of Christian sanctions is seen. For if Christian sanctions determine the use of machines, they will be good for man and they will cease to bring manifold evils in their train. And when you carry your thought to deeper levels and consider the power of the Christian religion to create men of good character and to transform the motives and the purposes of men of bad character, you see that the solution of the problems of the Machine Age is in the hands of the Christian religion. The debacle in the Machine Age is the debacle of machines in the control of evil men and used for evil purposes, or in the control of indifferent men who do not consider the evil thing they are inflicting upon the world.

There is, of course, also to be considered the tendency of the man who uses machines too constantly and becomes too much engrossed in mechanical processes to become something of a machine himself. Here, too, we can depend upon the vital energies which flow from the Christian religion. It knows how to produce men who can use mechanical formulas without ceasing to be free men using their freedom for noble purposes.

12. The Debacle of the Great Reversion

The outstanding political and social fact of the twentieth century is the Great Reversion. In the nineteenth century political democracy seemed to enter upon a period of something like finality. The parliamentary systems represented by Great Britain and the United States set the pattern for government everywhere. The parliamentary idea had attained a power over men's minds which was felt to promise its final victory. Even the governments which did not accept the democratic principle adopted the parliamentary form. Germany, for instance, had its Reichstag, which, though a glorified debating society, was a representative body and by the optimistic was considered a step in the direction of democracy. Even Russia played with the idea of the Duma. There were vast stirrings in the popular mind in all lands. The star of democracy had never been so high in the sky.

Then there broke upon the world a series of ideas which were held by men passionately impatient of democratic control. To them it seemed that waiting for the popular mind to catch up with great thoughts was an awful waste and might mean the failure of everything for which one cared. Democracy, it was said, was by its very genius inefficient. So the rights of brilliant minorities to secure control by whatever means were within reach were expressed first in appealing propaganda and then in dramatic action. So the Great Reversal took place. The dialectic of Karl Marx set the pattern for the victory of a communistic minority in Russia. And large phrases of social promise set the pace for the rise of Fascism in Italy and Nazi power in Germany. In each case a convinced minority gained power by a brilliant military tour de force. It was freely said that Mussolini gave to Italy an order and the promise of a life not within reach by means of the more orderly processes of popular control. And Hitler scornfully repudiated the sentimental incapacity of the Democratic states.

At this very moment the democratic powers were in the midst of a sentimental enthusiasm for disarming which played into the hands of the very powers whose increasing strength was a profound menace to their liberties. At the other end of the world Japan came under the full control of the military group and joined the company of the totalitarian states.

In 1939 the Great Reversal broke like a mighty tempest upon the world. The democracies were caught in lotus-eating dreams of appeasement. Mr. Neville Chamberlain and his umbrella dominated the councils of the sheep as they prepared peace offerings for the wolves. When war broke, the fatal folly of the democracies produced a situation where they were almost defeated even before they began to fight. Hitler's mechanized forces moved triumphantly over Europe. Mussolini, sure that the future was on the side of the Great Reversion, joined company with Germany. Britain stood alone—the island fortress of the world maintaining the human cause. After Dunkirk the democratic powers seemed in a hopeless position. But Britain held on grimly, and the United States showed its sympathy and provided some practical help.

The Russians seemed on the side of the totalitarian powers. But there was a real difference between the genuine passion for human welfare in Russia and the conscienceless will to power of Germany. Hitler sensed this and attacked Russia in 1941. It was a fatal mistake from a military standpoint, for it meant that fighting on two fronts which at all costs Germany should have avoided. But probably in any event Russia would have come to see that its real future was with the democracies. In December 1941 came the treacherous attack of Japan on the United States at Pearl Harbor. And now the battle lines began to assume their final form. France had crumbled. Germany had advanced by processes as ruthless and ferocious as any the world had ever seen. Britain stood steady in the darkest hours and the darkest days and the darkest months.

Now the far-flung energies of Russia and the utter courage of its fighting men were thrown into the scale. Slowly but surely the immense
resources of the United States in men and in matériel were prepared
for the great conflict. The victorious march of the totalitarian powers
was brought to a halt. The movement began to take the opposite direction. There were great Allied victories all about the world. The armies
of freedom swept across North Africa and invaded Italy. Mussolini and
his regime were overthrown. The Allied armies broke into Normandy
and at length invaded southern France. Within what had been the
French Republic men rose to support the Allies. France was freed from
German oppression. And in Europe the end was sure. In the South Seas
and the Far East the first dramatic victories of Japan were followed by
something like an impasse. Then the forces of the United States and
Australia began to make themselves felt with increasing power. The
Japanese dream came upon frustration. The Japanese forces with stony
eyes looked forward to inevitable defeat. So the great debacle came
upon the dark plot of the totalitarian states against civilization. The
Great Reversal was itself reversed. And civilized men began to feel that
after all the world might be a place in which they could live.

13. Democracy Faces Fate

Now the democracies themselves are in the crucible. Having conquered the foes which would have made the good life impossible, will
they themselves be able to achieve the good life? If the Great Reversion
has taught us nothing else, it has at least dispelled the myth of the
inevitability of progress. There are no automatic processes which insure
an outcome apart from human choices. There is no inevitable decline
of the West, as Spengler taught. There is no inevitable victory of democracy, as sentimental democratic thinkers have declared. There is no
inevitability in history. There is just constantly recurring the terrible
choice.

That democracy now confronts its supreme opportunity it ought not
to be difficult to see. That the great democracies themselves will be
judged by their action in this day of destiny also ought to be clear.
There are evil men in the democracies. There are evil forces in the
democracies. Will it one day be necessary to write of democracy as a
historical phenomenon what we have so often written in this chapter—
"good, but not good enough"?

There is at least reason for hope in the fact that there are multitudes
of men and women of glorious and impeccable good will in the democracies. And there are mighty forces of good whose strength is in the
honest purpose and sterling character of these multitudes of men and
women. If they can make their good will effective, then we may surely
say that as democracy confronts fate it will find that it is a good fate and

not an evil one. The good life cannot be achieved without democracy. But it must be a democracy which is more than the realization of the power of a popular majority which saves the world. The majority itself must choose and hold fast to the good life, or democracy will become the slave of evil. Here again Christianity offers to democracy that without which it cannot succeed and with which it cannot fail.

14. The Judgment of the Christian Sanctions

We begin to suspect that the Christian sanctions are on the throne. History is one long tale of the breakdown of states and of civilizations for lack of obedience to the Christian sanctions. No state has ever come upon debacle because it was Christian. No civilization has ever entered upon a process of decay because it practiced the Christian virtues.

Some curiously uncritical people talk about Christianity's being tested as if the fact that the world refuses to be Christian is somehow a reflection on Christianity. It is never Christianity which is tested. The human being is tested. The human state is tested. The human civilization is tested. It is always Christianity which sits in the seat of judgment.

And a close study of history makes clear another insight which is of the utmost importance. The Christian Church is always in process of judgment by Christianity. The fact that it bears the name of Christ does not give it immunity. The Christian sanctions maintain their place on the throne even when they must be the standard by which the Church itself is disciplined and chastised. They would maintain their place even if it were to become necessary that in their name a corrupt church should be destroyed. The very debacle of a corrupt church would be the victory of the Christian sanctions.

But there is no necessity that this dark possibility shall become a tragic actuality. Again and again the Church has regained its place as the representative of Christianity by a mighty act of expiation. And in the present situation a church which is ready to become Christian will confront its days of widest influence and its years of largest power.

We have spoken of the finality of Christianity in history. And it is indeed true that the destruction of evil is as much a Christian triumph as the victory of good. We may be sure that in one way or another Christianity always triumphs.

But we must remember that Christian sanctions are not abstractions which somehow have the power of enforcing their rule upon history. They are only names for those eternal principles which are alive forever in God and by which He guides his overlordship of human affairs. It is the living God who crushes recalcitrant evil. It is the living God who comes to the aid of every man who enthrones a good purpose and of every nation which accepts the law of moral love. In a way it may seem strange to come to know that this moral love which in our blind fashion we sometimes associate with the ineffective idealism of a pulpit—a pulpit possessing the secret of noble words rather than of powerful deeds—is after all the one supreme fact in history. As events work out they always reveal, if we have eyes to see, that in God the law of moral love is on the throne. It is the tragedy of history that so often He has had to come in judgment. But the God who brings evil purposes at last to frustration makes the most of every human good. How full is history of that story, too! And as men and nations choose the good, they bring the power of God and the God of power to their instant aid. The God of moral love is waiting to make effective every human purpose of good and to give it a secure place in history.

CHAPTER XXII

All the Streams Flow Together

HUMAN life is like a great river flowing in the center of a continent. It is watered by many tributaries and at last empties majestically into the sea. The tributaries of this vast stream of human existence are indeed many. But they all flow into the great river. They are united in one expansive, swiftly flowing stream. We have studied many aspects of human experience. We followed first over large areas that type of life and thought which eventuates in the evangelical tradition. So we found the central and definitive interpretation of life in the Hebrew-Christian corpus of thought. We inspected the vital and productive Greek tradition. We gathered something from the world-wide fields of criticism and poetry and fiction. Then we turned our attention to some of the great and characteristic movements of history itself. All this has been enough to convince us, if proof were needed, that human experience is a vast and varied and complicated and often confused matter. All sorts of tributaries flow through devious ways and come at last into the central stream.

Now dropping the figure, but keeping the insight, we want to see the way in which the varied elements of human experience come together and the fashion in which the Christian religion gives us clues for understanding them all.

1. Physical Well-Being

When we are thinking of human experience in the terms of its defining ideas, we may well begin with its physical aspect. Anyone who gazes at Athenian statues of the great period quickly comes to know how near the Greeks came to worshiping the perfection of the human body. The contrast between the Greek idealization of the human form and the ascetic denial and repudiation of the human body is one of the most dramatic contrasts we confront when we study the history of man's attitude toward his own life. And it cannot be said too strongly that Christianity meets these sharply antagonistic attitudes by a third. It does not worship the body. It does not repudiate the body. It accepts and disciplines the body.

Samuel Butler found something decadent in a religion which could subject a beautiful Greek statue like the Discobolus to scorn. So he wrote that scathing little poem "O God, O Montreal." But he made the problem somewhat simpler than it is. It is only after the misuse of the body that the scorn of the body appears. Debauchery is the mother of asceticism. It is always after the voluptuary has said, "Surrender to the body," that the ascetic cries, "Repudiate the body." Then the Christian appears and says, "Discipline the body."

For the body is like a magnificent horse. Unbroken and untamed, it is a wild and lawless thing. With the jockey firmly seated in the saddle, the powerful stallion goes magnificently down the track and wins the race.

It cannot be said too clearly that physical well-being is the sound basis of intellectual and moral well-being. An invalid may do a glorious day's work with his life, as did Charles Darwin. But that does not make the invalid the ideal scientist. A saint may conquer disease and be a glorious character. But that does not mean that disease is an ideal element in sainthood. All the advances in knowledge of the body and the fashion in which it functions most adequately and is kept in good repair are a part of the ongoing of the life of man. The body at its best is the true basis for the work of the mind at its best. So the Greek attitude, up to a point, was not only understandable but was correct. The human body in full strength, in fine co-ordination of all its elements, in noble use of its vital energies, in the genuine grace and harmony of all of its parts, is not to be despised and repudiated. It is to be accepted and honored. It is to be turned to good uses. Its beauty is to be appreciated and its strength applied to the high purposes of living. All this is sound Christian doctrine as well as good Greek doctrine.

But the specific Christian contribution to the understanding of the body is in what may be called the sacramental view of life. To the Christian it is, as we have seen, the very genius of the material to express the spiritual. It may be used to debauch the spiritual. But it was made to serve the spiritual. This is true of all material things. But it is very specially true of the human body. It is like a lamp. It is only truly understood when lighted. There are too many people whose bodies are like handsome unlighted lamps. It is when the body is aflame with the moral energy of the soul, quick with the intellectual energy of the mind, and glowing with the eternal energy of the spirit, that it becomes incandescent with a divine light. The body achieves its true well-being in serving these great purposes.

There is a cult of physical well-being which leaves out all the higher considerations. Its only moral code for man is a set of rules which will give him a healthy body. It says to him, "You can do anything which does not interfere with your health. Nothing is wrong which does not lessen your power to function as a well-fed animal in a state of complete physical well-being." When a great war is going on, some military men and some medical officers are always tempted to take this position.

That it is unchristian goes without saying. But it is unsound from every point of view. A soldier is more than a fighting animal even as a soldier. He is full of thought and emotion and purposes and ideals. And they must be co-ordinated with high purposes in control, even with the object of securing physical health. Many a soldier comes home a physical wreck for reasons which are not physical at all. We use the word "morale," paying sound if sometimes unconscious tribute to the moral basis of physical and personal efficiency. The soldier on the field of battle and the soldier on the even greater battlefield of life itself must have a body whose well-being is to be seen related to all sorts of laws of what may be called the complete sanitation of the body, but also to the fact that the body is controlled and mastered by something higher than itself which is the final secret of its vitality and the final security of its health.

Beyond this, physical well-being is dependent in part on a material environment which is the friend and not the foe of the good life. When Jacob Riis gave himself to a lifelong battle with the slums, he was mastered by a conviction that men and women and little children must live in surroundings worthy of their life as human beings. And the fashion in which the Christian religion has put its resources at the disposal of the struggle to secure a good material environment for men has been quite in accord with its own true genius. Only a decadent Christianity can be contented to leave men living in slums. And that is to say only a Christianity which is not Christian can ignore man's material environment.

2. Moral Well-Being

Man's life on this planet is always carried on in commerce with a world which makes moral demands upon him. This world of moral sanctions is viewed in the most various ways by men in different places and in different centuries and in different cultures. But the demand is there all the while. And the centuries have a way of recording manifold moral experiences which clarify the sanctions. That truth has rights which do not belong to falsehood, that loyalty has rights which do not belong to treachery, that there is a certain mutuality demanded of men who must live their life together, no civilized man would deny. And this is only an example of the fashion in which history and biography and literature reflect a corpus of thought about moral principles which is unerringly clear and is seen increasingly to be completely authentic as centuries go by. Living in loyalty to these great sanctions, the individual alone and the individuals in society achieve genuine well-being. Here the moral principles announced in the Old Testament and those set forth by the profoundest Greek and Latin thinkers and those revealed in the most penetrating and understanding interpretations of life in literature, meet and agree. If anyone reminds us of Machiavelli, we are ready to retort that he was a politician and not a moralist, and in the long run it turned out that he was not even a good politician.

But there are problems in moral well-being which must be faced. There is the possibility of being guided by a code alone, and so finding the moral life correct but uninspiring. There is the possibility of becoming so occupied by details that the great loyalties are lost in the fog. We know from the story of many of the sects that men who give first-class loyalty to second-class distinctions are likely to give second-class loyalty to first-class distinctions. There is the possibility of becoming so overwhelmed by the glorious amplitude of a moral ideal that it comes as a crushing weight and not as an emancipating energy. In all these ways moral well-being may be lost. And in all these ways Christianity has the key to the mystery. For in Christianity our fundamental loyalty is to a Person in whom goodness lives and not to abstract goodness. This changes everything. For the Person can understand motives as well as actions. He can appraise all that we try to do as well as all that we accomplish.

So the center of strategy in the moral life is changed. But more than this, our relation to the Great Person in whom all goodness dwells is determined by trust in what He is and what He has done for us, and not in dependence on what we have done for Him. Self-dependence always leads in the long run to self-stultification. Trust in God as He comes to us in Jesus Christ leads to the only true emancipation. So genuine moral well-being becomes possible only on Christian terms.

3. Intellectual Well-Being

"Come now, and let us reason together," cries one of the greatest of the Hebrew prophets. And the words might fall from the lips of Socrates as he addresses a stranger in Athens. "Choose you this day whom ye will serve," cries a Hebrew leader. And he might be a Greek standing at the parting of the ways and disciplining his intelligence for a great decision. Man is only securely a man when he becomes aware of himself as an intelligent being confronting alternatives. In every moral and spiritual crisis he must use his mind. So it is clear that he must have intellectual soundness if he is to have moral or spiritual security.

That the possession of a mind does not insure the right use of the mind, biography and history and all study of human experience make abundantly clear. A man may use his mind for the distortion of the truth. Clearly the matter of intellectual well-being is not a simple one.

Here again it will be found that Christianity makes contributions which are necessary and definitive. And by Christianity we mean Christianity and not multitudes of individual Christians who have missed or only partly understood the Christian secret. Indeed, one of the most important evidences of the divine source and quality of the Christian religion is that it has survived in spite of so many Christians.

But Christianity has done more than all the other influences in the world to produce minds who desired truth, however unwelcome or unpalatable to man's selfish lower nature that truth might be. The unselfish love of truth is essential to intellectual well-being. And century after century Christianity has produced just that.

But Christianity has also offered manifold clues which would enable men to go right where they might go wrong at the very subtlest places of intellectual decision. The first part of this book was devoted to setting forth a point of view respecting knowledge, reality, the being of God, the nature of man, the moral and spiritual history of man, and the Christian redemption which would meet the requirements of the mind and would satisfy the needs of man's moral and spiritual nature. It is the essential quality of classical Christianity that it does precisely these things. Both in its cleansing of the motives and the purposes of the thinkers and in the supplying of a corpus of thought in which critical intelligence can rest, the Christian religion performs a unique service.

The attempt to preserve the spirit of Christianity without the corpus of thought which is Christianity speaking to the intellect has always failed. The attempt to preserve Christian ideals without the sanctions upon which these ideals rest is doomed to frustration and failure. The attempt to preserve Christian ethics without Christian theology also goes down at last. Christianity is morally commanding because it is intellectually satisfying. You cannot have one quality without the other. The intellectual well-being which Christianity makes possible is a part of its secure hold upon the mind and conscience of man.

There is one other matter in connection with man's mental life. The idea that sin has so corrupted man's mind that he is unable to recognize or respond to truth except through something like a divine miracle in every individual case, is palpably false, as any appeal to life itself will show. Of course, all man's life is in and through God, and his existence and all his experience are matters at last of the divine grace. But the life which God has given him has not been so corrupted by sin that his mind is incapable of thinking God's thoughts after him or responding to those thoughts when they are offered to him. The tragedy of sin is that it may turn to bad purposes a mind whose structure is sound and good rather than that it takes away the structural qualities of that mind. It is noticeable that even the extreme Barthians are fairly sure of the intellectual dependability of their own dialectic. We owe so much to them for their reassertion of the place of God in human experience that we can criticize them sharply at the point we are now discussing without underestimating their great service. There is always something left in a man's mind to which God can speak when God addresses him.

4. Spiritual Well-Being

Once when I was lunching with Professor Irving Babbitt we fell to talking of Henry Adams. "The trouble with Henry Adams," said Professor Babbitt, "was that he could not find anything in the universe greater than himself." The realization that there is something in the universe greater than humanity, and the finding of the right relation to that great reality, is the source and the support of man's spiritual well-being. The matter has certain complications which deserve our close inspection.

Man is like the world below him in his possession of biological impulses. He is like the world below him in the possession of a body which is subject to the laws of physics. But his free intelligence connects him with the world above him. In his power to decide and in his power to create he is like the God who made him in His own image. Man's position becomes clear when we see that he is to master and control and use that which is below him, and he is to worship and obey the God who is above him. He is to be the king of nature and the loyal and loving servant of God.

But this intellectual awareness, this power to decide, this capacity to rule, this power to create, have qualities which easily intoxicate the possessor. He may want to repudiate the limitations of the human because he has been delivered from the limitations of the beast. He may want to know everything. He may want to decide everything. He may want to rule everything. With the limitations of a man he may want the powers of God. This, as we have already seen, is the Faustian fallacy. It arises from man's supposing that he is divine when actually he is human. It arises from his wanting to be God when actually he is man.

And this constitutes the very quality of spiritual ill-being. To mistake one's relative powers for absolute powers and so to become jealous of God for being what man is not, is man's ultimate sin. But this distaste for limitation, this refusal to accept the human estate, this attempt to climb on the throne of God, is the very characteristic of man's inordinate pride.

Spiritual well-being, then, consists in man's happy and friendly acceptance of his position under God and over nature. He is made to love and to serve God and not to attempt to usurp His throne.

Here once more Christianity possesses the keys to open all the doors. First it leads man into a moral experience which makes him completely aware of his limitations. And the more deeply he enters into this type of experience, the more clearly he sees that, while he must have God, he cannot be God. He needs a moral Master and Lord. He cannot aspire to that mastery himself.

Then in its revelation of the love of God for men, Christianity saps man's desire for usurpation. You cannot be jealous of a God who loves you. You cannot be envious of One who cares for you as you never dreamed of caring for anything or any person in all the world. And God's love for you reveals your haughty love of self in all its essential shabbiness. God calls you not servant but friend. And as He so speaks He captures your heart and makes you His own forever. To give in joyous love that which you ought to give is to rise from moral loyalty to spiritual emancipation. And this is the essence of spiritual freedom. The God who speaks from the Cross is unselfishness eternally alive. And fellowship with Him in unselfish love is the final spiritual good of man.

5. Social Well-Being

The Beloved Community is a great and noble social ideal. The social dream of the good society has haunted men of good will through many centuries. And once and again it has come to something like realization in particular social groups. The early Christian community revealed Christianity achieving a society where each did live for all and in a sense all did exist for each member of the group. It is easy to think loosely about the whole matter and to create social patterns of the mind which are built about great abstractions rather than about a sense of concrete actualities. Such patterns have a way of falling to pieces when the dream is confronted by actual human beings. For the real problem lies at last in the production of great numbers of individuals each of whom is a social individual in the sense that he is actually able to forget himself in the good of others. It may be said quite freely that Christianity has revealed a unique power in the production of just such individuals. And here the crux of the whole matter lies in the fact that every person who loves God, as God has come to him in Christ, is already the sort of person who can love his neighbor as himself. The type of man whose cosmos is all ego is already transcended in the person whose cosmos is all Christus. The spirit of outgoing has already triumphed over the spirit of incoming. But it is further true that, since Christ loves every individual with a perfect love, a man cannot love Christ with a complete devotion without loving the other persons who are the object of Christ's unbounded affection. In this sense spiritual well-being already has social well-being implicit in itself. The men who dream of a perfect society apart from Christ have discarded the one great dynamic for the production of that community of good will for which they long.

6. *The Tragedy of Ignorance*

Socrates felt that the whole human problem was one of ignorance. He could not imagine a person who knew what was good and yet deliberately chose to repudiate the good. This was actually the fatal weakness of the Socratic philosophy, as it is the fatal weakness of all those interpretations of life which fail to analyze and understand the darker aspects of human nature. If the replacing of Peter ill-informed by Peter well-informed represented the whole human problem, the life of man in the world would be very much simpler than it is. But at the moment we are insisting that, while this is true, it is also true that there is a problem of ignorance, and this problem is one of the great problems of human life. The tragedy of ignorance must be faced and must be clearly understood. There is also a problem of bad will united to intelligence. Of that problem we shall speak later. It is the problem of good will united to the bad judgment which comes from ignorance that we would now consider.

There has always been a vast amount of ignorance about the conditions which make for every sort of health. The capacity of men to learn from vicarious experience in these matters is a real capacity. But it does not become active with astonishing celerity. There has always been a vast amount of ignorance of the results of the trial and error method as these are recorded in biography and history. Someone once said whimsically that Horace Bushnell would have been the greatest of theologians if he had only been Adam. His originality and mental force were astonishing. But he never could persuade himself to master what men had done before he began to work. He used to say that if he tried to read a dull book, he put it down because it was dull, and if he tried to read a brilliant book, it so stimulated his mind that he put it down to carry on the processes of his own thought. In every field and especially in life, which is the most important field of all, there are many men who are quite ignorant of the material which is at their disposal coming from men's past experience and activity. There is an enormous amount of ignorance in respect of moral sanctions. Heedless men and women—especially, though by no means always, heedless young men and women—plunge into life without any secure understanding of its moral meanings, and when they come upon tragedy declare bitterly that they never really understood the meaning of what they were doing. The most difficult aspect of life comes from the fact that so many of our important decisions are made when as yet we can bring to them no secure body of knowledge and experience. Thus we might go on and on. What it comes to is this: A genuine part of the evil of the world comes from ignorance and not from bad intention. The literature of the world is full of tales of the unhappiness which comes from ignorance. And biography tells the same tale again and again.

7. The Solution of the Problem of Ignorance

The primary aim of education is to put the funded experience of the race at the disposal of those who are about to enter upon the adventure of responsible life. Dependable knowledge is to be given the place of ignorance. When Aristotle bases his political thinking upon existing forms of government and his *Poetics* upon existing examples of the poetic art, he is taking the line of the typical educator. He attempts to do his thinking in the light of a full knowledge of past accomplishment. The passing of the centuries has seen very great achievement in respect of this matter of putting knowledge in the place of ignorance. In many fields tragedies which were the result of lack of knowledge have become most infrequent or have ceased to exist. But the situation is not quite so good as it might be. Education is a discipline which worships many gods, and the history of the obsessions of educators would be a marvelous tale of human confusion. It is so easy to forget one important insight which grows out of adequate knowledge when we turn our attention to the pursuit of other knowledge and the insights which it carries. The educated by no means always have the right knowledge at their disposal when the crisis comes. There is a perpetual reappraisal of the knowledge of civilized men which often leads to loss at the very moment when we are proud of what we have gained. An age which knows much about things, for instance, is likely to be pitiably superficial in its knowledge of persons. At all events, there is only one cure for the diseases which come from ignorance. And that is knowledge.

Christianity has never claimed to offer men specific and concrete knowledge in all the fields of human experience. But it has offered knowledge which is not only relevant but decisive for the central moral and spiritual crises of life. And it has—when it has been aware of its own genius—created an attitude which furthered the dispelling of ignorance and the pursuit of knowledge. It has been the best friend of that education which gives men adequate knowledge for the tasks of living.

8. The Tragedy of Incompleteness

One of the saddest sights of human life is the spectacle of the unfulfilled. Despite the superficial optimism which would declare that there are no mute inglorious Miltons, because if the mute inglorious Miltons come to maturity they will become articulate, it is clear that there are no end of buds which never come to flower, there are no end of lives which come to frustration, not in the sense that they become evil, but in the sense that there is simply no fulfillment which in any way corresponds to the early promise. And the study of the human life of any period brings to the student the sense of possibilities which never at all become actualities. We see the sudden flowering of fifth-century Athens with great delight. We see all the blossoms of the Renaissance with something like rapture. But what about the centuries which never come to flower? What about the periods which never come to bloom? There is the flowering of New England but, according to a careful student whose judgment no one would question, after the flowering there comes the day of New England's Indian summer. And after the Indian summer one senses the coming of the frost and the cold of winter. We may try to be satisfied with an impersonal seasonal formula. But we cannot apply impersonal formulas to personal experiences. And so the problem of the human seeds which never come to flower and the human blossoms which never come to fruit remains. And it is more than a problem. It is a genuine tragedy.

When one thinks of the millions of human beings whose lives are only a hint of what they might have been and of the false dawns of history which never came to daylight, one has material of bitter and sad import. We cannot be contented with less than the full realization of the possibilities of every man who does not deliberately break his own life. We cannot be contented with flowering ages followed by ages which go barren to the grave.

9. The Solution of the Problem of Incompleteness

The philosophies of despair, of course, do not help. The interpretations which reduce history and biography to something expressed and controlled by a series of impersonal and mechanical formulas, of course, do not help. The revolutionary programs which deny the past instead of fulfilling it, of course, do not help. And here again the religion of the One who came not to destroy but to fulfill offers the guidance which the men who are seeking fulfillment need and possesses the secrets which would turn ages of frustration to ages of realization.

There have been Christian leaders who preached a gospel of denial rather than a gospel of fulfillment. But if they were in possession of the insights of classical Christianity, every denial was in the name of a greater affirmation. Christianity believes in and offers surgery for the sake of saving the whole organism. But it never destroys the whole organism for the sake of some ghostly spirituality which will remain when the organism has perished. It is not the foe of growth. It is the foe of malignant growth.

There is a type of voluptuary who is always complaining that the enemy of parasites is the enemy of life. The traveler in Florida is likely at first to be delighted with the sight of the draping, low-hanging mosses suspended from the live oaks. He is not so happy when he discovers that they are quietly devouring the life of the tree. There are a good many parasitic growths in human life. And Christianity is very skillful in discovering them and in destroying them. The foes of life must be destroyed before the true life can come to fulfillment.

The ascetic centuries cannot be used as the basis for an argument that Christianity has stood for a truncated, fragmentary life. One does not feed a patient who is recovering from typhoid fever the food demanded by a man in full health. Asceticism has a place in the religion of a convalescent man or a convalescent world. It does not belong to the state of full health either of the individual or of the social group.

Jesus was continually shocking people who did not understand his broad and generous humanity. He was always resurrecting and fulfilling hope where hope had died. He came that men might have life and have it abundantly. His was a religion of fulfillment.

The attempt to discredit Paul by claiming that he had a more provincial outlook is made only by those who have never understood Paul. The man who writes desiring that the fellow Christians he addresses "may be strong to apprehend with all the saints what is the breadth and length and height and depth, and to know the love of Christ which passeth knowledge, that ye may be filled unto all the fulness of God" believes in a religion of the amplest fulfillment. And if a man has doubts about the Pauline authorship of the Epistle to the Ephesians, there is no doubt at all that it came out of the very heart of the Pauline tradition.

We simply must not confuse Christian surgery with a refusal of Christianity to cultivate all the gardens of the Lord. Christianity has had to be responsible for a good deal of surgery first and last. But the surgery has always been for the sake of life. It has never been, to those who understood its meaning, a denial of life. And when once the malignant growths have been cut away, real life has the opportunity for the amplest fulfillment. Christianity has the power to complete every good thing inaugurated in the life of man.

10. The Tragedy of Sin

Man is ignorant. He must have knowledge. Man is incomplete. His life must be brought to completion. Of these things any student of the whole of human life as it is revealed in history and biography and literature becomes very sure. But it also becomes clear that humanity faces a problem far deeper than that produced by ignorance and far profounder than that produced by incompleteness. Man has deliberately created that which was evil because he has liked it and wanted it. He has made evil his good. He has put treachery in his heart when loyalty had a right to reign. He has put falsehood in his heart when truth had a right to reign. The deepest problem of human life is the problem of man's deliberate treachery in the presence of that which he knows to be good. It is in this precise sense that man has become a sinner. It is in this precise sense that man has corrupted his world. It is just this darkest element in the human tragedy which Socrates never understood. And for this very reason his brilliant thinking fell short of insights which it might have reached.

One does not need to shout aloud in telling of the profoundest insights in respect of the tragedy of sin. They lie embedded in the depths of every human spirit. They are written in the greatest masterpieces of human literature. They represent the corrosive poison at the heart of the human story. Shakespeare's Iago and Robert Browning's Count Guido Franceschini are human incarnations of the will to evil. Any man who has dealt with human life widely and deeply has come upon this central decay which is a rotting process infecting the very quality of the soul. And any man who has looked searchingly into his own soul knows that this deliberate alliance with evil is the thing against which he must wage his last war, the struggle which will involve his fiercest fight. This alliance has corrupted individuals and brought whole nations to decay. It is the thing which most desperately and finally threatens the good life for man.

11. The Solution of the Problem of Sin

It has not often been said bluntly and honestly enough that in a sense there is no solution for the problem of sin. If a man finally makes evil his good and in persistent inner antagonism to all the summons of moral and spiritual good will maintains this position as the last and central and eternal commitment of his life, not even God can rescue him. He must hear the word "Depart," as in that parable of terrible and magnificent conclusiveness in which Jesus described the great adjudication. Christ did not come to offer salvation to unrepentant sinners. He came to call men to repentance, and then to offer them a way from the defiling life of treachery to the eternal life of moral love.

We have already seen the fashion in which God in Christ assails the citadel of man's treachery and poisonous self-love. The suffering God makes His final appeal to men from the Cross. If a man can look at the Cross unmoved, one has to admit that God has said His last word.

But in millions of cases the great response *has* come:

> O Cross that liftest up my head,
>   I dare not ask to fly from Thee;
> I lay in dust life's glory dead,
> And from the ground there blossoms red
>   Life that shall endless be.

That is the mighty strategy of the Cross.

12. The Tragedy of Social Disintegration

We have said nothing in this volume of the picaresque novel. That form of fiction may be described as the literature which makes villainy fascinating. How far men have traveled from the good society is illustrated by the fact that in one century after another the man who violated the laws of society could be made a hero. And the man who drives through the forests near Nottingham and thinks of the tales of Robin Hood, must see clearly that only in a state which had reached a certain social disintegration could Robin Hood be possible.

This is merely a starting point, of course. Only the most terrible of Roman pens could tell the tale of the social disintegration of the Roman Empire at its worst. Only a moralist with a pen of fire could write adequately of the worst social vices which blackened the period which followed the Renaissance. And no one living has a pen equal to the task of describing the social disintegration which followed Hitler's armies in Europe from 1939 to 1945.

The inner social decay in many nations has been described with apocalyptic fervor by the apostles of social indignation. The sins of man against his brother man are known for what they are by all the world.

13. The Solution of the Problem of Social Disintegration

One cannot solve the problem of social disintegration by offering formulas of noble social co-ordination to companies of individual men, every one of whom is selfish at heart. The good society must be made up of men who have experienced a radical change at the very center of their lives. It was not an accident that after the Wesleyan Revival social reforms flourished all over England. It was not an accident that Wilberforce and the men who worked with him for the abolition of the slave trade were evangelical Christians. It was not an accident that the last letter John Wesley ever wrote was one addressed to Wilberforce, encouraging him in his great fight. It was not an accident that General William Booth became the practical foe of the slums.

Evangelical religion creates men who can be trusted with social tasks and without whom dreams of social amelioration and of the good society can never come to fulfillment. The strangest failure of insight in the modern Church is that which has put the gospel of individual regeneration over against the gospel of the good society. The New Jerusalem must come down out of heaven. And it must come first of all to the individual men and women who in Moffatt's fine translation become a "colony of heaven" even in the earth below. The individual and the social aspects of religion belong together at the heart of the Christian religion. Neither could survive permanently without the other. Jesus' teaching about the vine and the branches is the expression of a belief in a social organism living in vital connection with its source in his own life. The Kingdom of God is a kingdom into which men enter one by one. But it is also a good society living in joyous and creative fellowship with the God of moral love.

14. The Religion of Revelation

Humanity is the arc of a circle. And that circle can never be completed without God. This is the profoundest insight which comes from the study of the human adventure in the world. Man apart from God is less than man. Man with the aid of God achieves his true humanity. The debacles of history always come at the point of man's godlessness. The golden moments in man's life in the world are those when he is most conscious of his relation to the living God.

We have seen that the classical religion of moral love first comes to man as the speech of the Divine Voice. It is first of all revelation. "Thus says Jehovah," cry the great Hebrew prophets, and they proceed to say that which by every standard is worthy of the mind of God. We can compare the words of the great Old Testament prophets with the words in the world's literature and the words in the sacred books of the great religions. And always we shall find that when these words of literature and the ethnic faiths have proved good for man, they are words which fit into the great speech of the Old Testament voices. So they represent the light which lighteth every man coming into the world. But the Old Testament words go beyond them and deepen and fulfill them or cleanse and transform them. The God of moral good will who speaks in the Old Testament is the only God in whom civilized men can believe.

15. The Religion of the Incarnation

Sargent's great picture of the prophets shows the advancing messengers, each in a brighter light whose source is invisible but whose effulgence is undeniable. This is that true light whose shining is not the contradiction of Old Testament religion but its completion and fulfillment, not the contradiction of any true word ever spoken to man by poet or seer or religious leader, but the full light in which all lesser lights are lost.

The Incarnation is the pivotal event of history. It finally fixes man's place in the universe and determines his relations. In the Greek myth of Prometheus, heaven is against men. The friendly god has to steal fire from heaven to bless the life of man. In Christianity heaven is friendly to man. The very central life of heaven enters human life for the blessing of men. Man's essential kinships, then, are with that which is above him and not with that which is below him. He does not have the capacity to become divine. He does have the capacity for fellowship with the divine. Man cannot become God. God can become man. Man can become the friend of God. The fact that the Perfect Divine Person can express Himself in the very actuality of human life, gives to humanity a dignity which must never be forgotten. Indeed, as we have seen, man's worst sin is made possible by the fact that he is so like God that he can be tempted to try to be God.

But the Incarnation strikes that note of the giving of the unlimited to the limited, the giving of the perfect to the imperfect, which is the very glory of the life of God and makes possible a new kind of life for men. Jesus put it into powerful sentences: "Ye know that the rulers of the Gentiles lord it over them, and their great ones exercise authority over them. Not so shall it be among you: but whosoever would become great among you shall be your minister; and whosoever would be first among you shall be your servant: even as the Son of man came not to be ministered unto, but to minister."

The Incarnation also reveals the place of the material in its relation to the spiritual. Jesus lives a genuinely human life in a genuinely human body. He eats and drinks and accepts the material conditions of human life. But He makes the body and all material things the servants of His spiritual purposes. Self-conscious men of ascetic tendencies are offended by His frank attitude of being at home in the body and in the material world. He is at home. But He is always Master of the house.

The Incarnation establishes religion on the basis of personal relationships. "The training of the twelve," to use a fine phrase which Professor Alexander Bruce employed as a title of one of his books, was a training in personal fellowship. So must men think who are friends of God. So must men act who are friends of God. The Incarnation finally establishes that society of good will of which the God who reveals Himself in Jesus Christ is Master and Lord.

16. The Religion of the Cross

The religion of the Incarnation reveals God finding fellowship with human beings. The religion of the Cross reveals God saving sinners. Only a little thought would make it clear that the ultimate problem of a man in the presence of a radiantly good God lies just in the fact that man has played false with his own ideals and has betrayed his own best nature. How can the imperfect have fellowship with the Perfect? How can the sinful have fellowship with the Divine? The answer is that only by a process which destroys sin can God have fellowship with the sinner. God is never complacent in the presence of wickedness. He cannot possibly save men in their sins. But He can save them from their sins.

Moral evil makes a problem for God as well as for man. He must not only win man from evil. He must so deal with the dark tragedy of wickedness as to satisfy His own sense of loyalty to that perfection which is the essential quality of His own life. There is only one way in which perfection can meet imperfection except to destroy it. That is to suffer for it. Horace Bushnell in one of the profoundest words he ever uttered called it self-propitiation. When the All-Perfect says to the all-imperfect, "I will not destroy you. I will die for you," He touches the ultimate heights of moral grandeur. In the very hour that He wins men from devastating pride and moral selfishness and betraying sensuality, He expresses His own character as moral love in a deed which makes real in action all that He is in the inner quality of His own life. All of God's perfections shine in the white light of the Cross. The appropriation of the religion of the Cross is the glad acceptance of the divine surgery at the center of one's life. It eventuates in an eternal fellowship with the God of moral love.

17. Christus Imperator

So in every way Christ becomes the center of all human thought and of all human experience.

> That life, that death accepted by thy reason, solves for thee
> All questions in the earth and out of it.

As a sonnet condenses diffused beauty and sets it forth in forms of concentrated loveliness, so the diffused meanings of life come together in Christ.

> How still the pen lies in the poet's hand!
> How cold the thoughts within the poet's mind!
> No subtle artistry can he command.
> No flower of beauty in his soul can find.
> Then fiery joy suffuses all his thought
> And living words a disciplined delight
> In stately artistry securely wrought,
> Move like proud soldiers conscious of their might.
> The concentrated thought finds weighted phrase.
> Each sentence marches with majestic power
> And beauty finds its own imperial praise
> And truth has come upon its golden hour.
> So great the riches in a little room,
> The last two lines a flower of perfect bloom.

When Jesus meets men as He met the disciples going toward Emmaus and journeys with them and enters into the house, they never fail to have the sense that all things come together in Him. So great the riches in a little room.

Life can be misinterpreted. Literature can be misinterpreted. Biography can be misinterpreted. History can be misunderstood. But for those who will receive them Christianity brings the clues to understanding in respect of all these things. And in Christ all the streams of life and thought and experience flow together. Even our own confused and bewildered and sometimes sullen age can find an answer to all its questions and the satisfaction of all its needs in Him.

My days have come upon this circumstance
That what has been is lost and what would be
Passes bewildered through a devious dance
Of mad cross-purposes by men set free.
The old has brought to flower its evil seeds;
Its gracious good impatient men deny.
The new impetuous with explosive deeds
Holds tragic evils hidden from the eye.
But high above the deeds of this dark hour
There reigns a purpose holy and secure,
Turning the acts of men by its own power
To that which has the virtue to endure.
So I, for long betrayed by old and new,
Turn now with faith abiding to the true.

CHAPTER XXIII

The Tragedy of the Great Gregariousness

WHEN we have seen the meaning of the synthesis of the Hebrew-Christian witness and the humanistic tradition, one philosophy like a giant emerges in our path. This philosophy is pantheistic monism. It had its origin in India. To an appraisal of the claims of this philosophy and to a criticism of its inadequacies, we now address ourselves.

That very famous poem "The Bhagavad-Gita" is found in the sixth book of the *Mahabharata*. In a sense it is a revelation of the essential genius of India. As Krishna reveals himself to Arjuna, one discovers that it is the very nature of the divine to be all inclusive:

> Earth, water, ether, fire, and air,
>   Intellect, ego, brain:
> This eightfold subdivision serves
>   My nature to contain—
>
> My lower nature, but beyond
>   Is one more high and pure—
> The living soul, brave hero, which
>   Holds all that lives secure.
>
> Regard my nature as the womb
>   Of all that here draws breath;
> To all the world of life I am
>   Creation; I am death.
>
> Apart from me, brave Arjun, there
>   Exists no single thing;
> The universe is strung on me
>   Like pearls upon a string.
>
> I am the taste in water; sound
>   In ether; none the less
> Am I the mystic word that gives
>   All scriptures power to bless;
> I am the light in moon and sun;
>   In man, the manliness;
>
> I am the fragrance in the earth;
>   I am the heat in fire;

> The life in life; the energy
>   In men of stern desire;
>
> I am the everlasting seed
>   All forms of life to save;
> I am the wisdom of the wise
>   The courage of the brave;
>
> I am the strength of those too strong
>   For lust or passion's toll;
> And I am pure, permitted love
>   Toward every living soul.
>
> States good and passionate and dark
>   Are mine. . . .[1]

That is to say the being of Krishna includes everything. The divine gathers everything into itself. Everything is an aspect of the divine life.

So in a very fascinating fashion one meets in the Bhagavad-Gita the religion of the great gregariousness. It strikes us at first as gloriously cosmopolitan. It is free from all provincialism. It is free from all exclusiveness. Surely here is a vast religion, mother of everything and everyone, in which the mind can rest.

Of course, it includes whatever is noble and of good report.

> The man who hates no living thing,
>   Kind, patient, and humane,
> Unselfish, unpretentious, calm
>   In pleasure as in pain,
>
> Content, controlled, and disciplined,
>   From wavering fancies free,
> Whose brain and intellect and love
>   Are mine, is dear to me.[2]

But just because "Krishna is all," grave problems emerge. For so the divine includes all evil as well as all good.

> Behold the total world of life,
>   All moving things and still,
> Within my body; and therewith
>   Whatever else you will.[3]
>
> The generous heart, the level eye,
>   Denial, charity,

[1] *The Bhagavad-Gita*, tr. Arthur W. Ryder (Chicago: University of Chicago Press, 1929), pp. 55-57.

[2] *Ibid.*, pp. 96-97.

[3] *Ibid.*, p. 83.

> Content, fame, infamy—are states
> That life derives from me.[4]

> The serpent-king and wonder-cow
> Am I, of snakes and kine;
> Of missile arms, the thunderbolt;
> Creative love divine.[5]

When Arjuna has his revealing sight of Krishna, he cries:

> O master, these your mouths and eyes
> All numbering defy;
> Your arms, thighs, bellies, feet, and fangs
> Most horrid multiply;

> See yonder! Dhritarashtra's sons
> With all their hostile throng
> Of kings, with Bhishma, Drona, and
> With honored Karna strong,
> And with the chiefest captains that
> In our stout ranks belong,

> Are entering with hurried step
> Your jaws fierce-fanged and dread,
> While here and there between the teeth
> I spy a mangled head.[6]

So evil and good combine in the all-inclusive life of the deity. And we are not surprised that this moral confusion turns to moral indifference. The wise, we are told,

> . . . look alike on some good priest
> Matured in learning's vow,
> An eater of dogs' flesh, a dog,
> An elephant, a cow.[7]

Quite bluntly we are told:

> Who rates alike friend, lover, foe,
> Neutral, indifferent,
> Kinsman, the hateful, sinner, saint,
> Is deemed preëminent.[8]

The indifference becomes complete:

> I look on life with level eye;
> I have no foe nor friend;[9]

[4] Ibid., p. 75.   [6] Ibid., pp. 86-87.   [8] Ibid., p. 47.
[5] Ibid., p. 78.   [7] Ibid., p. 43.   [9] Ibid., p. 72.

In another mood devotion to Krishna is taken as a substitute for good character:

> Yes, even the most complete of rogues
> In whom no passions fight
> With love of me, is deemed a saint,
> Because his heart is right.[10]

Then again the sharp note of moral indifference:

> And he who neither grieves nor yearns,
> Released from hate and glee,
> Devotedly renouncing good
> And ill, is dear to me.[11]

So "difference melts into unity"—a genuine difference into a false unity. And thus we are introduced to the most subtly betraying kind of human thought. We confront a fascinating expression of that pantheistic monism in whose fogs so many minds have been lost.

1. The All-Inclusiveness of Hinduism

The Bhagavad-Gita is, as we have already suggested, more than a marvelous poem. Through it you look at the very soul of India. You see the very quality of the culture of this ancient land. Sir Sarvepalli Radhakrishnan once wrote: "The comprehensive and synthetic spirit of Hinduism has made it a mighty forest with a thousand waving arms each fulfilling its function and all directed by the Spirit of God." When the Aryans conquered the native inhabitants of North India, they did not laugh away their crude beliefs and practices. They joined them with their own. This joining of competing religions into a unity which includes them all has been called the Hindu solution of the problem of the conflict of religions. "Wherever you find a contradiction do not deny it, include it." This expresses the fashion of Hindu thought. So everything is included. So everything finds a place.

There is something most impressive about this vast comprehensiveness. You are dealing with something as rich as life. You are dealing with something as manifold as life. Surely you are dealing with life itself. Precisely, but you are not understanding life. You are not truly interpreting life. And you are not mastering life.

But we may pause for a little further inspection of the attractiveness of this vast panorama of thought and action which includes everything. Whatever you think, you find it there. Whatever you do, you find a place for it there. And there is a place for everything which everyone else has ever thought. And there is a place for everything which everyone has ever done. Forever you are delivered from the provincial. Forever you are delivered from the parochial. Everything belongs to you, and you belong to everything. Especially when you turn this general view into a catalogue of appreciations, it becomes impressive if not compelling by its very all-inclusive manifoldness. You give yourself to each separate point of view— *for a moment.* You make your own every separate aspect of experience *for a moment.* You vicariously do every sort of deed that has ever been done *for an instant.* And as you pass through the vast circle of this thinking and feeling and acting, you have an increasing sense of how rich and many-sided your own mind has become. You have ceased to be the thinker of one thought. You think all thoughts. You have ceased to be one person. You are every person. You cease to contemplate one thing. You contemplate everything. Indeed, you become everything by the ceaseless flow of an all-participating experience. You yourself look back at yourself from all other eyes. And all other eyes look out at the world from behind your own eyes. For you are already what you see, and what you see is already you.

Volumes would be required to amplify and illustrate this position. One would need not a Golden Bough but a golden forest. Indeed, when one comes to think of it, the forest would not all be gold. Or perhaps one ought to say gold would be everything else and everything else would be gold. And so with a shock we suddenly discover that in this vast comprehensiveness all integrity of meaning would be lost. Everything would all the while be engrossed in the process of becoming its opposite.

This actually happens in Indian thought. There is no intellectual position which is not *for a moment* defended with shrewd skill. There is no moral position which is not set forth with persuasive speech. There is no spiritual insight which does not flash *for an instant* before the mind's eye. All your intellectual and moral and spiritual affinities are found in this vast conglomerate mass. All your intellectual and moral and spiritual antipathies have their shining place set in a constellation of contradictions. As exercises in intellectual and moral and spiritual gymnastics, the various aspects of Hindu thought and the movement from one to another could scarcely be improved.

2. The Nest of Fallacies

Of course, by definition an all-inclusive position must include everything. It must include all false thinking as well as all true thinking. And if each is a part of the total reality, the false attains a temporary truth and the truth becomes a temporary falsehood. Because you try to have everything, there is no security for anything. You have allowed yourself to be corrupted by a word. That word is unity. You are fascinated by it. You find a certain hypnotic power in it. You surrender your mind to it. And soon you find that the more it gets, the more it wants. Your hand becomes the apple it holds. The apple becomes the hand which holds it. The arm which supports the hand is also the hand. And the hand is the arm. The eye looking at the arm is the arm at which it looks. And the arm is the eye beholding. So you may go on indefinitely. If unity means identity—and that is just what it does mean in Indian thought—then everything is all the while turning into everything else and everything else is turning into the thing which itself is turning.

Actually, the unity which is an all-devouring monster in Indian thought, ought itself to be subject to the mutability from which it receives such benefits. And if this were true and unity itself dissolved, then the whole vast structure of Indian thought would fall. As a matter of fact, Indian thought is a philosophy of phantasy. It is one vast phantasmagoria.

As long as you persist in looking at the separate things separately, you are fairly dazzled by the splendid pageantry which is an endless succession as vast and many-sided as existence itself. But while you are doing this, you are assuming your own identity as the watcher of the scene. And you are assuming the dependable individuality of each separate ingredient of the whole mass of existence. Actually you can do neither of these things. While you watch you are dissolving into the spectacle you behold. And every individual element in the spectacle is turning into every other element in one vast process of animated confusion. Really you have no right to be yourself long enough to perceive. And the object of your perception has no right to be itself long enough to be perceived. Your words are all the while turning into the lips which uttered them. And your lips are all the while becoming the other lips they kiss in fond affection. If everything is indeed everything else—and this is the meaning of unity—then logic is the perfect support of the illogical, and bad reasoning is the best defense of truth. But here we are really going too fast. For in this incredible unity, falsehood is the same as truth and truth is the same as falsehood. They are joined in a perfect wedlock. But again we are going too quickly, for union is one with separateness and separateness is the same as union—a nest of fallacies indeed!

3. You Cannot Affirm a Thing Without Denying Its Opposite

By this time it ought to be evident that we are dealing with a labyrinth of confusion. That it has darkened the light of a great and subtly gifted people is one of the tragedies of history. For the labyrinth is overhung by endless interlacing branches through which the bright shining light does not penetrate. But this false unity which blots everything out at last in a dissolving relativity is not merely a matter of history. There are men to the right of us and to the left of us, before us and behind us, who in one way or another are betrayed by this all-devouring unity which always comes to us at first as gently as a summer zephyr and finally becomes as wildly destructive as the most terrible tempest.

We need, then, to estabish some principles which will give us safety in the midst of this dissolving world of specious argument. And we need to do it always in the light of the fundamental assumption on which this book is written, namely, that experience is to be explained and is not to be explained away.

Perhaps the best place to begin is with an insight which is clear enough when you examine it but which has never come within the purview of the pantheistic monist. And the insight can be expressed in this statement. You cannot affirm a thing without denying its opposite. Or to put it in another way: There is a denial lurking at the heart of every affirmation. So a philosophy built upon assertions without denials is already self-stultifying. For assertions exist through the truth of the denials which are essential to their validity. A philosophy of unity is a vast assertion deprived of the denial without which that assertion itself becomes meaningless. Negations exist through affirmations without which they would fall apart. And affirmations depend upon negations which represent the opposite aspect of the truth affirmed.

The quest for a unity is a deceptive quest unless you understand perfectly that a denial will be found implicit in every affirmation. And it is precisely the lack of this understanding which makes pseudo unity *pseudo*. In other words, a thing cannot be its opposite. And its opposite cannot be the thing. A false unity is perpetually bringing together things which belong apart. The only true unity is in the process of thought which recognizes diversity for what it is and treats it honestly. Two opposite things can exist as objects of thought in a knowing mind. But the unity is in the mind and not in the objects whose contradiction the mind apprehends. Deeper than this, the mind becomes aware of itself as one as it apprehends contradictions in experience. And it is by seizing upon these contradictions with clear apprehension and expressing them with unhesitating definiteness that it expresses its own unity in the midst of the flux. Affirmation and denial are not foes. They belong together. When unity loses contact with diversity, unity itself ceases to have meaning.

4. A Relative Insight Is Not an Insight

The pantheistic monists are wonderfully friendly people. In the hierarchy of facts and values which they have constructed there is a place for every conceivable assertion. And at the level where it is possible to make that assertion, it is an insight. This gives a wonderful versatility and an exhaustless hospitality of mind to the holder of such a position. He can agree with everybody about everything. His only care must be that he talk to people of the same level at the same time. If he has to talk with people at different levels of understanding at the same time, he begins to stutter. And if there are too many different levels represented at once, he becomes incoherent. Probably the Tower of Babel was built by pantheistic monists determined to reduce all contradictory positions to one triumphant assertion. The contradiction stuck in their throats and speech became a jargon. Then particular groups, each with a common position, got together, and speech once more became possible.

The theory of relative truths and relative insights is a godsend to the politician who wants to win votes. Indeed, he becomes a master of what may be called conscienceless relativity. But that is just the point. Only a slippery mind can make the transition with comfort. For a relative insight is not an insight. And a relative truth is not a truth. You can organize various truths into a corpus of thought only if each truth remains itself. If each is constantly changing into something new and strange, there is no real thought, there is only nightmare.

It is fascinating to watch a facile Indian thinker meeting men on different levels of thought and with casual mental hospitality accepting the mores of the particular men for the time being. He is happy, and they are happy. But the members of one group will not be quite so happy when they hear him accepting the relativities of another group as a working hypothesis for another conversation.

5. A Relative Loyalty Is Not a Loyalty

The moral quality of a philosophy and a practice based upon the belief that everything is one with everything else is apprehended more clearly when upon such a basis you attempt to construct an interpretation of loyalty. While it lasts—be it only an instant—a loyalty has a certain shining quality. But you must understand that it is a relative thing. It depends upon elements which are constantly changing. And when the elements change, the loyalty must change. For this reason no loyalty has any stability. You cannot plan your future in such a way that it depends on the unchanging quality of the color of a chameleon. At this point the whole matter becomes very serious indeed. You begin by becoming so hospitable that you include everything in a great and spacious unity. Then you discover that the things combined are really hostile to each other unless in some subtle fashion you emasculate them. You do this by calling each one relative. That means that whenever it would become embarrassing by remaining itself, it quickly and graciously dissolves into its opposite. Thus you avoid collisions. But you avoid collusions by dissolving your universe.

When this is applied to the history of morals, the result is complete ethical disaster. At every stage you have a relative moral demand which has no dependable quality. All the moral positions you include in a great unity are capable of being united only when they are devitalized. They would fight each other if they were taken seriously. So each loses its commanding power in order to be united with its opposite.

By the same token loyalty itself becomes relative. For, of course, you cannot give a permanent loyalty to a relative distinction. And if you yourself must be prepared to dissolve into relativity in order to become part of the relativity of the universe, you could not give a permanent loyalty to a permanent distinction if you could find one. Clearly the relative loyalty of a relative person to a relative principle is falling apart before one begins to depend upon it.

6. A Relative Truth Is Not a Truth

The matter of getting contradictions together in a great unity is never more confusing than when we are dealing with matters of truth and falsehood. There is something imperial about truth. There is something very definite about falsehood. But if truth remains truth and falsehood remains falsehood, we cannot combine them in a great unity which includes both truth and falsehood. So the blessed doctrine of relativity comes in again. The true is relatively true. The false is relatively false. So we come in sight of a specious unity when truth and falsehood kiss each other. But that kiss is the kiss of death. For as they meet, truth ceases to be truth and falsehood ceases to be falsehood.

A mathematical example will illustrate the confusing nature of the situation when one comes to apply the conception of relativity to the structural relationships involving the truth and falsehood of propositions. We can take the quibble: If two and two made six, how much would three and three be? At once we move into a world of relativities. Numbers are not to keep their classical relations. But it may seem easy to work the matter out. If two and two made six, then the value of one would have increased by the difference between the old value of one as one, and the new value which makes four times one equal to six. That is to say one would now be in value one and one-half, since four times one and one-half would make six. But if one equals one and one-half, and four equals six, then three would equal four and one-half, and three and three would be equal to nine. The catch in all this lies, of course, in the fact that we have to bring in the old scale of values in order to work out the new equation. We decide that one has the value of one and a half by bringing in the old principle that four is four times one. But if one is one and one-half, it is not one-fourth of four. So one begins to be caught in endless confusion. After one has moved about for a while in a mathematical fog, one will conclude that the only way to think mathematically is to have a dependable scale of values.

If the doctrine of relativity as applied to the new physics is brought in, one begins by reminding the objector that there are two questions. One has to do with formulas which by a pragmatic test turn out to work as applied to nature. The other has to do with the consistent use of mathematical principles. The views of Einstein as to astronomy were not taken seriously until practical experiment proved that the calculations of Einstein had unexpected authentication. But a mathematician dealing with these unexpected relationships must use the classical scale of values to determine and record them and to calculate regarding them. A thing may seem to be true when it is not, because we do not know everything about it. But nothing can be false in the very sense in which it is true without the shipwreck of the whole mental process. A relative truth is not a truth.

7. The Ladder of Confusion

It is in the realm of philosophy and theology, of religion and the religious life, that the ladder of relativities on which one mounts to a blind unity becomes most confusing. In Indian thought you have the starkest primitivism combined with the subtlest and most sophisticated thought. You have theism. You have polytheism. You have atomistic pluralism. You have a substitution of evolution for creation. You have the yoga discipline. You have ritual and you have various metaphysical teachings, and all this and much more are combined into an amazing unity. Here again unity is possible only through relativity. These contradictory positions are not harmonized. They are brought to lie down together in peace, because no one of them means anything definite *very long*. Each loses its integrity in order to become part of its opposite. The apostle of unity through relativity in philosophical and religious thought can build his ladder as he pleases. It is not necessary for him to follow the Indian pattern. He can begin with animism. He can move on to polytheism. He can advance to theism. He can move on—if it is on— to an impersonal cosmic principle. He can build a Hegelian logical structure where the actualities of experience correspond to the formal relationships of thought. He can construct a materialistic corpus of thought based upon the interaction of forces or some other physical correlation. He can build a mystical other world of phantasy and see it as the ultimate reality. And he can do many other things in the process of building.

Each position is a rung in the ladder. It is sound and dependable at that stage of the climbing. But it is soon transcended. So in a sense each rung disappears the moment one steps on the rung next higher. The unity is a kind of unity of legerdemain.

But one question cannot be avoided. However you build the ladder and whatever be represented by the various rungs, when you get to the very top, what have you? When you get to the ultimate unity, what is it like?

Indian thought has no hesitation about the answer. In the ultimate unity certain distinctions are forever transcended. The distinction between subject and object is transcended. Subject and object are lost in a unity where neither continues to be. The distinction between being and nonbeing is transcended. You are in a universe where such distinctions have ceased to have meaning. The distinction between truth and error is transcended. You have passed to a region where you have found a perfect unity in which the contrast between truth and error has ceased to exist. The distinction between good and evil has vanished. You have found a unity which is indeed beyond good and evil. Your ladder is a ladder of confusion. No significant distinctions remain untouched. Significance has ceased to be.

8. The Great Gregariousness Becomes the Complete Blackout

This delightful passion for unity has thus become a very terrible and destructive thing. Nothing is left which has any meaning. Nothing is left which has any value. There is a blackout of the mind. There is a blackout of the conscience. There is a blackout of the will. There is a blackout of the spirit. The great inclusiveness has indeed led to the complete confusion. So pantheistic monism is revealed in its true quality. So we see how deceptive is the light which has come from India. The brilliant and fascinating mind of India has achieved every sort of understanding except the understanding of the treachery of that false unity in which it so deeply believes. No other civilization has offered to mankind such a magnificently brilliant way of committing intellectual suicide.

The deception is all the more alluring because each stage toward the great debacle is so full of rich and colorful experience. Everything you want is yours *for a moment*. But nothing you want is yours for long. The vast many-sidedness of the experience hides from the man, drunk with the intoxication of the moment, the ultimate disillusionment and frustration and futility. The sunset has all lovely colors in every combination of glorious light. Then, as night comes suddenly in the tropics, so the night comes down on life with unbelievable darkness. It is more than the flight of the alone to the alone. At last being itself ceases to have significance. The sense of awareness forever departs. The unity quite without quality is its own negation. And only a vast cipher is left.

Many a reader may be inclined to say, "But we should never think of carrying the principle of unity to such disastrous lengths." Perhaps not. But the great thinkers of India have no hesitation about going the whole length of the journey. And after all you only understand a position when you see that to which its logic leads.

There are many dabblers in pseudo unities. They have high-sounding watchwords. And when we are weary of paying the price of brave loyalty in thought or deed, it is easy to be allured by the summons of surrender to the peace which destroys understanding.

Lewis Mumford has carried on a great argument in his three large volumes *Technics and Civilization, The Culture of Cities,* and *The Condition of Man.* These learned books are full of materials of the utmost significance to contemporary men. He is often perverse. His writings have a curious and uncritical sensuality. And in one place or another in these volumes he manages to be driven to say what cannot be harmonized with many other statements. There is a dramatic change in the whole outlook as you get into the volume on *The Condition of Man.* Again and again the criticism is not only corrosive but splendidly right. Again and again he almost seizes the great distinctions. Again and again he almost sights the Christian sanctions which he so deeply misunderstands. But he comes at last to a curious thing he calls organic humanism, in which the relation of clear and controlling intelligence to the physical organism is not even suggested. If Mr. Mumford succeeds in being organic, he does not succeed in being human. And his suggested synthetic religion has all the dangers of the false gregariousness which has so often mistaken mental hospitality for intellectual insight. In the postwar world the apostles of pseudo unity will arise on every hand. If they have their way, we shall create a mental desert and call it peace.

9. The Great Distinctions

It is then the contention of this chapter and, indeed, of this book that everything depends on the preservation of the great distinctions. The distinction between being and nonbeing must hold eternally or existence itself would fall apart. The distinction between subject and object must continue forever. Only on the basis of that distinction has experience ever had any meaning. Only on the basis of that distinction does experience have any significance now. Only on the basis of that distinction can experience have any significance in the future. The distinction between truth and falsehood must be eternal. The end of that distinction would mean the end of intelligence, the end of thought, the end of any sort of validity of any kind whatever. The distinction between goodness and evil cannot come to an end. Goodness can triumph over evil. But the evil over which it triumphs will continue to be evil or the triumph would have no meaning.

Upon these great distinctions significant experience in time and in eternity rests. We have a supreme stake in their perpetuity. Without them nothing remains in which we could believe, for which we could care, or which could be the basis of hope.

Yet it is these necessary distinctions which a false doctrine of unity would destroy. It is these distinctions which a misleading monism would abolish. It is just these distinctions which can never be maintained in a world where pantheistic monism is triumphant. The battle against all these debasing pantheisms which would rob us one by one of each significant distinction until at last we would live in a great void, is the supreme intellectual battle which confronts contemporary man.

The matter of distinctions which must be maintained deserves further inspection. The distinctions between the free intelligence which is man's defining characteristic and the subhuman world of appetite and of impersonal mathematical forces is of the utmost importance. Man can become a beast. He can become a thing. But he loses his humanity when he does either. As a genuine man he stands with his free mind choosing between contending possibilities in the light of sanctions which are eternal. The distinctions between the imperfect intelligence, the imperfect goodness, and the imperfect power of man and the perfect intelligence and the perfect goodness and the perfect power of God must be maintained. The doctrine of the three levels—the subhuman, the human, and the divine—has been adumbrated by various thinkers and various writers in various centuries. Whenever it is remembered, you can approach life with clear and understanding eyes. Whenever it is forgotten, everything begins to fall into confusion.

The great distinctions all rest down on truths which belong to the world of reality and so may be called metaphysical truths. They have to do with the conditions of knowledge. And so they may be called epistemological truths.

There are earnest get-rich-quick thinkers, like those of the school of Kierkegaard, who are so impressed by action, by the world of the deed, that they would attempt to work out a whole philosophy of life on the basis of confronting action as an existential thing and ignoring all the problems of the being which makes action possible. So they sometimes slip along, passing by the very distinctions which actually make their own work possible. They become annoyed at theories of being and theories of knowledge. It is as if one should become annoyed at the earth upon which one walks or the air which one breathes. A false metaphysic would take away that world of action which includes all their interest. To do, one must be. And a theory of being is always at the basis of an account of doing.

The great distinctions upon which all action rests are not less important because we can cloud their meaning by expressing annoyance at words like "metaphysical."

There is one other distinction which in all sorts of ways is tied up with the matters we have been discussing. It is the distinction between freedom and necessity. On a subhuman, impersonal level, of course, there is no freedom. There is only mathematical and biological determinism. But there is no world of conscious intelligence without freedom. The person of conscious intelligence must always be able to say: "This is not that. And I choose this rather than that." Only on this basis is significant experience possible. The distinction between free intelligence on the free personal level and dependable necessary relations on the impersonal level is the foundation of everything we mean by civilization. It is that which gives individual life significance. It is the root of moral and spiritual demand. It gives importance to what happens in time and does not cease to be controlling in eternity.

10. The Living Corpus of Dependable Truth

From this long analysis of obsessions and this attempt to look directly at the truths which the obsessions deny, we come back to that world of correlated distinctions which makes possible and interprets that human experience which is the subject of this book. We have seen that the great gregariousness which includes everything at last takes from everything all significance. The vast inclusiveness brings the death of all real meaning, and so all these various things we seem to possess slip between our fingers. Unity, we see at last, is not what we need. Harmony is what we need. And harmony is found only in a world where the great distinctions are cherished. It is never found in a world where they are destroyed. So it is the living corpus of dependable truths upon which we must depend. Here we shall find a basis for significant experience with meaning not only for time but for eternity.

Men, the world God gives them; men and women and little children and their life together; the Great Person of moral love who made the people and who gave them their world; the persons of free intelligence which is God's image clear in them; the Person of perfect intelligence and perfect power—how the rhythm of it all fits into the meaning of true human experience! Man's adventures with himself, his adventures with his world, his adventures with his fellow men, and his adventures with the Great Person; the man in whom God came to the world and men; the good life and the good death against the pressure of a thousand treacheries—how it all fits with that strange darker rhythm of a man's battle with the evil in his own soul and the evil in the world! These things become real in a human brotherhood with the living Christ as

Savior and Master and Friend. They are only words until they become real in experience. And experience only finds true reality in them. All truth is alive in these personal relationships. And truth dies unless it becomes personal. The persons are at last truth and goodness alive as the grace of God in Christ does its masterful work in them.

Does this suddenly sound like a book of devotions rather than a philosophical or theological dialectic? Quite. And precisely because it is only when the dialectic becomes personal that it becomes invincible. It is only when it is so surgingly real that it is lyrical that it becomes finally victorious. The Divine Person and the human persons in growing fellowship in a dependable universe give us the sense of the final answer to all doctrines of the false unity. Here being is in everlasting contrast to nonbeing. Here subject is always over against object in harmonious mastery. Here truth is always sharp because seen against a clear perception of the black treachery of falsehood. Here goodness is seen as truly good in actual triumph over actual evil.

This corpus of living truth may give us a tragic view of life. It is tragic because it refuses to tell lies. It is glorious because it does not deny the possibility of battle but fights and wins. Its very realism is one side of the exhaustless splendor of its idealism.

There is a sense in which that pacifism which is as dangerous in a time of peace as in a time of war—perhaps more dangerous—is a part of that false dream of unity which cries for what can only seem to come when we deny the very facts of life. The unity of which the pacifist dreams is the unity of a world where moral distinctions become shadowy in the presence of the dream of peace. In the name of this false unity the sentimental idealist comes to feel that serenity is more important than righteousness, or, to put it in a way more just—or generous—to his own mood, that peace is the only righteousness. The doctrine of appeasement belongs to a world the center of whose thought has been corrupted already by that monism where sharp moral discrimination has already begun to be dulled.

In the real world of the permanent distinctions we cannot accept a peace which is based upon exploitation, we cannot accept a peace which is based on cruelty, we cannot accept a peace which crushes personality, we cannot accept a peace which is based on lies.

So one lives in a stern but glorious world. It is tender, too. It is as tender as the compassion of God, even as it is as stern as the judgment of God. The great truths remain in their full integrity; and, if there is no unity where all the great meanings are lost for the sake of a false peace, there is the hope of a harmony when the God of moral love is victorious. In as far as His mastery is accepted in human experiences, or rather by the men who have human experiences, there is harmony now. But all the lights are shining as eternal moral love achieves its triumphs.

CHAPTER XXIV

The Transfiguration of Ethics

THIS chapter is not to be a brief outline of Christian ethics. It will not be an endeavor to construct a *multum in parvo* expressing in sentences instead of chapters some such understanding of the practical outcome of Christian sanctions as is set forth in that clear and distinguished volume *The Principles of Christian Ethics* by Dr. Albert C. Knudson. It will not be a brief summary of the history of ethics coming to a final position in the Christian interpretation of the business of living, moving from the *Nicomachean Ethics* of Aristotle through the *De officiis* of Cicero and so down the centuries. It will not be a study of the ethical teachings set forth in organized Christianity. All these discussions would be deeply interesting and very important. But from the standpoint of that direct interest in human experience which is fundamental in this book, one question cannot be avoided: What does Christianity do to the ethical life? It is just the ethical life and not the analysis of ethical theory which is important for us. Of course, the ethical theory is important too, and at points where it confronts living experience we shall find it within our purview. But we are interested in ethical truth in experiences, and not in abstract ethical truth apart from experience. We have to do with living men under moral demand. And we are asking: What does Christianity do for them and in them?

1. Codes and Practice

It is the particular characteristic of ethical theory that it has a definite reference to practice. It is not constructed as a corpus of thought which has served its purpose when it has been inspected with intellectual satisfaction. It is meant to be a guide for life.

The *Bushido* code, which has had such profound influence on the life of Japan, is a system of knightly behavior. It is a warrior's code. Here you have something which moves from the good manners of the hero to his disdainful courage when he faces death. Here you have loyalty and self-control. It teaches men how to throw their lives away in the name of what they believe to be the greatest possible loyalty.

The ethical teachings of Confucius are based on the relations of ruler and subject, father and son, elder brother and younger, friend and friend. The code grows out of the study of actual relationships. It is shrewd and full of practical sagacity. In a sense it is the crystallized wisdom of a type of thought which does not attempt to rise to the height of religion or to probe the depths of philosophy, but is content to deal with the relations of men as it finds them. To use the jargon of a modern school of quite different thought, it is eminently existential.

The *Nicomachean Ethics* of Aristotle moves from code to deed. It perpetually keeps before you the menace of extremes. There are the deeds of the extreme right. There are the deeds of the extreme left. There are also the deeds of the middle way. And they are the best deeds.

Cicero's *De officiis* is engaged with the proper discharge of the duties belonging to the true life of man. Whenever appetite pulls or pushes, reason must consider. And the deed, when it comes, must express the control of reason over appetite.

Enough has been said to make it clear that the ethical code always exists not merely for the purposes of a philosophy of ethics but for the purposes of moral practice. The master of ethics keeps his eyes on men in the actual business of living.

2. The Man with Ethical Experience

Right at this point great problems emerge. The corpus of thought about deeds produces the ethical point of view. The actual practice of the principles, we are tempted to say at once, is the ethical life. Moral creeds and moral deeds would seem to sum up the whole subject. But the matter is not quite so simple.

There is the world of motives. As T. S. Eliot reminds us, it is possible to do the right thing for the wrong reason. And there is the whole matter of the relation of a man's inner life to his moral code and of the relation of the moral code to his inner life. Even when a man is sincere and earnest there is a loyalty which is the loyalty of the driven slave, as there is also a loyalty which is the loyalty of a free man. There is the question as to whether ethical demand comes like a master with a whip or like a friend with kindly inspiration. There is the subtle question of how you can combine moral authority with the release of free and joyous energy. When the ethical life is connected—as connected it must be—with religion, there is the question as to whether it is an attempt to satisfy the demands of a moral God and so to meet with His approval, or whether it is the glowing and eager expression of a relationship already established by the friendly God. Is the ethical life on the highest level an attempt to satisfy the moral demands of God, or is it the inevitable outflow of love for a God who by the offer of His friendship and by that alone makes the highest ethical life possible?

The man with an ethical experience is more than a doer of deeds. He is a man who would find the satisfaction of his deepest life in such a relation to the good and the God of goodness that his life is full of creative energy, growing peace, and productive power. He must pass his ethical life through the very central places of his soul.

3. The Personal and the Impersonal

As one contemplates the questions we have suggested, it will become clear, if he analyzes them carefully, that they are all related to another: Is the man of moral earnestness dealing with a set of abstract principles which have a right to rule his life, or is he dealing with a Living Person who is goodness alive? No end of problems center here. Abstract principles apart from personality have a certain hard and mathematical and, indeed, mechanical quality. They can never take account of one's motives. If, on the other hand, one's moral loyalty is to a Person, one can say:

> All that the world's coarse thumb
> And finger failed to plumb
> This I was worth to God.

The Great Person can take account of one's purposes as well as one's achievements. The Great Code can measure you only by your achievements. The Great Person can take account of your attempts as well as of your successes. The abstract standard can only be made the basis of judging you by your successes. The men under a moral law are in a difficult and precarious and terrible situation. The men under a moral Person are in an entirely new situation.

It is the perpetual tendency of ethics to get out of hand. The moral code leaps to the back of the horse and attempts to unsaddle the understanding person. There is a tendency toward the reign of impersonal principles rather than the reign of the Great Person to whom all action is the expression of the personal life.

Even when the code is seen to be one administered by a Divine Person, there is a tendency to look upon the Great Person as the servant of the code rather than the One who sees all principles in a new way because He sees them in their relation to personal experience. In a sense Mount Sinai sees God as the servant of the moral law, and Mount Calvary sees God as the Master of the moral law. Or to put it more adequately, the impersonal aspect of law is in emphasis at Sinai, the personal aspect of law is in emphasis on Calvary. So Christianity delivers moral demand from all impersonal rigidities and sees it to be not less but rather more regal as the instrument of the God of moral love, growing out of His own nature and the nature of the men whom He has made, and coming to fulfillment not in loyalty to an abstract principle but in glowing devotion to a Living Person.

4. The Great Dilemma

To the superficial and complacent man—and he may be a very respectable person—there is no moral dilemma. Conscience, with him, is
always a candle and never a searchlight. He considers that he does
rather well by means of the light which his candle gives. Of course, more
light may come his way. And then he will be startled out of his superficiality. But the man who makes the moral life the great enterprise of
his soul comes upon what seem to be stultifying paradoxes and para-
lyzing contradictions. Together they constitute the great dilemma.

You may put the matter in one way by saying that in the deepest ethical experience a relative person meets an absolute moral demand. And
the absolute demand is too much for the relative person. You may put
it in another way by saying that a creature in time meets the staggering
demand of a timeless ethic. And the shining light of that timeless standard overwhelms him. You may put the matter in still another way by
saying that an imperfect person is pursued by a passion for perfection
and that devouring passion literally consumes him. You may put it
again in this fashion: A human being meets a divine command, and he
is blinded by the awful splendor of this rushing of divine meaning into
his life. You may put it still again by saying that it is the very nature of
moral demand to become not only exhaustless but exhausting. Thus
it may come about that our moral ideals, which we feel ought to emancipate us, actually slay us. We may express it in a shrewd realistic
fashion by saying that we are more comfortable and those who must
live with us are more comfortable when we are not too much in earnest.
Or we may call it the self-defeating quality of the moral process. Put in
an extreme fashion, we may say that God has so made us that if we turn
altogether from ethical earnestness we commit moral suicide, and if
we become persons pursued by an exhaustless passion of deadly earnestness we are likely to become fit subjects for a madhouse. And the
dilemma assumes more terrible proportions in just the degree that our
moral earnestness increases. A white heat of moral intensity is within
possibility of becoming as destructive as a great conflagration.

5. The Solution of the Antinomian

The simplest solution of the great dilemma is to give up the problem.
Since the moral law plays such tricks with earnest men, we may say, we
shall have nothing to do with the moral law. Since we do not know any
way to be free in law, we can at least assert our independence and become free from law. There is at first a great sense of exhilaration about
the freedom of the lawless. We do not have to be bound by these moral
restrictions after all. Let us eat and drink and be merry and obey all our
impulses and put no restrictions upon our desires and enjoy the uncon-

fined liberty of those who acknowledge no law above their own impulses. But very soon we discover that our desires themselves are contradictory. And before long we are the victims of a civil war of our own impulses. It would seem, then, that we must establish a law of some sort over these mad desires or they will destroy each other and destroy us in the process. But a law of lawlessness is a contradiction in terms. And if we attempt to find a law to bend lawless impulses to lawful purposes, we have given up the freedom of license and find ourselves back in the world of moral meaning and moral tension and moral struggle.

The study of the contemporary literature of release from moral control is a revealing discipline. There is first the hot rapture of indulgence. Then there is the beginning of ennui. Then there is the emerging of contradictory desires. Then there is the civil war of the unlicensed appetites. The fiction which tells the tale is full of bitter tragedy. The poetry which sings its saga is full of intensity at first, then it passes through every stage of tension and conflict and disgust and disdain of life to a black silence at last. The final movement in the music of lawlessness celebrates suicide.

The argument of life itself is, of course, the big and conclusive argument. Tell the story of what happens to a man when he accepts a position and acts upon it, and one has revealed its secret. So judged, the way of the antinomian stands condemned by the arbitrament of life itself.

6. The Conventional Solution

There is a solution of quite a different character. It does not repudiate moral demand. It has great respect for authority. But the authority to which it submits is that of convention rather than that of moral principle. The pleasant aspects of this solution may be suggested by the resemblance of the word "convention" to the word "convenience." The conventional is likely to be the convenient. A conventional person is one who keeps on doing a thing after he has forgotten the reason for doing it because others still do it and so it represents the path of least resistance. The conventional represents the compulsion of fashion rather than the compulsion of character. In a way it represents a lazy man's morality. It accepts the mores of the clan, the fraternity, the political party, the ecclesiastical group, the social organization, without question and without critical analysis. It may chance that the track of convention and the track of real insight into moral values for a while coincide so that the man traveling on the train of convention finds that he is running on rails representing real moral values. But the conventional has a fashion of getting away from the real. Thus it happens that the man who solves the moral dilemma by accepting conventional standards is likely to dishonor true morality at the very moment when he pays it lip and hand and foot service. Even so one must reluctantly admit that convention is often the odd cement which holds a disintegrating society together and gives it a chance to discover genuine moral meanings in life. It is a poor thing at best, however, until the winds of reality blow through it. Then it may happen that a man will do just what other men of his group do but with a reason better than those which are possessed by any other members of his artificial society. The moment, however, that the winds of reality do begin to blow into a conventional mind, the great dilemma comes in sight again.

7. The Solution of Those Who Get Lost in Details

There are no end of people who give big loyalties to little insights and magnificent faithfulness to petty moral distinctions. This, of course, represents the scholasticism of ethics. Jesus met a good many men who were willing to die for things not worth dying for. Rabbinical thought became full of this dry overemphasis on the petty. But you cannot speak of that as if it characterized one group and did not characterize others. Let any group exist long enough and its fresh moral insights, if not renewed in central fires of moral energy, become cold and lifeless. Skeletons move about dexterously and insist on being treated as if they had vital organs. No religion and no religious group has been quite free from this dry rot of the moral sense. Some quite unimportant practice is made the symbol of an evil intent. Then those who abstain from that practice become the morally elect, and those who indulge in it are regarded as moral outcasts. The New Testament has a word for the person caught by this sort of thing. And that word is Pharisee.

Often those who get lost in details and so miss the big meanings seem to get no end of satisfaction out of their preoccupation with the morally microscopic. They become rather a nuisance in the society to which they belong. And often they organize cults of the unimportant. Their earnestness gets frittered away at last in endless preoccupations with the irrelevant. So the great hour comes and passes, and they do not see it. So the fate of the world is decided while they isolate themselves from the great struggle which they do not understand. But they cannot isolate themselves from destiny. They really vote for evil without being able to see its true quality. They fail to vote for the greatest good because they do not comprehend it. And when the tragedy they helped to produce comes to the world, they are innocently astonished. At least they are astonished. And they think that they are innocent. They have never learned to be suspicious of their loyalty to the good while the better and the best knock at the door. And they have never learned that the good ceases to be good when it turns their mind away from the better.

8. The Solution of a Shrewd Practicality

There is a solution which one is likely to view with a chuckle of amused tolerance, though really it is not good enough. This is the solution of the man of shrewd practical sagacity. He has no idea of repudiating moral values. He knows that they are the cement which holds society together. But he has a great fear of extremes, and he is determined that his ethical standards shall not make him uncomfortable. So when the absolute nature of the moral requirement begins to exercise its searching influence upon him, he decides on clever measures to meet the dangerous attack. He will be a man of moral earnestness, but he will not be a man of too great moral earnestness. It was in some such fashion probably that the eighteenth-century latitudinarians used to preach sermons on the text: "Be not righteous overmuch." There is often something quite dependable about the ethical loyalty of the man of shrewd moral sagacity up to a point. He is a respectable man. He is an honest man. He pays his debts. He is in a general way a good citizen. But he keeps a weather eye watching for the clouds no larger than men's hands which indicate the coming of moral tempests. And he gets under cover before the great storms arrive. He never climbs very high. He never sinks very low. He keeps in sight of the moral absolute. But he does not come too near the place where it exercises its awful power.

Sometimes he lives long enough to discover that really he depends upon men and women who are willing to take risks which he never faces. He never gets into a position where he might be condemned to drink the fatal hemlock. But he manages to be one of the citizens who vote for the acquittal of Socrates. We need not condemn him too harshly. He faces discomfort enough when he sees other men suffering for causes in which he believes in his heart but for which he has made no great sacrifices. Sometimes in the night he seems to hear voices which say: "We gave you the world in which you practice your safe virtues." And for a wistful moment he sees a man who might have been on the battle line of some great fight.

9. The Solution of Despair

Of course, despair is not a solution. So we have been putting together words which always belong apart, have we not? Let us examine the matter carefully. It may turn out that in the vast world of personal relations moral despair may lead to a sudden change of front when the greatest darkness will become the greatest light. But first let us inspect the darkness.

The men who make moral history accept none of the solutions we have discussed. They accept the full and terrible light of the most searching moral demand. And they come to see clearly that the moral imperative asks of them what they can never accomplish. They—finite beings—confront an infinite moral demand. They—creatures of time —confront the morals of eternity. They—children of imperfection— confront the awful demands of the Perfect. They realize fully the desperate nature of this adventure with perfection. But they refuse to give up the adventure. They will maintain their inner loyalty to the absolute demand, however far their actual practice falls below it. They would rather be condemned by the Perfect than crowned by the imperfect. So they come full upon despair. At last they realize their moral incapacity. And so they stand helpless in the presence of a perfection they cannot attain. Wave upon wave the bitterness of their lot sweeps over their consciousness like the billows of a stormy sea. They know at last the complete surrender of complacency, of dependence upon themselves, of pride in their own achievement. They fall on their faces in the presence of a moral demand which they fully accept at the very moment when they realize that they are unequal to the task of meeting it.

And in the very deepest depths of this darkness they suddenly discover that this is a strange kind of despair. For at its very heart, just when all hope in their own powers has been completely repudiated, there begins to be felt another dawning hope. In the depth of the gloom at its very abysmal center, there begins to shine a distant but growing light. Somewhere there is Someone who is glad that they have not given up the moral absolute when they realized its awful grandeur. Somewhere there is Someone who is coming to meet them in the heart of the gloom. The night of despair begins to sparkle with incredible promise.

10. The Solution of Faith

Then Christianity appears. And now the moral pilgrims who have carried their loyalty right through the gates of despair find the great light taking the place of the implacable darkness. For now trust in a Person takes the place of commitment to a task which can bring only frustration and defeat. And this Person who is the moral law alive makes the absolute moral demand strangely human in His own humanity. But He comes as the Great Sufferer who has borne agony when He might have inflicted agony. All the impersonal majestic principles become personal in Him. And they become redemptive. The act of trust which binds the pilgrims to Him in living fellowship is the end of that personal self-consciousness which is the tragedy of the moral life of man. It is His goodness in which the moral pilgrims rejoice and not their own. It is His suffering which opens the gates of joy to them and not their own. It is His death which is the secret of their life now and through all possible transitions of experience. So not only self-consciousness but selfishness is lost forever in the glory of the Cross. What

He is and has done takes the place of all men's dependence on what they may do. So the despair which has come from their own incapacity changes to joy in His perfect capacity to do for them what they cannot do for themselves. Indeed, their moral despair and this alone could interpret to them the need of One who would save them from the necessity of ever depending upon themselves again. So the way of trust takes the place of the way of moral self-assertion. And so the way of faith takes the place of the way of works.

But the works follow. Only the deeds are done in a new spirit. What you do for the love of God already yours is utterly different from what you do in a grim attempt to win God's favor. What you do because the joy of the great deliverance fills all your thought is utterly different in quality from what you do in a heroic attempt to deliver yourself. What you do as Christ's man is utterly different from what you do as the hard-pressed slave of the law. But just because the law is alive in the Person you love as you love no other person in the universe, your activities are suffused by a spirit which is the fulfillment of the law itself on a level only attained when law is set to music by a great personal devotion. You can find a glorious release in devotion to a Person such as you could never find in obedience to a law. And the law itself is transformed without losing its moral excellence when it looks at you through the eyes of a Divine Friend. You do not have a new system of morals. You have a vitalized system of morals. You do not have a new ethic. You have an ethic which has been transfigured. So faith in the Person who speaks from the Cross makes all things new.

11. The Searching Power Which Christianity Brings to Ethics

We see then the sense in which the Christian ethic has become transformed and made into a glowing and creative influence. But it has also become a more searching power than loyalty to impersonal principles could ever be. When loyalty to truth becomes a living devotion to a Person who is truth alive, it has a power to penetrate to the last recesses of the personality. No subtle sophistry escapes it. No evasive make-believe is able to hide from its clear light. Truth itself becomes a force in a fashion unknown before when it is truth in Christ. So every commandment belonging to the corpus of moral excellence is transformed because it is alive as a determining power in the beloved Person.

By a curious movement of moral experience, the impersonal code is often made the basis of curious casuistry. This happens so frequently that we may almost call it habitual. And when the moral life is shot through with casuistry, it loses its original force and power. Technical obedience takes the place of faithfulness to the spirit of the law. The grandsons of the prophets become Pharisees.

But the moment the Son of God who speaks to us from the Cross is made the center of moral allegiance and of spiritual devotion, moral scholasticism loses its appeal. For moral scholasticism always comes to have a subtle evasion at the heart of it. You may try to evade the too piercing power of an abstract moral principle. You have no desire to escape the moral lordship of the One who died for you. All moral values are seen in a new perspective at the Cross.

And here we can see the metaphysical foundation of all genuine ethical passion on the Christian level. We cannot get a theology of the deed of Christ upon the Cross which is not based on the *being* of the Person who achieved the deed. If He was God in human life, then the Cross has all this power. If He was a gracious and friendly man doing all this, then its central strategy at once disappears. Who He was is basal to what He did. And who He was is a matter of being. It is also true that the whole strategy of moving from loyalty to a thing to devotion to a Person is based upon the personal quality of the fundamental life of the universe. The being of God as a person is basal to the action of God. So every ethical question is at last a metaphysical question. A personal metaphysic gives the ethical life its truest authenticity and makes possible the final placing of loyalty itself on a personal basis. And here again the fact that the ethical life is based on the nature of the fundamental being of the universe gives it a new and searching power. The relations of persons are the ultimate relations. And so we come to the very bedrock of the ethical life.

But just because this is true we must take personal relations with the utmost seriousness. The shrewd schemer uses personal relationships for his selfish ends. He is rather proud of his capacity to manage other men. But if every man has his essential status as one God made for a full and free personal life, and one for whom Christ died, we cannot use him for selfish ends of our own. To treat any person as a thing is to sin against God and to sin against Christ. The human manipulator has no place in the fellowship of free persons made to be children of God. But the very freedom of a living devotion to Christ and the men who are also the objects of His love is one of the alternatives of the moral life. For a man may refuse to make the whole moral experience his own. At any point in the process he may say "No" to the great moral demand. He may refuse to be a responsible person in a personal world. And this ultimate refusal to accept moral responsibility leads to the final slavery, just as trust in the Great Person leads to the final freedom. There are stern and implacable elements belonging to the moral demand which is ultimate in the universe and is alive in the life of God. Because a man is not an automaton but a person, he can be a good person. Because a man is not an automaton but a person he can be a bad person. He may reject the suffering love of God which is offered to him in Christ. And so he enters upon a darkness not to be pierced by morning light.

12. *The New Spirit Which Christianity Brings to Ethics*

Paul's many-century-old distinction between a righteous man and a good man is relevant here. A righteous man is a slave of the law. A good man is one in whom the law has become friendly as he has met it in Jesus Christ. This new quality touches every aspect of the moral life, its motives, its resolves, its loyalties, and its actions.

The righteous man is often hard. The good man has kept all the moral incentive but has lost his hardness. The righteous man is self-conscious. And because he is always inspecting himself with a certain metallic rigidity, he is likely to treat other people in just the same way. The good man, precisely because he is depending upon the God who has come to him in rescuing love in Jesus Christ, finds all his thought of moral things in his own life and in the life of others suffused by this sense of gratitude for a great gift. Other men are also, if they will have it so, the recipients of this great gift. So he regards them as brothers at the banquet of God rather than as slaves to be judged by their circumspect performance of a task. He is able, even when he must be stern with others, to have a quality of gentleness in his heart. And even under the high presence of moral demand increased by a great devotion, he is able to see himself as the object of God's grace and to forgive himself in his acceptance of the forgiveness of God. It is always harder for a Christian to forgive himself than to forgive others.

So the moral life comes to be the life Christians live together in the society of the forgiven. And this new spirit, while it accentuates the ethical demand, gives it a gracious richness which is the soul of specifically Christian morality.

13. *The Lyrical Gladness Which Christianity Brings to Ethics*

Christianity does, then, actually set morals to music. A code becomes a symphony. A moral responsibility becomes an occasion for singing. The whole ethical life has gone through a process of orchestration and comes forth in glorious harmony. This singing quality of Christian goodness is the essential aspect of evangelical experience. When Christianity is interpreted in such fashion that it is accepting a way of life rather than trusting a Person and then walking in a certain way because it is the way of fellowship with Him, it loses the note of rapture. This has happened tragically and men have discussed the result under such subjects as the *Lost Radiance of the Christian Religion*. When Christianity is regarded as a living spirit first completely exemplified by Jesus rather than as a life lived in perpetual dependence on Him, again the glow and the rapture disappear. It is easy to discard the evangelical type of experience, but one cannot have the full Christian rapture without it. Not by accident was the Wesleyan Revival accompanied by a great outburst of sacred song. Charles Wesley was a living exemplification of what happens when life is set to music by the Great Evangel.

Sometimes the distinction between life at the pre-evangelical level and classical Christian experience is expressed by saying that the first is actually morality even though touched by genuine religious emotion. And morality consists in earning the sense of peace while religion consists of a great act of trust and the peace which follows it. Morality is earning salvation. Religion is accepting it as a gift. However one puts it, the sense of the gift and the act of trust create the Christian music.

14. Christianity and the Creative Ethical Life

A certain type of artist always claims that the very possession of standards limits the power of the vital impulses upon which art depends. The moralist may be in his way an excellent man, but the stern sanctions in which he believes have cramped his style, dulled his imagination, slackened the processes of his intelligence, and altogether depleted his productive force.

The charge deserves more critical examination than it has ever received. For while it is true that this charge is essentially false, it contains elements of truth whose understanding will help us to comprehend the moral life itself. Of course, on one side all art depends upon restraint and discipline and control. All truly classical art of every variety gives us this sense of power through discipline, and strength through noble control. In this sense the charge is palpably and completely false. But in order to have discipline and intelligent control there must be a vital and palpitating energy to control. And the significant charge is not an attack upon the control of vital energy but an attack upon a form of living which would deplete this vital energy at its very source so that there would be nothing to control. Now it is quite true that the stage of moral development when a man is giving self-conscious and grim allegiance to rigid and impersonal demands tends to harden a man's character and make him something not unlike a conscious mechanism. There is a depletion of the vital energies. But the moment moral loyalty becomes devotion to a Person who is goodness alive, all the hardness and rigidity disappear and the vital forces begin to flow with resurgent power. Only now they flow as a part of a great moral devotion. They do not flow apart from the moral life.

It is just at this point that Christianity becomes the reconciler of art and morality. Art without the vital sanctions of the Christian religion will tend at long last to become decadent with the false vitality of a lawless life. Morality without the creative union of love and goodness which the Christian religion brings will tend to become cold and lifeless and to turn into something not unlike a fossil in the end. But when ethical passion unites with creative joy, as is the case in the Christian religion in the classical form of its experience, one has the release of all the vital and creative energies and the maintaining of a living devotion to all the moral values. It is Christianity which will prevent art from committing suicide and morality from becoming a pillar of salt.

The problem is, of course, much more manifold and many-sided than we have suggested up to this point. A good home must have standards. It must have discipline. But if that discipline becomes hard and rigid and mechanical, it defeats the very purpose for which it exists. And it is the moral love which comes to fruition in the best Christian experience which sets the form for a home life where discipline itself shall be shot through with friendship, and order shall blossom with the flowers of mutual devotion.

In education the problem has been felt acutely. So-called progressive education is an attempt to restore the free and spontaneous elements to an education which had become formal and conventional and without creative energy. But the progressive education, in moving away from one extreme, goes quite into its opposite. If it was often true that in the old education one had discipline without the vital spark, it is very definitely true that in the new education in its "progressive" forms one has a lawless freedom which leads to chaos. Again that free loyalty which is at the heart of Christian experience suggests a pattern where education shall be so conducted as to combine high discipline with a respect for the integrity of the growing life and its free expression.

One might multiply illustrations in many directions. The truth is that when loyalty commands only the head, it will become cold and formal. When it commands only the will, it will become hard and rigid. When it comes only from a glowing heart, it will be temporary and fluctuating. When it comes only from a vision of great and eternal principles, it will become crushing in its magnificence. But when loyalty is the richness of a devotion to the Great Person who gave Himself for us and brought all eternal values to us in living experience, we find our minds satisfied, our wills made into steel, our hearts rich with a response which depends upon what He is and has done for us and not on our fluctuating moods. Thus the ethical life loses forever all qualities of rigidity and becomes gloriously creative, nobly free, and joyously powerful.

So it is in Christianity that the ethical life finds its interpretation, its goal, its completion. Here one finds the drama in experience in which the ethical life becomes fully fruitful. And here one finds the final meaning of that life in the relation of living men to the living God, and through Him their relation to each other in the fellowship of moral love. Ethics must find a fountain of perpetual youth if it is to do its work in the world. And in Christianity it finds that fountain, its waters sparkling with the very qualities of moral light.

CHAPTER XXV

Beyond These Voices

Leave Now for dogs and apes!
Man has Forever.

SO Robert Browning put with finality the distinction between the subhuman and the human. So he expressed man's audacious claim of his right to immortality. It is very important that we should see, as we take up the final matters connected with this discussion of the meaning of human experience, that we cannot get a satisfactory picture of human life if we confine man to time. This is indeed a matter of the utmost importance. The more we have studied human experience, the more we have discovered that there is somehow a touch of infinity about it. We cannot explain man's characteristic powers without a reference which goes beyond time and finds the explanation of man in the Great Person who inhabits eternity. Man's intelligence has full meaning only when it is seen in the light of the divine intelligence. His moral life requires sanctions which must be timeless and can only reach truly creative quality in devotion to a Great Eternal Person of moral love. His spiritual life cannot come to full fruition without fellowship with that Great Person who has made him and sustains him in life and who gives him the world in which he dwells. We never get very far with man without bursting the barriers of time and entering the boundless splendors of eternity. This is a really astounding fact about man. Whatever the original connotation of the phrase, when we say, "Thou hast put eternity in his heart," we are using a form of words which makes a stupendous claim and has an almost exhaustless meaning. To talk about immortality is not to enter into a process of wishful thinking but to discuss that which is implicit in the very nature of man.

1. The Creature Who Must Have Eternity

Rudyard Kipling whimsically wrote about what will happen to the artists:

> When Earth's last picture is painted and the tubes
>   are twisted and dried,
> When the oldest colours have faded, and the youngest
>   critic has died.

He declared that the Master of all good workmen would call the artists to work anew.

> Each, in his separate star,
> Shall draw the Thing as he sees It for the God
> of Things as They are! [1]

In all these words there is the restless consciousness that the artist is a person who must have eternity. It is the very nature of art to be exhaustless. And what Kipling says of the artist we must say of man. He must have eternity. It is the very nature of life on the human level to be exhaustless. It is quite true that men can try to become satisfied with things which do not deserve to continue beyond death. It is quite true that men have been interested in things which did not deserve to continue beyond death. It is quite true that some men have given their most eager activity to things which did not deserve to continue beyond death. And these are most sobering considerations. But it is also true that whenever you find a man giving his supreme interest to something which has no claims beyond the borders of time, you feel at once that he has prostituted his manhood. It was not for such things as these that the human story unfolded. It was not to be engrossed completely with such things as these that man was allowed to walk the earth.

When you study the activities of a man who has given his whole attention to the fleshly side of life so that at last he has had no interest beyond having as many and as vivid sensations as possible, at once you feel that he has lost the apprehension of the true meaning of manhood. These things have their place and are happy adjuncts to a life which has a deeper meaning. Even a Thanksgiving dinner which consisted merely of eating and drinking, with no gracious fellowship full of the memories of a common experience of life, of hopes and fears and joys and sorrows shared, and of a deep and quiet sense of gratitude to the Giver of all good things material and spiritual, would be something worse than a travesty. Material things somehow get their best quality at the very point where they are connected with something beyond the material. It was said of a group of men who with dull eyes but kindled hearts had walked unknowingly with the risen Lord that He became known to them in the breaking of the bread. The very homely intimacies of eating and drinking had connections which could rouse the spirit, quicken the imagination, and make men suddenly spiritually aware. Thus it is with all those material aspects of life which are made so gloriously to be the livery of the spiritual. But by this very token, when this larger meaning is taken from them, they become curiously deflated and, all alone, become more than meaningless. They actually come to have an

[1] From "When Earth's Last Picture Is Painted," from *The Seven Seas*, by Rudyard Kipling, copyright 1896 by Rudyard Kipling. Reprinted by permission of Mrs. Bambridge and Doubleday, Doran & Co., Inc.

evil meaning. For a creature meant to touch a clod and start a wing, there is something ignoble about perpetually having to do with clods and never sensing the presence of wings. For a creature who was meant to find every common bush aflame with God, there is something ignoble about perpetually having to do with bushes and never sensing the fiery presence. And the moment these deeper meanings are apprehended, man goes sweeping beyond time to something which is touched with the glory of the timeless. You can make machines and then in utter weariness dream of a mechanical world. But if you have one experience of true friendship, something has come within the range of your experience which laughs at mortality. And if you have ever known a deep and rapturous love, you know that within the borders of time you cannot possibly explore its meaning. Lovers always believe in immortality while they are in love. And if they forget that radiant faith which love has produced, it is not an argument against immortality. It means only that they have ceased to love. The same thing is true on all the loftiest levels of human life. When we experience even a little knowledge of spiritual fellowship, we begin to sing of that eternity when we shall know as we are known.

When we begin to ask real questions, we always find that they are questions which cannot be answered in time. The answers will require eternity. The moment we go beyond the immediate thought, the immediate desire, the immediate experience, we begin to touch something with an eternal reference. And it is the very nature of man, the moment he becomes aware of himself and knows a little of the real meaning of his life, to press against the walls of time and to call for the timeless. Man is a creature who must have eternity.

2. The Claims of the Unfulfilled

In Longfellow's well-known poem, Nokomis, the grandmother of Hiawatha, is asked by her little grandson to explain the colors of the rainbow. She replies by saying that the rainbow consists of flowers which never came to bloom in the world below but now are blooming in beauty in the sky. So in poetic fashion one of the great human problems is raised. What shall we say about the men and women who live and die without coming to any sort of fulfillment in the days of their human life? It is a delight to all of us to read the biographies of men and women who accomplish great things. And when they have to fight adversity and hostile circumstance at every step of the way, the tale of their achievement becomes doubly inspiring. But what about the others? What about those of whom Dr. Oliver Wendell Holmes wrote:

> Alas for those that never sing,
> But die with all their music in them!

The answer is just that if the human story does not go beyond the span of life during these mortal years, then there is no answer. There is a story of a well-known American businessman who once said that a great trust was like the American beauty rose. It was a wonderful consummation but any amount of potential roses had to be sacrificed in order to produce the final product. He was quite rightly criticized for being callous in his thought of the human beings whose frustration was involved in any practical interpretation of his figure. Human fulfillment is not something we can take lightly. It is something of the very greatest importance. We cannot pass casually by the problem of those who live and die without any real opportunity to bring the deepest meaning of their lives to consummation.

The conception of value is one of the most significant of the ideas which are essential to civilization itself. And this conception arises only with the existence of conscious persons. We have to have someone for whom a value exists in order to have a value. And the value exists in the conscious appreciation of the person. Civilization itself consists in the rise and development of the sense of values. But when we consider the rights of the individual, the very conception of values breaks down if the whole human story is told in this world. Actually most of the people who have ever lived have died without coming in sight of the great values for which human life is specifically made. It is all very well to talk of an ultimate consummation of human life in this world, an ultimate triumph of human values, and of everyone who at any stage made any contribution to these values as belonging to the choir invisible whose music is the gladness of the world. But this is cold comfort. Each life has a right not only in some far-off way to help to prepare for the fulfillment; it has a right to share in the fulfillment. There is something fundamentally wrong about a process whose benefits are enjoyed by only a few people at the end of long centuries and millenniums. The rights of those who perish on the way are ignored. If the values of human life, the values which give to civilization its very meaning, are to be justly distributed, they must be brought within the reach of all the human beings who are a part of the process of moving toward the realization of these values, even if they die while the period of realization is still centuries away. And this is only possible if human beings continue to live after they have passed from this life and in the period beyond death have brought within their reach the opportunities which they missed while here on earth. The choir invisible is likely to become the choir inaudible unless the values for which men strive are treated with seriousness and justice in the universe itself. It may seem very splendid to sing with Whittier,

> Ring, bells in unreared steeples,
> The joy of unborn peoples!

But the incentive for this gladness is taken away if as we sing the words we must believe that we shall have no share in the good of which we sing, and if we must believe that the great majority will fail of fruition in order that a small, far-off minority may obtain the felicity of true fulfillment. Indeed, so devastating is the effect of such a belief that there is a question as to whether the sense of values could survive if it became universal. If death is the period at the end of the sentence, it brings to an end something more than the lives of human beings. It brings to the ground that fair edifice of moral and spiritual hopes which man has based upon a belief in the fundamental spiritual and moral quality of the universe. We cannot deny the rights of those who fail of fulfillment in time to fulfillment in eternity.

And as we think about the matter, we can see that this claim embraces everyone. The human being who has entered upon the amplest heritage and who has come to death with the richest tale of achievement behind him still has fallen far short of the true fulfillment of all that is implicit in his life. Time itself not only at the worst but at the best cannot bring to man the realization of the full meaning of his life. The deep call for what only eternity can give rises from the soul of Everyman. Everyman has claims upon eternity.

3. The Claims of Those Who Cry Out Against the Injustices of Time

When Elizabeth Barrett Browning wrote "The Cry of the Children," she was striking her best blows against social conditions in England. And voices like hers were heard. Conditions were changed. But she was unconsciously more than a prophet calling for social change. She was expressing the claims of those who died before the social change could be made. These strange and stunted children who passed out of life before the beneficent transformations wrought by good laws could be felt are back there in the shadows, and the cry of these children is a cry for an immortality which will meet these children of injustice with an eternal hope. When Jacob Riis cried out that children born in certain districts of New York City were not born into the world but "damned into the world," his explosive indignation became so powerful that in some cases the battle with the slum was won. It was a great fight, and there was a great victory. But, once again, he was voicing a tragedy more far-reaching than the reader of his powerful books sometimes realizes. There were problems which could not be reached by the destruction of the slums, as splendid as one admits that achievement to be. What about those who carried the white leprosy of the slums to their graves and whose sentence of birth was indeed a sentence of death? Here again the cry for justice arises. It is a piercing cry coming from a vast multitude. Let what we have said of the slums stand for all the injustices perpetrated upon the bodies and the souls of men. Then the centuries become articulate with a cry for justice. It is a cry which cannot be answered in this world, for the voices are the voices of the dead. But it can be answered and, if justice means anything, it must be answered in a life after death. Injustice here, justice there; cruelty here, the healing of the ugly wounds there; treachery here, faithfulness there: so the great story must run. The moral imperative outruns time and claims the action of eternity.

4. Man Without Eternity

There is a very literal horror in the conception of man's being like the beasts that perish. And if we confront this tragedy with no hope beyond the anguish, we shall better understand that claim of humanity upon immortality of which we have already spoken. So many books have been written fouling the human nest that it is very easy for us to think of man's life as something essentially unlovely. Really, in spite of all the darkness, there has been much light. And its very nature has been of such a quality as to point to a sun arising from regions beyond these human shores and a sunset moving to regions beyond these mortal continents. If death brings the whole adventure to an end, all this glory begins to pale. First there is the twilight; then there is the dark.

Man has listened to a voice beyond the winds as he has heard them singing in the trees. He has felt a presence in the garden in the cool of the day. And as he has believed these subtle intimations, he has risen in stature. If all his delicate sense of meanings beyond the mortal voices is an illusion, then life itself is a delusion. Man without eternity lives in a time which has lost its noblest meaning, too. This is the precise sense in which there is truth in the French proverb: To understand time, you must have known eternity. Creatures of time already have the mark of the bar sinister upon their faces unless they are authentic children of eternity with a destiny beyond time. What is in time gains its glory from that which is beyond time. Take away this faith in eternity and life in time crumbles into the shadow of a shadow and then disappears.

Man has spoken to other men and called them friends. The very good fellowship of men with men has adumbrated waves of consciousness vibrating with a sense of the timeless. What you see in the eye of a friend is not subject to the inroads of mortality. But suppose that you are mistaken. Suppose that you are wrong. Then real friendship has no place in a world which denies it a sound basis in the reality of things. The butterfly has mistaken the radiance upon its wings for an eternal light. By and by butterfly and wings and light are lost in a final darkness. Man without eternity has a nature which is always asking what life is unable to give.

Man has knelt by his altar to speak to God. And he has heard a voice of gentle stillness replying in tones of unimpeachable authenticity. Or better still, before he has built an altar he has felt a strange compulsion which he is sure comes from beyond the borders of time telling him to worship. What if in spite of all this sense of finality he is mistaken?

A French philosopher wrote of the hour when he finally ceased to believe in God:

In vain I clung to my last beliefs, as a shipwrecked sailor to the fragments of his ship; in vain, terrified by the unknown waste in which I was about to float, I threw myself back once more upon my childhood, my family, my country. . . . This moment was frightful; and when, toward morning, I threw myself exhausted upon my bed, it seemed to me as if I could feel my former life, so cheerful and complete, die away, and before me there opened up another life, dark and dispeopled.[2]

So man without eternity falls into a deep abyss.

5. Eternity Without Man

Another way to approach the whole discussion is by means of an analysis of eternity without a destiny for man. We have already seen that the full view of the eternal reality which supports all life in time sees an Infinite Person of perfect intelligence who is moral love alive in infinite perfection creating and supporting all that lives in time. This Perfect Person who inhabits eternity has made man in His own image. He has made man with those powers of intelligence and mental and moral decision and spiritual hunger which we have found in human life everywhere. Now if He has made these characteristics to be the defining aspect of man's life, with longings and needs and capacity which can be satisfied only in eternity and yet has made man to perish completely at the end of his mortal experience, He has done something which contradicts both His own nature and His own character. So that we must conceive the Perfect Person of moral love as living on throughout eternity with the very creatures He has made for eternity condemned by His own fiat to a fragmentary life which never comes to the fulfillment which is required by the very nature He has given to man. Such a conclusion is so self-stultifying and so full of inner contradictions that it is clearly one which we cannot accept and in which the mind of man cannot rest. If God is the Perfect Person who is necessary for the very purposes of coherent thought, man's immortality is assured.

If we insist on taking the opposite horn of the dilemma and reach the conclusion that there is no Perfect Person of moral love, then the whole frame of coherent thought about existence falls apart. Man's intelligence has no basis in fundamental reality. His moral life has no basis

[2] Theodore Jouffroy, quoted in James Orr, *The Christian View of God and the World* (New York: Charles Scribner's Sons), p. 69.

in that which is actual in the ultimate life of the universe. His spiritual life is without any foundation in the ultimate truth of the universe. In every essential characteristic man is a sport without genuine meaning or essential relation to an order of which he is a part. But what possible reason could be powerful enough to cause us to subject the universe to this ultimate incoherence? We should be living in the midst of a cluster of effects with no adequate causes. Such a view is so self-stultifying and so subjects experience to a mass of utter inconsistency and incoherence as contradicts everything characteristic of the right use of the mind. We have a dead universe producing life, an unintelligent universe producing intelligence, and a universe without moral quality at its heart producing moral experience, and a universe without spiritual meaning producing spirituality. So we are driven back to a conception of reality capable of accounting for that which we actually find to be real in experience. The great denial by its very processes of self-stultification forces us back to the great affirmation.

6. The Faith Written in the Soul of Man.

Thus we come to see that the faith in immortality written in the very soul of man has the soundest basis in a coherent view of the universe in which every part supports the other parts and all join together with consistent and harmonious completeness. When man accepts his soul's invincible surmise, he is doing precisely that which the clearest and soundest use of the reason justifies.

This faith itself deserves a further consideration. It is clear at once that it gives to man a dignity which inspires in man the very loftiest thought and the very noblest action. That tug downward which every man feels and faces is confronted by a tug upward. He finds the real meaning of his life in that which relates him to a world in which his best thoughts receive confirmation, his noblest purposes are supported by a Divine Friend, and his highest aspirations are made valid both in time and in eternity.

Why then should man insult his humanity by denying the very faith which rises from the deepest depths of his nature and opens vistas of incredible splendor? This question, may we not say, involves just one answer. Man has a right to trust that faith which makes him truly human and gives him access to fellowship with the Divine.

And this position receives confirmation when we remember that man's triumph over nature, his analysis of its forces, all his achievements in science, all his creative accomplishments in art, have implicit in them the very view of humanity which fits in with the whole corpus of thought of which the belief in immortality is a part. The attack on man's humanity has many results when that attack seems to be successful. And one of the strangest is that it so reduces the human that every characteristic achievement of man becomes an anomaly. The foes of man could ask no more satisfying triumph than the overthrow of the doctrine of immortality and of all that is implicit in its compelling assertion of the dignity of man. And what possible reason can man have for joining the forces of his foes and defaming that humanity which is his great and characteristic gift from God?

This dignity, to be sure, carries with it tremendous responsibility. The creature with such a destiny cannot treat life lightly without being false to his great heritage. He does his work forever under the Great Taskmaster's eye. It is not an ignoble relation. For the Great Master is the Great Friend of men. He is the Eternal Lover of men. His only desire for men is that they shall be worthy of the great destiny which He opens before them. And the acceptance of the authority of the Great Master of men is the final use of a man's freedom in a complete and permanent decision to be worthy of the God who has made him and has made him for an eternal fellowship. When man turns from the Hound of Heaven who pursues him with such constant moral love, his sin against God is also in the completest sense a sin against himself.

And when man falters and turns from his high destiny, when he turns his face away from God, when with a strange jealousy of the Eternal he would rather be a beast living merely for sensations, or a being of hard calculation, violating the sanctions of the moral love which has given him his life, than an obedient friend of his divine Master, God does not accept even man's repudiation of the great and good things which He offers to him. He follows him with suffering love. He beats against the walls of man's selfishness. He attacks the citadels of his sensuality. He comes to him with the suffering love of the Cross. And so He answers to that deep faith in eternal meanings which man would feign stifle, by exhausting the very resources of the divine life to capture the devotion of the strange creature who is in process of becoming his own worst foe. It is only in the light of these eternal relationships of a love which bursts into time from eternity in a mighty deed of rescue that we can understand the deep words which God speaks to men in the God-man and His Cross. Christianity is only seen for what it is when we see God in suffering love contending with man to save him for his true destiny.

7. The Men of Social Passion Who Fear the Belief in Immortality

There is one inverted argument against immortality which we must consider. It is a psychological rather than a logical argument. It grows out of the fear of some men of social passion that a belief in immortality will lead men to patience with ugly wrongs in the present social order.

"We live in a world of social disorder, of ugly injustice, of hard cruelty," so runs the argument, "and it is our first duty to fight these things with all our might. If we give our minds up to the thought of immortality and of the righting of human wrongs in the heavenly country, we shall become so engrossed with that vision of a beatific future that we shall ignore our immediate duty. We shall allow dastardly evil, which we might overthrow, to become triumphant all about us while we dream of the Heavenly Kingdom. Therefore, let us turn from this treacherous dream of immortality, gird ourselves like men, and valiantly fight against the evils which surround us."

The sounding of the battle cry for the fight against contemporary evil is all to the good, and every one of us should respond to it with complete alacrity. But do we really believe that if we lower our estimate of the dignity of man, that will make it easier for us to fight against the evils which defile human life? Do we really believe that it is easier to do battle against injustice which falls upon the head of a creature of a day who is to live his little life and then to perish, than to do battle against the injustices which come upon a son of immortality? Do we really believe that it is easier to enter into the lists and join those who are fighting for the rights of man if we believe that man is so unimportant that all the millions who have died the victims of injustice, have died without hope of recompense for all they have suffered? Do we really believe that it is easier to fight for justice in a universe which is itself unjust?

The truth is that man has a greater stake in the essential dignity of humanity than in the outcome of any particular contemporary fight, however important that fight may be. If we can assure man once and for all that he is a child of eternity and that in the great consummation the wrongs of this mortal life will be righted and justice will be done, then he knows that the universe—or, to put it better, the God of the universe—is on his side in the battles with evil which he must fight here and now. One of the great leaders in social warfare in the nineteenth century said that he was fighting to make earth like heaven. The whole might of eternity is with us if as children of immortality we do battle for the enthronement of good in the very world in which we live and in the very life of which we are a part.

But actually profounder issues are involved. Where do we get our motives for the social warfare? What gives man any rights for which we must contend? What gives man such quality that we must not suffer his dignity as a true person to be attacked?

The truth is that the men who are fighting for human rights always inherit their belief in the dignity of man from those who believed in immortality and saw in man a creature of eternity. And when they want to keep the dignity of man and fight for it while they drop those beliefs about man which gave him dignity, they are cutting the ground from under their own feet. There is altogether too much of this attempt to seize the results of twenty centuries of Christian life and struggle and victory, to hold them tight, and at the same moment to throw away the Christian convictions which produced them.

There is just one inevitable result to this sort of folly. The sense of man's dignity is lost, and sooner or later the great social conflicts are given up. We can live for a while on the results produced by splendid old beliefs while discarding the beliefs. But in the long run only the belief which remains valid inspires a fight which is full of indubitable courage. The belief in immortality is actually the great support of that view of man which makes it worth while to fight every force which oppresses him and every evil which attacks him. The prophets of social passion who would belittle the man for whom they are fighting do not really understand the nature of man or the nature of the war in which they are engaged.

The tendency to corrupt the truth and even to indulge in brutal deeds for the sake of a social ideal is one which deserves careful and critical and constant inspection. We must have a cause as well as arms for the fight. We must have a map of human meanings as well as a strategy of attack and of defense. And the whole incentive will be lost from the social war if we discover that the man for whom we fight is not worth the pains we are taking for his emancipation. He is worth every bit of heroism ever expended for his sake because he is a creature of eternity and not a momentary flash in the night of time.

8. The Final Adjudication

After death—the judgment.

It is characteristic of the account of the words of Jesus in the Gospels that some of the tenderest and most gracious words of His which have come down to us are found in His account of the last judgment. The hosts of the men and women who have lived in the world are gathered for the great assize. And untold multitudes who have never heard the name of Christ and have never known of His existence stand in solemn awe before the Master of the universe and the Judge of men. With one of those swift turns of unexpected utterance so characteristic of Jesus, the Great Judge now on the throne, still the Gracious Friend of good will, declares that the masses of human beings on His right are there because of what they have done for Him. They have found Him hungry and have fed Him. They have found Him thirsty and have given Him drink. How can this possibly be, they ask, when they died not even knowing that He had ever existed? Then comes the swift reply. You never fed a hungry man without feeding me. You never gave drink to a thirsty man without quenching my thirst. When you had a heart of understanding for other men, you bound yourself to me.

The consideration of the final judgment should always be approached with this ineffable and understanding tenderness in our thought. We are not afraid to trust ourselves to the mind which could think these thoughts. We are not afraid to trust ourselves to the voice which could utter these words.

But there were those on the left. And in words of unutterable sternness they were told to depart. They were consigned to a fate prepared for the utterly evil. They had failed the Great Person. They had found Him in need and had not ministered to Him. But how could this possibly be, they asked, since they had died without ever knowing that He existed. Then came stern and searching words. You never failed a human being in his need without failing me.

The mighty Christ upon the throne finds that every person of every race and color and clime has forged an attitude toward life in his attitude toward his fellow men which has put either good or evil in command of his life. And that deep purpose expressed with perfect clarity in his treatment of other men determines destiny. All our sentimental and gregarious confidence in the superficial quality of evil and the inevitable triumph of good in every human life, in the essential goodness of the nature of man and the essential responsiveness of every human spirit, goes down before that stern picture of the recalcitrant hosts whose sin against love became the hard stuff of their very souls and sealed their doom.

They are now bent to the will of God by the sheer force of His omnipotent power. They who would not accept the will of God in loving loyalty now find that they must accept it as a stern necessity. Those who believe that the shining face of kindness will at last melt every hard heart find the basis for most serious thought as they confront this picture. Recalcitrant human wills are of such a nature that God must bend them to His purpose by force in the ultimate universe. And those who think that it is never lawful to unsheathe the sword and use force against evil in the struggles of time but that we should meet every situation through deeds of kindness and submission, find themselves in the curious position of asserting that men with their limited qualities can do in time what Jesus did not believe Almighty God could do in eternity. The phantasy of a world with no need of force goes down before the stern words of Jesus. In eternity persistent evil meets the forceful judgment of God and bends under the administration of His irresistible power. And as evil must meet the judicial force of God in eternity, so there come crises where the very welfare of humanity is at stake in this world and where hard and sinister evil must meet the military force of man.

When we attempt to probe the lot of the defiantly wicked in the ultimate universe, we are on precarious ground. We know that it is something for which the most tremendous material figures of speech were not deemed too terrible. We know beyond the peradventure of a doubt that it means the eternal loss of the fellowship of God. And we know that this comes not because God would not forgive but because man has become incapable of asking for or receiving forgiveness. What he is has become his fate. What he is, is hell. His soul has become incapable of responding to God.

But we know also that God's will is done in the ultimate universe. Those grim and terrible persons who have refused to become the friends of goodness must become the slaves of goodness. Hell is the lot of those who do the will of God because they must—hating it, protesting against it inwardly, but having lost all power of resistance. Only a man's will is his own. His deeds are God's.

If we are on precarious ground when we attempt to think clearly of hell, we are surely on ground far beyond our powers when we try to think of heaven. But even in this transcendent region some things are indubitably clear and finally certain. Heaven is eternal fellowship with the God of moral love who has come to us in Jesus Christ with all the strange sad glory of the Cross. The meaning of that fellowship is as exhaustless as the fullness of the life of God. "Eye hath not seen, nor ear heard" the things at which we can only hint in vast surmise. But again we can be absolutely certain that heaven is an eternal fellowship in moral love with a great company no man can number, of those who, like us, have walked the earth and have accepted the shining of the light of God in Jesus Christ. Together the human family of God is to live and grow and experience that amplitude of thought and deed which can be conceived only in the eternal world.

9. The Faithful God

> In the beginning God.
> In the end God.
> The Alpha and the Omega.

All of existence is the tale of the faithfulness of God. The Old Testament expresses this idea in the conception of the covenant and the covenant people. God enters into an agreement. And He keeps His plighted faith. He makes a mighty promise. And He keeps His word. When there is change, it is man that changes and not God. Man can break the covenant. Man can make the agreement void. Man can make the word of no effect. But the faithful God is always waiting to make secure and triumphant the best which He has promised men.

Our last thought, then, should be of our human fellowship with the Great Divine Person whose love is without a beginning as it will be without an end. The life of prayer can be understood precisely only as a life. It is the experience of the whole life turned Godward. All of the mind sets man's thoughts Godward. All of the heart sets man's affections Godward. All of the conscience sets man's purposes Godward. All of the will sets man's deeds Godward. That is prayer.

The best beginning of prayer is found when a child is taught by its mother to reach out beyond her to the Divine Friend who cares for them both. The best continuance of prayer is seen when a child hears its father's voice conducting the family devotions and comes to know that the little family is held in the love of God. The best enlargement of prayer is in that corporate worship of the Church when a child comes to feel that it is one of a divine society, all friends of one another because each is a friend of God. The best outreach of prayer is in those corporate acts of devotion wherein the Church devoutly calls upon God for His blessing upon the community, the state, and the whole country. So the child comes to feel at the center of constantly enlarging circles of the loving care of the faithful God. The ultimate outreach of prayer is that corporate act of worship in which the Church calls upon God for His blessing upon the whole world. And the child begins to understand what it means to think of all mankind as the object of the moral love of the Mighty One who inhabits eternity and whose face we have seen in the face of Christ.

The inmost reach of prayer is revealed in those hours alone with God when a man, perhaps an everyday Christian without much knowledge of the heights or depths, or a saint humbly climbing the precipitous cliffs of God, finds the ear attuned to secrets which cannot be uttered but which change everything else in all the world. It is a perilous and magnificent adventure to be alone with God. The tale of what may happen at such a time is told with direct and ultimate and searching power and complete simplicity of purpose in *The Private Devotions of Bishop Lancelot Andrewes,* still the supreme devotional classic possessed by the Christian Church. The light of God shines in. It illuminates all the dark places. It is completely revealing. And no man could bear that revelation of himself were not the friendly and merciful God nearer than his breathing, closer than his hands or feet. But it reveals such soaring possibilities, such heavenly beauty, such new meaning in the human life about, such exquisite capacity in souls one had never understood, that the land where one lives becomes a land of promise, one's city is the New Jerusalem descending from heaven, and one's own life has spiritual possibilities of which one scarcely dares to think. All this is the gift of the faithful God who has purposed good things for His children and is most full of desire to make His purpose true.

The man who has not met God alone has not met Him. The man who has only met God alone has not beheld Him as He is seen looking out of the loving eyes of a brother man. When a group of men and women worshiping together are aware of the presence and the blessing of God, we have the very essence of the Beloved Community, the human society of moral love, the Christian Church.

It is an expensive thing to pay the price of communal worship. For the faithful God demands with complete definiteness that we shall be faithful to our fellows. And as we pray together, their right to our fellowship, our co-operation, our deep moral and spiritual and social support becomes imperative. And the hand from which we receive all things touches our possessions and demands that we hold them as stewards of the great and good purposes of God.

It is a gracious and inspiring thing when men can find powerful and searching preaching in the Church. But whether or not they can find great preaching, they can always find a great experience of worship. In that experience they renew perpetually their membership in the Christian Church.

And in all this ample and many-sided experience of prayer, men in the little pockets of time are preparing for that perfect fellowship with God and that perfect fellowship with men which belongs to those regions where beyond these voices there is peace.

"Speech is but broken light upon the depth of the unspoken"—so once that strange and gifted woman George Eliot wrote. And so when one has tried to think and write of the meaning of human experience, there remain the vast unplumbed depths, the steep and unclimbed heights. We turn, then, from the thoughts to the life which includes and goes beyond what we have been able to think. We turn from the words to apprehend, at least in some dim way, the realities which are beyond all speech. There is tragedy, and there is splendor. There is mystery, and there is understanding. There is the perpetual demand for action. And as everything focuses upon the demand for deeds which shall express the very meaning of our inner life, the faithful God is with us if we will have it so. In His will is our peace.

Index